SPAIN

BY THE EDITOR

THE SPANISH TRAGEDY
CATALONIA INFELIX
SPAIN IN ECLIPSE
SPANISH—NOW
SPAIN, A COMPANION TO SPANISH TRAVEL
A HISTORY OF THE ROMANTIC MOVEMENT IN SPAIN
SPANISH MYSTICISM
STUDIES OF THE SPANISH MYSTICS
RIVAS AND ROMANTICISM IN SPAIN
RIVAS, A CRITICAL STUDY
RAMON LULL, A BIOGRAPHY

Translations

THE WORKS OF ST JOHN OF THE CROSS
THE WORKS OF ST TERESA
THE BOOK OF THE LOVER AND THE BELOVED
THE ROMANTICS OF SPAIN
BLANQUERNA
THE ART OF CONTEMPLATION
THE BOOK OF THE BEASTS
THE TREE OF LOVE

SPAIN

A COMPANION TO SPANISH STUDIES

EDITED BY

E. ALLISON PEERS

FIFTH EDITION
REVISED AND ENLARGED BY
Professor R. F. Brown

METHUEN & CO. LTD, LONDON
36 Essex Street, Strand, W.C.2

First Published 19 September 1929
Second Edition December 1933
Third Edition May 1938
Fourth Edition, Revised and Enlarged, 1948
Fifth Edition, Revised and Enlarged, 1956
Reprinted 1958

5.2

CATALOGUE NO 3817/U

PRINTED IN GREAT BRITAIN BY
JARROLD AND SONS LTD, NORWICH

TO

THE MEMORY OF

JAMES FITZMAURICE-KELLY

1858–1923

PREFACE TO THE FOURTH EDITION

ONE of the most striking features of modern education, both in the British Isles and in the United States of America, has been the revival of the study of Spanish in schools and universities.

The beginnings of Spanish studies in both countries date from an earlier period than is generally supposed. To consider the universities only, Trinity College, Dublin, can trace its Spanish teaching back to the eighteenth century, while the inaugural address of Antonio Alcalá Galiano as Professor of Spanish in the University of London is dated November 15, 1828. The famous Smith Professorship at Harvard, held successively by George Ticknor, Henry Wadsworth Longfellow, James Russell Lowell and J. D. M. Ford, was founded in 1816. Ten years later, Spanish studies began at Yale, and in 1830 at Columbia and Princeton.

But, although for so long Spanish has been taught, and taught efficiently—more assiduously in the United States than in Britain—it is only in the present century that educationists have given it serious consideration, and even during that time its vogue has suffered sharp vicissitudes. The first modern endowed Chair of Spanish in our country was that founded by Captain Gilmour at the University of Liverpool, and held by Professor James Fitzmaurice-Kelly from 1909 to 1916, in which year he was elected to the newly founded Cervantes Chair at King's College, London. Other universities followed suit in creating Chairs of Spanish, and there is now some form of Spanish teaching at almost every university in the British Isles.

In the schools, during this period, the claims of Spanish won some degree of recognition ; and by 1936, although ten times as many pupils were learning German as Spanish, and one hundred times as many were learning French, there were Spanish classes in over two hundred schools, and every year saw the formation of more. Then, unhappily, civil war broke out in Spain ; travel and study in that country became impossible ; and the numbers of classes and teachers of Spanish declined. The World War dealt the language a still heavier blow ; for most schools had only one master or mistress qualified to teach it ; and, if that teacher were called up for service, the supply was so short that it was difficult, and sometimes impossible, to find another. In this way Spanish disappeared from many curricula, including those of schools in which it had been taught with unusual success.

But it was also during the World War that the foundations were laid for a revival of Spanish teaching which has already brought it well above the level at which it stood in 1939. For the first time we began to realize the tremendous part likely to be played in the world of the future by the republics of Latin America. In the Western Hemisphere the language problem had already been solved : all its educated citizens understood either English or Spanish. How long would it be before these became the international languages of the entire world ? Even to-day Spanish is the mother tongue of well over 100,000,000 people, and Portuguese of 60,000,000 more. To this *international* argument for an increased teaching of Spanish had to be added three others. First, its *educational* value : the comparative simplicity of its pronunciation and accidence lead at once to rapid progress, while the richness of its vocabulary and the flexibility of its construction make the later stages of study an increasingly valuable discipline. Secondly, its *culture* : in literature and art, Spain rivals any other country in Europe ; its history is invariably found attractive by young people ; and it is a gateway to the culture of eighteen countries in Latin America. Thirdly, there is our *commercial* position : it is vital that we should recapture our export trade ; Spanish America is one of its most promising fields ; and even before the War most of our export trade with Spanish America had been lost largely because of our indifference to the people and their language.

These arguments were developed in a memorandum addressed in November 1942 to the Minister of Education by a body of business men and educationists which afterwards established itself on a permanent basis as the Hispanic Council. In the summer of 1943 the Report of the Norwood Committee laid considerable stress upon the importance of Spanish, going so far as to recommend that in certain areas it should be made a ' chief language '. In the same summer the Hispanic Council held the first of its vacation courses in Spanish, enrolling 250 members, nearly all of them teachers of other subjects anxious to qualify in another language. From that time the fortunes of Spanish have improved steadily ; more and more schools are teaching it, some of them not only as a ' second ', or a ' third ', but as a ' chief ' language ; and there is every reason to hope that, when in due course English and Spanish are recognized as the two international languages of the civilized world, we shall be in a position to provide our schools with all the teachers of Spanish that will then be needed.

One of the most hopeful features of the revival of Spanish studies has been the appointment to responsible posts, both in schools and universities, of English-speaking teachers with high qualifications in their subject. While one cannot be too grateful for the distinguished Spaniards who in the past have spared no effort to give the necessary impetus to the revival, it is generally recognized that the future of Spanish studies will be assured only by the creation of a strong body of teachers whose mother tongue is the same as that of their pupils and who can consequently appreciate the difficulties with which these pupils have to contend both in the elementary stages of learning the language and in the more formidable task of assimilating unfamiliar ideas and foreign cultures.

The present book is entirely the work of British scholars, specialists in the subjects of which they write, and it is dedicated, as a token of their deep respect for the pioneer of modern Spanish scholarship in their own country, to the memory of James Fitzmaurice-Kelly. Its aim is primarily to be a ' companion to Spanish studies ', to do something towards the broadening of those studies by providing all who pursue them with a fund of information which is necessary as a background to their reading, yet the whole of which is contained in no other single volume. It is hoped that the book will find its way to the table of every such student, and remain there as a constant source of assistance, until its contents become, as they should, a part of the equipment of his knowledge. As a reference book it hopes to be useful also to a far wider circle of readers, and, above all, it is ambitious to serve the intelligent traveller in Spain, who is not content with rushing through the country in a tourist car, but has time and inclination to read thoughtfully, and travel slowly, in what is one of the most difficult countries in Europe to understand.

In planning the volume, due regard has been had to the requirements of the traveller and the general reader, and considerable space has been allotted to the last century, trustworthy books on modern Spain being few in number.

The text of this fourth edition has been thoroughly revised, the final chapter enlarged and the bibliography brought up to date. That the book may continue to stimulate as well as to assist the study of the Spanish language and civilization is the hope of the Editor and of all who have contributed to it.

The University,
Liverpool,
September, 1945

E. ALLISON PEERS

PUBLISHER'S NOTE TO FIFTH EDITION (1956)

Professor Peers did not live to revise his book for this edition. The work has been carried out by Professor R. F. Brown, Professor of Spanish in the University of Leeds, who has made corrections throughout the book and has expanded Chapters V and IX to bring them up to date.

BIBLIOGRAPHICAL NOTE

The list of books recommended at the end of each chapter for further reading in connection with it has been compiled by the writer of the chapter and revised and co-ordinated with the other lists by the Editor. It is to be regarded as suggestive only and has been strictly compressed in compilation. It may usefully be supplemented by *A Handbook to the Study and Teaching of Spanish*, London, Methuen, 1938, and *A Practical Spanish Book-List*, Liverpool, Institute of Hispanic Studies, 1945. Two other bibliographical sources of a general kind will be found in the *Enciclopedia Universal* (Espasa) and *Encyclopædia Britannica*. The section entitled ' General Survey ' of the article ' Spain ' in this last-named work contains much useful geographical and statistical information which it has not been thought suitable to include in this book. From *Spanish Art* (No. 127, p. 215) the reader will be able to draw much bibliographical and other material on such subjects as ceramics, metal-work, glass and furniture with which we have also been unable to deal in a volume of restricted size.

The following selected list of periodicals dealing wholly or mainly with Spanish studies will often be found useful for reference. The place of publication of each is given in brackets :
Boletín de la Real Academia Española (Madrid) ; *Boletín de la Real Academia de la Historia* (Madrid) ; *Arte Español* (Madrid) ; *Cultura española* (Madrid) ; *Revista de Archivos, Bibliotecas y Museos* (Madrid) ; *Revista de Filología Española* (Madrid : see note on this review, p. 183) ; *Boletín de la Biblioteca Menéndez y Pelayo* (Santander) ; *Boletín de la Real Academia de Buenas Letras de Barcelona* (Barcelona) ; *Estudis Universitaris Catalans* (Barcelona) ; *Anuari de l'Institut d'Estudis Catalans* (Barcelona) ; *Revue Hispanique* (Paris and New York) ; *Bulletin Hispanique* (Bordeaux) ; *Bulletin of Hispanic Studies* (Liverpool) ; *Iberica* (Hamburg) ; *Hispania* (Washington, D.C., U.S.A.) ; *Hispanic Review* (Philadelphia) ; *Revista Hispánica Moderna* (New York) ; *Nueva Revista de Filología española* (Mexico). A large number of learned periodicals publish occasional articles on Spanish subjects : such are the *Modern Language Review* (Cambridge, England), *Modern Philology* (Chicago) and the *Romanic Review* (New York). Current literary production is best followed in the monthly *Insula* (Madrid).

CONTENTS

xi

LIST OF MAPS

xii

SPAIN

CHAPTER I[1]

SPAIN : THE COUNTRY, ITS PEOPLES AND LANGUAGES

TO the rest of Europe the Spaniard has ever been a man apart, one whose outlook on life refuses to conform to accepted criteria of logical behaviour, whose scale of values seems curiously remote from a modern age. He has been styled the supreme romantic and his country labelled vaguely as picturesque, tacit admissions of a complexity rare in the evolution of peoples. There is humour in the fact that nowhere has purity of descent (*sangre limpia*) been more vaunted than in a land where even the noblest dared not, in the Golden Age, trace his ancestry too far. For the peninsula has been the scene of many an invasion, now European, now Asiatic, now African, of which the shortest is reckoned by centuries, and all have left their trace.

To-day there is a sufficient semblance of unity to be mislead-ing. We speak of Spain, the Spanish people and the Spanish language in the belief that we deal with clear-cut, definitive con-cepts. But Spain was plural to the Romans, and its multiple aspects still submit ill to formulæ. Over its history the spirit of contradiction and contrast has long been a presiding genius. We think of a European State, and remember an African occupa-tion of eight centuries ; of ' Sunny Spain ', to recollect a winter sports season of many months and regions of perpetual snow ; of a fruitful garden of the Hesperides where toil were supererero-gatory, to see a vision of Castile. Turning from Spain to-day to that age of gold when she was mistress of oceans and continents, a dominant voice alike in world-politics and the graces of civiliza-

---

[1] For the maps used in this chapter the Editor is indebted to Professor J. Holmes.

1

tion, one asks where is the continuity, what the thread that, winding through the mazes of time, will give the clue to the pattern. The earliest known settlers in the peninsula, intrepid seamen come from distant Phœnicia, called the land ' Hidden ' (*Span* or *Spania*). Its mystery still awaits unravelling, and the most acute native thinkers can still find themselves, in all sincerity, completely at variance with one another.

Spain, with Portugal, forms the largest and most westerly of the Mediterranean peninsulas. Located once on the confines of the known world, the *ne plus ultra* of the adventurous navigator, its shores are washed by two oceans, and its boundaries completed by a barrier more formidable than any sea. The lesson came early, with Roncesvalles, and, taken in conjunction with a narrow strait of some dozen miles, gives point to the saying that Africa begins in the Pyrenees. Geographers tell us rather that the peninsula is a transition zone between the two continents, but the phrase stands as a key to more than one aspect of the country's story.

Next to Switzerland, the land is the most mountainous and that of greatest average altitude in Europe. Its dominant feature is the vast central table-land, fringed on three sides by a series of ranges, the Cantabrian mountains, the Iberian system and the Sierra Morena, while the fourth slopes westward to the Atlantic. The outline is completed by the Pyrenees to the north-east and the Sierra Nevada to the south-east, isolated from the central heights by the valleys of the Ebro and the Guadalquivir. Approximately one-half of the country's expanse is comprised in the *meseta central*, divided by a mountain system writ large in history, the Sierra de Guadarrama, into two plateaux, that to the north of an average altitude of 700 metres, that to the south of 600 metres, each cut into by a long river, the Douro and the Tagus, whose tortuous, precipitous courses are sufficiently indicative of the country they traverse. Two rivers alone, the Guadalquivir and the Ebro, are of noteworthy service to agriculture and navigation, and only in the rich valley of the former does Nature of her own accord clothe herself in smiling luxuriance. Life is good in Andalusia, but more typical of Spain are the cold, monotonous, all but barren expanses of Castile, ' land of saints and boulders ',[1] of rugged peaks and sudden ravines, where the earth conceives as in agony and yields a hard-bought sustenance to scattered hamlets.

No less striking are the variations of climate, determined

[1] ' Tierra de santos y de cantos.'

less by situation than by the general relief. The central table-land is characterized in winter by high pressure, low temperature and abundant rains, particularly towards the Atlantic seaboard, in summer by low pressure, torrid heat and drought, culminating at times in veritable monsoons ; and the transition is often violent and unforeseen. Even where the moderating influence of the sea is most felt, the contrasts in temperature are great and abrupt. The Atlantic winds provide on the west and north a heavy and constant rainfall (Santiago has 160 wet days per year) ; the Mediterranean fringe, on the contrary, suffers from abnormally dry periods (Alicante, 42 wet days per year), broken by sudden torrential bursts of rain, as when in 1882 there fell in Alicante more rain in one day than in all the rest of the year. The resultant inundations are as disastrous as they are inevitable and frequent. It follows that the Spanish climate, predisposing on the one hand to an existence of listless inactivity, and on the other making more than difficult the winning of one's daily bread, is a complex and important factor in the national life. ' Nine months of winter and three of hell ',[1] says the Castilian, alternately parched by a pitiless sun and pierced by the biting winds from the Guadarrama, ' that take a man's life, yet would not blow out a lamp.' [2]

A country's fertility will depend, after the nature of the soil, upon its water supply. Spain is rugged and mountainous ; its rainfall sins from extremes. The two factors in conjunction determine the character of its rivers, for there are wanting alike natural reservoirs and glaciers, save one in the Sierra Nevada. Flowing over high, broken country, they swell frequently into torrents. The Tagus, Spain's longest river, signifies in Spanish a cutting (*tajo*). With summer comes drought, and the same impetuous current degenerates into peaceful backwaters where cows stand knee-deep. The contrast is accentuated on the south-eastern slope ; there mountains dip precipitately to the sea, and the uncertain rainfall causes the short rivers to alternate between periods of ungovernable spate and of insignificant tricklings. The extremes call forth, and have called forth since Roman times, all man's ingenuity to solve the problem of irriga-tion ; although the alluvial deposits brought down to a tideless sea in the course of centuries, while ruling out good harbours, which require estuaries rather than deltas, make some amends by forming a littoral of remarkable fertility, justly known as the

---

[1] ' Nueve meses de invierno y tres de infierno.'
[2] ' El Guadarrama sutil
      que mata un hombre y no apaga un candil.'

garden of Spain. On the whole Spain's rivers, numerous though
they be (the Guadalquivir in its 680 kilometres counts 806
tributaries), are of little service to agriculture and industry.

To the contrasts in climate, in relief, in rainfall, there comes
as corollary a remarkably wide range of vegetation, typified
by the Sierra Nevada ('snowy range') whose slopes present
the whole compass from the tropical palm and the sugar-cane
to the flora of the polar regions. More than half the total area
is uncultivated, being either pasture-land or wholly unproductive.
In the remainder the predominant crops are, in the north, maize,

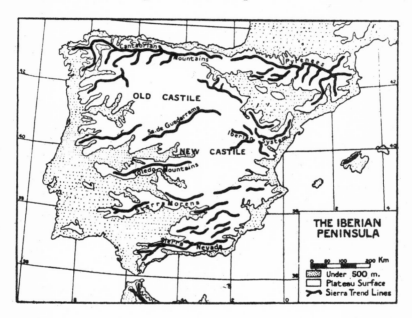

tubers and the cider-apple ; corn and other cereals, the vine
and the olive in the vast central plateau ; while the last two
with the orange become increasingly important in the south and
south-east. The coastal strip east of Gibraltar gives essentially
tropical products, cane, date-palm, cotton-plant and banana-
tree. From the east come rice, maize, hemp and vegetables,
with abundance of oranges and lemons. Forests are important
in the north and on the southern fringes of the plateau.

Spain is a predominantly agricultural country, and the yield
will be greatly increased when science has remedied the uneven
distribution of the water supply. It might be contended, never-

theless, that this orientation of the nation's energy is mistaken. Lack of communication, of capital, of enterprise cannot obscure a fact of respectable antiquity among Greek and Roman historians, to wit, that the country is exceedingly rich in minerals. The copper mines of Río Tinto, exploited by Phœnicians, Romans and Arabs, are still famous. Yet more important is the production of lead and iron. There follow zinc, mercury (the mercury mines of Almadén, likewise known to Romans and Arabs, are among the richest in the world), silver, manganese, gold and tin. The natural advantages of this rich subsoil are offset by the scanty yield of coal, the corner-stone of industry ; but one may still conjecture that, with improved organization and a freer hand for personal initiative, Spain's mineral production will in time rival agriculture as chief among the nation's resources

Spain, in its political configuration, is composed of fifty provinces. Their creation by an arbitrary decree of 1833 sprang from the servile imitation of things French, characteristic of the period, and, far from respecting traditional divisions, sought to abolish that strong spirit of regionalism which has ever made of the country less a unity than a confederation. But some changes politics cannot effect, and the entire subordination of considerations historical, geographical, and linguistic to mere administrative convenience has defeated its own ends. Spain is still complicated and heterogeneous, and one must still approach it through its various 'kingdoms'.

Galicia occupies the north-western corner with its rocky picturesque coast. It is a land of resourceful small farmers and hardy seamen, inured to perils and fatigues Ill-understood by the rest of Spain, their kinship, as descendants of the Celts who crossed the Pyrenees about the fifth century B.C., is with Portugal alike in language and literature. One attributes to them the epithets usually associated with the Celtic genius, ' impractical ', ' highly imaginative ', ' dreamers ', and one comes as far short of the truth as such generalizations usually do. The *gallego* is essentially industrious and severely practical. Lack of ambition and supreme patience make of him when he leaves home a manual labourer, laughed at for his equanimity and thickness of skin. But his intimacy with nature has brought understanding, and tranquillity, tenderness and a certain melancholy ; and the lyrical and musical gift is his in a special sense. From the twelfth to the fourteenth century Galician-Portuguese (it was then all one) was the recognized medium for lyric poetry. Alfonso the Wise drew up his *Primera Crónica General* and the *Siete Partidas* in Castilian, but his *Cantigas* are written quite naturally and inevitably in Galician. ' But lately ', writes the Marquis of Santillana (c. 1449), ' all poets and troubadours of these parts, whether of Castile, Andalusia or Extremadura, used to compose all their works in the Galician or Portuguese tongue.'[1] The phenomenon is explained largely by the pilgrim route to Santiago de Compostela, known to the devout from the tenth century. Along it came to Spain many a troubadour, and the full influence of the Provençal lyric, which, though it took deep root also in Catalonia, left Castile all but untouched. But much also is due to the introspective temperament of a people not concerned with the world at large, a people who even while adopting courtly forms have been able to inspire into their artificiality a breath of true feeling.

In Asturias we come on the haughtiest race of a haughty land. In this narrow strip between mountain and sea is Covadonga, and in Covadonga the Spanish nation was reborn invincible after the Muslim irruption. ' Land of torrents ' the name signifies, fitted for the restless existence of a people of fighters who knew no quarter. *Sangre limpia* was there a very present reality, for they had seen the vision of a Spain won back for Christendom, and every man was a crusader. Pushing beyond the Cantabrians and moving its capital from Oviedo to León, Asturias in time became merged in Castile, and its tongue, kept free from Moorish contagion, became the speech that was to impose itself on the country.

The Basques sit astride the Pyrenees, a people of mystery which their mountain home does nothing to dispel. Ethnographers see in the Basques of to-day the remnants of a people who were able nowhere else to preserve their identity, and find in their language the explanation of place-names which testify to a former occupation of the whole peninsula by a non-Aryan stock, though even this much is part conjecture and not universally accepted. The difference of race is further revealed in their considerable talent for industry and commerce : Bilbao is one of the most progressive centres in Spain. By nature kindly and hospitable, they are refractory to interference ; ' like saints, provided they be not angered,' says Cervantes.[2] ' Better be

---

[1] ' non ha mucho tiempo qualesquier dezidores e trovadores destas partes, agora fuessen castellanos, andaluces o de la Estremadura, todas sus obras componían en lengua gallega o portuguesa.'—*Prohemio al condestable de Portugal*, XIV.

[2] ' Son unos benditos como no estén enojados.'—*La Señora Cornelia*.

the head of a mouse than the tail of a lion ',[1] their own saying has it, and they steadfastly refuse to merge their nationality and their tongue, puzzle of philologists, in a larger whole.

Asturias for conscious pride ; Aragon for stubbornness. ' The *aragonés* knocks in a nail with his head,' [2] runs the proverb, and their history shows a greater tenacity in questions of personal liberty than is found elsewhere in the peninsula. Nowhere did the Cortes intervene more effectively in administration, and Alfonso I, confirming the charter of Jaca in 1187, tells that those of Castile, Navarre and other parts come to Jaca to study its charters and transfer them to their own country. The old Aragonese nobles, *ricos hombres de natura*, were always particularly turbulent, reserving to themselves the right to make war individually, and to throw off allegiance to the king—their peer—when it suited. The well-known oath to their monarch is a classic of independence : ' We who are as good as you swear to you who are no better than we, to accept you as our king and sovereign lord, provided you observe all our statutes and laws ; and if not, no (*Si no, no*).' Culture came early to Aragon. Huesca, chosen by Sertorius (*c.* 80 B.C.) as a centre where the youth of Spain were to be brought up after Roman standards, became an important focus of Roman influence. Ten centuries later, glosses from the monastery of San Millán de Berceo, whence was to issue the first poet known by name in Spanish literature, give the earliest example of Spanish written as an independent tongue.

In the supposed unity of Spain no element is more jarring than Catalonia. There is separatism in the very spelling of the name (Catalunya) by a Catalan, and his claim appears justified on numerous counts. Barcelona is to-day the most important city in the country, and the most European. Its cult of efficiency is utterly at variance with the outlook of the south, and its prosperity in face of difficulties implies a standing reproach to the indolence of those who benefit nonchalantly from the bounty of Nature or, where she is harsh and niggardly, resign themselves to poverty. Catalonia is poor both agriculturally and minerally, yet the love of toil and the will to succeed have converted it into a vast manufacturing region, where industries flourish even in towns distant from the sea and lacking alike in coal and in raw materials.

But the Catalan's uneasy feeling that his industry is helping to maintain others in idleness is only part of the problem, and

[1] ' Más vale ser cabeza de ratón que cola de león.'
[2] ' Un aragonés clava un clavo con la cabeza.'

is subordinated to his extraordinarily keen response to a tradition
of centuries of splendour in which Castile had no part. The
region through which Greek and Roman civilization entered the
peninsula has always been the most receptive of foreign influences,
and but for the impulse towards independence its destinies for
long would have been bound up with the other side of the
Pyrenees. The *marca hispanica* of Charlemagne, its counts soon
cast off allegiance to the Franks, and at the same time intensified
the campaign against the Muslim to such good purpose that by
the end of the tenth century their alliance or neutrality was
gladly bought at the price of territorial concessions. Union
with Aragon preluded trading relations with the Balearic Islands,
Sardinia, Sicily and Naples, and Catalonia was for centuries the
greatest trading nation in the Mediterranean (that is to say,
in the world) with a mercantile code, *The Consulate of the Sea*,
of universal acceptance. Things changed when, with the discovery of America and the new direction given to trade, the
Mediterranean became but a backwater, but it was left to Castile
to administer the *coup de grâce*, and the memory rankles. By
a codicil to the will of Queen Isabel her subjects in Aragon and
Catalonia were forbidden under pain of death to do commerce
with the Indies, and the sun had set, for the nonce, on their
economic greatness.

It is nevertheless in the realm of the mind that the Catalan
is most sure of his right to a separate existence. No argument
is so dear to the claimant of political concessions as the possession
of a special tongue, and if one hesitates to speak of Catalonia as
merely a province of Spain one dare not designate Catalan as
merely a dialect of Castilian. Its basic affinity must indeed
be sought inside the peninsula, for during the centuries of Roman
sway the whole country received the same Latin speech that
was afterwards to work out its own modalities in accordance
with regional tendencies and temperaments. Recent scholarship has revealed that affinity with the tongues of the West
to be a very real fact, though long obscured by the dissimilarities
of Castilian. But its evolution has been as long and as conscious
as that of any. It has been the speech of men who carved
out their own destiny. Historical circumstances, the Frankish
dominion, the later dream of a Pyrenean kingdom, and the
active part played here as in Galicia by the troubadours, have
caused it to develop in close kinship with Provençal, but it
remains a definite language, a legitimate daughter of Latin and
not a bastard offshoot. The proof is in the vitality of its literature. Its written documents go back to the early ninth century,

with a recommendation from the Church that preaching should be in the vernacular. By the twelfth there blossoms forth not merely court poetry but a rare wealth of fine prose, royal chronicles, political and commercial codes, romances of chivalry. Ramón Lull (see p. 107) bequeathed a truly encyclopædic heritage of philosophy, mysticism and science, establishing to all time the dignity and sufficiency of his native speech.

Centuries of ruthless castilianization succeeded in imposing the tongue of bureaucracy and in relegating Catalan to the country districts. There it persisted until with Romanticism and the cult of the mediaeval it once again leapt into prominence, not to lead a precarious existence merely as the handmaiden of a political movement, for languages cannot be forced into vitality, but because Catalonia had waked anew to the older glories of her race, and the key to the tradition was Catalan. Aribau's famous *Ode* of 1833 (see p. 186) was a first trumpet-call to an active pride in the past and the beginning of a movement to restore, purify, decastilianize a language that could stand by itself. To-day Catalan authors, writing to a potential public of five millions, can sometimes count on larger sales than Castilians, whose speech is the speech in Europe of four times that number.

The policy of centralization has never been fruitful in Spain. Land of many and conflicting tendencies, to one principle it has always been true, even to excess. Just as the individual refuses to merge into the regional, so the regional into the national. Catalonia can make a very notable contribution to Hispanic prosperity and Hispanic culture, not as a pale reflection of Madrid but as an entity combining something of the limpidity and light of that Greek thought which first reached its shores with the progressiveness of a people who have kept in close touch with European movements and have known how to make industry beautiful. Economically Catalonia would derive doubtful benefits from independence. Its agricultural yield is a mere fraction of its consumption, and its prosperity, dependent in great part on imported raw materials, could be all but stifled by tariff walls. It is for Madrid to make the gesture which will grant full scope to regional pride and initiative and yet leave Catalans glad to co-operate in the well-being of the country as a whole. The alienation of sympathies is perhaps the greatest crime which modern statesmanship can commit.

In Valencia one hears a tongue which is still far from Spanish though just intelligible to the Spaniard. It is Catalan facing south instead of north, influenced less by French and more by Castilian. The land, with its groves of oranges and lemons,

an unforgettable splash of gold against a spring sky, bespeaks
the transition to Andalusia, where the harsh facts of industrialism
are unable to acclimatize themselves and life is colour and music.
The Arabs found life pleasant there and sent the Berbers up
north to struggle for existence. For them was the delight in
running water, in delicate tracery in architecture, in poetry which
springs spontaneously to the lips, a tribute to the joy of living.
The places are few where one can still believe wholeheartedly
that time was made for cats and dogs. Andalusia is one of
them, and the traveller who goes there with a fixed itinerary
will find himself, and rightly, an object of scorn.

The *andaluz* is an exuberant conversationalist. So lively
are his impressions before the kaleidoscope of life that he must
exteriorize them or explode, and his eloquence is of a persuasive-
ness that ends by creating not only for his listener but for himself
a world far removed from reality. If the *sevillano* tells you that
two and two make six and a half, it is because he himself believes
that they make five, and under a sky so diaphanous that it
seems to reach up to the very gates of Heaven one's credulity is
not easily fettered, for mere facts are unavailing to disturb the
all-permeating peace. The dialect of Andalusia is a derivative
of the Castilian which from the thirteenth to the fifteenth century
spread south over the ever-increasing territory won back from
the Muslim. Its distinctive features are attributable partly to a
tardy evolution, partly to the effect on language of a temperament in which laziness takes from the energy of articulation
what vivacity adds to its rapidity. They may be briefly summarized. Intervocalic *d* and, to a less extent, *g* disappear :
na (nada), llegá (llegada), miaja (migaja) ; interdental *z* is pronounced as *s* (*seseo*), or, more rarely, *s* as *z* (*ceceo*) ; *s* at the end of
a syllable becomes a mere aspiration, ehta (esta), loh libroh (los
libros), or is assimilated to the following consonant, mul-lo (muslo);
r at the end of a syllable is often likewise assimilated—vihen
(virgen)—, at the end of a word it may become *n*—mejón (mejor)
—, and often again it is lost,—lleválo (llevarlo) ; initial *h* from
Latin *f* is aspirated : hilo, humo ; *ll* is weakened to *y* : caye
(calle) ; and *l* after a consonant tends to become *r*, prato, branco.
Several of these variations are definitely archaic ; many of
them are characteristic of South-American Spanish. For Spanish
America was colonized and exploited from the Guadalquivir,
and, if the *conquistadores* did not carry the King's Spanish across
the Atlantic, it was at least a considerable service that they
should have spread the same dialect.

The two Castiles, by way of contrast, complete the picture.

Perched high on a barren plateau, far from the sea and all its moderating influences, they strike a very distinctive note, a note of introspection, of austerity, of intimacy with the things that abide. The traveller feels it in his bones as he wanders across those monotonous landscapes, where man seems a pigmy in the presence of Nature, and realizes it. It is as naturally the land of crusaders and mystics as Andalusia is the home of bull-fighting. And it is the crusaders and the mystics who have formed Spain. Castile has been the leaven that has leavened the whole mass, standing out from the rest of the country as the peculiar home of individualism.

The transference by Ordoño II (914–924) of his court from Oviedo to León brings the first mention of protest from Castile that it should be subject to a distant tribunal, and we read of the election of two judges to decide all disputes in Castile as far as the river Pisuerga. Tradition has it further that the Castilians collected and consigned to the flames in Burgos every known copy within their territories of the *Fuero Juzgo*, the Visigothic code observed in León, in Aragon, in Catalonia and among the Mozarabs, decreeing that their justices should be guided by *albedrío*, free-will,—that is to say, by their own judgment and by customary usage,—and not by any respect for conventional authority. The change was epoch-making, for it marked out Castile as a dissentient, refractory to dictation and even to tradition when conscious that it had its own path to follow. The same ferment is at work in the development of its tongue, the predestined vehicle of epic as Galician is of lyric. On many points Castilian follows an evolution distinct from that ruling to east, west and south, and where the direction is the same it reveals greater surety in itself and reaches the definitive stage much earlier. At a time when codices from León bear glosses in Arabic, copyists in Castile comment or translate in Castilian. And it is this region of consuetudinary law and of vigorous romance speech which set the norm for the rest of Spain. When we speak of the Spanish language now, we mean Castilian, and it is the passage from Latin to Castilian that must here occupy our preferential attention.

National consciousness is closely bound up with a national tongue. It was no mere coincidence that 1492, Spain's *annus mirabilis*, the year of the fall of Granada, the expulsion of the Jews and the discovery of America, should bring to light the earliest known grammar of a romance language, Nebrija's *Gramática de la Lengua Castellana*. In all phases of the country's life it was clear that a long period of uncertainty and groping was over and that the time had come for systematization and taking stock. 'When I consider well with myself,' runs the dedication to Queen Isabel, 'and fix my gaze on the antiquity of all things which for our remembering have been preserved in writing, one thing I find and infer as a conclusion most certain, that always language has been the companion of empire, and did in such wise follow it that together they had their beginning, grew and flourished, and afterwards in their fall they were again

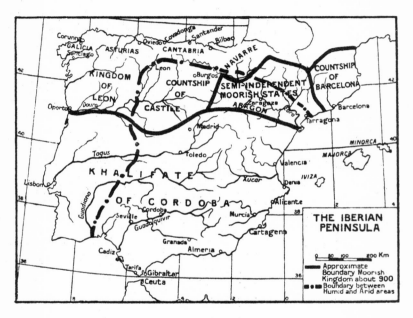

together.'[1] With the new reality of empire came the consciousness of a tongue worthy to follow it round the world and to impose itself on new peoples and continents.

There have been many stages between the speech of Cæsar and that of Cervantes, but the tradition is continuous, with the Senecas and Martial under Rome, Orosius and Saint Isidore

[1] 'Cuando bien cómigo pienso, i pongo delante los ojos el antiguedad de todas las cosas que para nuestra recordacion i memoria quedaron escriptas, una cosa hallo i saco por conclusion mui cierta : que siempre la lengua fue compañera del imperio ; i de tal manera lo siguió, que junta mente començaron, crecieron i florecieron, i despues junta fue la caida de entrambos.'

among the Goths, and the centuries of literary activity in the monastery until Alfonso the Wise made learning available to the ordinary citizen and taught him to have pride in his country's record. The kinship with the parent tongue is still easily traced. as in verbal forms, where whole tenses remain with but the change of a single letter as they were uttered by Cicero ; and dilettanti have left us compositions which are at once Latin and Spanish. The literature of the thirteenth century in Spain is readily intelligible to the modern reader, whereas the French of the period is to the uninitiated a closed book.

Many tongues have reacted on Spanish and left their mark on its vocabulary, but it is a tribute to the intensity of the Roman influence that not even the Goths, who found the moral authority of Rome at a low ebb, nor the Moors, in spite of their longer stay and of their cultural pre-eminence, could shake the hold of the Latin speech on the peninsula. Rome differed from other invaders in that it not only brought to Spain its customs, institutions and literature, but succeeded in creating a social cohesion and a civic sense so imposing that assimilation and full citizenship became the greatest ambition of the conquered.

The speech these rude tribesmen learnt was, needless to say, neither acquired from the *domine* nor steeped in the wells of pure Latin undefiled. It came primarily from contact with the soldiery, men who already in Italy expressed themselves in ways not current in the forum, and this ' vulgar ' Latin, domiciled now in regions far beyond the range of purists, marks out for itself distinctive tendencies of evolution which in the fullness of time produce a new romance tongue. Its domain was the entire peninsula, though least strong in the Basque country, a wild mountainous region of indomitable tribes and scant economic value and on the direct road to nowhere ; and its sway so absolute that pre-Latin traces in modern Spanish are exceedingly few (*páramo, izquierdo,* and several other words and place-names bespeak Iberian or Celtic descent).

The schools were there, and Spain produced its great names in Latin literature, but theirs was the speech of the erudite few, definitely modelled on Rome and finding its precepts in past authorities rather than in present practice. By the fall of the Empire, classical Latin was dead and its imitation a scholastic exercise ; not without influence, it is true, in the measure in which learning mingled with the outer world and imposed respect, but still something far removed from that principle of progress by which a language must constantly change, adapt and reju- venate itself if it is to keep pace with the movement of man's

mind. It is, then, rather in the development of low Latin
among the classes who used it as a living instrument and, ignorant
of linguistic science, developed it according to their needs that
one must search for the tendencies which have made modern
Spanish. That the same classes should be precisely those least
likely to leave behind written memorials of their existence is
the student's capital difficulty.

The first literary works are of the eleventh and twelfth centuries
(*Poema de Mio Cid, c.* 1140) and reveal Spanish as an accomplished
fact, but earlier notarial documents and ecclesiastical glosses
have done much to unveil the stages to that end. Scholars who
progressed backwards from romance texts to romance tendencies in Latin manuscripts found that, earlier than 1070, these
tendencies lost increasingly in number and significance before
a surge of low Latinity. Research from the opposite direction,
i.e. through the documents of the ninth and tenth centuries,
has recently brought to light a new richness of romance forms
appearing as marginal notes to elucidate or amplify the text.
These, too, decrease notably towards the end of the eleventh
century and vanish before that same low Latinity. One finds
then documentary evidence of a first gradual evolution towards
romance dating from the early centuries of the Middle Ages,
full of archaisms, neologisms and confusion with scholastic
Latin. There follows, with a reinstatement of this latter in
something approaching purity, a marked cessation of romance
elements, easily traceable to historical events.

The reign of Ferdinand I (the Great) of Castile (1035–1065)
saw a striking decrease in the extent of Mohammedan sway in
Spain. The Christian kingdoms were becoming alive to their
power and to their *rôle* as champions of religion, and the realization anew of their affinity to Europe and European culture
turned their gaze northward instead of to the south. The
suppression of Visigothic or Mozarabic rites (1078–1080) makes
the Spanish liturgy conform with that of the rest of Europe,
and the Benedictine monks of Cluny come to Spain to uphold
the ideals of religious austerity and papal supremacy. They go
further, and initiate a drastic cultural revision. Holding many
important sees, notably Toledo, they set themselves to restore
Latin grammar and scholarship among the clergy. Previous
literature is rendered unintelligible by the substitution of French
script for Visigothic, and the predominant influences in the new
age come from beyond the Pyrenees. It is about this time that
romance elements disappear from the Latin of notarial documents.
When, a century later, the purist influence has faded out, romance

reappears, not now uncertain and apologetic, but setting itself up as a definite norm alongside Latin. Thus, whereas in the earlier period one finds vacillation between many stages of development (e.g. *alteru, altro, autro, aotro, otro*), the latter is either definitely Latin, *alteru*, or definitely romance, *otro*.

The *sermo rusticus*, in Spain as elsewhere, early developed sounds new to Latin, and the earliest documents show scribes grappling with the inadequacy of the Latin alphabet to represent them. Among distinguishing features in the process of evolution one notes the formation of new diphthongs from accented ĕ and ŏ (ciento, bueno) ; the appearance of a series of palatal consonants evolved under the influence of the yod (daño, damnu ; mucho, mvltu ; Castilla, castella) ; the preservation or modification, rarely the loss, of the final vowel ; the sonorization of intervocalic voiceless plosives, with the subsequent loss of the unaccented vowel ; the reduction of initial *pl, cl, fl* to *ll* ; the passage of initial *f* to *h*, which has since become mute ; and the complete confusion between *b* and *v*. Documents reveal many conflicting forms of a word according as it is used by purists (e.g. *auctoricare*), by men not wholly insensible to romance influences (*obturicare, obtorigare, octoricare, octurgare, autorgare*), by pedants who mingle both tendencies (*otorekare*) or through ignorance cut across the instinct of the language (*otorkare*), or finally by those who know nothing of Latinity and reveal the popular tendency supreme (*otorigare, oturigare, otorgar*).[1] Continuity of record is lacking to give the chronological sequence, but it may often be reconstructed : *debita, debida, debda, deuda* ; *populu, pobulu, poblo, pueblo* ; *civitate, cividade, cibdad, ciudad*. In syntax, as with other romance tongues, the accusative is the only case of the noun, and its final *m*, tending to disappear in Latin, goes completely ; case relations are expressed by prepositions, and tenses enriched by auxiliary verbs.

Linguistic unity in Spain is still far from being a fact, and the language imposed by Alfonso the Wise was originally the speech of a minority, the inhabitants of Castile. Throughout the south and east, where the cultural influence of the invaders was greatest, education made men conservative. Cantabria, on the contrary, as the latest part of the peninsula to be romanized, and that never completely, shows a freer evolution, and low Latin develops many peculiar features ; and Cantabria was the cradle of Castile. Of the three vertical bands into which Spain is divided dialectally, Galician and Leonese, Castilian, Aragonese

[1] Menéndez Pidal, R., *Orígenes del español*, Madrid, 1926, p. 556.

and Catalan, Castilian was until the eleventh century hemmed in to a diminutive territory, and counted for little beyond its frontiers. The others had much in common, and were united in the centre and south by the speech of the Mozarabs. It is instructive to note the changing forms of a word as one moves across the north of Spain : e.g. Galician *leite*, Asturian *lleite*, *leiche*, Castilian *leche*, Aragonese *leite*, Catalan *llet* ; Galician *porta, tempo, peito*, Castilian *puerta, tiempo, pecho*, Catalan *porta, temps, pit*.[1] In each instance the dialects of east and west bear a closer relationship to one another than to Castilian. Then came political ascendancy, on which Alfonso VII set the seal in the partition of his realms in 1157 by leaving Castile to his first-born. Toledo had long since been conquered and to Old Castile was added the New. The language of the conquerors swept away Mozarabic dialects and, like a wedge, effectively broke the links uniting east and west, so that till recently it has been customary to look for the affinity of Catalan outside the peninsula, in Provençal.

In Cantabria, then, the nucleus of Castile, many of the distinctive traits of Spanish had their origin. The substitution of an aspirated *h* for initial *f* responds to the lack of this sound in primitive Iberian, which tongue persisted on both sides of the Pyrenees in spite of Rome. From Cantabria, too, came the contraction of the suffix *iello* to *illo*, the pronunciation *z* (modern *j, oreja, ojo*) in place of the *ll* or *y* of the remaining peninsular dialects ; the passage from *ct, lt* to *ch* (*hecho, mucho*). The diphthongization of *o* was a much less localized phenomenon, but again Castile took the lead in developing and later in propagating it. By the tenth century it had there reached its definitive form *ue*, while León and Aragon still vacillated between *ue, uo* and *ua*.

Some three hundred words are all that remain in Castilian to tell of the three centuries of Gothic rule in Spain. The paucity of the contribution is explained partly by the intellectual inferiority of the Visigoths as compared with the people they overthrew, partly by the long period of frontier contact with the Empire previous to their arrival, thanks to which their speech was already latinized to a considerable degree.

It is more surprising to find the linguistic influence of the Arabs utterly disproportionate to the cultural hegemony they so long enjoyed in the peninsula, a hegemony eloquently voiced in the lament of one Álvaro de Córdoba in 854. ' Many of my coreligionists ', he comments bitterly, ' read the poetry and tales of

[1] Américo Castro, *Lengua, Enseñanza y Literatura*, pp. 34, 47.

the Arabs and study the writings of the Mohammedan theologians and philosophers, not to refute them but to learn how to express themselves with greater elegance and correctness in the Arab tongue. Alas, all the Christian youths who become famous for their talent know only the language and literature of the Arabs ; they read and study zealously Arabic books, of which by dint of great expenditure they form extensive libraries, and proclaim aloud on all sides that this literature is worthy of admiration. Heu, pro dolor ! linguam suam nesciunt christiani.' But intercourse only served to accentuate the essentially different character of the two tongues. The same person often spoke the one and the other, but they were none the less immiscible, and romance grammar and pronunciation remained alike unmodified. Only in vocabulary are there any considerable traces. Spanish has derived from Arabic some 650 words, the majority concrete nouns which have been adopted with the objects they name ; many terms of war speak of the fundamental relationship between the two races ; others refer to the arts and sciences in which Spain had so much to learn, architecture, agriculture, industry or medicine.

Modern European tongues have entered Spanish mainly through literature. In their beginnings Peninsular letters are largely derivative. The eleventh century, as has been noted already, opened the way to French influence. Sancho the Great of Navarre remade the pilgrim route to Santiago, transforming it from a dangerous mountain passage into a highway of commercial and intellectual relationships, dotted with French colonies as the *Poema de Mío Cid* is dotted with gallicisms, *mensaje, palafré, vergel, vianda*. French still remains the most active influence on Spanish, especially in the eighteenth century, when the Bourbon dynasty and the preponderating influence of French thought throughout Europe introduced not only a multitude of words, terms of dress, social usages, warfare, but of phrases and idioms. The literature of no country is more translated in Spain, and the apparent ease of turning from one tongue to another closely akin is in reality a difficulty and a temptation to the careless or ignorant scribe. Such, for example, the deformation of ' à bride abattue ' to ' a brida batida ' by a seventeenth-century dramatist, to the disparagement of the proper Spanish idiom ' a rienda suelta '.[1] Only next to French comes Italian, whose cultural relations with Spain have been of the closest both before and since the days when Juan de Valdés, in the early sixteenth century, could write with legitimate pride that

[1] Noted by Américo Castro, *op. cit.*, p. 135.

' now in Italy, alike among ladies and gentlemen, it was counted refinement and elegance to be able to speak Castilian '.[1]

The contribution of Germany is recent, and consists in the main of scientific terms. English has loaned a considerable vocabulary of politics and industry, and has swept down all barriers in the domain of sport, even to the extent of endangering such a genuinely Spanish word as *deportista* with the spurious *sportman*. The language is to-day more receptive than ever, a state due partly to the ever-increasing internationalism of life, partly to the fact that in the more material branches of progress Spain has never aspired to leadership, and partly to lack of education and pride in its own ancient riches. Foreign terms are taken into the current vocabulary almost daily and adapted before one's eyes. A typical example is *lock-out*, which appeared recently first in its English dress, wavered momentarily between *lokout* and *locout*, and in less than a month had reached its phonetic form *locaut*.

But while foreign influences have been felt sporadically, as a corollary on politics and commerce, the language has constantly been renewing itself at the source. The latinizing tendency is inevitably strongest at the Renaissance, and is linked up with the varying fortunes of Spanish as a literary tongue. There had been a vigorous tradition of vernacular literature from the *Poema del Cid* onward, including such notable achievements as the *Libro de Buen Amor, Amadís de Gaula* and the *Celestina* ; but as a vehicle for learning it was long without repute. Conversation in Spanish was forbidden by statute among University students, and in 1546 Ambrosio de Morales wrote sadly : ' It is now almost sufficient for a book to be written in Castilian to be held of no account '.[2] Mariana wrote his history of Spain in Latin (1592), although, reflecting on the insufficiency of such patriotism, he had the perception afterwards to translate it into Spanish.

When there came men bold in their faith in the tongue and able to translate it into works, as Hernán Pérez de Oliva, whose version of the *Amphitruo* of Plautus was written designedly to illustrate the sufficiency of Spanish (*Muestra de la lengua Castellana en el Nacimiento de Hercules o Comedia de Amphitrion*, 1525), they proceeded from an intimate command of Latin as the fount of eloquence and turned there for enrichment. Hence many *cultismos*, terms which through their tardy and conscious adop-

---

[1] ' Ya en Italia, assi entre damas como cavalleros pasaba por gentileza y galania saber hablar castellano.'—*Diálogo de la Lengua.*

[2] ' Ya quasi basta ser un libro escrito en Castellano para no ser tenido en nada.'—Preface to *Diálogo de la Dignidad del Hombre*, by Pérez de Oliva.

tion have suffered few changes in form or content, alongside full romance forms of the same words current in popular speech since the days of the Roman soldiery. There are centuries between *bodega* and *botica*, *letrado* and *literato*, *cadera* and *cátedra*. The day of translation from Latin brought the discovery that many terms lacked correspondence in romance, and they were simply adapted. By the end of the sixteenth century the vernacular was triumphant. ' I have confidence in our Castilian tongue ', had written the same Pérez de Oliva in his dedication, ' that it will not let itself be worsted.' [1] The Golden Age brought, with Cervantes, Lope, Quevedo, a glorious justification.

Castilian is among the most phonetic tongues in existence. Added to its linguistic position between Latin and French, this suggests a tempting ease to him who would not go beneath the surface. In the richness of its vocabulary, the native vigour of its idioms and its precision in expressing the finer shades of meaning, the searching student, on the contrary, finds at once despair and joy. The vocabulary of Shakespeare has been computed. No one has yet fixed even an approximate limit to that of Lope de Vega, author of some hundreds of plays. The degree of exactitude permitted by the tongue may be exemplified by the fact that whereas English and French have but one word for ' to be ' and one for ' to have ', Spanish has in either instance two (*ser* and *estar*, *haber* and *tener*) to be clearly differentiated.

Such are the more obvious characteristics of a tongue that exercises a subtle power of creating enthusiasm. ' Speak to me in Spanish, for I understand it well and will take pleasure in it,' [2] Cervantes makes the Queen of England say, and the traveller from the north still experiences a charm hard to define as he listens. The emperor Charles V spoke Italian to his mistresses, French to his friends, German to his dogs ; in Spanish he communed with his God. For an earlier tribute we may go back to 1150, to the chronicler of a military expedition who writes of the Castilians : ' illorum lingua resonat quasi tympano tuba.' Sonorous, full of a weighty dignity, the speech of a race of *conquistadores*, it has also its tender side, helped by a wealth of diminutive endings.

The Spaniard delights in his tongue, and uses it lovingly. ' To talk ' (' tell ') is a prosaic word, of the counting of things ; ' parler ' is ' parabolare ', the search for effect ; but ' hablar ' is ' fabulare ', to invent, to romance, to revel in the joys of

[1] ' Yo tengo en nuestra castellana [lengua] confiança que no se dexará vencer.'
[2] ' Habladme en español, que yo le entiendo bien y gustaré de ello.'

conversation.   The sounds of Spanish are essentially short and
clear-cut, energetically enunciated and admitting of no slurring
and no diphthongization.   But the foreigner is impressed most
of all by its rich, flexible intonation.   Where the Englishman
is content with tones and half-tones, the Spaniard ranges through
octaves.   His meaning does not depend on the order of words
but on the rise and fall of the voice, and, in writing, interrogation
and exclamation marks precede as well as follow in order that
the reader may be prepared.

The mantle of Roman oratory passed to Spain, to the Senecas
and Quintilian, and the more meretricious facets of eloquence,
false emphasis, verbosity, a sought obscurity, have been recurrent
defects in Spanish literature whenever it has lost its grip on
reality.   But alongside the Senecas is Martial, and the gift for
pungent satire where not a word is lost is also inherent in the
language.   Quevedo wrote *La Política de Dios* ; he is also the
author of many a memorable *letrilla satírica*.   And against the
indictment of mere wordiness one remembers that nowhere is
the short, pithy saying more acclimatized than in Spain.   Sancho
Panza is the living embodiment of a Book of Proverbs.

Bearing in mind the diversity apparent in every aspect of
the peninsula, geography, race, history, language, it becomes
passing hard to form a broad estimate of Spanish character and
temperament which shall not be, *ipso facto*, false and misleading.
One may most safely begin by discounting the traditional picture
of Spain, familiar to all who have ever built castles, the Spain
of tambourine and guitar, of gypsies and light-hearted vagabonds,
of passionate love and equally passionate knife-thrusts.   ' Who
has not seen Seville has seen no marvel,' [1] says the Andalusian ;
it is still more cogent to say that who has seen only Seville has not
seen Spain, nor even the most characteristic side of Spain.   The
tourist who accepts an itinerary from a travel agency and goes
out cherishing the belief that, as in another equally maligned
and not wholly dissimilar country, there are no facts in Spain,
will find the inhabitants sufficiently sophisticated to humour
him.   He will see no facts, and he will come home to write a
book which, however unconsciously, will be a *guide à thèse*,
leaving truth where it was.

It must be confessed that one who turns from ingenuous
travel impressions to the reasoned analyses of native thinkers
will find his perplexity rather deepened than lightened.   Spain
has never been quite sure of its *rôle* in the world, and its most

_____
[1] ' Quien no ha visto Sevilla no ha visto maravilla.'

authoritative interpreters share the uncertainty. Angel Ganivet [1] has theorized on the peculiar destinies of a peninsular State. The continental country is concerned always to be prepared for possible invasion from its neighbours ; its policy is based on resistance. The island kingdom, with greater security and inelastic frontiers, must breed adventurers and found colonies or die of hunger. It tends as naturally to expansion as the other to conservation, and is characterized by an outlook essentially aggressive. Between them comes the peninsula. Doubtful which path to follow, it is likely to make an indifferent showing at either. It will recover from waves of invasion to burst into sudden activity as a colonizing power, forgetful till too late that there are still frontiers to be guarded. But in greatness or decline independence will be its keynote.

Spaniards have always been critical of their country. ' Hearing a man speak ', wrote Bartrina over fifty years ago, ' it is easy to tell where he saw the light of day. If he praises England to you he will be English ; if he speaks ill of Prussia he is French ; and if he speaks ill of Spain he is a Spaniard.' [2] Since 1898, when there faded away all hope of a colonial empire, the spirit of inquiry has been tenfold more intense, and Spaniards have interrogated not only the future but the past. Their findings are instructive for their lack of agreement. To Ganivet, an Andalusian, the greatest influence after the preaching of Christianity in the formation of Spain, that which gave birth to the spirit of quixotry, was the incursion of the Arabs. Unamuno, a Basque, professes towards the Arabs a profound antipathy, all but denies such a thing as Arabian civilization, and holds their invasion to have been the supreme calamity of Spain. [3] Certain fundamental attributes one can, nevertheless, distinguish beyond fear of contradiction.

Carthage was among the earliest cultural influences in Spain, and in Unamuno's adaptation of a line by a slave from Carthage, who indeed never saw the Peninsula, one finds the most fitting text for an appreciation of Spanish character : ' Homo sum, et nullum hominem a me alienum puto '. A broad humanity, founded on the belief that man is more important than his works and that his value is independent of the trappings of circumstance,

---

[1] *Idearium Español* (see p. 183 below).
[2] Oyendo hablar a un hombre, fácil es
    acertar donde vió la luz del sol ;
    si os alaba a Inglaterra, será inglés,
    si os habla mal de Prusia, es un francés,
    y si habla mal de España, es español.'
[3] Unamuno y Ganivet, *El Porvenir de España.*

underlies the Spaniard's every relationship with his fellows. It explains his refractoriness to authority and organization ; it explains also his inborn sense of pride, levelling the peasant with the highest in the realm and leading to the extreme and unreasoning cult of the point of honour, a dominant *motif* in classical Spanish literature. A belief in divine right secures inviolability to the king, but ' under the king, no one ',[1] and the wronged subject, who has held his peace in the belief that the offender was his monarch, discovers the real culprit and slays him without ceremony in the royal presence. It is a true democracy which comes out in the most aristocratic. Calderón was a Knight of the Order of Santiago and a Court poet who wrote conventional dramas of gallantry. A military expedition to Catalonia awoke other sympathies and he came back to write *The Mayor of Zalamea*, one of the noblest vindications in Spanish literature of the inalienable rights of the commoner against any overweening presumption of authority. Or it may be called an innate aristocracy that is very present in the humblest. There was a world of philosophy in the ragged girl who approached the writer on a severe winter evening in Madrid and asked, with that use of diminutives which can make the dignified Castilian tongue so tender and so moving : ' A little alms, young sir, we are all little brothers '.[2]

One of the most characteristic writings of the Spanish Renaissance is a *Dialogue on the Dignity of Man*.[3] The concept has often stood in the way of material progress, but it has always been cherished. The squire in the *Lazarillo de Tormes* had left his home in Old Castile because a neighbouring gentleman refused to doff his hat to him, and starved in Toledo rather than derogate from his gentle birth by putting a hand to toil. Few foreigners are not moved to anger by the beggars who are found in Spanish towns, but no true Spaniard will look down on them. The accidents of fortune can never justify a slighting *tú*, and he who cannot give has at least a ' Pardon, brother '. The beggar himself considers his place in society fully justified. It was in Toledo that one such sought alms ' for the love of God, for in the fullness of my youth He has taken away all desire to work '.[4] To an individualist the reasoning is perfectly sound.

---

[1] *Del Rey abajo, ninguno*, the title of a comedy by Rojas Zorrilla (1607–1648).
[2] ' Una limosnita, señorito, que todos somos hermanitos.'
[3] *Diálogo de la Dignidad del Hombre*, by Hernán Pérez de Oliva.
[4] ' Una limosna por el amor de Dios, que en la plenitud de mi juventud me ha quitado la gana de trabajar.'

For by personal dignity one must hold, whatever else be lost; and, as it is expected, so it is freely conceded even to one's enemy. ' Knights of Granada, although Moors, hidalgos,' [1] begins a border ballad.

It is an old saying, and not devoid of truth, that the gods denied to Spain one only blessing, a good government. Peoples probably get the government they deserve, and the extreme individualism of the Spaniard, producing an apathy in the face of organized society that is the despair of reformers, steadily refuses to believe that mere legislation can affect his fate. His practical philosophy is stoicism, expounded by a Spaniard, Seneca, who need not have gone outside Spain to formulate it. The true good of man lies within, in the knowledge of self that raises one above external events. Should they prove overpowering, the remedy is still in one's own hands, and Seneca's departure from life was head-high.

Seneca was born in Córdoba, but Andalusia was not formed till centuries later, and his doctrine might well have come from the heart of Castile. Yet there is no real antithesis between it and the frame of mind we associate with southern Spain. Unamuno may belittle the idea of a Muslim civilization, and it is true that the concrete visible results of a stay of eight centuries are surprisingly few. The Arabs gave to Spain a less tangible legacy, but something that speaks of a new value come into European life. It was a new creed, subordinating material gains to the pleasures of the senses, stressing the faith that this world can be a pleasant place when Time has fallen from his throne and become our servant, urging that the inscrutable future be left to work out the preconceived pattern of Allah while men's eyes feast only on what is beautiful in the present. In an age when the rest of Europe was obsessed by the conception of this existence as a dreary preparation for the next, the Arabs had brought to Spain a sense of the beauty and the joy of life. It is the conviction of the persistence of that sense, grafted on to the background of stoicism and personal dignity, that justifies one's belief in Spain to-day.

' The Spaniard's onslaught in battle', wrote Chateaubriand, ' is irresistible, but having once dislodged the enemy from his position, he is content to sit down, cigarette in mouth, guitar in hand, to celebrate the victory.' This supreme gift of detachment, which despises time, money, all our customary symbols

[1] ' Caballeros granadinos, aunque moros hijosdalgo ' (literally ' sons of something ').

of well-being, is the very antithesis of the spirit that informs our present age, but it is the distinctive feature of a land ' where peace comes dropping slow '. ' Spain is an absurd country ', to quote once more from Ganivet, ' and metaphysically impossible ; absurdity is its nerve and mainstay. Its turn to prudence will denote the end.' [1]

Yet Spain is not all vain imagination. If its head is in the clouds, its feet are very firmly on the earth. Realism, by which is meant not the search for the lurid and the ugly, but the acceptance of things as they are, suppressing nothing, explaining away nothing, is everywhere. Santa Teresa, who finds God no less among the saucepans than in the mystic trance ; Murillo, turning from portraits of monks to depict ragamuffins ; Don Quixote, the idealist who has in Sancho Panza not an antagonist but a necessary complement : all tell us that one rises above the trivial and the mean not by ignoring but by understanding. Spanish literature begins on a note of realism. Compare the *Poema de Mío Cid* with the *Chanson de Roland*. The latter abounds in romantic and idealistic incidents. The hero of the former is of human stature throughout, a tender husband and father, a stern upholder of the law—in whose finer points he is deeply versed— and of his personal dignity, punctilious in his relations with his king, and for all his Castilian gravity possessed of an engaging sense of humour. And no literary genre is so *castizo*, so genuinely Spanish, as the picaresque novel, the romance of roguery. But realism in Spain is tempered always by kindness and comprehension ; there can be no sting of bitterness for him who feels himself independent of the world. It has been noted that of the hundreds of characters who people *Don Quixote* not one is wholly bad or unreservedly frowned on by Cervantes. Yet the life of Cervantes was not laid in soft places.

From this firm basis, then, of fact, and not out of mere impracticality, springs the apparently superficial light-heartedness of the Spaniard. With more than a tinge of fatalism he can accept the present and await the future undismayed. What happens now has happened before and will happen again, and out of that vast fund of accumulated if uncoördinated philosophy to be found in his store of proverbs something will suggest itself to meet the case. No buffetings of fate can avail against ' There will be another day to-morrow '.[2] 'Patience and re-shuffle '[3] is

---

[1] ' España es una nación absurda y metafísicamente imposible, y el absurdo es su nervio y su principal sostén. Su cordura será la señal de su acabamiento.'—*El Porvenir de España*, p. 83.
[2] ' Mañana será otro día.'   [3] ' Paciencia y barajar.'

optimism in its essence. A group of peasants, carrying great bundles wrapped in newspapers and bandanna handkerchiefs, boarded a train at a tiny station between Granada and Antequera. They lacked alike hats, collars and coats, their garb coarse shirts and breeches and cord sandals. One would have said they were bound for the next station for market day. Yet their destination was Buenos Aires. ' And when will you be back ? ' ' Perhaps never, perhaps next year. Who knows ? '

Such casual acceptance of life's problems lay behind the greatness of Spain's golden age. *Ne plus ultra*, the ancients had said when they came to the pillars of Hercules. Charles V proudly blotted out the negative : *Plus ultra*. There was more beyond, there always is more beyond for the unshackled adventurer. Hernán Cortés on the shore of a new continent wrecked his boats and challenged the unknown ; and having won his way with a handful of men into the heart of a hostile empire and into the presence of a mighty monarch, ' it seemed good ', he writes home to his king, ' in the royal interest and for our own safety that that monarch should be in our power '.[1] And that idea he immediately translated into action, making Montezuma a close prisoner in his own capital.

As *conquistadores* they were supreme ; the problems of constructive colonization showed their weakness. Boundless energy in the thrill of action, great moments of vision ' silent upon a peak in Darien ', but scant patience for the routine task of consolidation, of reasoning, of laborious study. Spain's greatest authors have been men of intensely active life who have done things and forborne to theorize. Their drama is essentially one of improvization, born of contact with mankind. Lope de Vega was at pains to show that he knew all the rules and unities of the art of making plays, though he never applied them. His excuse, ' for since the man in the street pays for them it is only fair to address him as a fool to give him pleasure ',[2] is not so naïve as it may seem. The plain man, informed by a sense, however unconscious, of what is true to experience, will respond to the genuine and the durable in art with a surer criteiion than any evolved by the pedant in his study.

The genius of Spain is to a striking degree creative rather than critical. Criticism implies the recognition of a corpus of

[1] ' Me pareció . . . que convenía al real servicio y a nuestra seguridad que aquel señor estuviese en mi poder.'—*Carta Segunda de Relación*, 1520.
[2] ' Porque, como las paga el vulgo, es justo hablarle en necio para darle gusto.'
—*Arte Nuevo de Hazer Comedias*, 1609.

authority, of norms of conduct, of schools, a long preoccupation
with facts *qua* facts.   Against all such the Spaniard instinctively
rebels.   Of what should be an exact science he will make something essentially personal.   History, for example, as dealing with
the ways of man to man, he has always cultivated, but it has
become in his hands an art.   The *Estoria de Espanna* undertaken
by Alfonso the Wise began with the creation of the world, and
down the ages seized with a rare instinct on the human, the
eternal aspect of men and events.   The achievements of Nero
the Emperor fade before the account of his prowess in the art
of singing, his exercises in voice production as he lay flat with
a heavy sheet of lead on his chest, his recitals before an intimi-
dated audience.   When Al-Mansur, greatest of Arab generals,
ended his long career of campaigning against the north, the
monkish chronicler put a personal and very sincere touch into his
epitaph : ' In 1002 died Almanzor, and was buried in hell.'   And
Mariana, foremost of Spanish historians, is quite frank as to his
methods   ' I put down more than I believe ', he says, and seeing
no reason why legends should not have their crumb of truth he
allows them, too, to contribute to the panegyric of his country.
The study of man's record is humanized in Spain.   Mere facts are
only important in the light of the individual reaction to them,
and so are always changing and always averse to systematization.
The history of Spain's literature was written first by an American,
then by an Englishman ; that of its drama, by a German.

The results of this lack of continuous application, of rigorous
impersonal thought, are apparent in every manifestation of the
Spanish genius.   Its outstanding achievements are of the nature
of sudden flashes of inspiration, brilliant conceptions marred by
mediocre development and faulty judgment in detail.   The
idea underlying Calderón's *Life is a Dream* (*La Vida es Sueño*)
is of the noblest in literature, the struggle between free-will and
predestination, the victory of reason over the unchained passions
and appetites of man in his natural state, the vanity of earthly
pomp and power ; but its flaws are obvious to any tyro in letters,
and its ending is forced.   One often, indeed, gains the impression
that the playwright, conscious the allotted time is up, throws
verisimilitude to the winds, and rounds off his plot as readily
with a spate of murders as with impossible marriages.   Who
is he to say that the matter ends there, or to dare to write *Finis*
to any human action ?   Life itself does not end things, for there
is a beyond, and the belief enables him cheerfully to style the
blackest tragedy a *comedia*.

It is a notable revelation on the road to self-knowledge that things are not what they seem. There is a double truth, that of the immediate historical detail and that of the poetic whole. The first is static, isolated, of doubtful import in the pattern of existence. The second is the larger vision that supplies a faith whereby man may live. Spanish literature to most foreigners means Cervantes' *Don Quixote* and Calderón's *Life is a Dream*. Both are symbols of the Spanish people, and both are symbols of this latter truth of the imagination. One does not shut one's eyes to the former, but one goes further. ' That which seems to you to be a barber's basin ', Don Quixote informs Sancho, ' seems to me to be Mambrino's helmet, and to another it will seem to be something else.' [1] But basins and windmills led Sancho nowhere, whereas helmets and giants were stages in the career of Spain's greatest *conquistador*, one who discovered not new countries for Spain but Spain to herself. And in the end Sancho was converted.

The quest must be a lonely one, and in the long run facts are stubborn things. Crusades independent of facts ask for disaster in the eyes of the world, and Don Quixote, who for centuries has made the world laugh, recognized as he lay on his death-bed that he had been a tragic failure. His ' the immortal sadness of being divine '.[2] But true greatness is revealed in defeat, and the Knight of the Sorrowful Countenance, in following the gleam, saved his own soul, if all else was lost. ' Hic jacet pulvis, cinis, nihil ' is the legend over the tomb of an Archbishop in Toledo Cathedral. With the realization of the futility of material ambition the door is opened to the greater issues of man in his relation to eternity.

Eight centuries it took Spain to drive out the Muslim and make herself mistress in her own house, and four more were necessary to convince her that she should stay at home. Spaniards since 1898 are concerned for the prestige of their country in the scale of progressive nations, and full of theories. Unamuno would have Spain turn its back on a past of fantastic chivalry and become Europeanized with all haste. Ganivet maintained that the country must look south, to Africa, for its future. Perhaps it is not the true *rôle* of Spain ever again to loom large in international affairs, but rather simply to proceed along its own path of proud, impractical individualism, a standing reminder

---

[1] ' Y así, eso que a ti te parece bacía de barbero, me parece a mí el yelmo de Mambrino, y a otro le parecerá otra cosa.'—*Don Quixote*, I, 25.

[2] ' La tristeza inmortal de ser divino.'—Rubén Darío, *Soneto a Cervantes*.

28   SPAIN

of the value of man as man. But who can map out a nation's destiny? 'What are you painting?' inquired Don Quixote of one he saw busy with brush and canvas. 'That is as it may turn out', was the answer.

BIBLIOGRAPHY TO CHAPTER I

THE COUNTRY :
1. Azorín [J. Martínez Ruiz]. *El Paisaje de España visto por los españoles.* Madrid, 1917.
2. Echeverria. *España : el país y los habitantes.* Mexico, 1940.
3. Dwelshauvers, G. *La Catalogne et le problème catalan.* Paris, 1926.

THE LANGUAGE :
4. Lapesa, R. *Historia de la lengua española.* Second edition. Madrid, 1950.
5. Entwistle, W. J. *The Spanish Language.* London, 1936.
6. Menéndez Pidal, R. *Orígenes del español.* Madrid, 1926. [A small and readable textbook by the same author is *El Idioma español en sus primeros tiempos.* Madrid, 1927.]
7. Meyer-Lübke, W. *Introducción al estudio de la lingüística romance.* Trans. A. Castro. Second edition. Madrid, 1927.
[See also No. 68, which has a section on language and early literature.]

THE PEOPLE (from within) :
8. Altamira, R. *Psicología del pueblo español.* Second edition, revised. Barcelona, 1917. [With a Bibliography, pp. 285–335.]
9. Bergua, J. *Psicología del pueblo español.* Madrid, 1934.
10. Ganivet, A. *Idearium español.* Second edition. Madrid, 1915.
11. Madariaga, S. de. *The Genius of Spain.* Oxford, 1923.
12. Unamuno, M. de. *En torno al Casticismo.* Second edition. Madrid, 1916.
13. Menéndez Pidal, R. *Spaniards and their history.* Translated by Walter Starkie. London, 1950.

THE PEOPLE (from without) :
14. Borrow, G. *The Bible in Spain.* London, 1842. [Numerous later editions of this and No. 15.]
15. Ford, R. *Gatherings from Spain.* London, 1846.
16. Ellis, H. *The Soul of Spain.* Eleventh impression. London, 1929.
17. Trend, J. B. *A Picture of Modern Spain.* London, 1921.

CULTURE :
18. Castro, A. *El Pensamiento de Cervantes.* Madrid, 1926. [Renaissance thought in Spain.]
19. Haskins, C. H. *Studies in the History of Medieval Science.* Oxford, 1924. [The Arabs in Spain.]
20. Unamuno, M. de. *Del Sentimiento trágico de la vida.* Madrid, 1912. [The Spaniard's philosophy. *The Tragic Sense of Life* (London, 1921) is a translation of this.]
21. Peers, E. Allison. *Spanish Mysticism.* London, 1924.
[A large number of the works cited under other headings below will be found useful here also.]

CHAPTER II

SPANISH HISTORY TO 1492

THE influence of geographical conditions upon the course of Spanish history and upon the development of Spanish nationality is clearly perceptible. Spain stands in isolation from Europe and is divided within itself. Entirely surrounded by the Atlantic and Mediterranean waters, except where the Pyrenees separate it from France, the peninsula is also divided by mountain ranges into four regions : the narrow strip of coast-line on the north, the Mediterranean coast provinces, the southern province of Andalusia from Cádiz to Granada, and the great central plateau, which again is subdivided by the Guadarrama and Oretana mountains and separated from Andalusia by the Sierra Morena. Differences in altitude cause climatic differences, which have had their effect upon the history of the country ; the rapidity of the slope from the interior to the sea, which is greater on the East than on the West, makes river navigation almost impossible, except for short distances from the coast ; while the torrential rains which alternate with seasons of drought often cause disastrous floods. On the other hand, the coastal regions are remarkably fertile, especially in the East and South ; the mineral wealth of the peninsula has been famous from the earliest historical times.

To these facts are due in some degree the peculiar individuality of the Spanish people and also the differences between local populations ; the tendency to ' regionalism ' and the reluctance to combine during the earlier centuries may thus be partially explained. Foreign influence naturally became most potent in the fertile coast districts of the East and South, while the harder conditions of life in the mountainous centre and North produced a more virile type of character.

The primitive populations of Spain are a subject rather for the ethnologist than for the historian The first people of whom we hear in ancient history were the **Iberians,** and of them we know little more than of their predecessors, among whom the Cromagnon type appears to have predominated. Whether

29

they were the progenitors of the Basques, whether the latter preserve and continue their language, what were their relations with the **Celts** who followed them, and what ethnological significance belongs to the term ' Celtiberian ', are questions to which no certain answer is available.   The Roman historians appear to use the term ' Celtiberian ' as a generic name for the native populations of the country, of whom as individual tribes they knew very little.   Their descriptions represent the native Spaniard as a brave and hardy enemy, contemptuous of danger and pain, *prodiga gens animae*, generous and ready to forgive, but no less ready to avenge an insult or a wrong ; politically an individualist, inclined to separatism, not easy to lead and impossible to drive.   This race gave the Romans more trouble than any other native race within the Empire, and from them the Roman tacticians are said to have borrowed the famous short sword and the *pilum* or heavy spear of the legionary.

After Iberians and Celts came **Phœnicians,** who established numerous coastal settlements and were attracted in the first instance by the mineral wealth of the country.   Cádiz, Málaga, Seville and Córdoba were Phœnician trading centres, but their posts have been discovered on nearly all the coasts of Spain ; their Tartessus, perhaps the Tarshish of the Bible, has disappeared from the mouth of the Guadalquivir, if that were its position. The Phœnicians, who are said to have entered Spain in the eleventh century, were followed by the **Greeks**, who made their first voyage to Spain in 630 B.C.   These, according to Herodotus, were Phocians, and were followed by Rhodians ; they settled on the East coast, where Rosas and Ampurias yet recall their Greek titles and provide specimens of the earliest known Spanish coins ; the famous Saguntum, afterwards Murviedro, situated further south, was also a Greek colony.   The Greeks are said to have introduced the vine and the olive into the peninsula, an important contribution to its agricultural wealth.   Towards the end of the fifth century B.C. the Phœnicians invited their relatives, the **Carthaginians,** to help them in a quarrel with the native Spaniards, and the new-comers found the coast settlements so much to their liking that they remained and by degrees entirely ousted the Phœnician colonists.   These were all commercial enterprises, the promoters of which clung to the coast-line for the most part and made little effort to penetrate to the interior of the peninsula or to subdue any part of its population.

A new policy was begun by Hamilcar Barca, after the First Punic War, which ended in 242 B.C., with the Roman conquest of Sicily. He considered that Spain might be made a counter-poise to the Italian peninsula and become a suitable base of operations from which to attack Rome and restore Carthaginian supremacy in the Mediterranean, a policy followed by his son-in-law Hasdrubal and his son Hannibal. Southern and Eastern Spain were thus brought under Carthaginian influence and Hannibal's siege of Saguntum turned the attention of Roman historians to this part of the world. Our information upon Spanish affairs thus becomes increasingly detailed with the period of Scipio Africanus, who arrived in the country in 209 B.C. and completed the defeat of the Carthaginians, after which event Spain became a country of first-rate importance to Rome.

The history of the struggles of **Rome** with the native popula-tions from this time to 38 B.C., when Cæsar's genius secured a pacification, is far from creditable to Roman statesmanship, and is, in any case, a subject belonging rather to the colonial history of Rome than to the history of Spain. The exploits of Viriatus anticipated those of Pelayo or of Zumalacárregui, the siege of Numantia that of Zaragoza, while Sertorius showed that Hamilcar's idea of an independent Spain was no visionary project. It was left for Augustus Cæsar to consolidate the Roman power in Spain and to pacify the country ; the success of his efforts is perpetuated in the names of several towns, Astorga (Asturica Augusta), León (Urbs Septimae Legionis), Zaragoza (Cæsarea Augusta) ; Badajoz (Paz Augusta) especially testifies to the beneficence of his administration.

Modern Spanish is, in certain respects, nearer to Latin even than modern Italian, and the complete romanization of the country which produced this and other results, was effected during the four centuries which followed the reign of Augustus Cæsar. Spain became a part of the Empire no less important than Gaul. Spanish soldiers were as highly esteemed as were Spanish poets or rhetoricians ; Spanish corn was no less valuable to Rome than Egyptian. Cicero himself could find nothing more derogatory to say of the poets of Córdoba than that their style displayed ' pingue quiddam atque peregrinum ' ; Ovid, Mæcenas and Augustus himself owed something to the teaching of Marcus Porcius Latro, a native of Córdoba. In subsequent centuries Spain produced administrators, rulers and literary men of the highest rank ; the emperors Trajan, Hadrian and Marcus Aurelius were Spaniards, and to their days belong the high roads, the bridges and aqueducts which still arouse the admiration of the traveller. The two Senecas and Lucan, the nephew of the elder, belonged to Córdoba ; Pomponius Mela, the geographer, was from Algeciras ; Columella, the agriculturist, from Cádiz ; Martial was born near Calatayud and returned to die there ; Quintilian's home was at Calahorra.

In A.D. 406, the **Barbarians** at length broke down the crumbling defences of the Roman Empire, and Suevians, Alans and Vandals entered and ravaged Spain. The question is often asked, how it was that they met with so little resistance in a country which had for years defied successfully the power of Rome in her prime ; it is a question that recurs at the time of the Muslim conquest. But in this instance the answer is not far to seek. To begin with, the fighting power of the country had disappeared. Spain had given her best to the legions of Rome, and Rome had scattered them abroad upon the face of the earth. From the farthest limit of Northern Britain, where Spanish legions kept the Roman Wall against the Picts, to the provinces upon the Danube, where Spanish-spoken Latin survives as Roumanian, the Spanish soldier had fought and died. His own country had seen no fighting for four centuries, and the feeble garrison that sufficed for the preservation of order in this, the most peaceable of provinces, was not composed of Spaniards, but of degenerate provincials, who could not be trusted in posts of danger upon the outskirts of the empire. The population of Spain was too largely composed of slaves and paupers : *latifundia perdidere Italiam*, said Pliny, and the explanation is applicable in part at least to Spain. The growth of large estates worked by slave labour, the expropriation of the small farmer and the demoralizing results of town slavery had rotted the manhood of the country. Those, moreover, who had anything to lose had groaned for years under an iniquitous and oppressive system of taxation ; of what use to be Roman citizens, if they had to pay dues as such, in addition to their taxes as provincials ? If they had in any case to support a horde of rapacious officials, no change could matter much, and any change might be for the better. The native Spaniard had little for which to fight, and less inclination to fight for it.

It has been suggested that Christianity should be reckoned among the influences which weakened the resisting power of Roman Spain   The most that can be said is that some attention which might have been concentrated upon politics was diverted to ecclesiastical and theological questions and affairs. Christianity gained an early footing in Spain ; the rapidity of its dissemination and the number of important churchmen which it produced prefigure the earnestness and devotion, if not the bigotry and fanaticism, of later centuries. In Spain, a few years before the Council of Nicea, was held the first Christian Council of whose proceedings any record has been preserved. Among the bishops then present was the famous Hosius of Córdoba, one of the chief friends and supporters of Athanasius in his struggle against Arianism. Priscillian elaborated the heresy known by his name, and was executed as a heretic by Maximus, himself a Spaniard, in the year 384. At that time Prudentius, chief of the Christian poets of the age, had produced the greater part of his works, from which much of our information upon the social life and manners of Spain in the fourth century is derived. But there is no evidence that the Spanish church then exerted the important influence upon the government of the country which it certainly enjoyed under the Gothic kings.

The **Visigothic rule** is usually stated to have extended from 415 to 755, during which period thirty-five kings are named. Thirteen of these died violent deaths and the fact that ten of these deaths took place before 555 is sufficient to show the unsettled nature of the early Visigothic period, when Franks, Alans, Suevians, Vandals and Huns attempted to secure dominion in various parts of the old Roman empire, while religious dissension upon the Arian question was superadded to other causes of discord. This latter trouble was removed by the conversion of Reccared, the first of the Catholics. The labours of some few predecessors, especially those of Leovgild, had gradually welded the disparate elements of Spanish society into something homogeneous ; intermarriage between Roman and Goth, if nominally forbidden by law until 652, was none the less frequent ; Roman civilization had profoundly modified Gothic nationalism, and Reccared saw that Arianism was not likely to survive in Spain.

There were, however, more immediate reasons for a conversion to orthodox Catholicism ; the Gothic monarchy was elective ; the elector nobles were inclined to regard their nominee rather as their agent than as their ruler, and at the time of Reccared's accession, they had become wealthy, turbulent and disloyal. It was not possible for the king to solve the problem as Isabel afterwards did, by turning to the towns for popular support ; the small farmer class had almost disappeared and the middle and lower classes were generally in a state of serfdom. The one power that could be used to check the aggression of the nobles was the Church. After the ground had been prepared by previous negotiation and argument, the change of faith was formally announced at the Third Council of Toledo in 589, and the bulk of the people accepted it. The result was the transference of political power and influence from the nobles to the Church. In 633 the Fourth General Council of Toledo assumed the right of confirming the king's election to the throne and claimed to assert that right in the case of his successors ; the Church could and did use the weapon of excommunication against recalcitrant rulers.

From the fourth century the Church had continued to acquire the privileges and the wealth which afterwards made it a power in the land. During the Roman period, exemptions from taxation were allowed and some legal privileges conceded ; inheritances could be received and monastic life began. The Church here, as in other provinces of the Empire, was organized upon the basis of Roman law and administration, a system which persisted under Gothic rule. The title of Archbishop does not appear in Spain until the year 1085 ; the head of the Spanish Church was the metropolitan bishop of Seville or of Toledo, after the removal of the capital from Seville. Bishops were appointed by the king, and, in his absence, by the chief metropolitan. The country was divided into five provinces, each with a provincial metropolitan bishop, and the number of episcopal sees amounted to some eighty. The diocese of those days was in the nature of one large parish and tithes were paid directly to the bishop. Thus, when the Church became the king's counterpoise to the nobles, the influence of such bishops as Leander of Seville and his younger and more famous brother, Isidore, was almost unbounded. Isidore was a student as well as a statesman ; there were few subjects under heaven upon which he did not write, and his ' Etymologies ' range from disquisitions upon metaphysics to directions for shipbuilding, while his History of the Goths is an important authority for the events of this period. His work was continued by his pupil Ildefonso, an administrator and writer, who enjoyed the privilege of a personal visit from the Blessed Virgin, which has secured his continued veneration by the Spanish Church.

With the conversion of Reccared (586–601) and the consequent supremacy of Church influence, an unhappy period began for the Jews. Considerable numbers of Jews had settled in Spain and under the Roman Empire had enjoyed equal rights with all other citizens. When Constantine recognized Christianity, Jews were forbidden to have dealings with Christians in the Spanish peninsula, as in other countries, but persecution was not considered necessary. After the year 600, a complete change of policy was begun. Compulsory baptism was enforced upon Jews, and persecution was avoided only by those who

escaped to the South of France, where there were large settlements of their co-religionists. Until the Muslim invasion began,
the Jews were continually harried by the relentless intolerance
of the Church : they might hold no public office ; their children
were to be educated in convents or in Christian families ; mixed
marriages were declared void ; and relapse, after even compulsory baptism, was mercilessly punished. Jewish festivals
were prohibited ; the evidence of Jews was not accepted in
courts of law ; and such a king as Witiza, who succeeded to the
throne in 701 and treated the Jews with tolerance, while attempting to restrain the immorality of his own clergy, was held up
to later generations as a heretical and licentious monster. If
there be any truth in the accusation that the Jews, like the
Moriscos of later times, were conspiring with their brethren
in Africa and with the Muslim to overthrow the Visigothic rule
in Spain, some excuse for their action can be found.

The Visigoths had fallen under the influence of Roman civilization even before they reached Spain, and, after their settlement
in the country, the process of their romanization continued.
Their own language fell out of use and Latin became the current
vernacular. Roman administrative organization and methods
were retained. The Visigothic noble often preferred to live on
his own estate with his following of servants and retainers ;
town life was not, therefore, greatly increased or modified during
this period. The military power of these nobles was the chief
check to royal absolutism. Various attempts to make the throne
hereditary were failures, and the king was assisted by deliberative
councils of nobles and bishops. But, as he appointed the bishops,
summoned the nobles and could veto the proceedings of the
council, he had every opportunity of securing his own wishes
One positive contribution to Spanish civilization was made by
the Visigoths,—their legal codes. Many of their kings were
energetic legislators and they appear to have had as much respect
for law as the Romans themselves. The Breviarium of Alaric
II, prepared shortly before his death in 506, became the nucleus
of additions made by successive rulers, until Chindaswinth
established a code which reconciled the differences between
Gothic and Roman law ; this was revised by his son, Recca-
swinth, and promulgated as the Lex Visigothorum ; it became of
much importance in future centuries, when it was known as the
Fuero Juzgo.

In 711 came the **Muslim invasion.** A small band of Arab
marauders crossed the straits between Africa and Spain at the

spot where the town of Tarifa recalls the name of their leader. Seven years later, the Arabs were masters of the whole country with the exception of a few districts in the mountainous regions of the North. Subsequent generations, unable to account for the rapidity of this success, surrounded it with accretions of legend, and the collapse of the Goths was ascribed as much to Roderic's disregard of prophecy and tradition as to the treachery of Count Julian. It is likely enough that some one of the many quarrels between king and nobles provided the Arabs with their initial opportunity ; the degeneracy of the Gothic government supplies an adequate explanation of the rapidity of their conquest. The royal court was corrupt ; the majority of the nobles were selfish and idle ; there was no bond of unity, no feudal tie between the upper and lower classes ; commerce and industry were undeveloped in the absence of incentive to personal effort. Three centuries of peace, undisturbed except by the occasional turbulence of refractory nobles, had produced forgetfulness of the arts of war, and too large a share of political control was exerted by the Church. There was, in short, no sense of nationalism ; the noble was not loyal to the Crown ; the peasant was, at best, a serf, with little to lose by a change of masters.

Thus the Arabs overran the peninsula without meeting any serious opposition. When Tarīfa had shown the way and its possibilities, Tārik came with an army and reached Toledo, where he was joined by Mūsā, and the conquest was advanced to Barcelona and the Pyrenees. Their careers were cut short by the Muslim Caliph, who placed Abd ar-Rahman in command of Spain, to rule as emir under the governor of Africa, who was himself subject to the Caliphate at Damascus. The Arabs proceeded to invade Southern France, until they were checked by the great defeat of their co-religionists before Constantinople in 718, by the victory of Charles Martel near Tours in 732 and by dissensions among their leaders and among the aspirants to the Damascus Caliphate

The political connection between Arab Spain and Africa was loose ; nor was that between Africa and Damascus much closer. The several Muslim tribes and nations were often at variance among themselves, and though they admitted a nominal suzerainty on the part of Damascus, the only real bond of union was their religious faith and their belief in the brotherhood of all true believers. The conquest of Spain was not undertaken upon any preconcerted plan ; it was the outcome of a marauding raid, and the settlement of Spain was constantly disturbed by rivalries and factions fostered in Africa and often stimulated by the

Muslim priests. Berbers, Syrians, Egyptians and Arabs all required satisfaction, which was eventually attained by settling the various tribes in the districts which most nearly resembled their native environment. The government remained in the hands of the ruling race, the Syrians of Damascus. It was not until the tenth century that the civilization somewhat vaguely known as Moorish was firmly established and that its cultural achievements became possible.

This government made no attempt to crush the conquered, and the Moors in this respect repeated the policy of the Visigoths. Apart from some sporadic outbreaks of persecution, the Moors respected the religion, the rights and even the property of the Spanish population ; Christians retained their churches and were able to celebrate daily Mass under the countenance of the Muslim authorities ; living among Muslims, they were known as Mozárabes or Mozarabs, and the Mozarabic ritual was not replaced by the Roman until 1071 ; the only burden upon them was a small annual poll-tax. The subject population was certainly better off than it had been under the nobles and ecclesiastics, who had taken refuge in the northern districts. The Jews, who had perhaps suggested and had certainly welcomed the invasion, were not only tolerated but were distinguished by the consideration of the new rulers. Many Christians became Mohammadans, either to escape the poll-tax or to gain liberation from slavery, and formed the class known as *renegados* or *muladíes*. The new government took one-fifth of the land and distributed the rest among its adherents ; its own holding was allotted to Spanish cultivators who paid rent on the metayer system : the large estates were thus broken up and agriculture was improved in consequence.

For the first forty years after the Muslim invasion, some twenty emirs held the power in Spain at different times and with varying success. Progress and stability began with the reign of Abd ar-Rahman I (755–788), a member of the Ommeyad dynasty, who had escaped from the disturbances which had overthrown the Ommeyads and brought the Abbaside family into power. Abd ar-Rahman had to spend some years in struggle before the various tribes in Spain and the Abbaside rulers now established in Bagdad would recognize his authority ; but he succeeded in establishing his ideal of an absolute monarchy at Córdoba, which put an end to inter-tribal anarchy and strife. In his reign occurred the expedition of Charlemagne, who advanced as far as Zaragoza and was attacked during his retreat by the Basques in the pass of Roncesvalles, an event which provided the theme of the famous *Chanson de Roland*. Abd ar-Rahman did much for the adornment of Córdoba and the building of the great mosque was begun during his reign (see p. 220). Nine emirs or caliphs of Córdoba succeeded him and continued his dynasty until 1012, when a period of anarchy began which lasted until 1094. Of these nine, the most distinguished was Abd ar-Rahman III (912–961), who established peace in Spain under his absolute rule, created a navy as well as an army, and made the Caliphate of Córdoba respected as one of the most powerful and highly cultured states in Europe. Succeeding rulers became weaker and weaker ; palace intrigues, the government of favourites, religious dissension and the increasing energy of the Christian States in the North undermined their authority. A strong hand was needed to check the separatism of the several tribes, and the old Arab aristocracy was completely outnumbered. The end of this period saw Muslim Spain divided into a number of petty kingdoms, in a state of continual internecine warfare, while the Christian power advanced as far as Toledo.

The Muslim State was based upon monarchy absolute and hereditary. The Caliph was aided by various ministers of state (vizirs), while the several provinces were under governors (walis) with subordinate officials of their own. The judicature was well organized with judges for ordinary and extraordinary cases. The Koran was the only existing code of law and confusion between religious and civil law was the result. Religious toleration was the rule ; the aristocratic Arab appears to have been somewhat indifferentist, but the mass of the people were believers to the point of fanaticism. Such persecution as occurred was provoked by Christian defiance. The religious class were the leaders in the work of education which was highly esteemed by the people in general ; there was no system of public instruction and schools were carried on by private enterprise ; but there were few illiterates, and women could enjoy all the educational opportunities open to men. The Arabs introduced paper as the material of books instead of parchment, and books were comparatively cheap and numerous.

Through this civilization Greek culture was reintroduced to Western Europe ; the Arabs had become acquainted with the Greek classical writers and with Greek philosophy through the Byzantine Empire and the populations of Asia and Egypt ; mathematics and medicine were especially advanced, though the chief results in learning were attained after the fall of the Caliphate. Poetry was universally popular, especially love-poetry ; the extent of its influence upon early Spanish poetry is still a matter of controversy. In the tenth century Muslim Spain was hardly exceeded by any country in Europe for wealth and culture ; the descriptions of Córdoba given by the chroniclers approach the fabulous, but, when allowance is made for exaggeration, the city was undoubtedly a centre of magnificence. The great mosque is the most famous remnant of these glories, most of which have completely vanished. These developments were made possible by the improvements introduced into agriculture and the greater stimulus given to its pursuit. New products, sugar, rice and the pomegranate were established and much work was done by irrigation to increase the fertility of the soil, especially in Valencia and Murcia. Stock-breeding and mining were encouraged and new industries were started,—wool and silk weaving, glass-blowing, paper-making, the manufacture of weapons, leather work of various kinds and marble. Overseas commerce was vigorous, especially in the Mediterranean ; the Caliphs had a considerable navy, and Seville, Málaga and Almería became the chief centres of their trade.

The historians of Spain have always regarded the mountains of Asturias as the point where the scattered remnants of the defeated Christians collected for resistance to the invader. They elected one **Pelayo (718–737)** to succeed to the throne of Roderic ; the capital of the new king was at Cangas de Onís, near Oviedo, and in 718 he and his followers won a victory over the Muslims in the valley of Covadonga. Legend has naturally exaggerated the event ; but if the hero and his thirty followers in their cave did not destroy a hostile army of 400,000 men, there is no doubt that they won a victory which secured the Christians in the possession of their little kingdom.

In later years, the Reconquest was represented by popes, troubadours and chroniclers as a crusade ; if it occasionally assumed that form and was at times inspired by a crusading spirit, such was by no means its first beginning nor its invariable continuation. Pelayo, his nobles and bishops, and their immediate successors fought to recover their lands and to re-establish their authority in Spain, and these struggles were not necessarily racial or religious. In times of peace, we find members of Christian states trading and intermarrying with Muslims, and Christian princesses were thus united to Muslim princes ; Muslim towns were full of Christians, not only of Mozárabes, but of casual immigrants who came to trade or take service in the Muslim armies ; cases are found of Christians and Moors fighting side by side against other Christians, and even against their own countrymen.

The work of reconquest was facilitated by the civil wars and internal quarrels of the Muslims and was retarded by the same causes operating among the Christian States ; the antagonism between king and nobles which had existed during the Visigothic period was continued. The line of the Douro may be regarded as the southern frontier of the Christian power during this period, though it was not definitely held. It was not until the eleventh century that an advance in some spirit of nationalism began. To the east of Asturias was the little state of Navarre, which had its origin in the independent spirit of the Basques, who maintained some sort of autonomy against both the Frankish kings and the Muslim invaders ; the chroniclers ascribe the foundation of the State of Aragon to the same causes ; its name and history were confused with those of Navarre for some time to come. The modern province of Catalonia was overrun by the Muslims who invaded Southern France by that route ; but the Frankish kings were able to drive the invaders back and to establish a Spanish mark, ruled by counts nominally subject to the Frankish monarchy. Among these the counts of Barcelona became pre-eminent and one of them is said to have made himself independent in 874 ; the southern progress of Barcelona was blocked by the independent Muslim State which centred about Zaragoza.

Thus little progress was made until the fall of the Caliphate. **Alfonso I,** the Catholic (**739–757**), and **Alfonso II,** the Chaste (**791–842**), were the most successful kings during the first century after the Muslim invasion. In the course of their raids upon the enemy they were able to bring back many Christians from the conquered territory and so to re-populate their own kingdom. Alfonso II transferred the capital to Oviedo. Various legends arose about this time which have an importance for their influence upon literature as indicating the formation of a sense of nationalism ; to Roland and Roncesvalles we have already referred ; Bernardo del Carpio appears as the typical noble, intolerant of foreign interference and resolved to maintain his own independence. Finally, the body of the Apostle St. James was miraculously discovered to a Galician shepherd and Santiago de Compostela was founded, which became the most important place of pilgrimage in Western Europe ; a steadily increasing stream of pilgrims from all parts brought foreign influences and ideas into Spain, a trade in objects of piety sprang up, and Spain was provided once for all with a patron saint and a war-cry. But until the Caliphate began to totter, not much was done to advance the southern frontier. The Christian kingdom was divided against itself ; Galicia declined to acknowledge the supremacy of the Asturian kingdom ; the eastern part of the kingdom, known as Castile, from its numerous castles, had repeatedly shown a tendency to separatism, and in the reign of **Ramiro II (930– 950)** Count Fernán González took the lead and was able to make Castile, with Burgos as its capital, a province independent of León and Oviedo.

The civil wars which thus ended weakened the conquering power and inclination of the Christian States, and nobles and kings did not hesitate upon occasion to apply to the Muslim monarchs for aid against their own compatriots. Early in the eleventh century, however, a movement southwards began. **Alfonso V (999–1027)** and his uncle, **Sancho the Great (1000– 1035)**, respectively advanced from León and Navarre, and after the death of his nephew, Sancho succeeded in making himself master of Castile and León. He thus became ruler of all Northern Spain, with the exception of Galicia and Catalonia. Any prospects of union, for which Spain was hardly ready, were destroyed by his will ; he divided his kingdom among his sons, and Navarre, Aragon and Castile thus became independent units. Navarre lost its influence in a dismal succession of family quarrels, plots and assassinations, and its history is merged in that of Aragon and Castile. The King of León, Bermudo III, was killed in battle in 1037, and, as his line was extinct, **Ferdinand I (1037– 1065)**, King of Castile, the second son of Sancho the Great, succeeded to León ; a period of civil war left him the most powerful of the Christian monarchs in Spain.

Spanish civilization is the resultant of two streams of influence which converge in the eleventh century. One of these was oriental, exerted by Mohammedans and Jews. The other was European and, in particular, French : the extent of this latter has hitherto been under-estimated by historians. French influence was both ecclesiastical and military ; the monks of Cluny were invited to Spain by the King of Navarre, and after 1033 the effects of Cluniac influence are perceptible in Aragon, Catalonia and Castile ; Menéndez Pidal has shown that legal documents down to the early part of the eleventh century reveal an increasing number of romance forms, when a sudden reversal to a more ' grammatical ' style of Latinity occurs, and this fact he reasonably attributes to the influence of the Cluniac reforms. Boissonnade, again, has enumerated thirty-four expeditions, proceeding from France between 1018 and 1250, to support the Spanish states in their struggles against the infidels, of which ' crusades ' fourteen belong to the eleventh

century, fifteen to the twelfth, and five to the thirteenth. The
French *Chanson de Roland* was based upon an incident occurring
in one of these expeditions, and the French influences perceptible
in the composition of the *Poema del Cid* are easily explicable,
if these facts are borne in mind. The majority of these expeditions were sent to support the states in the North-east of Spain,
which were much more hardly pressed than were Castile and
León. They had few natural resources ; the ground they
occupied was far from fertile ; there was little sense of nationality, and Navarrese and Catalonians can be found fighting in
the ranks of the Muslim while their princes make alliance with
Muslim walis and emirs in furtherance of their own internecine
quarrels. The career of the Cid Campeador is sufficient illus-
tration of these conditions of life. While the collapse of the
Cordoban Empire brought some relief to Castile and León, the
powerful Muslim State of Zaragoza kept the north-eastern states
continually on the alert. French action was thus not entirely
disinterested.

The existence of the Muslim power so near the French frontiers
in North-east Spain was a menace that could not be ignored ;
the Church was continually urging war against the infidel, and
the prospects of adventure and booty were a strong attraction
to the French chivalry of the period. Spain was regarded in
the spirit of the sixteenth-century *conquistadores* advancing into
the New World ; a country of marvels, where salvation might
be won by the sword, where there were rich towns, replete with
all the wealth and luxury of the East, and where any competent
soldier, dissatisfied with his prospects at home, could carve out
a career for himself. With the warriors came not only the
churchmen, but also farmers, merchants, artisans ; the latter
classes remained, when their superiors in the social scale declined
permanent settlement, and went to increase the population of
the towns and to provide Northern Spain with those elements
of a stable and productive population which were much needed
at that period.

It was during this time that the towns began to develop
and to provide a counterpoise to the almost unlimited power of
the nobles. The higher nobility and the Church might acquire
lands for themselves, by conquest or other means, and rule them
in almost complete independence of the Crown ; the noble was
not liable to taxation and might leave the service of his king for
that of some other court. The king had, however, the right
to grant and to withdraw titles of nobility. There was no feudal
system, in the sense that land tenure implied an obligation to

military service ; but society was united by a system of depend-
ency known as *encomienda*, whereby the lower class became
retainers of the higher, giving military service in return for
protection, or paying rents and duties. In theory, the artisan
and labourer, as well as the noble, was free to break the connection and to commend himself to another lord, if he wished to
do so ; in practice, the disturbed conditions of life made any
such action extremely difficult, and many of the *encomendados*
differ little in status from the serfs descended from the old *colonos*,
who were transferred with the land upon a change of masters.
While the king was the source of legislative, judicial and executive
authority, and was absolute master of his own lands, he was
by no means in control· of his nobles. They raised their own
troops, collected their own taxes, and fought as they pleased
with one another and sometimes with the king. Bishops were
in a similar position. These ecclesiastical or civil potentates had
their own strong castles, from which they could defy the royal
authority, and were often more ready to plunder their neighbours
than to provide for the safety of those commended to them.

The king certainly retained powers of real importance ; he
could, if circumstances allowed, proclaim his intention of appointing judges to any district, of revoking concessions already made ;
he could summon an army to his standard ; he had the sole
right of coining money. But these and other powers were not
entirely adequate to deal with refractory nobles, and the kings
gradually realized that a check upon seignorial license and a
help in the establishment of order was to be gained from the
towns. Many of these were founded in frontier districts exposed
to the raids of the Muslims ; to attract population, and to please
the people, the natural enemies of the nobles, kings granted
special privileges to these towns or *villas* ; they might be exempted
from the payment of taxes or be granted a measure of self-
government which made them independent of the local governor.
Such privileges were stated in a charter or *fuero* ; some of these
became typical and were granted to new townships under their
first names ; the *fuero* of Toledo, for instance, implied a number
of privileges which were familiar to every one and enjoyed by
towns of a later date. Some towns were places of refuge, within
which slaves or escaped criminals recovered freedom. The
municipio, thus begun, administered its own affairs in a general
assembly or *consejo*, which appointed the executive officers. The
authority of such a *villa* might extend beyond its walls to surrounding villages. Nobles might also grant *fueros*, but only
with the consent of the king.

After 1031 the Caliphate of Córdoba was broken up into various petty states (*taifas*) which were constantly at war between themselves and from which Seville presently emerged as the most important. The Christian powers were therefore able to begin an advance which enabled them to reconquer the whole of the peninsula with the exception of the kingdom of Granada by 1248. During this period Spanish culture and civilization steadily improved. The kings gained more power as against the nobles. The towns and their citizens increased in numbers and resources. Two great kingdoms, Castile and Aragon, took definite form and were even able at times to act in concert against the common enemy, and some sense of nationality began to arise. Muslim civilization was still predominant ; many of its great scholars and writers then flourished ; some of them settled in Christian communities to avoid the troubles that beset their compatriots, and exerted a permanent influence upon Spanish life and thought. The rise of Portugal to independence during this period must also be noted.

Two revivals of the Muslim power delayed, but could not avert, the progress of the Christians. The ruler of Seville, Motamid. finding himself unable to make head against the forces of Castile, invited the help of the Almorávides, a fanatical Berber tribe. They crossed into Spain and defeated Alfonso VI in 1086, after which victory the Almorávide leader, Yusuf. returned to his own country, as he had promised the Spanish Muslim chiefs to do. Four years later he returned, whether on his own account or by invitation is not clear, defeated a Christian army and proceeded to make himself master of Southern Spain. The new government was at first energetically puritanical, and secured at any rate the observance of law and order ; but degeneracy soon set in, and as the central power grew weaker, *taifa* states began to reappear. But in 1125 a great religious upheaval took place in the Atlas mountains of Morocco, led by a Berber tribe who called themselves Almohades ; they invaded Spain in 1146, and speedily overran the old Muslim empire, which became a province of the Almohade empire with its capital in Africa. They drove out or destroyed the old Arab aristocracy, and vigorously renewed the war against the Christians, whom they utterly routed in the battle of Alarcos, near Badajoz, in 1195. However, in 1212, the united forces of Alfonso of Castile, Sancho of Navarre and Peter II of Aragon gained the great victory of Las Navas de Tolosa, and the tide then definitely turned. The petty states fell one after another, either by internal quarrels or by Christian conquest, until nothing remained of the Muslim power except the little State of Granada, which continued to hold out for some two hundred and fifty years longer.

Ferdinand I (1037–1065), who had made himself master of North-western Spain, followed the example of Sancho the Great at his death and subdivided his kingdom among his heirs. The result was a period of civil war, which left **Alfonso VI (1065–1109)** in power as King of Castile and León. He made Toledo a permanent possession and advanced into Valencia, until the Almorávides drove him back. Within his reign fell the exploits of the Cid, Ruy (or Rodrigo) Díaz of Bivar in the district of Burgos. He is first found fighting on the side of Sancho of Castile against Alfonso, and when Alfonso secured the throne, he found it advisable to show favour to Rodrigo and married him to Jimena Díaz, daughter of the Count of Oviedo and of royal blood. Rodrigo was then sent to collect the tribute due from the ruler of Seville and also to arrest García Ordóñez and other nobles who had attacked the King of Seville on behalf of the King of Granada. Rodrigo undertook some campaigning on his own account against Toledo, and Alfonso banished him in 1081. The Cid then took service with the Moorish king of Zaragoza and in the course of the next two years defeated several Catalan counts and the King of Aragon, Sancho Ramírez, who had attacked his master. He was then restored to Alfonso's favour and was in Castile in 1087 and 1088. Another quarrel led to a second banishment and the Cid returned to his former service against the Count of Barcelona, who eventually abandoned his claim to the protectorate of the Moorish lands and entrusted the responsibility of them to the Cid, who had won his confidence by his generosity in the moment of victory. The alliance was cemented by the marriage of the Count's cousin, Ramon Berenguer III, with the Cid's daughter María. Rodrigo then turned to the conquest of Valencia, which he captured in 1094, and held against the armies of the Almorávides ; he extended his power over Almenara and Murviedro, and in 1098 was able to restore the diocese of Valencia to the Church. After his death in the following year, his wife held out for three years against the Moorish attacks, but was eventually obliged to apply for help to Alfonso, who brought her back to Castile with the body of her husband and destroyed Valencia, leaving the Moors to overrun the province.

The Cid has become the national hero of Spain ; idealized by later generations as the leader of the Reconquest and as a brave and successful warrior, certain traits of character which a modern purist might describe as avarice, cruelty and treachery were forgotten. Like Bernardo del Carpio and Fernán González, he appealed to the people as one who had successfully defied royal authority and maintained the personal independence which was highly valued alike by nobles and towns ; when royal authority became a stringent reality, these personalities were regarded as typical of the old free times.

Alfonso VI had no son and was succeeded by his daughter **Urraca,** whose reign (**1109–1126**) was a period of anarchy. Her sister, Teresa, had married Count Henry of Lorraine and to him Alfonso had granted some territory in the north of the modern Portugal, an incident worthy of note as the beginning of the Portuguese kingdom. The confusion of Urraca's reign enabled this pair to increase their holding and to consolidate their position ; Teresa's son, Affonso Enríquez, fought against the Moors with some success and secured his recognition as King in 1143. **Alfonso VII (1126–1157),** who styled himself emperor, succeeded Urraca and attained to considerable power ; he was able to secure the acknowledgment of his supremacy from Aragon, Barcelona, Toulouse and a number of other petty states, both Moorish and Christian. On his death in 1157, he divided his kingdom among his heirs and **Alfonso VIII (1158–1214)** entered into a troubled inheritance. He was an able ruler, fully equal to the occasion and when he had secured domestic peace he turned against the Muslim forces. Defeated in the battle of Alarcos, owing to the defection of the contingent from León, he was able eventually to organize a combined effort ; practically all Christian Spain was represented in the great army which defeated the Moors at Las Navas de Tolosa in 1212 ; important foreign contingents were also present, including Englishmen.

The work of Alfonso VIII was continued by **Ferdinand III** (Fernando el Santo), his grandson (**1217–1252**), who conquered Córdoba, Murcia and Seville between 1236 and 1248 ; at the end of his reign the Moors were left with Granada alone as the remnant of their once great possessions. He also succeeded in finally incorporating the kingdom of León with that of Castile, on the death of his father, Alfonso IX of León, in 1230.

It was during this period that the three great military Orders were founded, possibly upon the model of similar organizations that the Moors maintained to protect their frontiers and their pilgrims and certainly under the example of the monastic Orders established during the Crusades for the protection of the Holy Land. The Templars were already in Spain, and were entrusted by Alfonso VIII with the defence of Calatrava, a fortress on the

border of Andalusia ; on the death of Alfonso the advance of the
Almohades obliged them to retire ; Sancho III offered the place
to anyone who would undertake its defence, and two Cistercian
monks successfully attempted the adventure in 1158 ; they raised
a force of volunteers (Church and State giving them money and
lands), drove back the Moors and distinguished themselves at
Las Navas de Tolosa.   The earliest in date, they were probably
the least important of the three great Orders, but they maintained their ground until 1587, when Philip II appropriated
their revenues and extinguished their independence.   More distinguished and far more wealthy was the Order of Santiago,
which came into existence about 1161, when certain outlaws
in the territory of León were converted to a religious life ; they
turned their predatory energies against the infidel with such
success that eventually the Archbishop of Santiago incorporated
them under his own spiritual leadership as an Order of Knights.
They rapidly amassed lands and wealth and at the end of the
fifteenth century were the richest of these three Orders.   That
of Alcántara was founded in 1156, when a fort was established
near Salamanca ; the garrison enjoyed the spiritual support of
certain Cistercian monks and became more ecclesiastical in
character than the other two Orders.

The Grand Masters of these Orders exerted over the members
an absolute authority, derived partly from the Crown and also
from the Pope, who was inclined to turn to them for support
when the Papacy was at variance with the Crown.   The master-
ship of an Order was thus a most influential position, in view of
the resources in men and wealth which it could command, and
when Ferdinand the Catholic assumed these positions as his
royal prerogative, he made a very considerable addition to the
prestige and power of the Crown.

In the year 1150, Petronilla, the daughter of Ramiro II of
Aragon, was married to Ramon Berenguer IV of Barcelona, an
event which proved to be of immense importance for the unification of Spain.   This couple had a son, who bore his father's
name, but changed it to Alfonso, when he came to rule over
Aragon and Catalonia united as one kingdom.   Catalonia, apart
from the inclusion of Barcelona, one of the most important
harbours in the Mediterranean, also held considerable possessions
in the South of France ; these came under the sway of Alfonso II,
who worked hand in hand with Alfonso VIII of Castile against
the Muslims, and made a treaty with him, regulating the division
of their respective conquests.   Peter II succeeded Alfonso II

in 1196, and was involved in the disputes engendered by the Albigensian heresy and crusade, which was ravaging many parts of his French dominions during the latter half of his reign, and produced, among other consequences, the Dominican Order of monks and the Inquisition. Peter was by no means inclined to countenance the heresy ; but he was equally determined not to allow Simon de Montfort to make himself master of the country. He was defeated and killed by Montfort and the crusaders in the battle of Muret, near Toulouse, in 1213.

Peter II left a son of six years of age, James (known to Spanish writers as Jaime, though Jacme is the correct Catalan form), who was to become famous as **James the Conqueror (1213-1276)**. Papal intervention freed him from the control of Simon de Montfort and he was educated under the Master of the Templars, while his great-uncle Sancho governed the country during his minority. James at an early age gave proof of sagacity and leadership ; the intrigues of his relatives and the rebellions of his nobles, together with interference from France and Rome, involved him in the vicissitudes of civil war at an age when he was little more than a boy. By 1228 he was master of the situation and turned his energy against the Moors, to the satisfaction of his Catalonian subjects who desired to safeguard and extend their Mediterranean trade. In 1229 he conquered Mallorca, and the remaining islands of the Balearic group were in his power by 1235. Then he attacked Valencia, which was conquered in 1238 ; here he checked his career in virtue of an agreement with the King of Castile to whom he had undertaken to leave the province of Murcia. In 1264, at the request of Alfonso X, he invaded the province and captured the town and fortress of Murcia, which he then handed over to the Castilian king, in a spirit of loyal co-operation of which there is no parallel example to be found in the previous history of the country. He projected an expedition to the Holy Land, but most of the fleet got no further than Aigues-Mortes ; he took his seat in the great Council of Lyons in 1274, and joined in recognizing the supremacy of Pope Gregory X ; he died in 1276, leaving Aragon, Catalonia and Valencia to his eldest son Peter, and the Balearic Islands and his possessions in France to his son James. He is certainly the most distinguished figure in Aragonese history ; tall and powerful above his contemporaries, and of indomitable personal courage, he was a strategist and tactician of no mean order ; religious at heart, he was licentious in character ; magnanimous to a beaten foe, he shrank from no cruelty to secure victory ; his violent temper led him to commit acts for which his after repentance was sincere ; he cut out the tongue of a bishop of Gerona in 1246, whom he suspected of betraying a confessional confidence and atoned by building and endowing a monastery. He left a book of autobiographical chronicles and a collection of proverbs, which reveal some respect for letters and culture.

After the death of James the Conqueror aggressive movements against the Moors ceased for nearly two centuries. Both Castile and Aragon were occupied with internal difficulties, and in particular with the struggle of nobles against monarchy ; with this should be considered the growth of the towns and the influence which they exerted upon the final settlement, the outcome of which was a more centralized government and a stronger movement towards national unity.

In Castile, **Alfonso X,** El Sabio (the Wise, or Learned), **(1252–1284),** marks the beginning of a new era. Alfonso aspired to the position of Holy Roman Emperor ; he married his sister Eleanor to Prince Edward of England, afterwards Edward I ; the journeys and negotiations which were thus necessitated are symptomatic of the fact that peninsularism was breaking down. Hitherto Spain had gone but little abroad ; she had her own crusade upon her own soil, and her chivalry lacked the experience and the broader outlook which knights of other lands gained by travel and service abroad. But when the Moors had been driven into Granada, a period of comparative peace supervened ; castles became homes rather than fortresses, and their inhabitants found time to take some interest in the refinements of civilization. The minstrel was welcomed ; the chronicler received consideration ; and Alfonso's literary activity responded to a general awakening of intellectual interest (see p. 102). This literary work had its political effect ; the realization that a national language existed worthy of literary respect was one step upon the road to national unity. Alfonso was a soldier as well as a scholar, yet his reign was a succession of quarrels with his nobles and his family ; he was an incompetent administrator with a strain of headstrong stubbornness in his nature which led him into action without due consideration for the consequences to himself or for the feelings of others. He gave away the province of Algarve to the King of Portugal and Gascony to England ; he irritated his people by his imperialist ambitions ; he squandered his resources in ill-advised liberality, and debased the coinage in order to improve his finances. He died in the course of a quarrel concerning the succession, with his second son, Sancho, who gained support enough from the nobles to enable him to occupy the throne as **Sancho IV, '** the Brave' **(1284–1295)**.

The reigns of Sancho and of his son, **Ferdinand IV (1295–1312)**, were chiefly occupied with friction between the Crown, the nobles and the towns. The next king, **Alfonso XI (1312–1350)**, was a ruler of genius, who reduced the business of playing off one noble against another to a fine art. Such public order as the preceding reigns had seen was largely the work of the Hermandades, or Brotherhoods, and in particular, of the Brotherhood of Castile. These were associations of towns, formed for mutual protection against the nobles, and even against the unjust demands of Crown officials. They had an efficient armed force at their immediate disposal and did not scruple to use it. They professed that their chief object was to secure respect for the king's authority, and more than one king was glad to avail himself of their help. Alfonso succeeded in improving the efficiency of local administration and of justice ; he also suppressed most of the refractory nobles. While his attention was chiefly directed to the improvement of internal affairs, he added the Basque province of Álava to Castile and also inflicted a severe defeat upon the Moors at Tarifa in 1340.

His only legitimate son, **Peter (Pedro) the Cruel (1350–1369)**, succeeded him, and the opposition of the eldest of Alfonso's five illegitimate sons, Count Henry of Trastamara, filled Peter's reign with civil war. Count Henry secured an alliance with Peter IV of Aragon, and the critical point was reached in 1366, when the allies, supported by the famous Bertrand du Guesclin, and an army of freebooters known as the ' White Companies ', invaded Castile and crowned Henry as king. Peter the Cruel had induced Edward III of England to send an army to his help, under the command of the Black Prince, and the Aragonese allies were completely defeated at the battle of Nájera (1367). The English then discovered what should have been obvious from the outset, that Peter was an unprincipled miscreant with whom no self-respecting leader could associate, and withdrew from the country. Count Henry was able to return with another army, and to defeat and kill his half-brother, whose death was a relief to Spain and whose character can be most charitably summarized as the outcome of homicidal mania.

Henry II (1369–1379) was obliged to make numerous concessions to the nobles and to the partisans of Peter, in order to secure his position ; he was also disturbed by the claims to the throne put forward by John of Gaunt, who had married Constanza, one of Peter's illegitimate daughters. This matter was eventually settled in the following reign, when Prince Henry, the heir of Henry II's son, **John I (1379–1390)**, married John of Gaunt's daughter, and they assumed the titles of Prince and Princess of Asturias, which became the regular title of the heirs to the Spanish crown. John I married the heiress to the Portuguese throne, but the Portuguese elected John of Avis as their king and an attempt to press the Spanish claims ended in the complete defeat of the Castilian forces in the battle of Aljubarrota in 1385.

John's successor, **Henry III (1390–1406)**, enjoyed a comparatively peaceful reign, and sent embassies to Constantinople and also to Tamburlane in the then unknown region of Central Asia ; a second embassy, which reached Samarkand, found a historian in one of its members, González de Clavijo, the John Mandeville of Spain. Henry also secured the Canary Islands as a Spanish possession. He died at the age of twenty-seven, leaving an heir only two years old, **John II (1406–1454)**. Until John was fourteen, the country was governed by a competent regent, Ferdinand of Antequera, who became King of Aragon in 1412. John proved a weak ruler, and left the business of government to his favourite, Álvaro de Luna, with whom the nobles were at constant variance, until they succeeded in securing his overthrow and execution.

These disorders grew worse during the reign of John's son, **Henry IV (1454–1474)** ; the nobles made the supposed illegitimacy of his only daughter, Joan (Juana), an excuse for disputing the succession, and proposed a series of administrative changes which would have left the Crown powerless. On Henry's death, his sister, Isabel **(1474–1504)**, was proclaimed queen by one party, while another supported the claims of Joan. Isabel had married Ferdinand of Aragon in 1469 ; Joan was promised to the King of Portugal, who therefore supported her party. Isabel's forces were victorious, she was recognized as queen in 1479, and Joan went into a convent. In that year, Ferdinand became King of Aragon.

In Aragon, James the Conqueror had been succeeded by his son, **Peter III (1276–1285)**, whose reign was chiefly memorable for the fact that he conquered Sicily and came into conflict with the Pope and the French over this acquisition. Peter had married Constance, the daughter of King Manfred of Sicily, a member of the Hohenstaufen imperial family, in opposition to which the papacy had called in Charles of Anjou. Charles defeated Manfred and executed his nephew, Conradin, in 1268. Though Constance had every claim to rule the island, Peter made no open move, until the outbreak of the revolt known as the Sicilian Vespers (1282). It then appeared that he had long been preparing for action ; he sent out a powerful fleet under the famous admiral, Roger de Lauria, and speedily made himself master of the island and the surrounding waters. The Pope replied by excommunicating Peter and offering Aragon to France ; a crusade was proclaimed and French forces advanced far into Catalonia ; the dissatisfied elements in Aragon grasped their opportunity and Peter was obliged to grant the celebrated General Privilege, which the Cortes thenceforward regarded as their Magna Carta. The French were defeated both by land and sea, but Peter died shortly afterwards.

Alfonso III, Peter's son, reigned for only six years (**1285–1291**), which were chiefly occupied with negotiations for the settlement of the Sicilian question. His brother, who succeeded him, **James II (1291–1327)**, agreed to abandon Sicily to the Pope in exchange for Corsica and Sardinia ; the Sicilians set Fadrique, the son of James, upon the throne, and the struggle went on, until 1302, when Fadrique married a daughter of Charles of Anjou and peace was made on the understanding that the succession should revert to the Angevin house.

Peter IV (1336–1387) is the most important figure among the next four kings, whose reigns were almost entirely filled with domestic difficulties. Peter was involved in a serious struggle with the nobles, which ended in the success of the Crown ; the powers wrested from his forerunners were reduced, and a centralized absolutism became a possible form of government. Sicily returned to Aragon, when Martin, the king of the island, succeeded to the throne in 1395. He died without issue in 1410 and **Ferdinand I (1410–1416)**, then regent of Castile, was elected to fill his place. The next king, **Alfonso V, (1416–1458)**, was chiefly occupied with warfare in Italy, with the result that disorder became apparent in the affairs of Aragon. Under the reign of his brother, **John II (1458–1479)**, a dangerous Catalan revolt broke out, in support of Charles of Viana, prince of Navarre and John's son by his first wife. John had married again and the stepmother fought for the interests of her own children, among whom was the future King Ferdinand. He married Isabel of Castile in 1469, and in conjunction with her, became ruler of the whole of Spain, apart from Granada, upon his father's death.

Forms of government, both in Castile and in Aragon, were modified during this period, not only by political and international events, but also by the slow development of class dis-

tinctions under the influence of increasing wealth and culture.
In Castilian history, the nobles appear as the disturbing element,
in continual opposition to the cause of order and centralized
government represented by the kings ; their decline was due as
much to economic reasons as to the increasing power of the
Crown.   The nobles took no part in trade and commerce, which
were steadily advancing, and their rents were diminished by the
gradual decay of the servile system.   At the end of the twelfth
century, the serfs began to obtain emancipation ; by the fifteenth
century the usual relationship between noble and commoner was
that of landlord and tenant, while the peasant was now able to
take service as and where he pleased, to marry without his lord's
consent and to secure legal definition of his liabilities.   The
consequence was a steady increase in the growth of town life,
to which many were attracted by the greater freedom assured
by a municipal *fuero*.   The clergy increased both in numbers
and wealth ; many men entered a religious order, while continuing their secular occupations, in order to enjoy the privileges
and immunities of the Church, which was not only exempt from
taxation but was allowed to collect a tithe from the produce of
lands not in clerical occupation, a portion of which, however,
the *tercias reales*, went to the king.

In Aragon and Catalonia, the peasant classes obtained their
freedom at a later date and with severer struggles ; in Valencia,
much of the agricultural work was done by Muslim tenants who
were in a state of practical serfdom.   The opposition between
towns and nobility was more marked here than in Castile.
The Moorish elements resident among Christian populations was
at this time very considerable ; these so-called *mudéjares*
enjoyed civil and political liberty, until towards the end of
the fourteenth century, when the Church began to proclaim
the necessity of religious uniformity ; the fact that much of the
commerce and industry of the country was in their hands was
a further cause of unpopularity.   The same observations apply
in greater measure to the Jews, whose numbers had been increased
in the thirteenth century by the persecutions of the Almohades
which had driven them into Christian territory.   In 1391 a
series of anti-Semitic riots broke out, the result of which was to
leave the Jew in a position considerably worse than that of the
Moor *mudéjar* ; Jews were confined to their own quarter, were
forbidden to trade with Christians or to hold public offices or to
carry arms ; many professed conversion and were known as
Marranos (pigs) by Christians, who were rarely convinced of
their sincerity.

The political interest of this period centres round the struggles of the Crown with the nobility and of the towns with the nobles and at times with the Crown. The natural aspiration of the Crown was complete control of the national forces and resources. The nobles were opposed to any form of absolutism ; their considerable wealth, their spirit of self-sufficiency and independence and the fact that the king was dependent upon their goodwill for the formation of an army, made them a difficult problem for any but the ablest of rulers. Alfonso X was the first ruler to formulate the rights which previous generations had gradually recognized as royal, the principle of hereditary succession and primogeniture, the right of coining money, mobilizing the army, making laws and exercising or delegating judicial powers. Alfonso was not himself particularly successful in asserting the rights which he claimed, but he has the credit of having formulated the ideal for future rulers.

As that ideal became realized, a Court bureaucracy began to grow up ; nobles sent their sons to Court to secure the king's favour and to gain some education ; by degrees the royal advisers became a regular council, the *consejo real*. A law of 1385 provided for some popular representatives as members of this council, which was to consist of twelve, of whom four were to be of the non-titled classes. It was found convenient that these four should be lawyers, as the council had certain judicial functions to perform. Judicial powers were also exercised by the provincial governors, the *adelantados*, appointed by the Crown, and by subordinate Crown officials, the *merinos*. The *alcalde* (mayors) of the towns acted as magistrates, and appeal could be made from their decisions to the Crown judicial authorities. There was, however, no uniform system for the whole country ; certain towns, certain corporations, such as the Mesta, the great sheep-grazing syndicate, the clergy, the universities were exempt from royal jurisdiction and had their own officials and their own laws. The general policy of the Crown was to curtail these privileges as much as possible by the substitution of royal for local officials ; the free Castilian towns, which had governed themselves and maintained their independence by means of their leagues (*hermandades*), received the king's judges, and in some cases invited royal intervention, when their internal quarrels became too acute. Alfonso XI was able to send a new official, the *corregidor*, to represent the interests of the Crown in the municipal assemblies. These officials became a permanent source of Crown influence.

The Cortes originated in the general councils of nobles and

prelates summoned from time to time by the king. The term
Cortes is first applied to a council of nobles in 1137. Representatives of the towns first appeared at the Cortes held in León
in 1188 ; no such case is known in Castile before 1250. The
Cortes thus came to consist of three estates, the nobles, clergy,
and the *procuradores* from the towns. There was at first no
limit to the number of these town deputies ; in the Cortes of
Burgos in 1315, 90 towns were represented by 192 deputies ; that
of Madrid in 1391 was attended by 126 deputies for 50 towns.
The Cortes met when the king chose to summon them, and at the
place where he happened to be ; some towns found the expense
of sending representatives a burden and induced richer towns to
represent them ; some allowed the king's officials to act as their
deputies, with the result that they eventually lost the privilege,
which was confined in Isabel's time to eighteen towns sending
two *procuradores* each. As the Cortes were chiefly concerned
with the grant of taxation and as the clergy and nobles were
exempt from taxation, these estates did not usually come to
meetings, except upon some important occasion, such as the
recognition of an heir to the throne. While taxation could not
be levied without the consent of the Cortes, they could not insist
that redress must precede supply ; they had a right to submit
petitions to the king which might become the basis of legislation
initiated by the Crown ; the Cortes had no legislative power ;
they could suggest and advise. As the royal power became
more centralized and absolute, so the influence of the Cortes
decreased.

Conditions in Aragon were somewhat different ; there were
separate Cortes for Aragon, Catalonia and Valencia, which might
be convoked simultaneously, but did not even then form one
whole. The Aragonese Cortes had four estates of the realm,
the nobility being divided into two classes. They could and
did insist that redress should precede any grant of taxation ; a
unanimous decision of the four estates was necessary to secure
the validity of a decision ; the opposition of one estate could
stop proceedings. Between their sessions a permanent commission of eight, two members for each estate, was maintained
to watch over the public interest as against that of the Crown.
The Aragonese Cortes were much less amenable to royal per-
suasion than the Castilian, for the reason that in Aragon nobles
and commons were united against the Crown, whereas in Castile
the opposition was of king and towns against the nobles.

The Crown was constantly in want of money for the public
services and for war ; apart from extraordinary taxation, the

resources under Ferdinand and Isabel were as follows. The king had the monopoly of certain mines and salt-works, and the patronage and estates of the three military Orders. There were also certain customs duties and duties upon traffic and circulation. There was the notorious *alcabala*, a tax, generally of 10 per cent., upon all pecuniary transactions ; this contradicted the very fundaments of the principle that a tax should be easy to collect and not readily perceptible by the payer. The *Bula de la Cruzada* was a tax authorized by the Pope to raise funds for the wars against the Moors, and was continued after the ostensible need had passed ; papal authorization was easily obtained for this and also for the *tercias reales* ; the Crown usually left one-third of the income to maintain church buildings. Loans forced or voluntary, the issues of mortgages (*juros*) on Crown lands and debasement of the coinage were other methods of meeting a financial crisis. The royal monopolies and the collection of the taxes were usually farmed out to individuals, and the evils attendant upon this practice were not wanting.

Castile and Aragon were not politically united by the joint reign of **Ferdinand and Isabel (1479–1504)**. But any clash of opposed policies was avoided and the way was thus paved in practice and in popular estimation for the closer union of later years. The Conquest of Granada (1492) was due as much to internal dissensions within the Moorish kingdom as to the military skill of the Spanish king, and was followed by a persecution of the Muslim and Jewish population which gave expression to the general religious intolerance of the age. The converted Moors formed the class known as Moriscos, and the Inquisition was established [1] to secure them from relapse and to increase their numbers. The revolts which followed cost heavily in lives and money and a period of tension began which (as will be seen in the following chapter) ended in the expulsion of that part of Spain's population economically most valuable to the country. Ferdinand was somewhat less fanatical than his wife and these measures were carried out with less stringency in Aragon, where the powerful landowners objected to see disturbance and hardship inflicted upon their most profitable tenants. From the

---

[1] The Inquisition was in existence in Aragon, and in Italy, during the thirteenth century. But it only became notorious after its introduction into Castile (1480), and its re-establishment in Aragon and Catalonia (1486–87). The Dominican Tomás de Torquemada, whose name is always associated with the horrors of the Spanish Inquisition, was appointed Inquisitor in 1482.

legal and ecclesiastical point of view, Spain was to be a land of Roman Catholic Christians only.

Both rulers did much to complete the process of centralizing all authority in themselves ; Isabel especially subdued the refractory nobles by force or diplomacy, secured the recognition of her officials in the towns, and with the help of Jiménez (or Ximenez) de Cisneros, Archbishop of Toledo, her confessor, purified the Church of some of its baser elements. The great event of the reign was the discovery of America, which immediately led to the final conquest of the Canary Islands to secure the route to the New World and to check any possible attacks by the African Muslim populations. Ferdinand's intervention in Italy and his acquisition of Naples were now to bring Spain into the current of European politics ; her adventures in America were to deprive her of men and attention which she needed for her own development and the treasure ships which her colonies sent her were no full compensation for the loss which they inflicted. Here, then, we see Spain at the parting of the ways ; at the moment when domestic and peaceful consolidation becomes a possibility, she is tempted to become the dominant figure in Europe and to make herself the chief colonial power in the world.

BIBLIOGRAPHY TO CHAPTER II

The following works will be found useful for both this and the next chapter :

22. Lafuente, M. (and others). *Historia General de España.* 25 vols. Barcelona, 1888.
23. *Documentos inéditos para la historia de España.* Madrid, 1842 ff. [In progress.]
24. *Cambridge Mediæval History.* Cambridge, 1911–36.
25. *Cambridge Modern History.* Cambridge, 1902–12. [Nos. 24 and 25 have useful bibliographies.]
26. Altamira, R. *Historia de España y de la civilización española.* Third edition, revised. 4 vols. Barcelona, 1913–14. Continued by P. Zabala, 2 vols. Madrid, 1930. [Has an excellent bibliography. English translation, in abridged form: *A History of Spanish Civilization.* London, 1930.]
27. Atkinson, W. C. *Spain, a brief history.* London, 1934.
28. Ballesteros y Beretta, A. *Historia de España y su influencia en la historia universal.* 10 vols. Madrid, 1919–41.
29. Chapman, C. E. *A History of Spain.* Second edition. New York, 1925. [Epitomizes No. 26.]
30. Hume, M. A. S. *The Spanish People, their origin, growth and influence.* London, 1901.

For this chapter only, the following are reliable works of a general character. Authorities such as Mariana, Zurita and Schmidt are not cited, since they need handling critically ; for these the student should consult the bibliographies mentioned above.

31. Boissonnade, P. *Histoire de la réunion de la Navarre à la Castille.* Paris, 1893.

32 Burke, U. R. *A History of Spain from the earliest times to the death of Ferdinand the Catholic.* 2 vols. Second edition. London, 1900.

33. Chaytor, H. J. *A History of Aragon and Catalonia.* London, 1933.

34. Codera, F. *Estudios críticos de historia árabe española.* Zaragoza, 1903.

35. Dozy, R. P. A. *The Moslems in Spain.* London, 1913.

36. Klein, J. *The Mesta.* Harvard and Oxford, 1920.

37. Makkari, Ahmed ibn Mohammed Al. *History of the Mahommedan Dynasties in Spain.* 2 vols. London, 1840–43. [Translated by Pascual de Gayangos.]

38. Menéndez Pidal, R. (*ed.*) *Historia de España.* In progress. 4 vols. in 6 (to 1954). Madrid, 1926 ff.

39. Merriman, R. B. *The Rise of the Spanish Empire in the Old World and in the New.* 4 vols. New York, 1918–34. [Vols. I and II fall under this chapter ; Vols. III–IV and Vol. II in part belong to the next. Very useful and practical bibliographical notes are given.]

40. Menéndez Pidal, R. *La España del Cid.* Madrid, 1929. Translated as *The Cid and his Spain.* London, 1934.

41. Scott, S. P. *History of the Moorish Empire in Europe.* 3 vols. Philadelphia and London, 1904.

42. Soldevila, F. *Història de Catalunya.* 3 vols. Barcelona, 1934–5. [Belongs partly to the next chapter.]

43. Watts, H. E. *Spain from the Moorish Conquest to the Fall of Granada.* London, 1894.

44. Whishaw, B. and E. M. *Arabic Spain : Sidelights on her history and art.* London, 1912.

[See also Nos. 6, 19, 45, 51, 55, 56, 76, 109, 111.]

CHAPTER III

SPANISH HISTORY, 1492 TO 1898

TWELVE years of life remained to Queen Isabel after the Conquest of Granada, a period characterized (as has been indicated in the last chapter) by rapid changes at home and significant happenings beyond the seas. By an edict signed at Granada on March 30, 1492, all Jews were given four months to become Christians or submit to banishment from the country, a step taken also five years later at the instance of the Catholic Monarchs [1] in Portugal. This intolerant policy was continued. The influence of Jiménez de Cisneros extended a like severity to the Moors, to whom the treaty, after the Conquest, had been not ungenerous. In 1502 Isabel decreed that all unconverted Moors in the Castilian realms should leave them on pain of death, as a result of which the number of Moriscos increased greatly.

Ferdinand, during these years, was occupied chiefly with a continuation of the projects of his predecessors for Aragonese expansion eastwards. By successive breaches of faith he first regained Roussillon, on his own borders, from his chief rival, France, and later, the important Kingdom of Naples. After Isabel's death in 1504, Ferdinand succeeded in driving the French from Italy, and added to his realms all Navarre south of the Pyrenees (1512). Powerful Spanish armies under the generalship of Gonsalvo de Córdoba (the ' Great Captain ') overran Northern Italy, making it clear that, having finally defeated her age-long adversary, Spain was now to be reckoned with as a force in Europe. Across the seas, the final conquest of Teneriffe (1494–1496) and the operations in North Africa which led to the capture of Bugia, Algiers and Tripoli (1510), showed that Ferdinand was prepared to follow up his victories over the Muslims, the more so since North Africa was a valuable strategic possession for operations against Italy.

But the crowning achievement of these years is of course the

[1] This title was conferred upon Ferdinand and Isabel by Pope Alexander VI in 1494.

part taken by Spain in the discovery of America. It should be needless to tell in detail how, with the blessing of the Church and the help of the Catholic Monarchs, Christopher Columbus set out from Palos on August 3, 1492, touched the Bahamas on October 12, and, after exploring parts of Cuba and Haiti, returned on March 15, 1493, and reported progress to Ferdinand and Isabel at Barcelona. On September 25 of the same year there set out a second expedition ; a third in 1498, and a fourth in 1502, made fresh discoveries. Before Columbus died, in painful circumstances, in 1506, other adventurers had begun to follow his example : of these the most famous was Núñez de Balboa who in 1513 crossed the Isthmus of Panamá and discovered the Pacific. Such exploits led Spain on to commitments in the New World as well as in the Old, preparing her greatness, and at the same time, though less apparently, her downfall.

On Isabel's death in 1504 it became evident that her daughter and heir Joan (Juana la Loca) was too mentally deficient to govern. Ferdinand therefore became regent of the thrones of Castile and León [1] until his death in January, 1516. In this year, fortunately for Spain, Joan's son Charles (b. 1500) came of age, and in November, 1517, the first of its Hapsburg rulers, **Charles I (1516–1556)**, landed in Spain, a foreign prince by education, surrounded by Flemish advisers, who only gradually conquered the esteem of the now united kingdoms and became one of the greatest rulers in their history. In 1519, on the death of his grandfather Maximilian, the young king was elected Holy Roman Emperor.[2] This event naturally strengthened in him the imperialistic ambitions which Ferdinand had inherited from his Aragonese ancestors. These, however, he could not indulge at once. Risings all over Castile (1520–1521) which were ended only by the Battle of Villalar, civil war in Valencia (1520–1522) and Mallorca (1521–1523) and Moorish insubordination occupied him even while he was preparing for the first (1521–1529) of the various wars against France which went on with brief intervals almost till the death of the ambitious Francis I in 1547. Charles's courage, determination and ability now became clearly evident to his Spanish subjects. Henry VIII of England, who had been coquetting with Francis, joined him (1523). The French had re-invaded Italy, and, in spite of the counter-invasion of Provence by the Imperialists, occupied Milan and besieged Pavia. But

[1] Joan's husband took possession of these thrones as Philip I, but died in 1506.
[2] Whence the title of Charles V by which he is usually known. His correct style in Spain is Charles I.

at Pavia (1525) they met their match. A great Imperialist victory was marked by the capture of Francis, who was taken to Madrid and released on the terms of his captor. Charles then pursued his campaign southwards as far as Rome ; the city was sacked by foreign levies ; and the Pope, who had abandoned his alliance with Charles, was made prisoner (1527). The French now retaliated with great vigour, pushing southwards to Naples and spending themselves there. Their final battle with the Spaniards at Landriano (1529) resulted in their total defeat.

With the Peace of Cambrai (' La Paz de las Damas ' : 1529) Charles I's real triumphs began. The acknowledged ruler of Lombardy, and the dominant power in all Italy, he could afford to place himself on free and generous terms with his fellow-rulers while he went to Germany (1530–1532) in an attempt to put down its rising Protestantism. Next he turned his attention to Africa, where the corsair Barbarossa, who ruled Algiers, not only attracted large bodies of Spaniard-hating Muslims to his side and service, but was slowly extending his kingdom and uniting his arms with those of the powerful Turk. Barbarossa's occupation of Tunis (1533) was taken by Charles as a direct challenge to reconquer a strategical position of such importance. After a fierce campaign he succeeded (1535) : it was a notable feat. But in the following spring the French opened a new campaign in Italy. Charles counter-attacked, unsuccessfully, in Provence. After two years of indecisive fighting a truce was signed for ten years (1538), but kept only for four. Late in 1541, Charles's disastrous attempt, made with an apparently invincible fleet, to crush Barbarossa once and for all and take Algiers, proved too great a temptation for Francis : only the re-alliance of Henry VIII with Charles saved the situation. Henry and Charles invaded France simultaneously : Francis made peace once more (1544) : three years later he died.

Then, with little gained save prestige from so many years' warfare, Charles once more turned to Germany. The first years of his French wars had seen a succession of movements on his part to overthrow German Protestantism, but it was not till Francis was removed that he was able to get to work effectively. The year (1546) after the Council of Trent assembled, Charles went to war against the princes who had embraced the reform, and in 1547 won an overwhelming victory at Mühlberg. By dint of imperial edicts and Spanish garrisons Germany was completely catholicized, and the Emperor, victorious on all sides, seemed almost to be without occupation. But religious observances cannot for long be imposed by force of arms. The Spaniards were hated in Germany, by people as much as by princes, and a new and more powerful revolt ended in the decision of the Diet of Augsburg (1555) that Catholics and Protestants should worship side by side in freedom.

And what of Spain during these five and thirty years of bold but unproductive Imperial adventure ? Through no direct doing of her sovereign, Spain was flourishing. In the so-called Indies, conquest was succeeding discovery. From Hernán Cortés the motherland received Mexico ; from Francisco Pizarro, Peru ; from Pedro de Valdivia, Chile. Explorations and settlements were proceeding continuously in what are now Argentina, Bolivia, and the Central American republics. Among the results was the development of an enormous trade, exports of manufactured goods of all kinds in great quantities—especially of wine—being balanced by the influx of gold and the import of American raw materials. From Seville, which long had the monopoly of American trade, transshipments to the Indies were made, not only from other ports of Spain, but also from foreign countries. The sudden rise of mercantile transactions on such a scale created machinery of all kinds in advance of that known elsewhere. All these conditions of commercial prosperity outlived not only Charles I's reign but also the sixteenth century.

The constitutional history of the reign it would take too long to relate in detail. It was well that Charles's solid virtues came to be appreciated by his people, and that he took a wife, not from England as he had at first thought of doing, but from Portugal. For he was not unnaturally compelled to strain his relations with the Cortes by the persistence of his demands upon them for money, which, as a rule, they granted him, while, on the other hand, though he learned wisdom from his initial difficulties, he inclined towards absolutism in his refusal to redress grievances as a preliminary to the granting of subsidies. Ferdinand and Isabel, as we have seen, had used the Castilian Cortes for their own purposes, and only called them or the Cortes of Aragon when to do so was unavoidable. The decline in power of the two privileged Orders dates (as already suggested) from before 1492 ; the third estate, weakened by the defeat of Villalar, was quietly undermined throughout Charles's reign. Side by side with this goes the prominence given to the advisory Councils such as the Council of the State, the Council of Italy and the Council of Flanders. The important Council of the Indies, too, was created in 1524 for purposes of colonial administration.

A ruler whose projects were so vast could hardly have failed to exercise much thought about the succession to his Crown and Empire. Both he would undoubtedly have bequeathed to his son Philip (b. 1527), but his brother Ferdinand had aspirations to the Empire and it was clear that the Germans would not tolerate a continued Spanish union under Philip, even if he were to succeed not his father but his uncle. As a result he turned again towards union with England and married Philip to its Roman Catholic Queen Mary,—a union which thwarted his dearest hopes by proving childless. At length, in the fortieth year of his reign, growing weary alike of power and disappointment, he determined to abdicate. First the Low Countries (1555), and then Spain (1556), he made over to Philip, and retired to the Monastery of Yuste, in Extremadura. In 1558, his brother Ferdinand was elected to succeed him as Emperor, and Spain was severed from the Holy Roman Empire.

The reign of **Philip II (1556–1598)** continued the tradition set by his father, who, indeed, had both educated and practised him in government. Less efficient in several ways than Charles, he was no less industrious, determined or devoted to the cause of Catholicism. He inherited a throne still beset with troublesome possessions : his European activities were to bring him glory and bitterness in equal measure. The American colonies continued to develop throughout his reign, and with them the material prosperity of the mother country.

No sooner had Philip ascended the throne than his European wars began. A short struggle with the Pope over his Italian interests was succeeded by a more serious one with France, in which Philip was able to obtain the support of England, and won the battle of St. Quentin, though he failed to follow up his victory by marching upon Paris, as Charles would undoubtedly have done in his place. Some further fighting and prolonged negotiations ended in the Peace of Cateau Cambrésis (1559), which Philip thought to seal in the same year by taking as his third wife the young Princess Elizabeth, eldest daughter of Henry II of France.

A Spaniard to the core, more at home and more often at home in his kingdom than his father, Philip now returned there. He had already made it perfectly clear to the Castilian Cortes that he intended to govern without their aid if he so desired, and he took definite personal control, the effective governing bodies being the various central Councils. There followed a brief and badly needed period of retrenchment after the wars abroad which even Spanish prosperity was beginning to find exhausting. It was marred by a serious rebellion of the Moriscos of Granada

(1568–1571), the cause of which was the harshness of the Inquisition and some legislation more intolerant than that to which Granada was accustomed. As a supposed but mistaken remedy, the Moriscos were expelled from Andalusia (1570). A worse trial still was the Turkish menace in the Mediterranean. This a Spanish fleet had twice failed ignominiously to check in 1560–1561 ; in 1565 the Turks besieged Malta, which held out after the most appalling horrors ; but when next they came out on the offensive, Philip's help was more efficient, and it was mainly a Spanish fleet that in 1571 won the really decisive and crushing victory of Lepanto. Philip's bastard brother, John (Don Juan) of Austria, who was in command, would have followed up his victory had the money been forthcoming, but he was forced to be content with taking Tunis, and, like Ferdinand the Catholic, with dreaming dreams of a North African Empire.

Meanwhile the supreme trouble of this reign had already begun : the wars in the Netherlands. For a long time dissatisfaction had been fermenting, for Philip tried to govern the Flemings like the Spaniards, and to maintain Spanish officials, Spanish troops and even the Spanish Inquisition there. The unrest, which was largely due to political causes, began soon to assume the character of a religious rising. Hardening a heart incapable of compromise and gentleness, Philip sent the Duke of Alba to quell the rebels, which he endeavoured to do (1567–1573) with such brutality that the revolt now resembled a war of independence. Alba was at length recalled in favour of Luis de Requeséns, whose gentler methods were more successful. Upon his death (1576), John of Austria was sent to succeed him, but a mutiny of the Spanish troops made things harder for him, and the Flemings presented a united resistance. After more than a year of open warfare he died (1578) of fever.

Leaving the Netherlands to be tranquillized by the diplomacy of Alexander Farnese, we now turn to a field in which Philip won an almost bloodless victory that might well have become the most significant of the century to future ages. The young King Sebastian of Portugal had just died, and Philip saw his opportunity of succeeding to the vacant throne, to which he had a claim through his mother. None of the other claimants could stand against him, and a show of force, together with a few essential promises, was sufficient to bring the whole Peninsula under Spanish rule (1581) for a period of sixty years. Unhappily, although Philip kept the promises he had made and respected the Portuguese nationality, the cleft between Spaniards and Portuguese was too deep for Iberian unity to become permanent.

Yet, when one considers the vastness of the Spanish empire as reinforced by the Portuguese colonies in three continents, it is impossible not to feel that this was the day of Spain's opportunity and that all else should have been subordinated to realizing the ideal of permanent union.

So far as Philip was concerned, the year 1581 marks a climax. Troubles both personal and political began to overwhelm him, and his disposition became gloomy and embittered. His child-wife Elizabeth had long ago died in a confinement ; Charles, his half-witted son, had died at the age of twenty-three : now his fourth wife died also, and two of her three children. Not only the Netherlands but Naples was in rebellion ; the Pope and the Spanish Bishops had recently defied the royal authority ; while England, eyed by the King throughout his reign with misgiving, had been aiding the Protestant Flemings, and France seemed likely at last to emerge from the religious insecurity which had made her impotent.

It was a wretched enough outlook, but Philip hoped, by one bold stroke, to bring good out of some of this evil. Only policy had kept him from attacking England in the past, for not only did she defy him in the Old World, but her pirates were stinging him continually in the New. Now with his enfeebled vision he believed he saw a way to the English throne which in the past had seemed to be barred to him. He would dethrone Elizabeth, and give Mary, Queen of Scots, her crown, on the understanding that she made him her heir. Though Spain was totally impoverished, a superhuman effort was made to raise a fleet which could be termed ' invincible '. Troops from Flanders and ships from Naples were pressed into service ; the Pope, under certain conditions, promised a subsidy ; forced loans and illegal taxes in great number were resorted to, not for the first time, but more freely than ever before. The story of what happened is well known : how in 1587 Drake ' singed the King's beard ' in Cádiz Harbour, and how, on May 30, 1588, the great fleet sailed from Lisbon to its doom. Every kind of mistake was made in organization : and the worst mistake of all was the appointment as commander of the totally incapable Duke of Medina Sidonia. Before ever the fleet reached La Coruña its commander advised Philip to recall it. When at length the engagement began, off Plymouth (July 31), defeat was followed by panic, and panic by storm and shipwreck. Out of 131 vessels and 24,000 men, only 65 and 10,000 returned.

Philip lived for ten years after the rout of the Invincible Armada. In that time he saw the end of the religious strife in

France, the accession of Henry of Navarre to the throne, which
he had done his best to prevent, the contempt of England
expressed in the light-hearted sack of Cádiz by the Earl of Essex,
and an insurrection in Aragon which was put down with some
severity. His last days were passed in the agony of a horrible
disease which he bore with unflinching fortitude, lying in the
simplest chamber of his great sombre palace of El Escorial, till,
on September 13, 1598, death claimed him. During his reign,
Spain's inward decay had set in. Even in Charles's day the
Cortes had had difficulty in finding money for the royal exploits.
Now the country was bankrupt, oppressed, corrupted and all
but ruined. Both agriculture and craftsmanship had suffered
from the expulsion of the Moriscos. Fishing had been ruined
by the commandeering of all boats for warfare. Manufactures
had ceased from pure inertia. The population, already drained
by the Americas, was thinned still further by war, disease and
exile, though it was not till some time later that the seriousness
of its decline became apparent. Nor were social conditions any
better. Excess of luxury in the upper classes contrasted with
miserable poverty in the lower. The King's religious fanaticism
bred hypocrisy in his court and people, and testimonies of every
kind speak of a moral tone that sank continually lower.

It may be said at once that this social and political degrada-
tion continued through the reigns of all the three remaining
Hapsburgs, which form one period of frank decline. **Philip III
(1598–1621)** succeeded, at the age of twenty, to possessions
much more manageable than his father's, since the Netherlands
had been left to his half-sister Isabel. But he had not even the
elements of a ruler : weak, fatuous and extravagant, he was
entirely governed by favourites, notably the Duke of Lerma,
and he replenished his coffers, when the Cortes would not fill
them, by selling honours far and wide to those who would buy.
The story of his reign makes pitiful reading, even compared
with the splendid failures of his father. Its characteristics are
indecision and inefficiency. Since 1560, the capital of Spain
had been Madrid : it now (1601) became Valladolid, and after
four years Madrid once more. A new invasion of England was
planned,—and a new storm dispersed the fifty ships which set
out for it. A fantastic attempt was made to support the rebellious Earl of Tyrone and conquer Ireland ; a pathetic one, to
help Isabel against the Flemings. At last these pretences of
activity petered out, and Spain, at peace with England, Holland
and France, might have recuperated her forces had her mis-

governors known how this could be done. As it was, they used their freedom from foreign wars to commit a supreme act of folly. Attempts were made to check the menace of Moorish pirates, and activity in the Mediterranean, not being considered sufficient, was followed by the expulsion of the Moriscos from the kingdom of Valencia (1609). Nor was this all : the expulsion, accompanied by quite unnecessary cruelty, was extended to all other parts of Spain where Moriscos were still left : Aragon, Catalonia, Murcia, Andalusia, La Mancha, Extremadura and Castile. Thus any number up to half a million of Spain's most profitable and industrious subjects were expelled, and with the continuance of peace she grew not richer, but poorer. An inconclusive war with Savoy and an impolitic entry into the Thirty Years War, on the side of the Emperor, concluded an inglorious reign.

Philip IV (1621–1665), son of Philip III and Margaret of Austria, was even weaker and more frivolous than his father. The Duke of Lerma gave place to the Count (Conde-Duque) of Olivares and the misrule of Spain went on much as before, with the additional burden for the country of new and ruinous wars. A truce which Philip III had made with Holland expired in the year of his death and Olivares haughtily resumed hostilities. Though the young King had married the daughter of Henry IV, he went to war with France also. Naval victories over the Dutch and the capture of Breda put heart into the Spaniards again, but with the entry of France (1635) into the Thirty Years War the tide of fortune turned against her. In Guipúzcoa, and in Roussillon, France made incursions into Spain ; at sea, a Spanish fleet was destroyed by the Dutch ; and things were heading fast for the disaster of Rocroi (1643), where the French gained so decisive a victory over the Spaniards that it may be said to have killed the once world-wide reputation of the Spanish army.

Meanwhile Philip had worse troubles at home than any abroad. It was hardly to be expected that the wise government of Portugal would continue under Lerma and Olivares, and the latter's open attempt to castilianize that country brought it into a complete accord against Spain which he could do nothing to alter. In a single day's revolt the Spanish rule was overthrown and the Duke of Braganza was chosen by the Portuguese for their King (1640).

To this disaster was added in the same year a serious rebellion in Catalonia caused by disregard of Catalan liberties. An endeavour was made to put down the revolt with troops and slaughter, whereupon the Catalans called on the French, who responded by an invasion by land and the bombardment of Tarragona by sea. At the same time Louis XIII was openly proclaimed King. When the French had occupied the whole of Catalonia and part of Aragon the spirit of Philip IV was stirred at last. He took command himself of his troops, dismissed Olivares (1643), and did his best to make peace with his rebellious subjects, hampered as he was now (1646–1648) with a fierce but abortive rebellion in Naples. Unhappily, the Catalan rebellion wore on, though its force was largely expended, and the Catalans began to realize that the French were no more ideal rulers than the Spaniards. The Treaty of the Pyrenees, between Spain and France, in 1659, restored Catalonia to Spain, while Roussillon and Cerdagne became French again. María Teresa, Philip's daughter, was given in marriage to Louis XIV of France, and Spain had now peace once more, since the end of the Thirty Years War had come eleven years earlier.

The state of the country at this time can hardly be imagined. What the taxation was like may be judged from the fact that one-third of the income of the nobility and one-eighth of the value of all staple articles of diet went directly to the State, together with 14 per cent. on the values of all sales. These unpopular taxes were known as the *millones* and the *alcabala* [1] respectively. Industry of almost every kind was at a standstill ; foreign trade was non-existent, and, for the most part, forbidden. Yet Philip, still favourite-ridden and desperate, devoted the last four years of his life to fruitless efforts for the reconquest of Portugal. His son Baltasar Carlos, immortalized by Velázquez, had died in boyhood, and his second wife, Mariana of Austria, had given him a weakly epileptic child, who succeeded him at the age of four as **Charles II (1665–1700)**.

It was seen, almost from his accession, that ' Charles the Bewitched ', as he was later unkindly named, was likely to be the last of Spain's Hapsburg rulers, and as a result intrigues for the crown went on throughout most of his reign. Nor did wars abroad cease with the desire for them. In 1668, the independence of Portugal was finally acknowledged, but the ambitions of Louis XIV, now approaching the height of his power and fame, involved Spain in unprovoked wars with France. First, the cause was Louis' invasion of the Netherlands, where he succeeded in retaining his conquests (1667–1668). This gave him the chance for a second invasion in 1672, from which he emerged six years later with fresh possessions. Unhappy

---

[1] See p. 56 above. The *alcabala* had greatly increased since the time there referred to.

Spain, from being first a great power, and then at least a valiant fighting people, became now almost at the mercy of the Roi Soleil. In 1681, Louis began to lay hands on those few European outposts of Spain which former treaties had left her, and after a three years' campaign and a brief interval, he again attacked her in 1689. This last war continued till 1697, by which time Louis had determined that his grandson, Philip, Duke of Anjou (b. 1683), should succeed the last of the Hapsburgs, and was therefore no longer anxious to appear too depredatory. Charles himself, who was near to death, would have preferred an Austrian successor, for his mother and wife were both Austrian ; but, yielding to persuasions on all sides, he at length bequeathed his kingdom to the young Bourbon Duke, making the important proviso that France and Spain should never be united under the same monarch. On November 1, 1700, he died.

Philip V (1700–1746) soon showed himself to be acting under the orders of his grandfather, and the century of Spain's regeneration under the Bourbons began ominously in 1701, when England, Austria, the Empire and the Protestant Netherlands formed the Grand Alliance and supported the Archduke Charles of Austria against France and Spain. The King had hardly celebrated his marriage (to Louis XIV's nominee, Marie Louise, daughter of the Duke of Savoy) when he had to leave to quell a revolt in his kingdom of Naples. On his return, hearing that an English and Dutch army had landed at Lisbon, he was forced to invade Portugal (1704). In the same year, the English took Gibraltar, which they have held ever since, and, in 1708, Menorca, which they kept for over seventy years (see p. 72). Elsewhere in Spain, Philip struggled bravely to hold his own. Catalonia quickly became disaffected and the Archduke was proclaimed King in Valencia and Barcelona (1705). While Philip was engaged here, another allied army marched through Portugal and took Madrid, holding it only four months (1706). Outside Spain, the War of the Spanish Succession, as it was called, centred round the victories of the Duke of Marlborough, at Blenheim (1704), Ramillies (1706), Oudenarde (1708), and Malplaquet (1709). It seemed likely, at this point, that he would be able to impose his own terms on Louis. But in 1711 the Archduke, somewhat unexpectedly, became Holy Roman Emperor (Charles VI), whereupon the plans of the Allies were completely changed, for their real motive in the war was the maintenance of the balance of power in Europe, which the union of Spain and the

Empire would have upset as disastrously as that of Spain and France. So the Treaty of Utrecht was drawn up (1713), which confirmed Philip in his kingdom, but made him formally renounce any right to the crown of France and surrender his Italian possessions to the Emperor. England, too, was given the important monopoly of the slave trade with the colonies of Spanish America, and the right of setting up trade agencies in certain of their ports.

During the latter stages of the war Philip had suffered severely in his own country. Not only had the Archduke again taken Madrid, but, even after the Treaty, Barcelona held out, and flatly refused to recognize the Bourbons. In the end, after a hideous carnage (1714), the city was reduced by sheer force, and it may be imagined that Catalonia was not the more contented, though she can hardly have been surprised, when some of her traditional and valued privileges were taken from her.

As a result of the long struggle, Philip had endeared himself to the Spaniards as a brave soldier, and still more had his spirited young Queen become respected when again and again she had been able to stir up the people to action. Both in morals and in *morale*, Spain was already improving greatly ; corruption and favouritism were on the decline ; and taxation was at least effective though still ruinously heavy. In 1714, Marie Louise died, and Philip quickly re-married, his bride being Elizabeth of Parma (Isabel Farnese). The dominating feminine influence on Philip during the first fifteen years of his reign (and he was always easily moved by women) had been the Princesse des Ursins, an old lady of great skill, who had been sent to Marie Louise by Louis XIV : she was faithful as a rule to Philip's best interests, supporting him more than once when he kicked against Louis' wishes. His new queen, however, dismissed her, so as to rule her husband alone, and, through him, his country. She was a forceful and aggressive personality, and her dominating ideas,—separation from France, advances in Italy and the aggrandizement of her own children—prevailed until the end of Philip's long reign. His ministers, in particular, were markedly Italian, chief among them being the Cardinal Alberoni, who (while still a simple priest) had been responsible for his second marriage.

During the rest of Philip's reign no events of primary importance took place, beyond a series of wars and wrangles in the interests of the Queen's ambitions. A belated and unwilling peace (1720) with the Empire was forced on Spain by the hostilities of the Quadruple Alliance. Four years later came Philip's somewhat startling abdication, during one of his recurring periods of intense melancholy, in favour of his son, Luis I, who, however, died after a reign of seven months. In this difficult situation Philip re-assumed the crown. An unsuccessful attempt to reconquer Gibraltar was followed by a war on Austria with the object of reconquering Naples and the Two Sicilies for Isabel's son Charles. This end was attained (1734), but at the price of the three duchies of Parma, Piacenza and Guastalla, which Philip was compelled to renounce. A further conflict with England, in which France joined Spain, grew into the War of the Austrian Succession (1740–1748) : as a result of this Isabel was successful in obtaining the three duchies above mentioned, which she gave to her son Philip, who had married a daughter of Louis XV. But ere this took place Philip V had died (1746), to be succeeded by Marie Louise's son, **Ferdinand VI (1746–1759)**, a young man of thirty-four, who proved to be a patriotic and peace-loving king, kept Spain from foreign wars and foreign influences and allowed her ample opportunity for recuperation. Sad to relate, the melancholia of his father was accentuated in him, and the death of his Portuguese consort, Barbara of Braganza, broke his heart and caused him to lose his reason.

Those very foreign influences which, under the first of the Bourbon kings, were so frequently resented, were in many ways the best thing that could have happened to Spain. More efficient administration did much to better her fortunes, and, had not the Succession wars and Isabel Farnese's ambition continued to drain her resources, many of the oppressive taxes might have been abolished, as indeed a very few of them were. Constitutionally, as will readily be understood, the Bourbons continued the absolutist policy of the Hapsburgs. The Cortes of Castile were now scarcely ever summoned ; the Councils lost much of their authority ; only the King lost nothing. Philip did as much as he dared towards depriving the provincial kingdoms of their few remaining privileges, not so much from enmity towards the kingdoms as in the interests of a centralized Spain. Except in Catalonia, little hostility was aroused by what was done, and the provincial Cortes were hardly more alive than those of Castile. Finally, the Inquisition, which was active under Philip V, weakened considerably with his successor ; and the next reign was to see further changes in the relations of Church and King.

Both Philip and Ferdinand were lovers of art and literature. Learned societies, academies and libraries were founded (see p. 155) under Philip, and under Ferdinand they had time and

opportunity to flourish.[1]   New theatres sprang up all over the
country. Fashions were predominantly French, but the middle
and lower classes, in recovering something of the stability of
their existence, reverted to their simple and homely customs of
old which we still know to-day.

Ferdinand's successor was his half-brother, **Charles III
(1759–1788)**. A man of mature years, with experience of
government as King of Naples, he was welcomed heartily on his
arrival in Spain by a people no longer cowed by defeat and hunger.
He proved to be well deserving of his popularity : far-seeing,
patriotic, enlightened, the best ruler Spain had had for generations.   In his foreign policy he opposed England, and looked
towards France, allowing himself, as his brother had refused to
do, to be drawn into the Seven Years War (1756–1763) on the
side of France, and making with Louis XV a ' family compact '
(1761–1762) which was a defensive alliance against all the world
and an offensive and defensive one against Britain.

The principal result of the War to Spain was a reshuffling of
her American possessions.   A few years later (1770) she quar-
relled with England over the Falkland Islands, and, France not
aiding her, had to yield.   A more successful American quarrel
was with Portugal who had attacked Spain's colony of Buenos
Aires and was forced to grant her some territory in reparation
(1777).   But America influenced Spain in a much more serious
way when, after the United States had declared their independence and France had supported them against England, Spain
(unwisely for a great colonial power, it may be thought) joined
France.   Once again she used her opportunity to attack Gibraltar
in great strength by sea and by land, and once again she failed
entirely.   Menorca she did recapture, after which she returned,
once more in vain, to the siege of Gibraltar (1782).   When peace
was made in the following year, Menorca was kept by Spain and
the Rock by Britain.

It cannot be too much emphasized—there were those who
foresaw it at the time, even in Spain—that it was the example
of the United States in the first place which fomented unrest and
eventually brought revolution in Spanish America.   Though
Spain had lost islands or patches of territory here and there, her
possessions still included practically the whole of South and
Central America (with the important exception of Brazil)—
territory ruled, either by viceroys or by captains-general, with

---

[1] From Chapter V it will be seen how large were the contributions made
to knowledge by the literature of this epoch, though creatively it was
weak.

the same absolute authority as that of the Kings of Spain, and contributing not ungenerously to the coffers of the mother country. Among the reforms of Charles's early years had been the reorganization of his departments for the colonies, which had undoubtedly in the past been greatly neglected. But it was not till after the Declaration of Independence that the viceroyalties of Buenos Aires and Peru began to rebel, and stern suppression was only of avail temporarily.

The remaining wars of Charles III's reign were fought against the Moors, who attacked the Spanish possessions of Ceuta and Melilla in 1775, as a reply to which an unsuccessful Spanish attack was made upon Algiers. After the European peace of 1783 fresh attempts were made by Spain to solve the age-old problem of Moorish piracy. What war could not do was in the end effected by diplomacy, and the Muslim States came to a working arrangement with the Spaniards which put a stop to organized piracy at least, and went a long way towards making Spain's South and East coasts prosperous.

Turning now to the internal history of Spain under Charles III, we have to record amazing strides in her prosperity. At long last her taxes were lightened : the *alcabala* and the *millones*, the most crippling of all, were greatly reduced and in some circumstances abolished, while other taxes were both distributed more equitably than in the past, and collected more economically.[1] Largely through the importation of skilled craftsmen from foreign countries, Spain's former manufactures were revived and new ones started. Agriculture, mining and fishing came to life again spontaneously. New roads and waterways were constructed in great number. Stricter police regulations, at first resented by the people, led to greater national security in the cities. Schools and universities, hospitals and asylums, museums and archives, savings banks and patriotic unions of workers—all came into being in this reign or developed with unprecedented rapidity. It was as though Spain had suddenly awakened to the strides which other nations were making, and indeed this phrase not inaptly describes the effect of Charles's reforms upon her.

Some account must be added of the King's relations with the Church. Conflicts between King and Pope had not been infrequent in the time of the Hapsburgs, and the Bourbons had not been mollified by the support which Rome had given to the Archduke Charles in 1700. But while neither Philip V nor

---

[1] A new code of laws, known as the Novísima Recopilación, was (in 1806) substituted for the existing code of 1567.

Ferdinand VI was disposed to yield to the Pope his royal
authority, Charles III, a good Catholic but a progressive one,
went farther in asserting himself than any sovereign who had
preceded him.   All papal communications, he ordered, must be
submitted to the King before publication.   The powers of the
Inquisition were regulated in some directions and curtailed in
others.   The Jesuits were expelled from Spain (1767) with
unnecessary dispatch and rigour,—a prelude, as it proved, to the
suppression of their Order by the Pope, six years later, which
lasted until 1814.   Together with these drastic measures, a large
number of minor reforms in the Spanish Church were made by
the King, the general results of which were to increase its efficiency, to curtail the jurisdiction of the ecclesiastical courts and
to subject the clergy, inferior and superior, to the King's authority.
All these things were done by Charles without reference to his
Cortes, for, like his predecessors, he was a thoroughgoing despot :
his chief adviser during the first part of his reign was the Count
of Aranda, no mere favourite but the responsible ' President of
the Council '.   This Council, composed of sixteen members,
assisted Charles to govern, while a more intimate Council,
including chiefly the five secretaries of Departments, was chosen
from its members.   But Charles and Aranda, together with the
Counts of Campomanes and Floridablanca, were the real rulers,
and they had undoubtedly some infusion of the new and modern
spirit which was shortly to sweep over France with such violence.
More prudent than the Bourbons of France, they prepared a
foundation on which those very forces that in France worked
revolution might have built a prosperous and progressive Spain.
Alas, that they had none to carry on their work and that Spain
was shortly to sink lower than ever !

Charles III, as he lay dying, knew, as surely as Philip II had
known, that his son (b. 1748) was no ruler fit to succeed him.
And, of all Spain's royal failures, **Charles IV (1788–1808)** is
the most tragic in relation to his country's possibilities.   Weak
and fearful by nature, he was content to become a nonentity,
to be influenced by his wife, Maria Luisa of Parma, and to rely
entirely on the counsel of his favourites ; nor did he long retain
his father's prudent ministers, Floridablanca and Aranda, exalting
to the presidency the notorious Godoy, then (1792) a youth of
twenty-five, to the disgust and wrath of his subjects, whom the
thirty years' rule of Charles III had educated to expect better
things.
The Revolution and the Terror in France left Spain untouched

and, in spite of her disapproval of them, on the one hand, and of France's offers of an alliance on the other, she was able, until the beginning of 1793, to remain neutral.   Then, with the execution of Louis XVI, Spanish feeling was roused, and Spain joined the first coalition, though it was France who actually declared war.   Considerable enthusiasm was shown by Spaniards for the alliance, but the campaigns were sorely mismanaged, and it was a servile populace in Madrid that welcomed the conclusion of the war (1795) by bestowing on Godoy his well-known title of ' Prince of the Peace '.   By the Treaty of San Ildefonso (1796) the countries now became firm allies, but on terms by no means advantageous to Spain, who found herself pledged to join France in any war with Britain.

In 1799, Napoleon Bonaparte, with the lustre of his Eastern exploits fresh upon him, returned from Palestine to Paris, over-threw the French Directory and became First Consul.   It quickly grew clear that under Napoleon France would dominate Spain still further.   The general dislike for Godoy, who was now not only Prime Minister, but Commander-in-Chief of the Spanish army and navy, and the Queen's lover, gave him the opportunity to foster the growth of a party which centred its hopes on Charles's young son Ferdinand (b. 1784).   With this weapon ready to his hand, he made increasing use of Spain, leading her at last into a war with England of which the chief event was the disastrous naval battle of Trafalgar (1805).

By this time the supporters of the young and popular prince Ferdinand had grown so greatly in numbers that Napoleon saw no insuperable obstacle to the dethronement of the Bourbons in Spain and the setting up in their place of a puppet under his orders.   In 1807, the preliminaries were accomplished in the conquest of Portugal, which could offer but little resistance, Napoleon having persuaded Godoy to allow him to bring his troops through Spain.   This conquest was accompanied by the occupation of parts of Northern Spain with hardly a plausible motive.   Both Godoy and Charles now divined Napoleon's intentions.   The favourite was for resistance and war, but Charles was too craven a soul for anything but submission, and he was supported by the Prince's party, who believed that Napoleon's aim was only to get rid of the favourite.   But Charles knew better.   A project between Godoy and the King and Queen for their escaping together to Spanish America was interrupted by a riot at Aranjuez (whither the Court had been transferred), and the capture of Godoy by Ferdinand's followers (1808).   Charles now lost all discretion, and on March 19 abdicated in favour of his son, who succeeded to the throne as **Ferdinand VII (1808–1833)**.

His reign began badly, even ludicrously. Napoleon, by announcing a visit to Madrid, enticed the young King first to Burgos, and then as far as Bayonne, to meet him ; had him arrested forthwith and forced him by threats to restore the Spanish crown to his father, who, having arrived at Bayonne also, thereupon handed it to Napoleon (May 6). Four days earlier, the famous ' Dos de Mayo ' insurrection had taken place in Madrid, when the inhabitants rose in a body against Murat and the French garrison. Although after much bloodshed on both sides they were put down by superior force, the news of their courage flashed through Spain, and even before Napoleon had nominated his brother Joseph as King, the whole country was in arms in defence of Ferdinand.

This was the real beginning of the Peninsular War, known in Spain as the War of Independence. On July 19, 1808, the Spaniards gained a decisive victory at Bailén. Joseph Bonaparte at once fled from the capital and the entry of England on the side of Spain, together with the success of Palafox' magnificent defence of Zaragoza, made things look black for Napoleon, who had badly under-estimated Spain's powers. He had taken the precaution to summon a council of Spanish notabilities at Bayonne (June 15), which naturally (since the more patriotic of those who were summoned refused to attend it) acquiesced in his arrangements. But in Spain the great cities and chief provinces had taken the law into their own hands. They appointed emergency *juntas*, sending representatives to a supreme Junta Central, varying from twenty-four to thirty-five members, which first met at Aranjuez on September 25 and combined legislative functions with executive. In the following January, the Junta Central made a bold bid for the help of Spain's American colonies ; in May it decreed the re-establishment of the Cortes. But November saw the Spaniards sorely beaten at Ocaña ; Joseph Bonaparte returned to Madrid and resumed his reign ; and in the provinces not only did Zaragoza fall to the French after a two months' siege, but the hardly less heroic stronghold of Gerona fell, and a number of other towns in the east. Napoleon, repairing his error, had poured his battalions into Spain ; the British, who had been engaged in Portugal, advanced to meet the invaders, but had to retreat from Astorga to La Coruña, where Sir John Moore was mortally wounded. Their action in diverting so great a part of the French forces gave the Spaniards time which was sorely needed, and indeed may be said to have

saved Spain.   The Junta, late in 1809, left Aranjuez for Seville,
and again, in the New Year, for the Isla de León, near Cádiz.
Here it dissolved in favour of a Regency of five members, and a
National Assembly of three estates met in September, 1810, the
members of which were of necessity chosen arbitrarily since
so great a part of Spain was cut off from Cádiz by the enemy.
This body was strongly liberal in character : the tasks before it,
as may be imagined, were almost insuperable, and not made
easier by the determined opposition of the Regency.   It was
simple, however, for the Assembly to nominate a new Regency
of three, of purely nominal authority.   On March 19, 1812, the
promulgation of a new constitution followed.

This Constitution of 1812 was markedly democratic, to the
degree of being revolutionary.   Political though not religious
liberty is secured by it : the nation alone is sovereign, and the
King, who is head of the executive, is required to obey his responsible ministers.   The legislative authority is to consist of a single
Chamber elected by a manhood suffrage granted to all over the
age of twenty-five.   These are only a few articles of the new
constitution, but they are typical of the rest.   It was too progressive for the country as a whole : even under the artificial
conditions of the day it was only passed after a struggle, and,
with the final defeat of the French invaders, it was doomed.

This defeat had already been prepared, before Ocaña, with
the return to Portugal of Sir Arthur Wellesley (later Duke of
Wellington), who had been originally in command there.   He
had driven Soult out of Portugal and won the Battle of Talavera
(1809).   Then he was forced to retreat, but while Andalusia was
being conquered and Cádiz besieged, Wellesley was establishing
himself immovably in Portugal.   Masséna, when he attacked
him, could do nothing against the famous lines of Torres Vedras,
constructed between the Tagus and the sea.   He retreated, and
Wellington, after an unsuccessful attempt in each case, took the
important cities of Badajoz and Ciudad Rodrigo, both near
Spain's Portuguese frontier.   One further victory at Salamanca,
in the summer of 1812, and both Joseph and the French armies
began to retire.   A huge and determined counter-attack by the
forces which retreat had concentrated caused Wellington to fall
back again behind Ciudad Rodrigo while Joseph returned to
Madrid.   But it was for the last time.   On June 21, 1813,
Wellington gained a brilliant victory at Vitoria, and by the
following spring Spain was once more her own mistress.

This, in effect, meant that Ferdinand VII, whom she
welcomed, on his return from captivity, as *El Deseado* (March

22, 1814), became her master. He was an even more unpleasant
character than his father, spoilt from boyhood by unreasoning
adulation, cowardly in adversity and in prosperity tyrannical.
The majority of his people were undoubtedly with him when he
immediately (May 4, 1814) annulled the decrees of the Assembly,
and the Constitution of 1812, which it had proclaimed in Madrid
after the Battle of Salamanca. His next acts—the arrest and
harrying of those known or believed to harbour Liberal opinions
—were less popular in Spain, and resented and condemned both
by England and by France. From 1814 to 1820, one piece of
the purest tyranny followed another. The King and the little
circle of favourites known as his *camarilla* did what they pleased.
For the most innocuous offences against the new *régime*, malcon-
tents were summarily executed. Ministers were dismissed by
caprice, and imprisoned or exiled without trial. Periodicals,
with few exceptions, were suppressed, and foreign publications
confiscated at the frontiers. It is not surprising that the *doceañistas*
(supporters of the 1812 Constitution) endeavoured to foment
revolution, nor that after no more than six years of absolutism
they succeeded. The American colonies were getting more and
more restive, and it was the assembling of a large Spanish force
for service in America that set Spain on fire. On January 1,
1820, an Asturian called Rafael Riego proclaimed the 1812
Constitution and started a rebellion which spread hardly less
quickly than that of 1808. Ferdinand, on March 6, capitulated
without a struggle, summoned the Cortes, announced all kinds
of reforms, and took the oath, almost cheerfully, to observe the
1812 Constitution. The people, incredibly trustful of an un-
trustworthy king, acclaimed his submission, and three years of
Liberal reaction and so-called constitutional government followed.

These years were by no means, however, peaceful. The
return of many exiles swelled the numbers, and augmented the
violence, of each and all of the discordant progressive parties.
Plots for a *coup d'état* were rife from the beginning. Eventually, in 1822, when the Cortes of 1820 dissolved, and a more
radical government, under the presidency of Riego, came into
power, Ferdinand began to appeal to his supposed friends abroad.
In January, 1823, Russia, Prussia, Austria and France intervened
by common consent to save Ferdinand from his enemies, who
were known as *exaltados* or progressives. Britain, suspect-
ing the motives of French intervention, remained neutral, but
France prepared for invasion and the radical government for
defence. The invasion took place (April, 1823) ; the government carried Ferdinand off to Seville and later to Cádiz. Since

he went unwillingly, they appointed a Regency to act for him. Once more adversity brought this unbelievable tyrant popularity : no stronger condemnation of the Liberals than these events can be imagined.   By August, the French, openly welcomed by the Spanish people, besieged Cádiz ; in October, Ferdinand, set free by his captors only when they saw that no other course was possible, began a new career of tyranny which completely eclipsed his earlier period of freedom.

This third section of his reign lasted from 1823 until his death ten years later.   It began with the arrest and execution or banishment of those to whom he had been compelled to promise free pardon, a proceeding which called forth the protests even of the French invaders.   Riego was naturally hanged without question of pardon.   Coercive measures hitherto unknown were employed for the persecution of everything resembling Liberalism. Not only was the Press muzzled, but universities, societies and clubs were closed as being possible centres of insurrection. Rather than re-establish the recently abolished (1820) Inquisition, the King created a secret body of like aims.   His most frenzied supporters are said to have founded in various parts of the country a ' Society of the Exterminating Angel '.   It is un-necessary in a brief sketch to give further examples of a tyranny of which the general nature is only too evident.   The name of Calomarde, inappropriately named Ferdinand's ' Minister of Justice ', stands to Spaniards for the terrors associated with that epoch.

The Liberals being duly suppressed, a new source of danger sprang up to Ferdinand's rule.   Impossible as it may seem, there were those who thought he had not gone far enough, and when they found that, under the influence of some tem-porarily popular adviser, he occasionally slackened his perse-cution, they began to plot against him in favour of his brother Charles, who, as Ferdinand had no heir, would naturally succeed him.   The ' Apostolic ' or ' Carlist ' party—the first name gave place later to the second—organized in 1827 an open revolt in Catalonia and was temporarily suppressed :   the occasion was an opportune one for Ferdinand to receive more protestations of loyalty and acclamations from his loving subjects, which he duly did.

After the Revolution of 1830 in France a number of attempts were made by exiled Spanish Liberals to cross the frontier and revolt once more against Ferdinand.   The last and most tragic of these, led by Torrijos, an ex-officer living in London, resulted in the betrayal and slaughter of the leader and his fifty-two

companions, and was the occasion for renewed severity. A
fresh expectation, however, had been given to the Liberals, when
Ferdinand's third wife died and he married the girl-princess
María Cristina of Naples, whose leanings showed themselves
quickly to be progressive. On October 10, 1830, she gave birth
to a daughter, and the Liberal hopes rose still higher, while
those of the Carlists sank correspondingly. Neither party,
however, was completely at ease, for the Salic Law had been
declared in force in Spain in 1713, and confirmed by the 1812
Constitution, while on the other hand, Charles IV, in 1789,
and now, more formally, Ferdinand VII, seven months before
his daughter's birth, had declared it to be void. On September
29, 1833, having, in spite of much pressure from the Carlists,
bequeathed the crown to his infant daughter, the spoilt, deceitful
and tyrannical monarch died.

A complex situation in Spain was produced by Ferdinand's
death. For his daughter, proclaimed Queen as **Isabel II (1833–
1868)**, María Cristina acted as regent. At the same time, Charles
(then in exile) was proclaimed King by his followers, and civil
warfare, largely of the guerrilla type, dragged on in Spain till
1840. During most of these years the predominant force in
power was moderate Liberalism, partly because otherwise the
Carlists would have drawn away the Cristinist adherents, and
partly because of the return of the twenty thousand Liberal
exiles. Accordingly, the Conservative, Zea Bermúdez, Ferdinand's right-hand minister, was, though loyal to the Cristinists,
succeeded in power by the very lukewarm Liberal Martínez de
la Rosa. Being only a transition-minister, Martínez resigned
after establishing a partly elective parliament of two chambers
(*estamentos*), with consultative functions only, and remaining at
its head for a year. He was succeeded by his more Liberal
supporter, the Conde de Toreno, who in three months gave
place to the still more Liberal Mendizábal. The Moderates had
done little for Spain but promulgate Martínez' colourless attempt
at a constitution called the Estatuto Real. The Radicals, under
Mendizábal and (later) José María Calatrava, first restored the
1812 Constitution and later produced a modified and more work-
able one which is known by its date of 1837. The Moderados,
however, were considerably more powerful than the Exaltados,
and in the next year (1838) their party was in power again.

Meanwhile, the so-called Carlist War, especially in Navarre
and the Basque provinces, and in Catalonia and Aragon, drained
the strength of what might have been years of returning prosperity. The Carlists for the most part came from the country

districts: the large towns were Cristinist. In the western storm-centre Tomás Zumalacárregui led the Carlists of Navarre to various useful victories, while Merino concentrated an army at Logroño. The Cristinist armies, under Espoz y Mina and Rodil, were strengthened by the support of Britain, France and Portugal. When the Carlists, hoping for supplies from Austria, Prussia and Russia if they could capture a seaport, besieged Bilbao, they were defeated and Zumalacárregui was mortally wounded.

From this point things went badly with the Carlists. They had Charles among them, 'reigning' in Estella, but their leaders fell, their foreign friends gave them no help and more than a few of their adherents began to despair of gaining their ends by open warfare. The inhuman savagery which from the beginning had distinguished the encounters on both sides was increasing with the losing party's exasperation. The Cristinists had meanwhile discovered the most successful of their generals, Baldomero Espartero, who at the end of 1836, with great brilliance, raised a second siege of Bilbao, and prevented an attack, threatened in desperation, on Madrid. For a time after the Pretender's consequent retreat, his cause seemed to be improving. But his last great general, Ramón Cabrera, left him, with large numbers of men, and an agreement between Espartero and the Carlist leaders brought civil war to a virtual end in 1840.

In politics, as well as in war, Espartero was to become an active if less distinguished participant. Soon after the promulgation of the code of 1837 he joined the Progressive party, and, having triumphed over the Carlists, devoted himself with lightning effect to politics. The Moderado government of 1838 had been succeeded in the next year by an entirely Radical lower chamber, of which Cristina was pleased to show her disapproval by dissolving it. The elections obediently gave a Moderado victory. But this was not Espartero's idea of politics. Cristina's continuous alliance with the Moderates made a Progressive *coup d'état* very practicable. Espartero achieved it: the Queen Mother abdicated and fled to France (October 17, 1840) and he himself became Regent in her stead.

For three years he remained at the head of the executive, a military hero whose popularity, well merited but in peace inclined to be evanescent, could not overcome his political mediocrity. Although he was able to frustrate a conspiracy to seize the young Queen, and a revolt in Barcelona, his hold over the people lessened visibly. Some years before, he had been successful in driving from the country a rival general, Narváez. Now Narváez returned, and Espartero, within an ace of a complete fall and its consequences, left the country immediately for England.

From 1843 to 1854 the Moderates were again in power, the young Queen, though only thirteen years old, being declared of full age by parliament to avoid further problems of the regency. Though a bad queen from first to last—unprincipled, capricious and headstrong—she could look back upon the first years of her rule as comparatively prosperous ones for her country. In 1845, the new Constitution promulgated by Narváez' government, and more conservative than that of 1837, met with general approval. In the next year the Queen made an unfortunate but popular marriage with her cousin Francisco de Asís, Duke of Cádiz; and when the events of 1848 swept over Europe, Narváez, who was again, after a brief interval, in power, proved himself both able and determined to quell such risings as threatened what he complacently considered his 'Liberal' administration.

In 1851, he was succeeded in power by his late finance minister, Bravo Murillo, who began by making financial reforms which were of mixed benefit, and proceeded to an important Concordat with the Pope (see p. 262). Although the Constitutions had one and all upheld the Catholic religion in Spain to the exclusion of every other, relations with Rome had, since Ferdinand's death, been strained to the last degree possible. The suppression of convents, the confiscation of their property, the plundering of almost all the regular Orders, the new suppression of the re-established Jesuits, the abolition of the tithe and the disendowment and nationalization of the secular clergy were an unexampled series of rebuffs. The most flagrant of these were now atoned for, and a number of ecclesiastical reforms, long overdue, agreed upon. Bravo Murillo resigned at the end of 1852 and a period of stress succeeded, culminating in a revolution in the capital which was attended by the loss of a few lives, and the re-elevation to power of none other than Espartero, who had long since declared his willingness to serve his country in this way if it so desired. He was greeted with an effusion of sentiment which recalled his past popularity, and General O'Donnell, the real leader of the revolution, had to be contented with the post of War Minister.

Espartero the Progressive and O'Donnell the Conservative worked together in a coalition for two short years, at the end of which time, as had been generally foreseen, O'Donnell succeeded to the premiership, though not without violence. The 'Liberal Union' continued, Narváez' 1845 Constitution remaining in vigour. From 1856 to 1868 came a constant alternation of governments, three of them under O'Donnell, and three under Narváez. In 1857 the birth to the Queen of a son made the dynasty for a time reasonably secure. Commercially these were years of prosperity for Spain ; while abroad a short but brilliant campaign against Morocco brought into the limelight another military hero and amateur politician, General Prim. Less fortunate were Spain's relations with America. Space has not permitted us in this chapter to outline the history of how nearly all her colonies in America obtained their independence between 1810 and 1824, so that only Cuba and Porto Rico now remained to her. Peru; however, had fallen behind the other colonies in her degree of independence, and certain rights which Spain still retained in the young republic became the cause of a brief war which ended indecisively. Prim chose this very time to negotiate a military revolt which was handled by Narváez and O'Donnell with their usual severity, and thus failed. When O'Donnell died in 1867, and Narváez early in 1868, it was evident that any other such attempt would have a greater chance of success. In September, 1868, hastened by impolitic acts of González Bravo, the new premier, the attempt came. Starting as a mutiny, in Cádiz, the Liberal fortress of sixty years before, the revolution spread quickly to Seville, Granada and the east : Madrid and the north-west followed. Isabel, who was at San Sebastián, moved quickly into France as a measure of safety. It was as well : she was dethroned without bloodshed and by the voice of general opinion. Both her private life and her public life had been a disgrace to the title of Queen.

The dethronement of Isabel brought the country face to face with serious problems. There was a two to one majority in parliament for a monarchy, but where could a monarch be found ? The Bourbons were now taboo : Espartero, it appeared, might have been elected but was unwilling to succeed the queen to whom he had once been regent. Abroad, the King of Portugal, Ferdinand of Saxe-Coburg his father, and Leopold of Hohenzollern all refused. Not till the end of 1870 did **Amadeo** of Savoy, Duke of Aosta, accept the crown. He was unlucky as well as unhappy, for Prim, who could have helped him and had chiefly desired him, was assassinated on the day of the new sovereign's landing. No single group in the country welcomed his rule, while three groups, strong and increasing in strength daily, were respectively Republican, Alfonsist and

Carlist. After five ministries had fallen and he himself had been fortunate enough to escape assassination, Amadeo abdicated (February, 1873).

This short experience of a foreign ruler turned the country even more completely republican than it had recently been monarchist. A majority in parliament of no less than eight to one established a Republic, which in 1873 alone had four presidents, and was entirely unable to restrain anarchy or prevent a vigorous recrudescence of the Carlist War. This, especially in Catalonia and Aragon, spread rapidly; once more long-suffering Bilbao was invested; and when that siege was raised, Irún. Pi y Margall, Castelar and Sagasta were better statesmen than the generals of the preceding generation, but they must all have seen that Spain would only be content with a monarchy. One simple event sufficed to prove this. Isabel's son Alfonso attained the royal age of majority (sixteen years) in November, 1874 : the next month he issued a prudent manifesto in which he endeavoured to unite in his favour all the parties. Sagasta and a few convinced republicans held out, but only for a time, against the inevitable. At the beginning of 1875, the boy-king entered Spain as **Alfonso XII (1874–1885)**.

Perhaps it is from 1874 that one should date Spain's still rising prosperity. The country as a whole received Alfonso gladly; a year was sufficient to end all serious Carlist risings; the Republicans in a body, Sagasta included, became liberal monarchists, and the Powers and the Holy See both recognized the new *régime*. Alfonso's greatest boon was the support of Antonio Cánovas del Castillo, the greatest statesman of his age, who as a youth had been an adherent of O'Donnell but was now a man of mature and moderate views and in his prime. The Constitution of 1876, which was his work, was based on that of 1845, which he admired greatly. It declared Spain a constitutional monarchy, with two legislative chambers of equal powers : the Senate, of 360 members, partly hereditary, partly appointed, and partly elected, and the Congress of 431 deputies elected by taxpayers. The problem of religious toleration was solved by a compromise, to the satisfaction of all but extremists. Wise provisions were made for local government. Provincial privileges (notably in the Basque provinces) were, with the slightest exceptions, abolished.

For eight years Spain had been at war with Cuba, though events at home had overshadowed the fact, and it was only now that a determined attempt was made to end the conflict. Peace was concluded in February, 1878 : it may be said at once, however, that Spain continued to be troubled by Cuba until her misgovernment of it led to the Spanish-American War of 1898.

Little more need be said of Alfonso XII's reign, during which the country continued to make slow but steady progress. Cánovas was for the most part at the helm, and the ideals of the Liberal leader Sagasta were not greatly unlike his own. But tragedy befell the throne. The young King, when twenty years of age, married his cousin, to whom he was devoted, and who died of fever a few months later. In the next year he married María Cristina, daughter of an Austrian Archduke, and six years later died, leaving his queen with two infant daughters and in expectation of another child, pending the birth of which Spain was in effect without a sovereign. Alfonso XII was a well-meaning ruler, of undoubted culture, vicious habits and indomitable bravery,—a King for whom one cannot but feel sympathy, the more so in view of his troubled life and private sorrows.

On May 17, 1886, the Queen Regent's son was born and became, at birth, King **Alfonso XIII**, 1886–1931, died 1941. During the dramatic months of the interregnum all parties had rallied round the dynasty and behaved with great moderation ; Sagasta remained in power till 1890, while María Cristina for her part was equally ideal as the regent of her country and the mother of her delicate baby son. The ex-Queen Isabel molested her daughter-in-law as she had molested her son, but was forced at length by public opinion and private pressure to leave the country. Sagasta was succeeded in office peacefully by Cánovas, who found himself faced with universal suffrage, of which he himself disapproved, but which Sagasta had introduced before his resignation. Two questions only presented grave difficulties during the 'nineties : the first was connected with the few but clamant Radical extremists, the second with America.

Neither Cánovas nor Sagasta, either jointly or alternately, could conciliate the small band of Republicans which had not already turned Monarchist. In the industrial centres of Spain, such as Barcelona and Bilbao, the rise of socialism, not to say communism, and anarchy, caused the authorities grave misgivings. Bomb-throwing was bad enough, but that the ultra-progressive forces should unite and sink their differences would be worse. Financial reforms in 1893 bade fair to provoke such a climax when a welcome diversion arose in a brief dispute in Morocco, upon the cessation of which Sagasta was able to hold the reins of government firmly until the less welcome American diversion dwarfed every other question.

That Cuba's independence was imminent few doubted when a new revolution broke out there in the spring of 1895 just as Cánovas was for the last time succeeding Sagasta. Ever since 1874, Cánovas had demanded complete submission from the colony and had promised reform as a reward for this only. The Cubans were obdurate ; their insurrection became a warfare, which extended to the Philippine Islands ; and to make matters worse for Spain, the United States now supported the insurgents and for four months took up arms in defence of her. The shortness of the conflict was caused by the ease with which Spain was defeated. Off Cuba and the Philippines alike, her navy was routed. In the autumn of 1898 came peace, bringing Cuban independence, the cession of Porto Rico to the United States and the sale to the States of Spain's remaining possessions in the Pacific. Thus came to an end the extensive colonial system of a great people. The event is more important than it might at first sight appear. For Spain began now to turn her gaze exclusively upon herself, and though unrelieved introspection may be harmful in the extreme to an individual, it is seldom a remedy too drastic for an unhappy nation.

BIBLIOGRAPHY TO CHAPTER III

Besides Nos. 22–30, the following are outstanding works on this period :

45. *Historia general de España, escrito por individuos de la Real Academia de la Historia.* Madrid, 1892 ff.
46. Armstrong, E. *The Emperor Charles V.* 2 vols. Second edition. London, 1910.
47. Blasco Ibáñez, V. *Historia de la Revolución Española, 1808–1874.* Barcelona, 1890.
48. Cánovas del Castillo, A. *Estudios del reinado de Felipe IV.* Madrid, 1889.
49. Clarke, H. Butler. *Modern Spain, 1815–1898.* Cambridge, 1906.
50. Fernández Duro, C. *Armada española desde la unión de los reinos de Castilla y de Aragón.* Madrid, 1895–1903. 9 vols.
51. Hume, M. A. S. *Spain : its greatness and decay, 1479–1788.* Third edition, revised by Edward Armstrong. Cambridge, 1925.
52. Hume, M. A. S. *Philip II of Spain.* London, 1897.
53. Trevor Davies, R. *The Golden Century of Spain, 1501–1621.* Second edition. London, 1954.
54. Hume, M. A. S. *Modern Spain.* London, 1899.
55. Irving, W. *Conquest of Granada.* New York, 1829. [Various modern editions.]
56. Lea, H. C. *The Moriscos of Spain.* New York, 1901.
57. Lea, H. C. *A History of the Inquisition of Spain.* 4 vols. New York, 1906–7.

58. Llorente, J. A. *Historia crítica de la Inquisición de España.* Barcelona, 1835–36.
59. Oman, C. W. C. *History of the Peninsular War.* 5 vols. Oxford, 1902–14.
60. Pirala, A. *Historia contemporánea.* Madrid, 1900.
61. Pirala, A. *Historia de la Guerra Civil, con la Regencia de Espartero.* 3 vols. Madrid, *n.d.*
62. Prescott, W. H. *History of the reign of Ferdinand and Isabella the Catholic.* 2 vols. New York, 1838.
63. Prescott, W. H. *History of the reign of Philip the Second.* 3 vols. Boston, 1855–58. [Various modern editions of this and No. 62.]
64. Robertson, W. *History of the reign of the Emperor Charles the Fifth.* 3 vols. Philadelphia, 1770. [Edited by W. H. Prescott in 2 vols., London, 1857.]
65. Rodríguez Villa, A. *El Emperador Carlos V y su corte*, etc. Madrid, 1903–5.
66. Sabatini, R. *Torquemada and the Spanish Inquisition.* Sixth edition. London, 1927.
67. White, G. F. *A Century of Spain and Portugal* (1788–1898) London, 1909.

[See also many of the works referred to under Chapter IX below, and Nos. 16, 32, 39, 76.]

CHAPTER IV

SPANISH LITERATURE TO 1681 [1]

I. The Mozarabs

THE irruption into Spain of Tārik and his Berbers in the year 711, though it severs the ancient from the mediaeval history of the Peninsula, did not occasion great displacements either of wealth or of population. The Jews had been active partisans of the invasion, the Hispano-Romans stood by their estates and cities, and a powerful faction of the Goths had even proved to be the cause of the success of the invader. Andalusia therefore retained that supremacy of comfort and education which Bætica had possessed in Roman times, and it was from Andalusia that one would expect to get the first dawn of a new modern literature. But though the Spanish mass of the new state continued to use their own dialect of Romance and were not harassed by persecution or proselytization, the attraction of the Arabic language and culture proved so great that by the ninth century it seemed to be on the point of superseding entirely the native speech for all politer uses. The language of Islam inferred a peril to Christianity, and the more zealous Christians deplored the inability of their co-religionists to write a tolerable epistle in the tongue of Christendom. In furtherance of a programme of religious and linguistic renaissance, Eulogius, a priest of Córdoba, was dispatched to Navarre in search of satisfactory models of classical Latinity. On his return, his policy reached a crisis through the fanatical denunciation by a Spanish Moor of the ' apostasy ' of his sister, a beautiful girl named Flora, who had, though the child of a Muslim father, been reared in the tenets of our faith by a Christian mother. This unnatural prosecution was repugnant to

---

[1] While it is impossible, in this chapter and the next, to indicate precisely which of the many authors treated are suitable for reading by those who are not professed students of Spanish literature, it may be noted that, with few exceptions, the names of the most important authors and works are followed by their dates (where these are known), while the less important are undated.

88

Christians and Muslims alike; but Eulogius and his biographer
Álvaro developed their defence of Flora into a doctrine inciting
the Christians to seek martyrdom voluntarily by infringing
Koranic principles.   An orgy of suicide raged among the most
ardent adherents of Latin and Christianity, and, though their
leader died as he had advised others to die, his propaganda suffered a fatal check both on its religious and its literary side.
Towards the end of the same century a Mozarab, Omar ibn
Hafsun, attempted to organize revolt among the Spanish elements on a racial basis, to which he later added a religious
motive; but he, too, failed, and the Caliphate of Abd ar-Rahman
III appeared to be more homogeneously Muslim and Arabic than
the Emirate had ever been.   Later in the tenth century the
religious wars of Al-Mansur began to infuse bigotry into Cordoban
statecraft, and the fanatical rule of the Almoravides and Almohades in the two centuries that followed, besides bearing heavily
on Muslim philosophy and science, drove the more intelligent
and resolute Jews and Mozarabs into the districts which the
Christian kings were rapidly subjugating in the Tagus and Ebro
valleys.

Thus the rise of a Hispano-Latin literature in Andalusia was
frustrated, but the work of the Mozarabs was not wholly undone.
They brought a high standard of culture with them into the
north, and numerous important writers of the Alfonsine period
appear to belong to their numbers.   They brought to Christendom their knowledge of Arabian science at the moment when it
was being extinguished by orthodox bigotry in its own territory.
Their dialect succumbed to that of Castile, but to the latter they
added the rich vocabulary of Arabisms which had adorned their
own.   They first, as it seems, appreciated the historic value of
the Cid, and they created and brought with them one of the
most fecund of Spanish historical legends, that of Don Rodrigo
or the Destruction of Spain.

II. The Alfonsine Empire

The terms ' empire ' and ' emperor ' were first used by the
kings of León in order to mark their hegemony over the other
princes who occupied the ancient realms of the Visigothic kings.
They asserted the unity of the Peninsula as a heritage from the
Cæsars, and this unity and hegemony were in a manner acknowledged by the other petty kinglets-of the Christians.   The most
reluctant of the Spanish territories was the county of Castile
under the renowned Count Fernán González ; but when, in the
eleventh century, the balance of power in the joint kingdom of

Castile-León lay in fact in the eastern member, the terms served to cover the aspirations of Castile herself to control the destinies of the Peninsula not only in her own province but also in the kingdom of Aragon and the county of Portugal. The title was favoured by a succession of Alfonsos, notably those numbered VI, VII, VIII and X, during the twelfth and thirteenth centuries. This, however, was the epoch of the pullulation of the literature of Christian Spain, and nowhere is the ' empire ' more distinctly felt than in the earnestness with which the emperors forwarded the interests of learning. Works of history were performed at their orders and inspired by their ambitions. They invited foreign scholars and poets to their courts. The eighth and tenth Alfonsos were conspicuous for their hospitality to the troubadours of Provence ; the sixth was the most zealous partisan of the civilization of France. Under his auspices the abbots of Cluny filled the benefices of Spain with their monks, reformed the handwriting of the scriptoria, restored Spanish Latinity, purged the ritual. They fomented mass movements of French-men into Spain, whether as pilgrims to the shrine of St. James or as crusaders ; and the pilgrims and crusaders trod out the ' French Way ' from the Pyrenees to Compostela and formed ' French suburbs ' in the cities on the route. It was in these movements that certain French epics, notably the *Chanson de Roland*, appear to have found their inspiration. But the French pilgrim-*jongleur* would find at the court of an Alfonso VII numerous Castilian *juglares* just as the Provençal troubadour there met the lyrists of Galicia. The reports of Jews and Mozarabs, particularly those resident at Toledo, made an awaken-ing Europe aware of the treasures of Greek learning concealed in the commentaries of Avicenna, Averroes and their peers ; and accomplished Latinists began to cross the frontiers to find in Toledo not only the new light but also the active favour of the king and the archbishop, the necessary dragomans, and not infrequently Spanish benefices to supply the means of existence.

The Hispano-Latin literature of the north of Spain takes to itself an unwonted dignity, and aspires to a purity and elegance unknown since the days of Isidore of Seville. The feats of Alfonso VI fire with patriotism an unnamed monk of Silos, though his Chronicle does not reach to that monarch's reign ; the more pretentious seventh Alfonso (the *emperador* above all others to the epic poets) has his special record in history ; his Chronicle even aspiring to include a specimen of the author's skill as a Latin poet, viz., the well-known ' Song of Almería ' (captured in 1147). A Latin chronicle, longer than these of the kings, celebrates not unworthily the career of Ruy Díaz de Bivar,—' My Cid ',—and his astonishing fidelity in banishment and uninterrupted career of victory. The Cid also had his meed of Latin verse, the semi-popular Sapphic poem, which opens with a minstrel's invocation to the people :

> Eia, laetando, populi catervae,
> cuncti venite . . .

In the early years of the thirteenth century historical writing acquires more philosophical and more popular content. World history is attempted first by Lucas, Bishop of Tuy, in the province of Santiago de Compostela, and Rodrigo, Archbishop of Toledo, the latter being both a competent Arabist and a historian of more acumen than many of his successors. With their wider horizons, both Lucas and Rodrigo unite a more intense interest in the riches of the national intellect, for both make what use they can of the colour and vivacity with which historical events were invested by the singers of the national epics. The epics of France were the more peculiar interest of another archbishop-ric of the ' empire ', that of Santiago, which, in support of its claims to the primacy, forged and put into circulation the notorious Codex Calixtinus, of which one portion, the Life of Charlemagne and Roland, fathered on to Archbishop Turpin of Rheims, was one of the most influential works in mediaeval European literature.

In addition to histories, sincere or perfidious, the Alfonsine empire made important additions to the Latin literature of law, romance and science. In the domain of law it kept in circulation the Forum Judicum, or code of the later Visigoths, an expression of the legal unity of the Peninsula. To the development of the novel the converted Jew, Pedro Alfonso (his second name is an allusion to his royal patron), contributed his eleventh-century collection of apologues entitled the *Discipline of the Clergy*, in which he drew copiously on the stores of apologues transmitted by the Arabic invaders and settlers from Syria, Persia and India. The exploitation of Arabian science was especially the province of scholars from beyond the Pyrenees, such as Gerard of Cremona, Robert of Retines, Daniel Morley, Michael Scot, and others ; but among the earliest and most clearly characterized of these thinkers are Gonzalo of Segovia and his interpreter, John of Seville. One of the latest of the strangers, Herman, became not only Bishop of Astorga but also a collaborator with Alfonso X in the first vernacular Spanish translation of the Psalms, and it may be said that the mechanism of translation from the Arabic used by Alfonso in his vernacular works on scientific subjects is an inheritance from that association of Latinists with Jewish and Mozarabic interpreters which is frequently termed the ' School of Toledo '.

The Hispano-Latin literature of the period attracts attention not to itself but to the vigorous and almost vocal vernacular. The national epics and those of France can be perceived in action behind the prose of the historians and the Pseudo-Turpin. The laws of the Visigoths were soon to be applied to the special case of Córdoba by Ferdinand III, and under Alfonso X to become part of a great advance towards the unification of the Spanish codes. Apologues of oriental origin appear among the earliest examples of vernacular prose ; and the means were created for enriching Spanish literature with some of the history, astrology and other sciences or pseudo-sciences of the more cultured South.

From a very early time clerics in their sermons and public entertainers in their performances must have felt the necessity for employing the language of the mass of the people, with the result that a species of spoken literature in the vernacular tongue considerably antedates extant documents. By the twelfth century these entertainers had come to be known as *juglares* and were especially numerous in the court of Alfonso VII ' the Emperor ', but could also be met with in the courts of prominent nobles, at fairs, weddings and pilgrimages, and wherever crowds gathered together. Clad in picturesque garments, the *juglares* travelled on horse or on foot from place to place, and also were wont to undertake journeys in order to learn from celebrated minstrels a new trick, tune or poem, to add to their repertory. The whole art of public entertainment was termed *juglaría*, from bear-wrestling and sword-swallowing to music and poetical recitation, but for literature only the last-named groups are of importance. The *juglar* was a performer, an artist ; the public did not think of the author, except in the courtly branch of literature which came with the troubadours from Provence. We can thus make the convenient distinction that the national epics constitute the *mester de juglaría*, of anonymous authorship, learned by rote and then considered to be the property of the performer who ' represented ' the story ; while lyrical poetry can be styled the *poesía trobadoresca*. Within lyrical poetry, however, the words ' troubadour ' and ' minstrel ' have a further special application, owing to the ambition of the authors or troubadours to arrogate to themselves the whole faculty of composition, and to restrict the minstrels to mere performance of the works of others; owing further to the social division between the troubadours, who ranked from squires to kings and ostensibly did not work for pay, and the minstrels, who were commoners and professional entertainers. The word *juglar*, which covers all entertainers, covers also those clerics who used vernacular literature to spread among their less erudite contemporaries a knowledge of religious legends, classical history or foreign tales; but the special description and grouping of these authors, and their insistence on a reformed versification, gives their art the name of *mester de clerecia*. The earliest poetry of Spain, therefore, is the work of *juglares* who wrote and performed national or Carolingian epic poems or *cantares de gesta*, of *trobadores* who composed the music and words of lyrical compositions for minstrels to sing, and of *clérigos* who aspired to give their works greater artistic perfection and learned content. In respect of language, the *juglares* (in the limited sense) employed by preference Castilian, the *trobadores* Galician, and the *clérigos* mixed literary dialects with a Castilian basis.

The *cantares de gesta* were, as we have seen, composed by a *juglar* or professional entertainer, and taught by rote to other *juglares*, who then became owners of the matter and at entire liberty to refashion it. The tradition was essentially oral; manuscripts served chiefly as mnemonics. For that reason, and others, written records of their work are extremely difficult to come by, and when found are seen to be executed with the greatest haste and slovenliness. Only the *Poem of the Cid* preserves a form sufficiently similar to that in which it was composed, and this in a manuscript so late and so careless that the labour of editing it has outlasted a whole century of the most acute scholarship. A second poem, dealing with that hero's youthful exploits, is still later; it is incomplete, extravagant and constantly lapsing into prose. A hundred lines survive describing Charlemagne's visit to the stricken field of Roncesvalles, and about an equal number have been excavated from later chronicles relating the tragic history of the Seven Princes of Lara. But the great mass of the *cantares de gesta* or *mester de juglaría* has to be inferred from the prose renderings in the various redactions of the *General Chronicle* (*Estoria de España* or *Primera, Segunda, Tercera* (etc.), *Crónica General*), of which the first dates from 1289. From these prose texts we find that a large number of narratives, historical in subject and poetical in manner, were in circulation during the thirteenth century and earlier, and that these already constituted a running poetical history of the country. The tale of King Roderic (Rodrigo) the Goth and his illicit love for Count Julian's daughter, which led to the Arab invasion and the ruin of Spain, arose among the Christians of Andalusia, and from them passed not only to the Christians of the North but also across the Pyrenees into France, where it gave rise to the epic of *Anseïs de Karthage*. Its existence as an epic in Spain is less firmly assured : here it gained satisfactory expression twice, as a tradition repeated by Muslim historians, and as a fifteenth-century novel of chivalry, the *Crónica Sarracina*. The story of Bernardo del Carpio has the singularity of being a Leonese work : its principal matter relates to the hero's efforts to liberate his father from a tyrannous incarceration, but the ascription in one of its episodes of Roland's defeat and death at Roncesvalles to Bernardo's exploits rapidly overshadowed the rest of the work, and became very popular with the anti-French patriotism of the sixteenth and seventeenth centuries. The theme of the liberation of Castile from the suzerainty of León furnished a subject to an epic called by the name of the first independent count, Fernán González : the epic has been obscured by its rehandling in the *Poema de Fernán González* (see p. 101), a clerical and erudite work which was alone reported by the scribes of the first redaction of the *General Chronicle*, but the second redaction of that history (1344) contains important reminiscences of the *cantar de gesta*. As we have it in the clerical poem, this epic has flashes of national and regional spirit, but is overloaded with historical and hagiographical matter, while the metrical alterations have made it frequently wordy and didactic. The son of the first count was himself the subject of a short adaptation of a French epic plot, but is better known as the ruler of Castile during the story of the Seven Princes of Lara (*Los siete infantes de Salas o de Lara*), a sanguinary story of murder and vengeance, which is the most vehement and tragic of all the stories that have come down to us. The terrible scene in which Almanzor (Al-Mansur) displays to Gonzalo Gustos the seven heads of his sons is tragic to the point of horror, and the scene of their requital by Mudarra, a personage born only for vengeance, at the expense of the treacherous Ruy Velázquez de Lara, is a fitting conclusion, to which Victor Hugo has done much less than justice in a celebrated *Orientale*. The most powerful of the *cantares de gesta*, this poem is also probably one of the earliest.

Poems whose action belongs to a later date have been attracted into the orbit of Ruy Díaz de Bivar, known as Mío Cid (' My Cid '), who was compared, even in his genealogy, with Fernán González, the founder of Castilian greatness. Before 1160, a poem was composed relating to the death of Sancho of Castile before the walls of Zamora, and as reported in the Chronicles it was completed by an account of a duel, of undecided result, intended to determine the complicity or otherwise of the inhabitants of the town. In this poem the Cid functioned as the sage adviser and supporter of Sancho, and the arbiter of the succeeding contest : he is clothed with the gravity which he shows in the celebrated *Poema de Mío Cid* (*c.* 1140). In this latter a *juglar* tells in rugged metre and rapid style, redeemed with few touches of imagination, almost wholly devoid of the supernatural, sage, virile, and sublime by the mere importance of its matter, the story of the last banishment of the hero, how he wins the renewed favour of his king, and how, in the king's court, he obtains formal satisfaction for the injuries inflicted on him by his enemies the powerful Beni-Gómez. The lever whereby the Cid overthrows his enemies is the wanton outrage inflicted on his daughters by their husbands, two of the Beni-Gómez, notorious for ever under the style of the ' infantes de Carrión '. Relatively little prominence is given, despite the manifest historicity of the poem, to the Cid's ' crowning mercy '—the capture of Valencia in 1094. The whole of the Cid's military career is looked upon as his means of reconciling his king, estranged through slanderous counsel ; and the poet displays a lively interest only in campaigns and journeys within a comparatively short radius from Medinaceli, of which he may have been a native. The date *c.* 1140 is generally, though not universally, ascribed for its composition. A third poem on this hero, the *Mocedades del Cid*, was recorded only later than the *First General Chronicle*, and is best known from the degenerate and prosy *Crónica Rimada* or *Cantar de Rodrigo*. It was written round the tradition of the Cid's five pitched battles (' cinco lides campales '), fought and won in his youth, which had already occupied the pen of the writer of the dog-Latin Sapphic verses. This is the Cid of the ballads, arrogant, lawless, braggart, extravagant in his insults to his betrothed, his king, and to pope and emperor. This Cid has the heady insolence, but not yet the licentiousness, of Don Juan.

At the court of Alfonso VII, the emperor beloved of the epic poets, figured the earliest known minstrel of Galicia, Palha (' Straw ') by name. To his court, too, came courtly lyrists from Provence along with the minstrels of the *chansons de geste ;* and the troubadours increased in numbers and importance when Eleanor of Aquitaine became Alfonso VIII's queen. Their permeation was doubtless assisted by the prolongation of their lyrism at this time throughout the whole Catalan-speaking region, which belonged in politics and in culture essentially to the South of France until Northern French influence became paramount in Provence and Toulouse by the Battle of Muret (1213). Catalan troubadours are only faintly distinguishable in style from their instructors : they are, as one might expect, of later general date, their tone is more didactic, their versification less free and rich, and their preoccupation with linguistic purism, in face of the increasing divergence of Limousin and Catalan, gave rise to interesting grammars for the use of poets, and even to the first chair of a modern language ever established in a European university. This stream of influence from the southeast met, in the courts of Castile and León, a stream from the north-west. The monarchs were themselves generally educated in Galicia, and to them Galician would be their mother tongue; the speech of affection and sentiment, even when another dialect might be used for administration,—the speech of the lyrical muse, though the epic and historic might use Castilian. This is not to deny the existence of native Castilian or Leonese songs, which we can dimly perceive arising out of the necessities either of lonely workers, such as sentinels, reapers, travellers, etc., or of companies performing the same action to the same rhythm, dancers or pilgrims. It is only to aver that what has survived to us, being transmitted solely in collections of courtly origin, is stamped by the preference the monarchs gave to the Galician idiom, which is used for these purposes by Portuguese, Castilians and even Italians as well as Galicians of pure descent.

A further reason, however, for the use of this idiom is the unbroken predilection of the Galician people for lyrical expression. Their idiom is destitute of all successful narrative, whether in prose or verse, but in the mouths of women is improvised with startling facility into snatches of song, whether humorous, elegiac or sentimental. In our day these improvisations are generally in the form of quatrains : in the Middle Ages they were *cossantes*. The *cossante* centres on a brief refrain or lyrical cry, themes which could be collected into one poem (as in a famous case by Airas Nunes) or variously glossed : in one or two cases, indeed, they have furnished the refrain for Castilian *villancicos*. In the *villancico* the refrain is glossed in lyrico-narrative verses, frequently of eight octosyllables : in the *cossantes* the gloss consists of little more than an indication of circumstances, very faintly sketched in, and developed in couplets of almost identical meaning but diverse assonance. The first and second couplets

are identical in sense ; if there be a third and fourth, these are
identical in meaning to each other, and their first lines are the
second lines of the first and second couplets ; and so further
verses may be added. The device is of the simplest, but so are
the thought and the language ; and in their unaffected beauty,
echoing cadence, alternation of treble and bass intonation, and
sincere, universal emotion, the *cossantes*, mostly expressed
through the mouths of women, are clothed with persuasive charm.
In our authorities they are generally accompanied by the names
of male poets, who either composed or collected them, or were
the authors of new or adapted music; among the most eminent
are King Diniz of Portugal (d. 1325), who has passed on to us
the most graceful of *cossantes* as a relief to the over-elaboration
of his Provençal Muse, Airas Nunes of Santiago, João Zorro, a
minstrel, author of delightful barcaroles, Martin Codax, singer
of the Bay of Vigo, Admiral Pai Gomez Charinho, who carries the
sea into his verses, Meendinho and others. The *cossantes* are
heard for the last time in the plays of Gil Vicente.

These charming songs make their appearance in the official
collections of lyrics only at a late date and by way of relief to
troubadours who felt that the artificial style of verse and tune
was becoming monotonous to themselves and their hearers.
The earliest such collection is the *Cantigas de Santa María* by
Alfonso X of Castile-León (see p. 49), in which only every tenth
piece is truly lyrical. The remainder, from among some four
hundred poems, are narrative or episodic, brief accounts of
miracles performed by the Blessed Virgin, either as they were
recorded in standard collections or as they happened within the
King's own experience. The narrative is of a convincing *naïveté*,
which conveys to a modern reader a pleasant, though erroneous,
sense of humour. In his versification, Alfonso, who here worked
more personally than elsewhere—though the illuminations of
the Escorial manuscript show that he was not without clerical
assistance—displays great curiosity and employs a considerable
variety of lines, combinations and rhyme-patterns. He is not
the most lyrically gifted, but he is the ablest and most fluent
technician of the Galician school. In profane verse he carried
this technique to the point of scurrilous controversy, insisting on
the necessity of still further provençalizing and elaborating both
the manner and the matter of the courtly lyric, denouncing the
vague, naïve Provençalism which had satisfied the poets of his
father's court at Seville, Bernardo de Bonaval and Pedro da
Ponte. In this protest he was followed by his grandson, Diniz
King of Portugal, to whose son Pedro, Count of Barcellos, is

ascribed the collection of the courtly lyric into a song-book or *Cancioneiro*, which remains to-day in three manuscripts known respectively as those of the Ajuda and Vatican Palaces and the Colocci-Brancutti text. Primarily a collection of the songs in favour at Diniz's court, these manuscripts contain also what was then remembered of the lyrical activity of the courts of Alfonso IX, Afonso III of Portugal, St. Ferdinand, Alfonso X, as well as works posterior to Diniz. The *cossantes* enter as *cantigas de amigo* or songs directed by the lady to her lover, or under other denominations. The poems of courtly lovers are styled *cantigas de amor* and are stiff with the feudal conventions and protestations of the Provençal muse, without any touch of its later philosophism. In these two classes almost a thousand lyrics may be entered, the most considerable artists being Alfonso X, Diniz, Estevão da Guarda, etc. Minor erotic poems are styled dance-songs, pastorals, barcaroles, hill-maidens' songs (*serranilhas*), dawn-songs, etc. They are usually popular in style and simple in construction, with a notable absence of narrative or realistic tendencies. Apart from love we have the motive of scorn (*escarnio*), and in that vein some hundreds of satirical verses which, if they do not attain to poetry and are normally frivolous and insincere, powerfully document the social life of the time, and particularly the day-to-day incivilities of the Court. They tell us better than any other source what were the pretensions and disappointments, what the rivalries and vices, the clothes and conversation of minstrels at a mediaeval court in their dealings with ' minstrelized ' nobles and kings.

We must not forget that the text of these songs was conditioned by their tune (*som*). Unfortunately the Ajuda scribe failed to enter the notes, and all the tunes have been lost save two settings for Martin Codax' Vigo poems. The music of Alfonso X's book of sacred lyrics is extant, though it would be risky to generalize inferences based on so personal a work ; on the other hand, the miniatures which adorn his manuscript are of the highest use as a commentary and extension of the social information contained in the satires of the *Cancioneiros*.

Codes of law and documents of the archives indicate a considerable mimetic activity during the Middle Ages in Spain, displayed especially during religious and civil festivals, together with notes as to cost, decoration, tableaux and the difficulties of controlling the license of performers. But literature offers us only the fragment of the *Auto de los Reyes Magos*. Written probably in the later years of the twelfth century, and approximating to the model of the Orléans Twelfth Night play, it is one of the oldest documents in Spanish literary history, while its orthography makes it probably the oldest in actual condition of record. The piece is not without a certain humour, shown in the truncated squabble of a couple of rabbis : it is written in rhymed couplets, whose varied length seems to anticipate an important feature of the technique of the *comedia libre*. Whatever may have been the content and interest of this lost dramatic literature, it is safe to say that the highest dramatic talent of the Middle Ages found its expression in other moulds, as in Juan Ruiz's *Libro de Buen Amor*.

The clerks (*clérigos*) distinguished their style from that of the minstrels (*juglares*), just as the troubadours from their *juglares*, by the test of counted syllables. This has been held to imply that the epics were composed in lines distinguished by medial pause and final assonance, but without rhythm or reckoning of syllables (*poesía amétrica*); but other authorities hold that the difference on which the clerks insist is, like that of the Galician troubadours, rather one of degree, that the minstrel trusted to his ear and the cleric to his fingers. The clerical lines are, however, still far from regular in scansion, even when all deductions are made for doubtful cases. They use by preference the alexandrine in longer poems, the nine-syllable line (which represents a French octosyllable) in shorter : their alexandrines are formed up in quatrains of one rhyme, which, with their obligatory medial pause, have a slow ponderous movement, forcibly contrasted with the single line unit of the epic singer. These quatrains (*cuaderna vía*) were esteemed for their greater artifice (*maestría*) ; but, apart from this formal advantage, their quadruplicity extending into the style itself makes them an easy prey to padding and *longueurs*, and demands from a successful author as a conspicuous quality a tireless volubility. These poems are all narratives, apart from the fragment of drama already discussed ; they draw on varied sources, and being written in connection with monasteries rather than with the Court, they characterize the Alfonsine period chiefly by their indecision of literary speech, ranging from the Leonese Castilian of one manuscript of the Alexander story, through the Riojan of Berceo, and the Aragonese Castilian of the Apollonius of Tyre poem, to the *Libre dels tres Reys d'Orient*, with its Catalan connections. As the work of clerks, the new poetry of the thirteenth century was from the beginning recorded in permanent written form, though the authors did not the less aspire to public recitation (Berceo styles himself a *juglar*) and were actually so performed : for this reason their works have persisted to our day in numbers that much exceed their merit, especially when we think of the almost total loss of national epics in their original dress.

To the clerks belongs also the first name of Spanish literature, that of Gonzalo de Berceo, a lay member of the Benedictine community of San Millán de la Cogolla, in La Rioja, who lived through the first sixty years of the thirteenth century. Very few of his myriad verses go aside from the ' fourfold way ', and with this monotony of metre goes a monotony of matter, which is with him religious only, and a monotony of style. Berceo would be the last man in the world to claim to be a great poet, but beneath a uniformity not dissimilar to the Castilian uplands of his birth he masks homely and endearing qualities. Many shrewd touches in his lives of St. Millán and St. Domingo of Silos are suggested to him by his personal knowledge of day-to-day monastic life ; his humility gains a reader's attention, which is then held by his naïve garrulity and transparent sincerity. Before long one begins, as it were, to answer back when Berceo colloquially invites the reader to advise him how the tale shall be told, and the candid local patriotism of his three lives of Spanish saints (Millán, Domingo de Silos, and Oria) comes upon us with a subdued but steady glow. His most ambitious work is the collection of twenty-five *Miracles of Our Lady*, which have parallels in Alfonso X and Gautier de Coincy, even if some of them be not drawn from the latter's more ample narratives. To Berceo a Paris manuscript ascribes the Book of Alexander (*Libro de Alexandre*—after 1218), which a Madrid codex of Leonese cast attributes to a certain Juan Lorenzo of Astorga, whether as author or copyist. Nothing is further from Berceo's style than this, the most pretentious and erudite of its class. The poet, far from concealing his skill, parades his reading and technical efficiency. His verse (he says) is not *juglaría*, but the syllables are counted, the lines are rhymed in sequences of four, and the whole is to be taken as ' great mastery '. The length of the poem equals all Berceo's assured productions, and, amid the *longueurs* of this interminable mediaeval tale, the poet is at his best in moments of display, when he is describing the pomp of King Darius or the procession of the months or of Spring. A third early work of this school is the Book of Apollonius of Tyre (*Libro de Apolonio*), which versifies at one or two removes the Greek novel, whose matter is to be found in Gower and in Shakespeare's *Pericles of Tyre*. The author has to struggle against the naïve improbabilities of a Greek romance of adventure with its arbitrary separations and unlikely reunions; but within the defects of his matter the poet contrives to be nervous and concise, to make the lumbering metre do double its usual work, and to create in the *juglaresa* Tarsiana a character of quite unexpected charm and actuality. This unknown cleric is, despite a certain dryness, probably the ablest of the earlier versifiers in the ' fourfold way '.

Very far from this eminence stand two other poems. The *Poema de Fernán González* (*c.* 1255) is termed by the scribes of the *General Chronicle* a ' history ', and rightly so. A rambling preface versifies the *Chronicon Mundi* of the Bishop of Tuy, and when the tale of Fernán González's exploits is at last reached it is loaded down with the interests of the author's monastery at Arlanza and with historical matter which in no way forwards the main action. The poet is an unskilful metrist and not infrequently at a loss for a rhyme or half line. Even at this he is superior to the anonymous Muslim who wrote in Arabic characters the Poem of Joseph (*Alhadiz de Yuçuf* or *Poema de José*), who struggles with his illiteracy in the attempt to produce the most considerable unit in a depressed literature, that of the Muslims subject to Christian rule. This *literatura aljamiada* or ' barbarians' literature ' flourished chiefly in Aragon and during the sixteenth century, the date of Mahoma Rabadán, with a repertory of tales, exhortations to devotion and treasonable hopes for the success of the Turks cloaked in the impenetrability of the Arabic alphabet. As for the Joseph poem, it is not easy to determine its date, which may ascend as high as the thirteenth century.

Of lesser clerical poems we recall three Debates : those of Wine and Water, of the Soul and Body, and of the Knight and Cleric known as *Elena y María*. To the first of these is prefixed an irrelevant but charming lover's vision of his lady, which is one of the earliest lyrics in the Spanish tongue, and not one of the least in estimation : the author or the copyist was named Lope de Moro. The Life of St. Mary the Egyptian (*Santa María Egipciaca*) is in irregular nine-syllable lines, and is more entertaining during her sinful than during her saintly days. The *Libre dels tres Reys d'Orient* has nothing to do with the Magi, but begins to recount the tale of the Penitent Thief, which is swiftly truncated.

The commencement of vernacular prose in the Peninsula was later than the creation of the more important epics, *cossantes*, and even certain of the clerical poems. It constituted itself the heir of Hispano-Latin literature, from which it adopted its first

forms of expression—chronicles, science, history, the apologue,—
leaving others, such as theological dissertation, still in the learned
tongue until the Renaissance. It took over the task of
europeanizing the culture preserved from Classical antiquity by
Islam, and also the same technique of translation. Above all,
it inherited the courtly patronage and imperial purpose so evident
in its Latin forerunners. As in the development of the courtly
lyric, as in the history of University education, so in prose it was
Ferdinand III (see p. 46) who projected the first important
works in the vernacular speech : as in the lyric, it was his son
Alfonso X the Wise who carried on this task, with which his
father had from the beginning closely associated him, who gave
it amplitude and, doubtless, quite novel direction. Works
planned by Alfonsö the Wise were sometimes executed in his
reign, sometimes completed in the days of his successors, and it
was probably only in his great-grandson's time that his plans
were fully realized. The place of the monarchs in this development of prose style may have varied considerably. It is impossible
to separate Ferdinand's influence from that of his son, who was
from the beginning the chief patron of the rising literature ; to
Alfonso we ascribe the architecture of the more important works,
in the sense that as general editor he determined the order of
passages for translation by his subordinate editors, and he is
known to have revised the style of works completed in his reign,
so that there are sometimes important variations recorded between
the rough copies and the official codices inscribed on parchment
for the royal library. A miniature in his song-book shows him
in the centre, flanked on the one side by clerks who consult
manuscripts and on the other by musicians who tune their instru-
ments ; and in his prose works there must have been an even
greater delegation of function to his assistants, several of whose
names are known, though their literary personalities are lost.
Under Sancho IV the standard enterprises have less polish, and
it is possible the plans may have been extended to include translation not only from Latin and Arabic, but also from French and
Provençal. The first original novel appears under Ferdinand IV,
and in the latter half of Alfonso XI's reign (1312–1350) there is
leisure to embark on enterprises additional to those we may be
inclined to associate with the name of his great-grandfather.
This long and glorious reign is also noteworthy for three advances
in literary development : the curial tendency changed into an
aristocratic patronage of literature, since not only the royal
court but also the establishment of Prince Juan Manuel favoured
literary enterprises conducive to the common good ; style gained

its first personal attributes in Juan Manuel and in Pedro of Barcellos ; and Portuguese prose detached itself from the main current of Castilian-Leonese. The dialects of the centre crystallized into one literary idiom, from which only Aragonese, for political reasons, stood somewhat apart, and this idiom, first consciously exemplified in Juan Manuel and Juan Ruiz, has remained uniform and constant as the literary Spanish tongue to our day, which is bounded by the Portuguese and Catalan areas on either side.

It is recorded that Ferdinand III's restoration of the University of Salamanca was due to the perception that the gains of chivalry could only be retained by culture. By this he understood, primarily, the legal and administrative union of his dominions, and in giving to the conquered city of Córdoba the Fuero Juzgo as its special charter (which was soon translated into Spanish), he initiated that centralization of social polity which was so powerfully advanced by Alfonso X's code of the *Siete Partidas* (1256–1263). The latter only became a source for Spanish law by a resolution of Cortes passed under Alfonso XI. It is not so much a code of laws as of social counsels : how must a king preserve his gravity ? what are the duties of chivalry ? how much liberty should be conceded to centres of instruction ? what is the most desirable rule of succession ? how should public entertainments be regulated so as to afford the maximum of recreation and the minimum of scandal ? The *Siete Partidas* has a breadth and humanity unusual in a legal document, and is one of the primary sources for the social history of the times. History had, under Ferdinand III, continued to employ the Latin speech : under Alfonso X it became vernacular, and subserved his two imperial claims—his ' empire ' of the Spains and his majority election, never ratified, as Holy Roman Emperor. The latter interrupts the composition of his Spanish history, and is expressed in the *Grande et general Estoria*, or world-history, which combines a core of Biblical history from Adam to Christ, with Roman history from Saturn's golden age, through Æneas to the Cæsars. As it is unfinished, we cannot judge how it was to have been linked with the author's futile claim to world-empire. As successor of the Leonese ' emperors ', Alfonso traced his right from Tubal and Hercules, through the Cæsars and their lieutenants the Visigoths, followed by their heritors the Leonese kings, in the *Estoria de Espanna*, better known as the *Primera Crónica General* or *First General Chronicle*. It is not certain whether the whole plan be Alfonso's : it is known that only half was revised by him, the remainder, more crude in finish but richer in matter, being reserved for the days of Sancho IV (completed 1289). This second part contains the celebrated ' prosifications ' of the epics of national history, a process that had already been indicated by previous historians ; and if the prosifications tended to supersede and so destroy the original *cantares*, they are the principal source of our knowledge of Fernán González, Bernardo del Carpio, the Infantes of Lara, the siege of Zamora, and many minor poetic narratives. The amours and tragedy of Rodrigo, the last of the Goths, are better represented in the *Second General Chronicle* (1344), which also relates the youthful feats (*mocedades*) of the Cid, and has additional information concerning all the *cantares*. The historiography of the Middle Ages was, apart from particular chronicles, wholly concerned with the refundition of the *General Chronicles*, the most influential being the so-called *Third Chronicle*, on account of its issue in print by Ocampo (1541) and its extensive use as a source book for Spanish history among the ballad-mongers and dramatists of the Renaissance. In the Chronicles the prose is naïve and impersonal, efficient in narrative, and often, under the influence of the epics, striking, unskilful in evolution and in the expression of the abstract. Alfonso's scientific works include the important Alfonsine tables of astronomical bearings, corrected for the latitude of Toledo, and a curious book on the virtues of precious stones : he caused to be translated from Arabic the book of *Kalila and Dimna* (1251) and his brother patronized the version of the Book of Sindibâd, issued under the style of the *Book of the Deceits and Tricks of Women* (*Libro de los engaños e los asayamientos de las mugeres*) (1253), thus incorporating into Spanish literature two of the most important collections of oriental apologues.

Under his successor, Sancho IV, the process of ' prosification ' was extended to a foreign epic, the *Chanson de la Croisade*, which was amalgamated with William of Tyre's account of the Crusades in the *Grand Conquista de Ultramar*. The King's hand appears in the *Book of Counsels for his Son*, a collection of apophthegms similar to several others of about this date. Translation from modern foreign languages was exemplified in the Spanish version of Brunetto Latini's *Trésor*, and the leading Arthurian novels were acquired for the Peninsular literatures probably under his reign or that of his successor : they were the tales of Tristan, Lancelot, and the vast Quest of the Holy Grail. Though translations, and perhaps not always of great literary merit, these novels, with the sentimental story of Floire and Blanchefleur, profoundly influenced Spanish prose, giving it a flexibility of narration, a capacity for architecture, a variability and in the end a cadence, which could not have been reached through the blunt virility of the epics nor the lumbering straightforwardness of the chronicles and apologues. Under their general inspiration an unknown writer (perhaps the archdeacon Fernán Martínez, mentioned in the preface) wrote, before 1305, the first independent Spanish novel, the *History of the Knight of God whose name was Cifar* (termed briefly in Spanish the *Caballero Cifar*), which adapts in the first book the adventures of St. Eustace to the author's hero, in the second retails an already translated book of apophthegms, and in the third constructs a chivalrous romance round Cifar's son Roboan and his adventures in the realm of Tigrida. To the chivalrous hero, the writer has had the wit to attach a shadowy forerunner of the earthy Sancho Panza, thus beginning that wedding of ideal to real which is Spain's supreme contribution to the most popular of modern literary moulds. More uniform, and equally successful in modern times, was the book of Amadis of Gaul (*Amadís de Gaula*), which rivalled the Arthurian stories in popularity during the whole Middle Ages, and felicitously inspired the imagination of Cervantes. It is known to have circulated in Central Spain from 1350 and to have been in three books, probably the same in outline as the first three of the extant romance. It cannot have been undistinguished in style, as it is far from undistinguished in plan : but it suffered a rejuvenation during the Renaissance which has led to the destruction of the original. Much ink has been spilt in the controversy as to its author and native language. To the present writer it seems probable that the author was a Galician troubadour, João de Lobeira, attached to a Prince Afonso of Portugal ; that the work was executed during the latter's expatriation in Castile (from 1304 to his death in 1312) ; and that the language employed was probably conventional, approximating as closely to the Spanish literary idiom of the Court and of Juan Manuel's sub-Court as the author's birth permitted. Strong claims have been put forward on Portugal's behalf. The question of dialect is not of prime importance before the differentiation of the literary idioms, which was carried out at a time later than this date : but the Portuguese claim has to meet the objections that the work is recorded in the centre of the Peninsula a century before it is in the west, and that its mention in the west (about 1450) follows too closely the date of Juan de Baena's *Cancionero* (1445), where it is extensively cited by Castilian poetasters.

Under Alfonso XI's reign the Alfonsine prose reaches its conclusion. The *General Chronicle* was recast, and an anonymous official, who may have been Fernán Sánchez de Tovar, added chronicles of the kings who succeeded St. Ferdinand. Though increasing the extent of historical literature, this work does not mark an advance of style. Among its sources is a *Poema de Alfonso Onceno* (*c.* 1344), written in tiresome octosyllabic quatrains, with considerable national patriotism. It is marked by Galicianisms and is connected in subject with a lost Portuguese poem on the Salado Battle, also in octosyllabic quatrains. This latter bears the name of Afonso Giráldez : in the former we read

> Yo Rodrigo Yáñez la noté
> en lenguaje castellano,—

verses of sense too cryptic to tell us whether we are dealing with a translator, or a Galician's infirmities in handling Castilian. The Trojan Chronicle, rendered Spanish in this reign, has the oddity of being translated later into Galician prose, which has almost no other literary document.

But the principal interest of this reign is the passage of literary patronage to certain great nobles, and the emergence of personal style. This was, in Spain, the work of Don Juan Manuel, who was disposed to consider himself the literary, and even the political, heir of his uncle the Wise Alfonso. Much of his work is in common form : he abbreviated the *General Chronicle* and composed works after the manner of the *Partidas* on social divisions and the duties of chivalry. He described the aristocratic sport of hawking, and detailed his own great pedigree. The 'Fifty pleasant tales of Patronio' (*Libro del Conde Lucanor o de Patronio, c.* 1335) is but one more book of apologues and aphorisms, the former set into a wooden frame of Lucanor's request for instruction on points of conduct and the moral verbosely deduced by Patronio from a fable. But the tales are free and varied ; though the sources are diverse, they flow from the author as of his own invention and experience, stamped with his aristocratic reserve and covering the fluctuating embarrassments of baronial politics. Above all, they are couched in a grave, aristocratic Castilian, influenced by Leonese, parsimonious of effort and full-voiced in word, practical, somewhat dry, realistic, which has conserved its appeal and intelligibility to our day. From the *Book of Patronio* Spanish literature ceases to be an amalgam inspired by ' empire ', and becomes homogeneous and national. National existence was conferred on Portuguese prose by the third and fourth *Books of Lineages* (*c.* 1350), which are connected with the name of Pedro, Count of Barcellos, the reputed collector of the *Cancioneiros*. The genealogies there related are those of all Spain, and the materials had already served Alfonso the Wise or his successors. Amid the formless name-lists, the author intercalates a few of the myths wherewith the vanity of nobles crowned their ancestry in a prose utterly unaffected in its simple charm.

III.   CATALAN·NATIONAL LITERATURE

The literature of the north-easterly portion of the Peninsula commences as part of a foreign culture, and after a national efflorescence independent of, but similar to, that of Castile and Portugal during the fourteenth and fifteenth centuries, merges itself with the Renaissance into the general culture of Spain, reappearing in our own days not as a national literature but as the most important of the regional cultures.   It was the Battle of Muret (1213) that cut off Barcelona from its aspirations after hegemony in southern France, and the campaigns against the Balearic Islands and Valencia (1229–1238) brought the kingdom of Aragon wholly within the Peninsular line of evolution.   The first national writer, who was also the greatest of this literature, was born in one of the conquered territories, in Mallorca.   Ramón Lull's (1232–1315 : modern Catalan prefers the spelling Llull) was a mind of infinite variety :   poet, novelist, missionary, educator, reformer, logician, scientist, traveller, martyr.   His life is known from a biography, largely dictated by himself, and issued four years before his death in 1315, but his intimate aspirations find better expression in the grave, melancholy, wooden but sincere *Cant de Ramón* and *Desconort.*   These show his mainspring to have been a passion for evangelization, and in particular for the conversion of the Muslim world.   To this end he demanded the creation of missionary colleges, with oriental languages as their special study.   As fully as any other mediaeval theologian, he believed that conversion arose from intellectual conviction, which he proposed to achieve through an ' Art ' or system of dialectic applicable to all subjects.   This ' Art ' is expounded and applied in innumerable works, principally extant in Latin :   its leading feature is that, in opposition to the Averroists who insisted on the validity of sense-perception, the Catalan author desired to invest certain abstract categories with absolute validity, the sum of these categories being the definition of God. He achieved no system of philosophy, still less a serviceable dialectic, and must be understood to be an idealistic protestant against the materialism of Siger of Brabant.   Not a logician, Lull is a poet.   His works in metre are often unpoetical owing to his notion of using verse as a jingle to assist in the memorizing of his ' Art ', and we must seek his high watermark in the prose of the *Book of the Lover and the Beloved* or the *Book of Ave Maria* (*c.* 1284). The same poetical qualities characterize, though less intensely, his novels of *Blanquerna* (*c.* 1284) and *Felix de les Meravelles* (*c.* 1286). In these dissolving views of the society of his time, both ecclesiastical and civil, Lull contrives to voice his idealistic protest and to make many striking suggestions for reform, which are not the less stimulating for being altruistic and impracticable. Lull has exercised a profound influence on the literature of Central Spain from Don Juan Manuel to our day.

The central pillar of Catalan nationalism is the sequence of four magnificent chronicles written in the thirteenth and fourteenth centuries. That of James I (*Libre dels Feyts del rey en Jacme*), extant in Catalan and Latin, reflects the hardy good sense of that monarch in language that must be largely his own. His successor, Peter III, is the subject chosen by Desclot, in a chronicle as impartial and sober as its subject is fantastically chivalrous : in Desclot the anonymous author of the fifteenth century novel of *Curial i Guelfa* found inspiration. Ramón Muntaner, the Catalan Froissart, is also inspired by the great reign of this Peter, but his most brilliant and valuable chapters treat of Roger Blum's expedition to the Orient which caused the establishment of the Catalan quasi-republic of the Morea : personal, picturesque and intensely patriotic, Muntaner's book of adventure supplied much matter to Martorell's *Tirant lo Blanch* (published in 1490). The fourth chronicle is that of the shrewd, cynical, accomplished and national monarch Peter IV, the Ceremonious, or ' he of the Dagger '. Again we are frequently in face of the ruler himself, despite the known assistance yielded in its composition by writers like Descoll : the chronicle was inserted in his general compilation by the archivist Miquel Carbonell at the end of the fifteenth century, and is the best part of his compilation. In that century general history superseded in interest the record of contemporary affairs, and there is a notable failing in historiography. At length antiquarianism usurped the whole field.

The reign of Peter the Ceremonious marks the high watermark of Catalan nationalism. His letters and those of John I and Martin show the intimate association of the Court with every phase of national sentiment, and their astonishing absorption in culture. They governed their realm through parliament, and both the first- and last-named had high repute as orators ; specimens of their eloquence still remain. Peter completed the codification of maritime law in the celebrated *Libre del Consulat del Mar*, which has profoundly influenced the legislation of all

Europe. Above all, from our point of view, they served letters by standardizing the official idiom. This is best to be studied in the works of the secretary Bernat Metge, author of innumerable official dispatches, of the *Somni* (1398) which shows him to be the firstfruit of the Renaissance in Catalonia, and translator of Petrarca's *Griselda*. Dante's *Divina Commedia* was known through an accurate rendering by Andreu Febrer, and there is an equally felicitous anonymous rendering of the *Decamerone*. Metge is thus one of a circle of humanists inspired by Italy, and in respect of syntax and diction is of the highest authority in the definition of standard Catalan ; his matter is, however, of less importance than that of two of his contemporaries. Francesc Eiximenis (d. 1409) is a practical moralist, whose life-work one may sum up in the words of a title chosen for one of his books : his writings are the ' compendious doctrine of just living and occupying with zeal and loyalty all public offices '. Such is his *Life of Christ*, such his more amous *Christian* (*Lo Crestià*, 1381–1386), commenced at the instance of Peter the Ceremonious. Always sane and balanced, Eiximenis shows real genius for preaching in his delightful fables, interspersed throughout the book, told with charm and with a freshness that never disappoints the reader either in respect of felicitous phrasing or unforeseen turns in the narrative. Eiximenis was a preacher on paper : St. Vincent Ferrer swayed the multitudes in market-place and cathedral, though his surviving sermons scarcely account for his rhetorical appeal. We have, therefore, to set beside Eiximenis, not a brother churchman, but one of the most amusing renegades and rascals of the age, Fra Anselm Turmeda, known in Tunis as the holy sheikh Abdullah. A natural polygamist, Turmeda could not remain a celibate priest in his own land, but from his exile in a Tunisian harem had the effrontery to send his *Book of Sound Cautions* (*Libre dels bons Amonestaments*) to more honest Christians than himself. His greatest work is the *Book of the Ass* (*Disputa del Ase*), of which the Catalan text is lost and our authority is an early French translation : in this he adopted an ancient fiction, perhaps of Indian origin, whereby in public dispute man demonstrates his superiority to the animal creation. But in Turmeda this demonstration is accomplished with such scandalous difficulty, the contrary arguments of the Monkey are so damaging, and salvation by aid of the Ass so humiliating, that the work becomes the best Spanish piece of goliardic satire.

It was only in the fifteenth century that a school of poetry, specifically Catalan in aims and manner, arose. Lull and Muntaner wrote their poems in a conventional dialect of Limousin, and the same unreality pervades the poems of Bernat Metge and of Torroella, the latter the author of an interesting Arthurian *Faula* (*c.* 1381). Their *codolades* and *noves rimades* are pedestrian metres destined to serve later satirists. With Pere and Jacme March, Catalan poetry acquires consistency if not masterpieces, and shifts its centre of gravity to Valencia, in which city it reaches its height in Jordi de Sant Jordi, ' crowned ' poetically by a great Castilian contemporary as the greatest lyrist of his day—a mighty but not incomprehensible hyperbole,—and Ausiàs March (1393–1459), the most Petrarchian of those poets who owe no direct debt to Petrarch. Ausiàs March is a sophist of love, who takes his point of departure from the more abstruse Provençal singers. Neither his Songs of Love nor Songs of Death say anything specific in description of the lady he is alleged to hymn ; in view, indeed, of his practices, much doubt may be felt as to the existence of any one pole-star of his life. His ' lily among thistles ', who is ' full of sense ', nowhere overwhelms our poet, who through lack of abandon, perhaps, has missed his place among the great lyrists of Europe ; his style is concentrated, subtle, casuistical, and in its best moments given over to a passion of noble thoughts, and in his Prayer to God (' Puis que sens tu algú a tu no basta '), though profoundly mediaeval, is bound by no formula, but in the aristocratic dignity of his soul March can stand up and enter into not unworthy colloquy with his Maker.

The argumentative eminence of March, and even the chivalry of Jordi de Sant Jordi, did not prove to be the level at which Valencian literature was to rest. This was determined by Jaume Roig's light, comprehensive and entertaining satires on society in his *Book of Women* (*Spill o Libre de les Dones*). Like all the most entertaining items in the controversy as to the nature of womankind which agitated Spain in the later fifteenth century, Roig's verdict is unfavourable to the sex. Satire, however clever, sacrificed the intellectual and emotional eminence towards which the Marchs had aspired, while Roig's short stabbing verses banished from prosody the grave alexandrine octaves of serious poetry. Satires perpetuated themselves in Valencia, but it is perhaps not surprising that the next Catalan name in serious poetry, Juan Boscán Almogáver, should have elected to employ the idiom of Castile, thus integrating the literary expression of his country with the main current of Peninsular culture.

IV. THE EARLY RENAISSANCE

The work of Juan Manuel (1282–1348) shows Spanish literature emerging from the impersonality of its curial epoch into the individuality which is the characteristic quality of his humbler contemporary, Juan Ruiz, Archpriest of Hita (? 1283–? 1350). The biography of this author is known only from his work, and is so wrapped in humour that one cannot know where literal truth begins.   He suffered an imprisonment, and concluded his work in bonds; but it appears that he was also a person of sufficient gravity to deserve the confidence of an archbishop, and to be entrusted with a message to clerics guilty of the ecclesiastical vice of *barraganía* or legalized concubinage.   Whatever the real character of this author, he has been pleased to describe himself in goliardic terms, and to attribute to his own experience lengthy and picaresque adventures translated from well-known authors. But this characterization has been so skilfully, vividly and consistently carried out, including even the physical details appropriate to a figure of sensual appetite, that it becomes the sole connecting link of the disparate matter contained in the *Book of Virtuous Love* (*Libro de Buen Amor*), which is in reality not one poem, but a selection from the author's works, completed in 1330 and amplified in 1343.   The author explains that his poems lead towards virtuous love if the reader steadily avoids the examples of foolish human love which they exhibit, but they may also serve to guide those perverse ones who prefer folly !   Commencing with an exordium which mingles in one the invocations of priests and jugglers and the general proposition that ' man in all his trials ought always to seek entertainment ', Juan Ruiz plunges into a collection of versified fables, told with incredible verve and comic spirit.   The principal item in his poem is a narrative version of the twelfth-century Latin drama *De Vetula*, which the Archpriest ascribes to his own life history; the Trotaconventos of this tale is the grandmother of the go-betweens of Spanish realistic novels and dramas, and is not inferior in vitality to the most scandalous of her offspring.   The battle of Lent and Carnival is an admirable parody of epic pomps, and the five songs of hill-women (*Serranas*) in their broad farce and unsparing realism contrast forcibly with the pastoral suavity of the Galician *pastorelas*.   In these songs, and in his devout lyrics, the Archpriest is a lyrical poet,—the first Castilian to leave behind a considerable body of songs,— who enjoys an independence of Provençal traditions such as seems to indicate behind him a considerable lost tradition of Spanish lyrism.   His most quotable moments are satirical songs, such as those on the power of money or the pleasing qualities of little women, the indignation of the polygamous chapter of Talavera or the Rabelaisian account of his own appearance, expressed in his dominant metre, the alexandrine quatrain.   Ruiz alone has the exuberance and fancy required to fill the verbose ' fourfold way ', which becomes in his hands pliable, bubbling with broad humour, and even, as it would seem, the one literary mould ample enough to give free course to his roistering spirit of fun.

Nothing is further from Ruiz's verbosity than Rabbi Sem Tob's parsimony of words and ideas. His *Proverbs* (*c.* 1350) are in quatrains of heptasyllables, where Ruiz uses lines of fourteen ; in the ' fourfold way ' the phrase coincides with the verse, but in Sem Tob, who borrows his manner from the antithesis of Hebrew wisdom, each verse contains two contrasted phrases. Tense and concentrated in manner, his matter is invariably grave and serious ; he advocates a practical and estimable morality, uninspired by any ideal, unblemished by any goliardic excess. Grave and sufficient for his purpose, the Jew is a poet of consideration and weight, whose thought becomes striking, despite its nearness to the commonplace, by the exotic, apposite illustrations which he draws from Talmudic lore. Pure poetry is also absent from the spirit of Pedro López de Ayala, Chancellor of Castile (1332–1407), who heads the great line of historians in this era. His poetical work is given a fictitious appearance of unity in the *Rimado de Palacio*, but its composition extends over a large space of the author's life, probably from his imprisonment in Gascony (the ' Inglaterra ' of one manuscript) after the Battle of Nájera (1367), certainly from his stay in Portugal (1385), up to the agitations connected with the Great Schism in the early years of the following century. The title refers to a brilliantly incisive satire on court life, the evils of favouritism, the insolence of office, the rapacious exactions of the tax-farmers, the royal passion for war, the sanguinary outrages which Peter the Cruel took for justice. But Ayala is equally stringent in his castigation of ecclesiastics, and the introductory portion of his work is occupied by a series of pieces which measure his own conduct against the rules of life, and find him guilty of breaking all the Ten Commandments, neglecting all the works of mercy, stained with all the deadly sins, etc. Such a character does not deserve to live. We must regard his self-denunciations as too systematic to be sincere, and suspect the same excess of bitterness in his denunciations of others. He took up his pen only when it was dipped in gall ; in his happier moments he was himself one of those courtiers, councillors and patrons of Jewish tax-gatherers whom he satirized from prison or retirement. We may deny to him, as to Juvenal, the title of poet, but verse gives points of iron to his scourge, he is an undoubted master of expression, and his knowledge of society is unrivalled for authority. He is, in respect of his versification, the last great master of the 'fourfold way'.

Ayala is also one of the oldest contributors to an important trifle, Juan Alfonso de Baena's *Cancionero* (1445). This records the lyrical diversions of John II's Court, endless in vituperation and rhyming tricks ; in these the compiler is especially interested, to the exclusion of all the really noteworthy lyrical effort of his time, but he documents two important evolutions of the Spanish lyric,—the Castilianization of the Galician muse, and the beginnings of Italian hegemony. The diversions of Alfonso the Magnanimous' Aragonese Court at Naples, collected by Stúñiga, are less important as historical sources and not more worthy as poetry. The minor poetry of the second half of the fifteenth century is recorded in a number of similar collections, such as those of Herberay, Castillo, etc., of which we need only signalize the *Cancioneiro de Rèzende* (1516) because it is the first sign in a hundred and fifty years of poetical activity in Portugal. Rèzende's collection is as frivolous as any, and is heavily castilianized ; but it contains one poem by its compiler which Portuguese literature will not suffer to be forgotten.

The greater poets of the fifteenth century are Santillana, Mena, and the two Manriques. Iñigo López de Mendoza, first Marquis of Santillana (1398–1458), is the most gifted of a literary aristocracy, which included in one family his grandsire, López de Ayala, Pérez de Guzmán, the Manriques, and, in the full Renaissance, Garci-Laso de la Vega. A great lover of books, his admirable *Proemio* or letter to the Constable Peter (or Pedro) of Portugal, himself a poet, is the first monument of Castilian literary criticism. He was profoundly impressed by the genius of the great Italian poets of the *trecento*, sought to naturalize among his countrymen their allegorical and quasi-philosophical methods, and himself introduced their metres by his forty sonnets made in the Italian style, whose halting versification rendered them of no influence in the history of Spanish prosody. His sympathies embraced the Catalan courtly poet Jordi de Sant Jordi, and the fiery preacher St. Vincent Ferrer, thus anticipating in literature the political and cultural union of the Golden Age ; but he was equally in touch with Portugal in the west. Serious as are his claims to historical recognition, his fame now rests almost wholly on his unequalled pastorals (*serranillas*), with their easy movement and musical expression, and on his appreciation of popular wisdom as recorded in proverbs. Santillana was, further, the patron of the most admired poet of the age, Juan de Mena, whom Nebrija described as the Vergil or pre-eminent bard of Spain.

Mena, who died young (in 1456), is linked to the metrical novelty termed the *verso de arte mayor*, which banished the clumsy four-fold alexandrine from literature (it has been restored by the Modernist movement) in favour of another, not less weighty, phalanx of syllables.   Serious weight is the characteristic merit of his *Labyrinth of Fortune* or *Las Trescientas*, an intricate allegory of Fame unrelieved by Dante's genius or the least spark of Chaucer's wit.   The language of Mena is 'aureate', stiffly Latinized in vocabulary and in syntax, a thoroughgoing but uninfluential gongorism, from which Nebrija drew illustrations of all the Classical tropes.   In prose Mena shares with Enrique de Villena the distinction of being the most unreadable of Spanish writers.   Of the two Manriques, Gómez (*c.* 1415–*c.* 1490) is the more equable and talented, and is interesting for his experiments in simple dramatic forms ; but Jorge (*c.* 1440–1478) is immortal by reason of his lines on his father's death (*Coplas de Jorge Manrique* : *c.* 1476).   Their heavy, clangorous movement has escaped Longfellow in his otherwise admirable translation.   There boom, like a tocsin, grave re-echoing commonplaces in verses regularly punctuated by sobbing half-lines.   Death is common and the consolations open to us are commonplace, nor have they ever, anywhere, received such inevitable expression as in Jorge Manrique's muffled lines.   It is, perhaps, the only Peninsular work in the Middle Ages which may be adjudged to be perfect.

The prose of the later fourteenth and the fifteenth centuries is no longer curial, but is profoundly aristocratic, being composed by and for those whose wealth, leisure and culture enabled them to acquire and peruse manuscripts.   To the nobles had descended the enthusiasm for learning and elegance which had marked the 'emperors' down to Alfonso the Wise, and in the later Middle Ages important libraries were gathered by López de Ayala, Santillana, Fernández de Heredia, Santa María, etc., as well as by such royal figures as Duarte of Portugal, Peter IV and John I of Aragon, the Prince of Viana, Isabel the Catholic.   For these illustrious patrons translations from the classics were executed, such as Livy's *Decades* or Homer ; and these models begin to mould style, now that the secret of personal expression had been discovered.   Among the most zealous of these humanists before Humanism was Pedro López de Ayala, whose Livian studies shaped his chronicles of Peter I, Henry II, John I, and Henry III of Castile.   From Livy he learned to make annals politically instructive by reviewing the course of action in set speeches attributed to named or anonymous characters ; and

as in the latter reigns he had himself intervened in all the more
important councils of state, as the policies urged were frequently
his own or policies which he had rebutted, we must assign to them
a high degree of historical probability. From Livy he learned the
trick of drawing summary thumb-nail sketches of his personages,
and these rapid characterizations were made without historical
context by Pérez de Guzmán and Hernando del Pulgar in succeeding reigns, so as to give us an invaluable literary portrait gallery
of the worthies who played their part during the Trastamara
dynasty. From Livy, and perhaps yet more from the Arthurian
novels, Ayala learned to build up his incidents so that the narrative should itself point its moral, as in the Tacitean character of
Peter the Cruel, inexorably condemned by the naked sequence
of events recorded. Resolute in style and weighty in political
content as he is, Ayala fails in prose as in verse to win the favour
of the Muse : he has intellectual eminence devoid of the æsthetic
charm which marks the Portuguese chronicler of the same events
Fernão López (c. 1380–c. 1460) whom Southey considered to be
the greatest chronicler of all times and ages. López has no
Peninsular rival but Muntaner for patriotic sincerity, vivid
impressionism and picturesque imagination ; and he is superior
even to Muntaner in his intense popular sympathies. It fell to
him to narrate the epic of Portuguese independence in his
chronicles of Peter I of Portugal, Ferdinand the Handsome and
the first two parts of John I's reign, and in these works the real
hero is the Portuguese people, the commoners or *gente miuda*,
whose activities he records with almost Macaulayan detail and
with a sympathy and warmth beyond the reach of a Macaulay.
He lacks political insight and has no sufficient understanding
either of the theory or practice of war, which Ayala had studied
in Vegetius ; but he is inferior to the Castilian Chancellor neither
in industry, nor in good faith, nor in copious variety of information.
An anonymous life of the victor of Aljubarrota, Nuno Alvares
Pereira, forms a considerable part of López' narrative, which
some have supposed to be an early work from his pen. Such
an attribution cannot stand in face of López' assertion to the
contrary, and the author was most probably the Constable's
secretary, Gil Ayras.

Ayala's life of the third Henry was cut short midway, and we
have to supplement his narrative as best we may from the *Vitorial*
(c. 1431) of Gutierre Díez de Games (c. 1379–1450). The *Vitorial*,
however, is not primarily a work of history : it is the characterization of the ' happy warrior ', found by Díez de Games not in the
regions of imagination, but in the person of D. Pedro Niño, Count

of Buelna, whose naïve triumphs in love and war are related by his lieutenant with a schoolboy's romantic ardour.   The same reign gave occasion for Clavijo's celebrated journey to Samarkand, in which the envoys of the King of Spain took precedence over those of the Chinese emperor in the presence and tent of Tamburlane (1405).   Clavijo's account is sober and precise, strictly discriminating things seen from things heard.   This distinction is partially lost in Pedro Tafur's *Andanzas* (1435), a tourist's trip through the Near East and Germany, which compensates in brilliance for its diminished evidential value.   The reign of John I⟨ⁱ⟩ (see p. 51), in which Tafur's trip took place, cultivated the elegances rather than the realities of life, and its chroniclers take on a chivalresque tone, which is profoundly indebted to the Arthurian novels and *Amadís*, incessantly quoted by the poets of the Court.   Such is the manner of the anonymous writer of part of the Chronicle of John II, which was begun by Álvar García de Santa María and perhaps completed by Fernán Pérez de Guzmán ; it is also the manner, in an exaggerated degree, of the author of the *Libro del Paso honroso*, or defence of Orbigo Bridge by Suero de Quiñones against all comers during the whole of the year July, 1439, to August, 1440. A private chronicle of the great favourite Don Álvaro de Luna presents a favourable opinion of this bitterly hated minister, whom John II sacrificed to his enemies : in the succeeding reign the biography of Lucas de Iranzo is important less as political than as social history, in its picture of the profusion and ostentation practised by the great Spanish nobles.   The complicated official history of the reign must be sought in the pages of Alfonso de Palencia and Enríquez del Castillo, who are continued into the reign of Ferdinand and Isabel by Hernando del Pulgar and Andrés Bernáldez.   For these years Diego de Valera's letters and *Memorial de Diversas Hazañas* are of great import ; the same compliment cannot unfortunately be paid either to his, or to any other, work of general Spanish history, though several were issued in the fifteenth century.

After López had ceased to write, owing to age, the best work in Portuguese historiography is that which follows the maritime urge given to the country's destinies by Prince Henry the Navigator. All Gómez Eanes de Zurara's (*c.* 1410–1474) laborious and scrupulous scholarship was directed on transmarine enterprises— the capture of Ceuta in 1415 by the sons of John I, its defence by the two Menezes, and above all the invaluable *Conquest and Discovery of Guinea* (*Chronica do Descobrimento e Conquista da Guiné*), which narrates the African explorations down to the discovery of Sierra Leone in 1446.   A private biography of great

interest is Fr. João Alvarez' account of the imprisonment and
sufferings of the ' sainted prince ' Ferdinand, held a prisoner in
Morocco during seven years (1437–1443). His words move us to
compassion as only those of an eye-witness have power to do.
There is a steep descent in manner after Zurara demitted office
as chief archivist, and to his successor Ruy de Pina we owe the
destruction of Fernão López' narrative of the first seven kings of
Portugal : Pina, Rèzende and Damião de Góes carry the line of
royal chronicles down to the end of the mediaeval period.

History is the principal achievement of both Spain and
Portugal during the fifteenth century, and the other classes of
literature are rather sparsely cultivated. Historical romance has
a noteworthy representative in Pedro del Corral's *Crónica Sarracina* (*c.* 1440) which gave to the legend of Roderic and the
destruction of the Visigothic empire a suitably ornate and exotic
expression, using material from the extended version of the
fable offered by the second redaction of the *General Chronicle*.
Corral was himself refunded at the end of the next century by the
rogue named Miguel de Luna of Granada. Otherwise both in
Spain and Portugal the continued circulation of already existing
novels, notably of *Amadís*, the three Arthurian pieces and *Flores y
Blancaflor*, is of greater significance than the new creations. The
most valuable of these are sentimental novels of slight activity,
in which the analysis of psychology is carried much further than
even the chivalrous novels encouraged. Round the lives of the
troubadours Macías and Rodríguez del Padrón a sentimental
history evolved, and the latter's *Free Slave of Love* (*Siervo libre de
Amor*) gave rise to Diego de San Pedro's *Love's Prison* (*Cárcel de
Amor* : 1492). The former has an autobiographic interest that is
not readily perceptible in the latter ; in both, action is sacrificed
too often to pathological curiosity. Among the humbler branches
of romance we find the books of anecdotes and apologues for the
use of friars. The largest and most independent of these is the
Leonese Clemente Sánchez de Vercial's *Libro de Enxenplos por
a b c* (between 1400 and 1421), with some three hundred tales
briefly outlined and provided with morals to match : from English
authors Spain obtained Odo of Cherinton's stories which circulated under the title *Libro de los Cuentos* (miswritten *gatos*), the
Espejo de los Legos of Hoveden, and Gower's *Confessio Amantis*,
translated into Castilian from Robert Payne's Portuguese version.
Gower, rendered into careless prose and divided into more than
three hundred chapters, is but one more book of friars' apologues.

The odd controversy suggested by Boccaccio as to the virtues
and vices of the gentler sex raged in Castile as in Catalonia, pro-

voking scurrilous defamation followed by sanctimonious restitu-
tions. No less a person than Don Álvaro de Luna intervened in
the conflict, a resolute champion of female virtue ; but the chal-
lengers carried off the credit of the fray, in Catalonia with Roig's
verses, and in Castile with Alfonso Martínez de Toledo, Archpriest
of Talavera's *Libro* (without other specification), which has been
given the convenient title of *Corbacho*. The suggestion for his
penetrating and unscrupulous record of feminine vanities and
frailties appears to have come to the author from his tours in
Catalonia. He has carried out his task without vindictiveness,
but with a boisterous, picaresque humour which justifies the
epigram that he was as good an archpriest in prose as his colleague
of Hita in verse. It is odd to reflect that this spirited archpriest
was also the author of a singularly dull and spiritless *Watchtower
of the Chronicles* (*Atalaya de las Crónicas*), made up of snippets
from the General Histories of Spain.

Didactic work is best represented by Portugal, which wholly
lacks original novels in this period. John I (1365–1433), founder
of the Aviz dynasty, discussed hunting as a fine art, and passed on to
two of his sons his literary tastes. The elder, Duarte (1391–1438),
amassed a fine library in his palace at Lisbon, and was perhaps
the best read monarch of his time. He dedicated the cream of his
studies to his wife in the book entitled the *Loyal Counsellor* (*Leal
Conselheiro* : *c.* 1430), valuable not merely for its encyclopædic
information, but yet more for the simplicity and sincerity of the
king's mind. Virtue was pursued with the same zeal by his
brother, Pedro, the illustrious but ill-fated Duke of Coimbra,
author of a Senecan treatise on Beneficence. The duke had
enjoyed the advantage of a grand tour in Europe, which became
legendary in the Peninsula and in the mid-sixteenth century
attached to his name a spurious work of travel that was patched
up from Mandeville, Tafur and less reputable sources. In Castile,
didactic prose is best represented by the Jew Alfonso de la Torre's
survey of the liberal arts in his *Visión delectable* (*c.* 1440), noteworthy for the part played in it by the speculations of Maimo-
nides, and Juan de Lucena's Ciceronian *Libro de vita beata* (? 1463).
Both works belong to the last years of the century, and indicate
that full Renaissance Humanism is not far off.

Attention was drawn to the interest of the *Romancero* or
corpus of Spanish ballads by Romantic critics who hoped to
find in them the popular origins of epic poetry, in accordance
with the arbitrarily created theory which supposed that the
greater national narratives were centos of episodic narratives

stitched together.   At the first competent inspection, that of Milá y Fontanals, it was seen that the process was, in Spain at least, inverse, that the ballads were generally posterior to the ' prosifications ' in the chronicles, and still more to the *cantares de gesta* ; but it was also seen that the ballads were the most universally appreciated of Spanish literary forms, and their extension out of Castile into Portugal, Catalonia, Spanish Jewry in Salonica or Oran, and South America, marks, as does no other cultural manifestation, the limits of the Iberian spirit.   Milá's investigations were amplified in Menéndez y Pelayo's treatise on the ancient ballads, and await definitive statement under the hands of the greatest of Spanish scholars of all time, Don Ramón Menéndez Pidal.   This modern renaissance of the ballad corresponds to an earlier renaissance in the first half of the sixteenth century, when a series of collections of traditional and of erudite *romances* appeared in Antwerp, Zaragoza, Valencia and elsewhere, together with the issue of numerous broadsides (*pliegos volantes*).   These sources have been vastly augmented by modern research, from manuscripts and the texts of comedies, and from the oral tradition of peasants or Spanish-speaking commoners who have been in some way subtracted from the changes of literary fashion during the eighteenth century.   Many of the most primitive and interesting pieces have lingered on only among the villagers of Asturias, or in the Azores, or on the lips of Salonica Jews.

This vast mass of material is represented in greatest numbers by the two volumes edited in 1849–51 by Agustín Durán, but first received critical treatment from Wolf and Hoffmann (1856), who applied to printed sources the criterion of age, which Menéndez y Pelayo's issue of their *Primavera y flor de romances* applies to oral and non-Castilian sources also (1899–1906). This critic has divided the material according to time and to matter.   The oldest ballads (*viejos*) are fragmentary and episodic, anonymous and unconscious of effect, frequently in close contact with the *cantares de gesta* ; less ancient are the minstrels' ballads (*juglarescos*), complete short narratives, anonymous but possessed of a simple technique ostentatiously used, and best represented by the Carolingian poems ; to these fourteenth and fifteenth century types there succeeded in the sixteenth century erudite compositions (*eruditos*) by named authors, consisting of the prose of the chronicles carved into verses that imitate, generally without success, the manner of the ancient and minstrel types ; artistic (*artísticos*) lyrico-narrative poems by the great poets of the seventeenth century and later sixteenth, Lope de

Vega, Góngora and others ; and plebeian pieces produced in the
epoch of the full decadence of the type (*vulgares*). The histories
of bandits and bullfighters are of as little interest as their ballads
are numerous ; the artistic pieces belong to the criticism of
their several makers ; the erudite *romances* are simply constructed,
and generally, save those of the ' Cæsarian knight ', too uninspired to serve for more than stopgaps to complete series ; so
that criticism is principally concerned with the first two types—
the *viejos* and the *juglarescos*. The subjects of the ballad-
mongers form certain great cycles : the history of Spain is
mirrored in epic ballads (Rodrigo, Bernardo del Carpio, Fernán
González, Infantes de Lara, Cid), in the sub-cycle of Peter the
Cruel and in the frontier ballads (*fronterizos*) ; chivalresque
ballads include a copious collection of Carolingian poems which
includes various sub-cycles, and three ancient pieces concerning
Arthurian heroes ; and to these classes we add miscellaneous
romantic narratives, which include some of the most enchanting,
and lyrical ballads, of late date, whose principal sub-group is occupied by conventional love-lyrics in Moorish disguise (*moriscos*).
    The ballads of the frontier wars deal picturesquely with
events trivial in themselves, and by their help and that of one
of Peter the Cruel's cycle, we can carry back the date of composition of the earliest known pieces, despite their sixteenth-
century form, as far as the year 1368.   In that period the earliest
known ballads meet the latest *cantares de gesta*, and, as the word
romance (vernacular composition) is common to both, earlier
prolongations of the ballad are necessarily the province of theory.
The notion of the anteriority of ballad to epic, favoured by the
Romantics, has been almost universally abandoned, but latest
speculations suggest that the earliest epics may have had an
extension similar to that of the longest ballads, while the octosyllable has been traced back to the tenth century.   The dominant theory of our times considers the earliest ballads to have
been the disintegrated fragments of epics ; fragments torn from
their context on the ground of their superior interest and ' represented ' with no more than a line or two of preface and epilogue.
Such an explanation tends to become mechanical, and on that
account it is supplemented by a theory of authorship.   The
ballads are not ' popular ' poetry, as the populace is never a poet ;
but they are ' traditional ' poetry, in the sense that, once composed and put into circulation, their text is refashioned in accordance with the inclinations, taste or barbarism of each reciter.
Hence they survive in numerous variants, extending in one case
to over a hundred and fifty, happy or infelicitous, and such

as when taken together establish, not one text, but a history of transformations.   In one noteworthy case, the charm of the most romantic of all the ballads—that of the Count Arnaldos— is due to a mechanical alteration, by which a situation has lost its commonplace solution and remains hauntingly unfinished in the reader's imagination.   Compression is a conspicuous feature of ballad technique.   Description is almost wholly avoided by the ancient ballads, but increases as the centuries pass and in the end ousts more virile qualities.   Action is reported sparingly, but speeches with dramatic frequency and length.   Ballad influences ballad, and contamination is one of the methods of composition most in vogue ; successful formulæ rapidly extend their range of application, and the need of assonance leads to certain special alterations in syntax.   In the ballads of minstrelsy a single assonance dominates the entire poem, but in earlier times assonances change in conformity with the tirades of epics or chapters of Arthurian romances.   The metre is described by modern scholars generally as consisting of lines of sixteen syllables with medial pause and final assonance.   This metre approximates to that of the later epics, and supports the theory of epic disintegration ; but the only ancient authority in its favour is Nebrija (1492), whose opinion was coloured by reminiscences of the Classic tetrameters.   For Encina (1496), a musician, the ballads are octosyllables with alternate assonance, and his music was composed for quatrains.   Encina's views commend themselves to champions of the antiquity of the octo- syllable, admittedly the most national of Spanish metres.   In the ancient ballads the phrase coincides with the assonance, but in the artistic ballads there is a perceptible tendency to compose in quatrains, the difference being due, perhaps, to some change in musical fashions.

The Spanish ballads are of varying value in all the epochs of their composition.   They provide no escape from reality, and in respect of the more ethereal qualities of imagination they may disappoint one who comes to them directly from our own English balladry.   They are profoundly human and realistic, and, above all, they are tenacious of the soil on which they have their birth.   In this way they bind together all that is Spanish in Spanish literature, making a grand sequence from epics and chronicles, ballads, historical comedies, to modern legends and novels.   Native to Castile, they migrated to all the Spanish- speaking world, and even into the territories of Portuguese and Catalan tongue : in these lands they were adopted, adapted, nationalized, refunded and conserved even when forgotten by

Castile, so that the extension of their use as popular and traditional literature defines the widest range of that one culture in three languages which we call Hispanic or Iberian. Other forms of art occupy more than a single linguistic area, but usually with some degree of specialization : only the ballads occupy evenly the whole.

V. The Golden Age [1]

There is no rigid division between the Spain of the sixteenth and seventeenth centuries and the Spain of the Middle Ages, and yet the greater intensity of her life and the acceleration of her cultural development gives to the ' Golden Age ' a character of its own. The invention of printing did not cancel the industry of transcribing manuscripts, and its texts were at first the classics of the Middle Ages, many of which are conserved to us wholly by the early printed editions ; but the printers made literature accessible to a far wider class of readers, and in its reaction upon authors created a profession. The Press was a powerful ally of the new humanism acquired by Spanish scholars in Italy. The pursuit of Classical knowledge had been a feature of Spanish culture from the days of the ' magni reges ' of León and had never a more distinguished exponent than Alfonso the Wise : in the period we are now discussing it gains greater momentum through contact with Italy, and carries with it the mass of the nation. The union of Aragon with León-Castile, and the completion of Peninsular unity by the conquest of Granada, accentuated the feeling of Hispanic patriotism, for which a motive was sought, not in history, but in religion. It is crusading zeal that, in Camões' lines, distinguishes the twin empires of Spain and Portugal from the remaining nations of Europe. The Catholic spirit, surprisingly in the background during the actual period of the Peninsular crusades, was intensely and increasingly felt during this period : in capital errors, such as the establishment of the Inquisition and the expulsions of Jews and Moriscos, as well as in the moral reform of the religious Orders, and the new vitality which streams from the visions of the great mystics. The Catholicism of Spain, however, was national : the Inquisition was an instrument of government ; the ecclesiastical dignitaries

[1] The Golden Age (*Siglo de Oro*) of Spanish Literature and Art lasts from about 1580–1680 (from the beginnings of Lope's and Cervantes' activities to the death of Calderón or from El Greco's arrival in Spain to the death of Murillo). From 1492 to 1580 is a period better described as the Spanish Renaissance ; but as several literary types reach perfection before 1580, the phrase ' Golden Age ' has been here extended to include both the Golden Age, strictly so called, and the Renaissance.

were nominees of the Crown, and, especially in colonial administration, its trusted assistants ; and the Popes suffered more
personal danger from Charles V and Philip II than from Henry
of England or the German Protestants. Having no quarrel
between Church and State on their own soil and having achieved
the moral purgation that their fifteenth century required, the
Spanish monarchs and theologians were incapable of appreciating
the motives of those who sacrificed the unity of doctrine and
polity in order to attain precisely these ends : at Trent, therefore, they stood forward as the champions of a reunited Christendom, forcing spiritual reforms on the reluctant Italians and
attempting the re-conversion of the protesting Germans and
Dutch, towards which end Spain created the disciplined phalanx
of the Jesuits and utilized the spiritual exaltation of the mystics.
In another chapter have been described the events which made
it evident at last that Spanish predominance could not indefinitely
persist. The political decadence which dates from the Battle
of Rocroi (1643) was followed, with a generation's interval, by
spiritual exhaustion ; and from the death of Calderón (1681)
until the subjects of the Bourbons started to rebuild the fabric
of national culture in the second quarter of the following century,
we find the nadir of Spanish literature. The great cycle begun
by Alfonso the Wise had run its whole course, and the modern
Spanish literature of European inspiration had not commenced
its rise.

The humanists completed the vernacularization of literature,
perhaps in their own despite. By insisting on the need for classical purity in Latin diction, they made composition in that
idiom the preserve of technicians ; and at the same time their
programme for the advancement of the vernacular speech
towards a parity with the ancients powerfully stimulated its
use in departments of study hitherto considered too grave for
its employment, notably in theology and philosophy. They
themselves cultivated the learned speech, with the result that
many of the most influential Spanish treatises of the sixteenth
century are composed in Latin. Antonio de Nebrija or Lebrija
(1444–1522) stands at their head, a grammarian of no great
logical distinction when compared with his Italian masters,
but a pedagogue of tireless iteration, who impressed on the
reformed University of Salamanca the doctrine of humanism.
He was inferior as a Latinist to the brilliant Francisco Sánchez
de las Brozas (1523–1600), to whose commentary on Garci-
Laso de la Vega we owe the circumstance that that poet is the
best edited of all writers of the Golden Age. The influence of

Erasmus is seen most clearly in the Valencian Juan Luis Vives (1492–1540), the greatest of the group; he served as tutor to Mary of England, and his treatises on feminine education are among the best early discussions of that problem; his prayers are a principal source for the Book of Common Prayer; his letters to More and Erasmus are delightful in phrase and, with his other works, document the period of transition from scholasticism to humanism, together with the resurgence of scholasticism in his native land; while his little dialogues, written as school texts to assist in the acquisition of Latin, add to excellence of diction great charm of matter and manner. Vives, in his insistence on experiment as the only source of knowledge, was a Baconian before Bacon. To these names of general interest we must add those of certain specialists: of Hernán Pérez de Oliva (?1494–1531), who, with Sánchez de las Brozas, represents the progress of Hellenism in the Peninsula; Benito Arias Montano (?1526–1598), the librarian of El Escorial; Fox Morcillo, who reconciled Aristotle and Plato; Francisco de Vitoria, the forerunner of Grotius in the domain of international law; García Matamoros, author of the treatise *De asserenda Hispanorum eruditione* (1553); the philosopher of the Jesuit Order Francisco Suárez (1548–1617); together with such brilliant Portuguese as André de Gouvêa (d. 1548), the reformer of the University of Coimbra, and Aires Barbosa. Though the works of the Humanists and Latinists have suffered from the neglect of their compatriots, it is not possible to forget, even in a short history, that theirs were the first apologies for the vernacular tongue, theirs the theories of its advancement which Herrera and Góngora followed; theirs was the science of Camões and theirs his esteem for the epic *genre*; theirs was the reasonable humanity of Cervantes. We cannot forget that Fray Luis de León was one of them; that Mariana composed in Latin before Castilian; and that apart from the disputes of Báñez and Cano the most subtle plays of Tirso de Molina and Calderón are wanting in system and context.

Lyrical poetry during the Golden Age reflects more than any other the influence of Italy and Italian prosody. It may be dated from the year 1526, when the Venetian ambassador suggested to Juan Boscán Almogáver (?–1542) the attempt to compose Castilian poems in the metres and manner of Italy. In Boscán the Catalan muse became Castilian: he was a talented rather than an inspired fashioner of verses, and his experiment would have failed had he not secured the support of his friend

Garci-Laso de la Vega (1503–1536), one of the most equable and tactful minds of the age. Garci-Laso's stay in the Neapolitan viceroyalty gave him a deeper appreciation of the Italian style than was possible for his friend, and the slender volume of his poetry, though not without shortcomings, combined tact in adaptation with inspiration in invention and musical charm of execution. He gave a patent of naturalization to all the leading Italian metres, but was pre-eminently successful in the canzon and eclogue, his ' Flower of Gnido ' (*Canción a la Flor de Gnido*) and first Eclogue being unsurpassed in their kind. Garci-Laso's diction is of elegant simplicity, choice but not averse to racy phrases, copious, flowing and harmonious. In respect of matter, though the poet is resolutely third-personal and prefers objective fashions such as that of the eclogue, he yet incorporates into Spanish poetry a greater fullness and subtlety of personal allusion than can be discovered in the *Cancioneros*. The same service was performed for Portuguese letters by Francisco de Sá de Miranda (1485–1558) on his return from Italy in 1527, and his early experiments were renewed on receipt of the published works of Garci-Laso and Boscán, in 1543. Miranda, however, like Santillana, committed the error of admitting into his adaptations too great an admixture of the irregular lines tolerated by previous Hispanic poetry. Despite some noble sonnets, Miranda's best work is to be found in traditional metres used with a new seriousness, as in his famous address to John III ; still more is he to be credited with the restoration to poetry of the Portuguese tongue, thus withstanding the Castilianization of his country which was almost complete in the Court of Manuel the Fortunate.

The succeeding course of poetry in Portugal is similar to, but more simple than, that of Castile. All the lyrists save Antonio Ferreira are bilingual, and in virtue of his Castilian pieces alone Camões would deserve a prominent place in this essay. His lyrical poems in Portuguese—the Babylonian roundels, some eclogues and sonnets, and the autobiographical pieces—place him on the summit of Peninsular achievement as one of the greatest lyrists of the world : he is full of passion, profoundly melancholy, deep of thought, but also versatile, courtly, satirical, an absolute master of all the resources of his prosody from the gravity of octave and canzon to the wit and dexterity of the motto and gloss. In the ' Simonides ', ' Vinde cá ', Mondego and Socotra canzons, Siamese roundels and sonnet on the death of his Chinese slave-girl he has no rival in the Peninsula ; but much of his work is in common form and on a lower level. The eclogues have, in particular, a certain cloying sweetness combined

with conventionality of outlook which came to be the characteristic of the Camonists, especially as it was also the manner of
his nearest Portuguese rival, Diogo Bernárdez (d. 1605), whose
pastorals derive their music from the tune of the waters of
Lima River.   In the work of his brother, Agostinho da Cruz, the
religious lyre of Portugal finds its most inspired master.   While
the bulk of Portuguese poetry is Italianate and bucolic, three
senior contemporaries of Sá de Miranda worked in traditional
styles : the charm of Gil Vicente's farces consists in his attentiveness to popular lyrism, including the last echoes of the *cossante* ;
while in the work of the two friends Bernardim Ribeiro and Chris-
tovam Falcão, particularly that of the former, the traditional
octosyllables run with smooth cadence in expression of the
characteristic Portuguese mood of *saudade* or vague pervasive
melancholy.

In the centre of the Peninsula there was greater variety
of lyrical experience.   The Italian innovations triumphed over
the witty and far from obstinate opposition of Cristóbal de
Castillejo, and in the third quarter of the century evolved in
two directions.   Fray Luis de León (?1527–1591), and the humanists who surrounded him, sought the perfection of style in simplicity and sincerity, and in real depth of thought.   They
proposed Horace as their model, preferred short stanzas, and
especially the *lira* (7.11.7.7.11.), but generally failed to impose
order and architecture on the poem as a whole.   In their leader,
Horatian influences gave way to Platonic, and all became inspired
by intense Biblical study : his lyrics are informed by the sublimest
concepts of Platonic philosophy, and in their faithful and unsophisticated reflection of his experience they reach the zenith of
personality.   There is a certain lack of variety and the more
elemental emotions : but an unrivalled intellectual eminence
persists throughout all León's work in a passionate aspiration
after truth, beauty and justice.   Human passion finds a vent
for itself in the expression of Divine longings when we pick out
the slender, but imperishable, body of San Juan de la Cruz's lyrics
from the morass of prose that surrounds them : it would seem
that the genius of central Spain could not achieve self-forgetful
abandon save under the goad of religious ecstasy.   San Juan
de la Cruz shares simplicity of stanza and structure with the
Salamancans, though he was not one of León's circle : but
the Sevilian Fernando de Herrera (1534–1597), ' the Divine ',
sought for perfection not in sincerity but in pomp and magniloquence, not in an unsophisticated sequence of simple stanzas,
but in the weight of odes, the artifice of sonnets, the riches of

Latin vocabulary and syntax, the elegance and parade of mythological allusion. Less truly learned than the Salamancans, less rich in content and in thought, Herrera's Pindaric genius found its fitting expression in national odes on the victory of Lepanto, the defeat of Alcacerquebir, or the career of St. Ferdinand. Less interest now attaches to his sonnets, though they attracted the attention of his contemporaries, among whom his influence was predominant, both because of Andalusia's fertility of poetic talent, and because he took the precaution of publishing his work, while that of the Salamancans yet lay in manuscript.

In the later years of the century, an equilibrium established itself in Madrid between the traditional and the Italian prosodies and between the rival schools of style. The two Argensolas represent this equilibrium in Aragon ; and in the capital there were immense hordes of poets, including all the dramatists, at whose head we must place Lope Félix de Vega Carpio (1562–1635). Lope de Vega's volume of production in lyric verse is immense ; he is brilliant in burlesque, and happier than any of his contemporaries in catching the echo of truly popular sentiment. In the expression of simple emotion, including simple religious emotion, he is without a peer. His diction is copious and fluid, endless in word and rhyme, profuse and prolix, lucid to the point of banality. Popular acceptance was his criterion in lyrical poetry as in the drama, and thus he drifted into a position of disagreement with the tenets of all Renaissance criticism. Herrera had insisted on the right of the poet to choose his audience, and on his duty to attend only to the plaudits of competent critics (los doctos) : Luis de Góngora y Argote (1561–1627) did no more than carry on the tradition of Herrera when he latinized his syntax, increased his vocabulary, complicated his allusions and subtilized his expression to the point of passing beyond the comprehension of a careless listener. Gongorism, named after its most illustrious champion, or Culteranism from its appeal to the cultured, is a stylistic vice arising out of the exc ssive cultivation of expression, as Conceptism (championed by Quevedo) is a vice caused by the over-cultivation of the concept : but as hyper-refinements of thought cannot but be reflected in the phrase, gongorism is the more general vice. Gongorism is, however, as fully developed in Juan de Mena as in Góngora, and it is as flagrant in Góngora's ode on Tapia's Camões (1580) as in the Polifemo and Soledades (1611 and 1613). If we grant the poet's right to pick his audience, these poems need not be regarded as unintelligible, for they yield their meaning duly to an attentive reader ; their classicism is no greater than that of an average man of culture who knows his Ovid well, their neologisms have been admitted by the language, their inversions are no more than the remains of conjugations and declensions can amply bear. More peculiar to Góngora than his gongorism is the unexpected music of his lines and verse-paragraphs, and his sustained metaphorical manner. We may go further. In the *Polifemo* the natural background is of more consequence than the story, in the *Soledades* the story is a shadow and natural scenes succeed one another as reflections of the poet's soul. Góngora is on the road to that philosophic interpretation of nature, not as an external tableau but as part of one's inner experience, that is the peculiar glory of Wordsworth. Both Góngora's poems remain unfinished, perhaps because his vision was incomplete.

It was the lesser and not the greater quality of Góngora's work that formed his school, which, apart from Villamediana and Jáuregui, is continued by the later dramatists. In Portugal, where there was no drama of consequence other than in Castilian, Gongorism met Camonism in the bucolics of Francisco Rodríguez Lobo (*c.* 1580–*c.* 1625) and his successors. Lobo is the most notable figure of his century in Portuguese letters, which, under the Philips and even under the first Braganza kings, was suffering a process of renewed Castilianization, which affected the stage (Matos Fragoso) and serious prose (Manuel de Melo, Faria e Sousa) so as to leave to the nymphs of Tagus, in the decadence of epic inspiration, almost only the lyric string.

The artistic regeneration of Spanish literature by the Renaissance is best illustrated in the evolution of the schools of lyric poetry ; its moral and religious effect by the sequence of great mystics. Together with the mystics we consider didactic writers because whenever the mystic is diverted from his proper business of communion with the Divine, or when inspiration fails, his writing becomes didactic. The true Spanish mystic is unconscious of an audience, conscious of no more than two realities—his soul and God,—and of but one purpose in existence—the union of his soul with God. But this state of absorption is one to which only rare souls may attain, and that not for the whole of their experience ; on cooler levels their sound and prudent advice on daily conduct, or their instructions for the attainment of the experiences they have enjoyed, belong to the sphere of didacticism.

Before the rise of Spanish mysticism, three writers of importance practised the moral or critical treatise. Juan Boscán Almogáver's workmanlike translation of Castiglione's *Corteggiano*

(1534) was not only an excellent model of perspicuous prose, but presented to his countrymen a classic of gentlemanly deportment which had in Spain, as elsewhere, a profound influence on society. The 'estilo cortesano' of the sixteenth century was a necessary corrective to the gross realism of the fifteenth, and performed services analogous to those of the Arthurian models of chivalry in the thirteenth and fourteenth, 'under which vice itself lost half its evil, by losing all its grossness'. No such ends were served by the famous works of the Bishop of Mondoñedo, Fray Antonio de Guevara (c. 1480–1545), celebrated in his day for the 'golden book' of Marcus Aurelius, otherwise known as the *Reloj de Príncipes* (1529), the 'golden letters' addressed to his friends (1539–1542) and the *Menosprecio de corte y alabanza de aldea* (1539), which has received modern praise. The argument of the 'Princes' Watch', that a prince must be, firstly, a good Christian, then a good father, and in the third place a good ruler, shows us that we are dealing not with a conquest effected by the human intelligence, but with a rhetorical disquisition whose justification must reside in its style. It was the 'aureate diction' of Guevara which captured the attention of Europe and made him more celebrated and influential than many better writers, so that in our land, for instance, Lord Berners' translation is a collateral source of Elizabethan euphuism. If Guevara's secret lies in his words alone, his contemporary, Juan de Valdés (?–1545), claimed to deal with ideas only: 'I write as I speak : I merely take care to use words that clearly indicate my meaning, which I declare with all possible simplicity, because I consider affectation unsuited to any language.' And, in fact, Valdés' 'Dialogue of the Languages' (*Diálogo de las Lenguas*) is the best model of the plain, unrhetorical manner in the Spanish tongue; besides being, with Santillana's *Proem* and Luzán's *Poetics* (see p. 156), one of the very few first-rate contributions to literary criticism made before Milá y Fontanals. Unfortunately, Valdés being an unorthodox Catholic, if not a heretic outright, his work did not come before his fellow-nationals until the eighteenth century, too late to correct the tendencies towards over-ornamentation in prose style which dominated the whole of the Golden Age.

An immediate forerunner of Spanish mysticism can be discerned in the posthumous *Dialogues concerning Love* (1535) of the expelled Jew, León Hebreo or Judas Abrabanel (c. 1460–1520). The work is extant in an Italian text heavily impregnated with hispanisms, in which the metaphors and metaphorical ratiocination of the Spanish writers is already in full bloom. The movement in the

Peninsula was delayed until the mid years of the sixteenth century, and by its conclusion was already in decline amid an increasing mass of reiterated precepts. Arising from the fervour engendered by the Catholic Counter-Reformation, it shared with Jesuitism a distrust of Reason, which had proved to be the source of so much discord in the Church, and stressed obedience and implicit trust in the received dogmas. So firmly are these dogmas held that they never come under discussion, and for that reason the Spanish mystics are singularly free from theological bias. They argue about nothing : their whole business is to realize emotionally, with all possible intensity of self-abandon, those primary tenets of our faith which most identify the individual soul with the Divine. As mystics they have no concern with any other being, though as didactics they may offer sound and sane spiritual advice or even intervene effectively in mundane administration : as mystics, they endeavour to abstract their hearts from the world, and when this degree of seclusion is gained through meditation and spiritual discipline, to eject their Ego from their own souls, filling these in their entirety with the Divine influence. In the effort to give concrete reality to spiritual experiences they are supported by metaphors,—the stair whereby the soul ascends to God, the rooms through which it may progress, the chains that bind it, the flame that burns without destroying, the dark night when the soul is voided of self and has not yet received the full glory of its Maker. Metaphor is the language of emotion, and in emotion the intellect had to be submerged ; the consequence of which was that such intellectual giants as Luis de León or St. Ignatius Loyola, despite their good-will, are never pure mystics. Religious emotion, too, has not the capacity for variety that is possessed by intellectual religion, so that after the gamut of metaphors had been run through, few chances remained for fresh descriptions of the same emotional experiences ; as early as the writings of Fray Juan de los Ángeles repetition sets in and the didactic element rises into prominence.

At the head of Spanish mysticism stand two figures, a woman and a poet. The greater is Santa Teresa de Jesús (1515–1582), in the world Teresa de Cepeda y Ahumeda, the reformer of the Carmelite Order, who describes the whole of her religious experience, with biographical detail, in her *Life* (*Libro de su vida* : c. 1562) and idealistically in the *Moradas* (1577). The former is a spiritual autobiography of the same style and excellence as Bunyan's *Grace Abounding to the Chief of Sinners*, whose title expresses the same thought as the alternate title (' Libro de las

misericordias de Dios ') used by the Spanish saint. The narrative is sparing of dates and facts, but follows from experience to
experience, from childish aspirations after sainthood and girlish
rebellion against parental authority, to contrition, illumination,
spiritual retirement and final union with God. In the *Moradas*
the same progress is detailed systematically as a progress through
the rooms of a spiritual castle into the innermost chamber of
complete identification with the Divine. The books of the
Relations (*Relaciones*) and of the Foundations (*Fundaciones*) are
supplementary sources for her biography, the latter being concerned with the monasteries founded by her efforts, and in the
Letters (*Cartas*) she appears in a singularly attractive light, in
her heroism under persecution, her humility under correction,
her admiration for excellence in others, her sanity in counsel,
her ever-present wit and good humour. All her works are
written in a style tenacious of the soil, racy, sane, humorous :
it is the language of the peasants of Ávila, transferred to paper
with the least possible literary sophistry. The words are all
current coin, yet virile and often of surprisingly exact intention :
the sentences are colloquial, with frequent inversions, suppression of pronouns and the machinery of precise relation, with
rapid and astonishing transitions : qualities which, however,
differ from mere incorrection by their constancy in the style,
and by their intimate relation to the sincerity of the writer's
thought. It is in a sense the simplest and most natural of Spanish
prose styles ; and it is assuredly the least capable of imitation.
Much narrower are the excellences of Juan de Yepes y Álvarez
or San Juan de la Cruz (1542–1591), disciple of St. Teresa, and
reformer of the Carmelite monks. His description of the mystic
life is concentrated on the last two only of the *Moradas* in his
*Dark Night of the Soul, Ascent of Mount Carmel, Living Flame of
Love* and *Spiritual Canticle between the Soul and the Bridegroom.*
In these lyrics there is a passion more vibrant and moving than
can anywhere else be found in Castilian literature, which can only
be equalled by Camões at his best. The white heat of the
author's emotion is luminous, but the shades gather round
him when he attempts to explain his meaning in prose, and what
intelligibility is found in the commentaries is a reflection from
his verse.
     Two great prose stylists are aggregated to the mystics, though
neither claimed to have attained to the high state of union,
namely, Fray Luis de Granada and Fray Luis de León. Granada
(1504–1588) is above all a preacher, master of a rotund paragraph
in what is perhaps the most oratorical of the languages of men.

His Ciceronian genius was expended on a variety of religious works : - translations, meditations, sermons, biography of contemporary saints, compendia of Christian doctrine. His four cardinal works deal with Prayer, the Christian Life, the Symbol of our Faith, and the Guidance of Sinners (*Guía de pecadores* : 1567). In the prose of Fray Luis de León we instantly recognize the poet. He was strongly attracted throughout his life by the poetical books of the Old Testament, and especially by the Psalms, Job and the Song of Solomon. To comment and expound these worthily was the supreme object of his life, for which he formed his own admirable style as a lyrist, and in which he intended to find employment for his varied talents as poet and scholar. Fine and sensitive as are his commentaries, they are subservient to his translations from the sacred texts : and his prose reaches its noblest achievements when it approximates to his poetry, or rather when it is using the very words and ideas of his greatest lyrics. These opportunities happen more frequently when he is not bound by the versicles of a text, but is free to adorn so general a theme as the thirteen Names of Christ (*Nombres de Cristo*), a work (1583–1585) famous for its two admirable prologues, its description of the Tormes at Salamanca and the *granja* of La Flecha, and such supreme passages of lyrical prose as the chapter on the Good Shepherd. A lower level is held by his treatise (1583) on the Perfect Wife (*La Perfecta Casada*), in whom he expects to find the virtues of King Lemuel's mother.

In Fray Juan de los Ángeles (?1536–1609) the mystical life becomes matter for precepts, and contemplation passes into preaching, whether he treat of the spiritual struggle between the resisting soul and the love of God, or of the conquest of the secret kingdom of heaven. The *Conversión de la Magdalena* of Pedro Malón de Chaide (?1530–1596) also attains to the front rank in this style of composition, and he shows the stimulus of Luis de León's teaching in the abundance and excellence of his verses, his varied picturesque prose and his defence of the employment of his mother tongue on so serious a subject. The attainments of Portuguese writers in this manner are not so high as the Castilian. Frei Heitor Pinto's (*c.* 1528–*c.* 1584) *Image of the Christian Life* is a series of dialogues on general topics, philosophy, religion, justice, tribulation, the solitary life and the thought of death. In the Augustinian Tomé de Jesús (1529–1582) the style gains warmth and colour in its account of the sufferings of Christ (*Os Trabalhos de Jesús*), from the author's experience of the Moroccan prisons after the humiliating disaster of Alcacer-

quebir (1578). In Manuel Bernardes (1644–1710), author of
Luz e Calor and *Exercicios Espirituaes*, religious didacticism has
been the source of the most pithy, graceful and finished writing
in the Portuguese language, modest, humorous, precise, intense
and restrained.

The *Consolation for the Tribulations of Israel* (*Consolação
das tribulações de Israel*) by Samuel Usque, printed at Ferrara
in 1553, escapes all classification. Its matter is historical, being
a catalogue of the persecutions of the chosen people, and of the
ruin of their enemies ; its form is that of a pastoral novel in dialogue ; its spirit is the spirit of vengeance, without stint or pity,
for the consolations promised by Nahum and Zecharia to the
long-suffering Jacob are the utter obliteration of the Christian
nations, his persecutors, even as Rome and Babylon had been
obliterated. The indictment of Christendom is terrible and just,
denounced with a sombre gravity, unrelieved by any lighter
touch of fancy.

Among the later Spanish didactic writers two names are
outstanding. Francisco de Quevedo y Villegas (1580–1645)
ranks next to Cervantes as a Spanish prose writer, and has been
converted by his countrymen into a legend. He is much more
admired than read, for if the attractiveness of his style lies largely
in his abundant and racy vocabulary, his innuendoes, puns and
allusions, it must be admitted that these are almost as obscure
to his compatriots to-day as to the stranger within the gates.
As a poet Quevedo is best in the more prosy styles, satire and
burlesque. His activity in prose was insatiable, and covers
treatises on moral and political subjects, literary polemics in
support of his doctrine of Conceptism, humorous and general
journalism, etc. He remains in the memory for two works
principally : his Dreams (*Sueños*), a kaleidoscopic satire on fantastic subjects which caricature the society of his time (1606–1627
or later), and the picaresque novel entitled *Historia de la vida del
Buscón* (1626). Deficient in grace, form and humanity, Quevedo
alienates the reader through his want of sympathy : his unhappy
hero is merely a butt for the shafts of his pitiless wit, and as we
are unable to feel our common humanity in him, we turn against
his maker. The Conceptist doctrine was also championed by
the Jesuit Baltasar Gracián (1601–1658), who preaches ' discretion ' of style in his *Agudeza y Arte de Ingenio* and of political
conduct in his *Héroe*. Merit he regards as wholly due to ' discretion ', which involves a Machiavellian subtlety in the politician,
and extreme compression of language in the stylist. In the
Criticón he rises to a rather more philosophical height. To

Andrenio, the natural man, and Critilo, the man of understanding, residence in Spain, France and Rome reveals with impartial satire the sorry customs and texture of the world, from which they are rescued by timely disillusionment.

The literatures of the Spanish Peninsula are rich in the consequences of Columbus' discovery of America (1492) and Vasco da Gama's voyage to India (1496), giving rise to a series of reports from eye-witnesses, which have the freshness and vivacity that is to be expected of men looking for the first time in history on the inhabitants of another world. In the front rank we have the reports of the great discoverers and conquerors themselves. Columbus' letters and journal, together with his *Life*, by his son, illustrate his amazing mind, easily erected by success and dejected beyond measure by misunderstanding, but tenacious of his great designs because with him the dream had already become a reality before its realization. Balboa's reports show him sage and prudent amid improvident adventurers, and the five letters of Hernán Cortés, especially the fifth, are not unworthy to stand beside Cæsar's commentaries for their unspoken but implied defence of his conduct and their penetrating and exact information. Of Magellan's voyage we have only reports of strangers, but Vasco da Gama's is related in Alvaro Velho's quaint log (*Roteiro*), irregular in style and unsophisticated in its candid wonder. The foundations of Portuguese dominion in India, which are the foundations of our own, were laid by the great Afonso de Albuquerque, and the *Comentarios* published by his son Bras represent doubtless the words and sentiments of his father in the hazardous turns of his undertaking.

Behind the great figures there lies a cloud of witnesses, various in literary and evidential value, but all noteworthy for the originality of their information. The disastrous attempt to employ the feeble Arawaks of Hispaniola by forced labour gave rise to Bartolomé de las Casas' (1474–1566) warm-hearted protests (*Brevisima relación de la destrucción de las Indias*). It is the work of an advocate, and in its championship of the indigenes it coincides with one of the principal duties undertaken by the Church in the New World : the exploitation of the Arawaks was stopped as soon as its consequences were clear. Las Casas' work has gained additional celebrity for political reasons, but Humboldt's calculations of mortality made on the narrow basis of ten years' experience give as their results figures higher than the total probable population of the New World in that era! The conquest of Mexico is detailed from two sides : Gómara writes an apology for Cortés, drawing upon the latter's despatches as well as on personal experience ; from Bernal Díaz del Castillo (1492–c. 1581) we learn the soldier's point of view, in language of great vividness and in a manner that is transparently honest. The Peruvian conquest is less happily represented in literature by Cieza de León, but in the *Florida del Inca* and the *Comentarios reales* of Garci-Laso de la Vega el Inca, son of a Peruvian princess, we have a species of historical Utopia, the perfect socialistic state, which has clouded all subsequent investigations into South American antiquities. New Granada also has its historians, but a special interest attaches to the colonies established on the Paraná in the modern territory of Paraguay, seeing that there alone did the Spanish invaders lack a pre-existing civilization as the basis of their efforts. The history of the enterprise, which also led to the foundation of Buenos Aires, was arduous, but it occupied only half the colonial activity of Álvaro Núñez Cabeza de Vaca, who, before his eventful governorship of the South American colony, had experienced the worst privations during ten years among the Indians of Louisiana, being the first man to behold the Mississippi. In the *Naufragios* of this traveller we learn, better than from any other source, the heroism and suffering which was the cost to Spain of her magnificent discoveries.

Portuguese narratives are concerned principally with Africa and Asia, with a slight interest in Brazil, and in the Moluccas they meet the westernmost extension of Spanish historiography. Concerning Africa the principal documents are Zurara's account of the Guinea explorations, already mentioned, and Francisco Alvarez's (c. 1470–c. 1540) *True Information concerning Prester John's Lands* (*Verdadeira informação das terras do Preste João :* 1540). But Africa was not tamed by the Portuguese, and its most enduring monument in literature is the collection known as the *Historia Trágico-Marítima*, which describes the most celebrated wrecks that occurred on its inhospitable shores, and the privations of those who were unfortunate enough to escape the sea. In India our documentation is denser and more sprightly. Fernão López de Castanheda, Gaspar Corrêa and Diogo do Couto are frequently the eye-witnesses of what they describe, and always enjoy authority from the circumstances of their residence in the east, supplemented in Couto's case by the most careful research in the archives of Goa. But the palm is borne by a traveller, indeed, but one of low credibility. Fernão Mendes Pinto had no intention of deceiving the public, and indeed only wrote for the amusement of a child ; but in his repeated imprisonments and shipwrecks he lost the notes of a quarter of a century's

wanderings, and in place of written mementoes he had his astonishing gifts of imagination. When travelling in known territories,
as in Sumatra or Siam, the general lines of his wanderings are
clear, even if the details be open to doubt ; but when he is
beyond the range of observation, lack of data and excess of imagination combine to form a narrative that is remarkable indeed.
But in all parts of the work, whether we have our feet on terra
firma or are wandering in a geography of the imagination, the
reader is the slave of Mendes Pinto's picturesque manner of
narration. His *Peregrinações*, which were early turned into
Castilian, and from thence into the other European speeches,
is the classic of pure adventure, and the journey from Hangchow
Bay to Nanking and Peking, not knowing whether he was travelling to life or to death, is a classic that every schoolboy should know.
Mendes Pinto alleges himself to have been one of St. Francis
Xavier's companions in Japan : that great missionary to the
Orient is the subject of a special biography by João de Lucena.

These great events, together with the sudden expansion of
Spanish influence throughout Europe, gave a great impulse to
history, which had to be rewritten in terms no longer of nations,
but of world empires. The historiographical activity of this
era rivals its literature of travel in extent, but, save for historians,
has a less ready appeal to modern readers. It is sufficient here
to notice certain general tendencies which differentiate the
writings of this age from its predecessors. Humanism greatly
stimulated archæology, and as early as Nebrija we meet the
will to reject the system of etymologies proffered by the General
Chronicles : in Florián de Ocampo this manner is complete.
Ocampo etymologizes with all the *naïveté* of Alfonso X or Rodrigo
of Toledo, but in a manner more in keeping with the prejudices
of his age, and his work powerfully stimulated antiquarian
research, which was carried to its height by Ambrosio de Morales,
Argote, and the historians of the great religious Orders. In
Jerónimo Zurita's (1512–1580) *Anales de la corona de Aragón*, the
taste for research was combined with scientific method and
infinite patience, so that both his work itself, and his marginalia
wherever these can be found, have their place among the primary
authorities for the subject to this day. Unfortunately Zurita's
gifts did not include that of style, and he yielded pride of place
to a less veridical historian, the Jesuit Juan de Mariana (1535–
1624). In Mariana the influence of Livy reached its highest
point of development in Castilian historiography, as it did in
Portugal with João de Barros' celebrated *Décadas da Asia*, or

history of the first years of the Indian viceroyalty. Livy's influence was already prominent in Pedro López de Ayala, but in Mariana and Barros it extended to the structure of the sentence (Mariana's history was first composed in Latin) and to the conception of history itself. For these authors the primary object of history is not truth but glory. Truth, of course, they pursue, but without feeling an obligation to resolve its many doubts : probability is their guide when facts are difficult to attain, as, for instance, when Mariana details Roderic's words and acts before the disaster of 711. But they hold with Livy that history's purpose should be to preserve noteworthy events from oblivion, and their plans lead them to a heroic panegyric of their respective nations, which could not find ultimate expression in so cold a medium as prose, even if that prose be heightened by all the artifices of the periodic style. In Barros and Mariana, history borders on the epic, and clamours for verse. Diego Hurtado de Mendoza's (1503–1575) *Guerra de Granada* (published in 1627) offers the peculiarity of being modelled on the sententious manner of Sallust and Tacitus, to the extent of paraphrasing speeches and descriptions from these authors. The rising of the Moors in the Alpujarras (1568–1571) is not an event of primary importance, but acquires significance from the author's competence as a man of affairs, who has access to good information and can criticize with knowledge the movements of troops and the plans of administrators.

We may pass summarily over the chroniclers of the reigns of Charles V and Philip II, as well as the authors of the *Monarchia Lusitana*, in order to mention the three important historians of the seventeenth century, Solís, Moncada and Melo, who alone seem to maintain their poise and gravity in the *débâcle* of Spanish letters under the last Hapsburgs. Solís' classical and well-informed history of Mexico enjoyed fame as the principal authority on that conquest, until Prescott's masterpiece appeared. In Moncada, Muntaner's old tale of Roger Blum's romantic expedition to the Near East was clothed in a Castilian not unworthy of its original exposition, though with less than Muntaner's vivacity and warmth of patriotic sentiment. Francisco Manuel de Melo (1608–1666), a Portuguese, who later wrote clever conceptist essays and verse in his own tongue, is principally remembered for his classic account of the Catalan insurrection of 1640–1642, in the *Guerra de Cataluña* (1645).

Both the astonishing events of the early sixteenth century and the Livian theory in history, fortified by the critical views

of a Vida or a Tasso and by the prestige of Ariosto and his followers, required an expression of national experience in the form
of a classical or national epic.   We find, therefore, all the outstanding lyric poets promising their patrons to sing of higher
things, and contemporary literature is rife with prognostications
as to the Vergil that was to be.   It remained to find the subject
and the man.   As for subjects, the most varied and diverse were
attempted, after the initiation of the fashion in or about 1550.
Many imitated the Italians, whether in the free romance of Ariosto
or in the more cloistered manner of Tasso : Lope de Vega had
leisure to imitate both.   The Gongorists (and Lope de Vega)
sought to re-tell classical legends, principally those already much
more happily told by Ovid.   Others looked to religion : to the
life of Christ, the legend of the Virgin, the lives of saints (here
also we meet Lope de Vega with his *San Isidro Labrador*).   Contemporary history was ransacked for epical possibilities, as in
Lope de Vega's *Dragontea* (Drake) and *Corona trágica* (Mary
Stuart).   The old national legends supplied a secondary masterpiece in Balbuena's *Bernardo*.   More success attended the cult
of exotic and transmarine topics.   In Portugal this produced
respectable verse chronicles such as Corte Real's second siege of
Diu ; in America the manner gave rise to Juan de Castellanos'
unending *Elegías de varones ilustres de Indias*, the most noteworthy
product of literature among the Spanish colonists in the New
World.   From America Alonso de Ercilla y Zúñiga (1533–1594)
brought the better cantos of his *Araucana*.   The subject of the
Araucanian resistance is truly epic in grandeur and in incident ;
Ercilla adequately realizes the possibilities it offers for appreciation
of deeds of heroism, and the author is exceptionally brilliant in
description.   The order of events is chronological, but after the
close of the first part fantastical elements intrude, love affairs and
episodic allusions to contemporary events, and the parade of
erudition.   Despite these defects, however, Ercilla retains his
rank as the leading Renaissance epic poet of Castile, and is
placed among the highest of those who have won the commendation but not the favours of Calliope.

   A secondary cause of Ercilla's fall in the latter two-thirds of the
Araucana may have been the powerful influence exercised by Luis
Vaz de Camões (? 1524/5–1580), whose *Lusiads* had appeared in
1572 and was the most adequate example of the Vergilian epic
demanded by the æsthetic feeling of the Renaissance.   In the
Lusiads national history conceived in the manner of Livy meets
with the ocean-wide romance of the age of discoveries, the

Italian forms of art with the inspiration of Classical studies, and national spirit finds an issue in national channels of expression. The author's troubled life is reflected in its diurnal course in the corpus of his lyrical poems, from his witty glosses in the hey-day of his popularity among the aristocratic exiles in Goa to the plangent notes of his great canzons, octaves and elegies : it is also found sublimated in the great epic, which was lived out in the twenty-five years of his wanderings and sufferings in the East, so that the spirit of Camões in all its nobler or more gracious aspects—in its permanent values—is, in fact, that ' illustrious heart of Lusitania ' which is his real hero.   It is this conception that gives novelty to the *Lusiads* among the epics of the world : the hero is a nation as a whole, not impersonally conceived, but not wholly identified with any of the personages that carry on the narrative.   Vasco da Gama is, in fact, not the hero, but merely he whom Destiny called upon to execute the most typical feat of Portuguese history, the discovery of the road to India. His character surrenders many of its distinguishing marks to the Genius of Portugal, and his voyage is surrounded with mythology and allegory.   Not so those parts of the poem in which the domin-ating personality of Portugal ran no risk from the prominence of individuals, the books of the kings (cantos iii and iv) and heroes (canto viii) and the book of the viceroys of India (canto x). The composition of the poem covers the whole of its author's life.   The book of the kings was doubtless inspired by Camões' journey from the University of Coimbra to Lisbon in 1542, when his road passed through Batalha, Aljubarrota, Alcobaça, Leiria, and all the most historic ground in Portugal.   Towards 1552, whether spontaneously or through reading the first of Barros' *Decades*, he was led to select Gama as his central figure, and his journey to India in 1553 furnished the details of Gama's voyage (cantos i, iii, v).   The episode of the Twelve of England (canto vi) depends on Jorge Ferreira de Vasconcelos' *Triunfos de Sagramor* (concluded about the 5th August, 1552).   When shipwrecked at the mouth of the Mekong (1559), the author escaped with only the manuscript of his poem, which breaks off in a celebrated aposiopesis (canto vii, 78).   For the book of the viceroys he would require the use of the Goan archives and the aid of Diogo do Couto or other friends (1561 ff.—canto x).   The poem was completed in Mozambique (1569), and the initial and final verses were appended in Portugal (1571).   The *Lusiads* is, therefore, rich with the whole experience of his much buffeted life.   It is a poem magnificent for its patriotism, full-blooded in its passion for action and for beauty, spacious as the ocean, somewhat deficient in allegorical skill, and often of disconcerting pessimism ; the diction is clear, smooth and swelling, a ' voz sonora e eloquente '. The *Lusiads* has fixed Portuguese nationality and the Portuguese speech, and is a principal bond of union between Portugal and Brazil.

The influence of Camões is marked in the work of Bocage and those poets of the Arcadias who re-established the independence of Portuguese literature. Though the seventeenth century was, like the later fifteenth, characterized by a tendency towards the formation of one literature for the whole Peninsula, especially in the departments of history and the drama, the achievements of Camões' genius could not be forgotten, and were a rallying point for Portuguese nationalism in literature. With the re-assertion of this nationalism, the severance between Spanish and Portuguese literatures was finally established on lines that have persisted to our day, and from Camões' time onwards we cease to treat Portuguese literature together with Spanish in our narrative.

The changes in fashions for prose fiction during this epoch are curiously correlated with the course of its political events. In the days of discovery and conquest, when new worlds could be expected to appear and empires fell to an adventurer's sword, the mood of elation translated itself into the romance of unlimited personal action, the chivalrous novel. Somewhat later in the century a more chastened ideal was offered by the pastoral novelists, working under the influence of humanist utopias, but with the end of the century disillusion gives rise to the realistic and picaresque novels which view life only on its under side, and contemplate its shortcomings. When the seventeenth century brought its disasters in the political sphere, the picaresque novel was almost the only narrative prose in existence, and it alone partially resisted the imaginative stagnation of the eighteenth.

The new movement took its rise in Montalvo's redaction of the old mediaeval romance of *Amadís de Gaula* (first known edition 1508), which his preface declares to have been inspired by the chivalrous deeds of the siege of Granada. To the original three books Montalvo added a fourth, not inferior in manner though unnecessary in fact, and revised the whole style until he formed a manner pleasing to his age, smooth and inclined to magniloquence, but flexible : a style already indicated by the *Tristan* romance and later carried to its classic development by Cervantes. More immediately influential was Montalvo's device of announcing in the tail of one book the birth of the hero of the next. This trick led to the invention of strings of romances linked by a common genealogy, and of the twelve parts of Amadís' cycle, all inferior to the first, we need only notice the ninth, which announces the advent of the pastoral fashion. A rival to the Amadises was found in the family of the Palmerins, the most distinguished of whom was the third, *Palmeirim de Inglaterra* by Francisco de Moraes (prepared for publication in 1544). The immense mass of chivalric novels produced during the first half of the century, with a notable diminution of output thereafter, is chiefly remembered for its condemnation to the flames by Cervantes' priest, but it so toned in with the temper of the age as to gain an immense popularity and become a source of peril for the austerer forms of morality. The companions of Cortés saw in Mexico the magical scenery of their chivalrous romances, and named California after an island in one of them ; and in literary consequences it is sufficient to allude to Cervantes' amazing knowledge of their contents, which still exceeds that of his most industrious commentators.

The pastoral tradition first appears about the year 1530 in the ninth *Amadís*, as we have noticed, and was carried further by Bernardim Ribeiro's *Menina e Moça*, in Portugal, an autobiographical love romance of dissolving views, interspersed with charming lyrics in the popular vein : the most complete example of Portuguese *saudade*. With another Portuguese, Jorge de Montemor or Montemayor, the pastoral romance in Castilian reaches its maturity. Montemayor's *Diana* (*c.* 1559) is a medley of prose and verse, in which the prose—flowing, graceful, somewhat languid and effeminate—is superior to the verse ; a relationship which is reversed in his successor Gil Polo, the Valencian. Their novels depend wholly for interest upon their style, as the subject-matter is colourless and conventional ; but in their own day they offered the intellectual attraction of being representations of that ideal state of Nature which the humanists had declared to be original in human development and attainable by the use of reason and right conduct. For this cause Cervantes retained to the end his affection for his *Galatea* (1585), of which he never ceased to threaten a second part ; and Lope de Vega took pride in his *Arcadia*.

Two other idealistic currents have to be distinguished in the Spanish romances of the Golden Age. The Byzantine novel of adventure exercised a powerful influence through translations of Heliodorus and Amyot's Longus, and had as their principal result Cervantes' last work, the *Persiles y Segismunda* (1617).

On the other hand, the Moors of Spain, once defeated, had been sentimentalized and adorned with all the attributes of Arthurian cavaliers ; the principal agent in this process (which has given American literature Washington Irving's *Conquest of Granada*) is Ginés Pérez de Hita's (? 1544–? 1619) historical novel *Guerras civiles de Granada* (? 1604), which is adorned with admirable frontier ballads. Pérez de Hita is the creator of the famous legend of the Abencerrajes, as well as of others which have received less world-wide notice, and he is the ultimate source of that excessively sentimental and chivalresque explanation of the Spanish temperament which is preferred by many strangers to the real Spain, and dubbed by them, again in deference to this author, 'Moorish'. Of the same class is the delightful little sentimental romance of *Abindarráez y Jarifa*, interpolated in Montemayor's *Diana*, after that author's death (1561), and possibly due to Antonio de Villegas in whose *Inventario* (licensed in 1551, printed in 1565) it also makes its appearance, though it probably must be attributed to some unknown predecessor. Simple, rapid, full of colour and affecting sentiment, there is no better short story than this in the literature of Spain.

In face of the romance that looks at life only through rose-coloured spectacles there also appeared that of smoked glasses. Realism is never far beneath the surface in the literature of Central Spain, and distinguishes this region from Portugal and Galicia where sentimentalism is supreme ; and even in the flush and glory of conquest and colonization, realism persistently recurs, while it dominates the period of disillusion and decay. As early as 1499 arose one of its primary masterpieces, Fernando de Rojas' *Tragi-comedy of Calisto and Melibœa*, better known (from its principal character) as *La Celestina* (? 1499). It is a novel in dialogue, too long for any stage and manifestly not intended for representation, carried out in the Terentian manner and with Terentian characters. It was doubtless intended to consist of five acts, like its principal derivative the *Eufrosina* of Jorge Ferreira de Vasconcelos, but the plan was altered after the completion of Act I, and the remaining ' acts ' have the length and content of scenes. The distinction between the first and the other acts lies deeper than that noticed between the sixteen acts originally published and the five added in 1502, which all belong to the plan. In the central figure of the go-between Celestina, the tradition of the archpriests of Hita and Talavera is carried on in terms of the Renaissance ; and she with her court

of scamps, her arts and sorceries, her crudity of speech and
wealth of popular expressions, stands out against the conventionality and sentimentalism of the hero and heroine, whom passion
leads to death. A second protest of realism occurred in the
mid-most years of the century, in the anonymous *Lazarillo de
Tormes* (1554). Lazarillo was already a proverbial character
before the appearance of this work, and figured, doubtless in
chapbooks, as a graceless simpleton who passed rapidly from
master to master. The original form of his japes may still
be distinguished in the additional tales of the Alcalá edition, but
in the *Lazarillo* they have been arranged into a simple, but
consecutive narrative, of which only the first three chapters have
been fully developed along with the conclusion. This is the
first and best of the picaresque novels,—that is, of those which
describe all the shifts of a *pícaro* who adopts every contrivance
for filling his belly save that of honest work : it differs from
Guzmán de Alfarache by its absence of sermonizing, from the
Buscón by the sympathy we feel for the comic hero.

It was only at the end of the century that *Lazarillo* bore
fruit in Mateo Alemán's *Guzmán de Alfarache* (1599), to which a
false and a genuine second volume were added later. Alemán's
life was as unfortunate as that of his hero, and his notes on
military service in Italy are of especial realism. Francisco
López de Ubeda's *Pícara Justina* (1605) describes the female
of the species in a series of disorderly episodes, and Vicente
Espinel's *Marcos de Obregón* (1618) is of very diverse contents,
but includes as a special feature the roguery of students at
Salamanca. Quevedo's *Buscón* (1626) might easily have been
the greatest of the series, which is never distinguished for formal
merit as art, had the author been able to control his excessive
wit, and not gone so far as to gain for his victim the loathing,
as well as the pity, of the reader ; but Quevedo has dispensed
entirely with human sympathy, and his treatment is mordant,
cruel and mocking.

The short stories of the era are not, perhaps, in their majority,
realistic, but their principal interest is seen to reside in their
serviceability as social documentation, whether for the facts or
for the conventions dominating mutual intercourse. In them
the influence of Italian story-tellers is noteworthy, of Boccaccio,
Straparola, Bandello, Cintio. Cervantes is their only exponent
of front rank, but Lope de Vega and Tirso de Molina also cultivated the *genre*. Merit of a special kind attaches to Trancoso's
Contos e Historias de Proveito (1575, ff.), which contain in addition

to Italian matter, tales derived from popular Portuguese tradition expressed in direct and effective vernacular. In Castile the most industrious cultivators of the short story were Salas Barbadillo and Castillo Solórzano, while a high documentary value is ascribed to the tales told by a talented lady, María de Zayas y Sotomayor (*Novelas ejemplares y amorosas*: 1637). A place apart must be conceded to Luis Vélez de Guevara's (*c.* 1578–1644) *Diablo Cojuelo* (1641) which stands half-way between the fantastically expressed satire of Quevedo's *Sueños* and the picaresque novel : like Quevedo, Vélez sports with language in puns, metaphors, extravaganzas and innuendoes, which pass the wit of commentators to explain. His work inspired the *Diable Boiteux* of Lesage, whose *Gil Blas de Santillane* (see p. 160) is indebted to three Spanish picaresque novels and to several comedies.

It was in this field that the most important single contribution by the Spanish Peninsula to world-literature was made, when she gave birth to the true novel by expressing the ideal in terms of the real and presenting to us the three dimensions of life. This is the significance, historically speaking, of the *Don Quixote* of Miguel de Cervantes Saavedra (1547–1616), who is now known to have been far other than the untutored genius of Romantic criticism. There is a strange discrepancy in æsthetic value between his various works, and those on which he most prided himself fall lowest in the scale. The unity of his work is, in fact, not artistic but intellectual, and has been described in this sense by Dr. Américo Castro in his penetrating *Pensamiento de Cervantes* (1926), the principal document for the study of our author. Cervantes' thought was educated during his stay in southern Italy amidst the humanists and liberal thinkers of the Neapolitan viceroyalty. To them he owes much of his humanity and his persistent rationalism. To avoid conflict with the theological identification of the Divine with the arbitrary and miraculous, the humanists based their arguments on the conception of Nature, wholly good and wholly reasonable. This ideal found literary expression in the pastoral novel, and persisted with Cervantes, who was an incurable optimist, from the publication of his *Galatea* in 1585 to the posthumous *Persiles* in 1617. As the ideal was attainable through perfect reason, all things were to be regulated by precept : and Cervantes never tires of setting forth the correct conditions of things, the true principles of drama, or of courtship or of knavery or of local government ; he calls for the public examination of poets and provosts to test their fitness to be either ; he discourses on ideal matrimony and

ideal justice.   His thought falls into place as a system, singularly
independent of the local conventions of his day, when textually
compared with the writings of Erasmus or Telesio ; but we must
not expect of Cervantes that his system be logically watertight.
Indeed, his principal appeal comes from the impingement upon
his ineradicable optimism of an alien view of life, the doctrine
of authority, infallibility, and disillusion which emanated from
Trent and gained strength from the manifest insufficiency of
humanism.   Cervantes is conscious not only of the ideal, but
also that the ideal is never actually attained.   He notes the
discrepancy between his pastoral fictions and the actual conditions
of shepherds in a state approximately that of Nature.   In all
his work, therefore, his dream is accompanied by the shadow
of reality.   In the drama, this sardonic comment is external to
the personages and prevents the author from ever becoming
one of them ; so that his plays lack dramatic life, and are remembered because, like the *Trato de Argel*, they reflect the author's
experiences, or in the *Numancia* express his fervent patriotism.
Only in short sketches of type (*entremeses*) is Cervantes happy,
as he usually is, like Velázquez, when his eye rests on the living
model.   In the *Novelas Ejemplares* (1613) the two principles
lie disjoined ; some pieces belong wholly to the Italianate convention, and are excellent only in fleeting moments of direct
observation of fact, while in others observation predominates,
giving rise to those admirable short tales, *Rinconete y Cortadillo* and
the *Coloquio de los Perros*.   The *Licenciado Vidriera* is of peculiar
interest, since it adopts the device for putting the critic of reality
into a state of mental abnormality, thus serving as a preliminary
study, among many others, for the great masterpiece of Spanish
literature.   In *Don Quixote*, the real and the ideal are at grips
with each other everywhere throughout the novel, optimism is
criticized by fact, and reality is criticized by the ideal.   It is
the optimistic and the ideal which is the master, the real which
must necessarily serve, and in this way Sancho Panza and Don
Quixote express the whole spiritual conflict of their creator's
soul, their age, and human aspirations as a whole.
As first planned, the *Don Quixote* (1605) seems to have been
no more than an exemplary novel similar to the *Vidriera* and
contrasting with fact those ideals of chivalric romance which
are expressed in the ballad cycle of the Marquis of Mantua.
With the entry of Sancho Panza into the story and the scrutiny
of the hero's library of chivalric romances, the true matter of
the book begins ; but though, from that moment, *Don Quixote* is
primarily a satire on novels of chivalry, the influence of Caro-

lingian ballads is only second to that of *Amadís* throughout the book. The first part differs from the second (1615) in the evidence it affords of Cervantes' lack of technical assurance, which leads him to diversify his history with extraneous matter in more conventional moulds, such as the exemplary novel of *El curioso impertinente*, the pastoral of Grisóstomo, and the artificial romance of amatory adventure which bulks so largely in the latter half of the first part : whereas in the second the story is wholly concerned with Sancho and his master. Both parts received less scrupulous revision of style than did the relatively insignificant *Galatea* (1585), but there is little that even hyper-criticism can object to the second until, in the fifty-ninth chapter, the conclusion is abruptly hastened by receipt of Avellaneda's spurious and malignant continuation of the original novel (1614). This technical insecurity becomes, however, one of the leading merits of the tale, if to it we owe the changing character of the protagonists, who, as they gradually know each other better and as their author becomes better acquainted with them, actually evolve and live from page to page, until the realist is not far from dreams and Don Quixote dies at the touch of disillusioned sanity. Much of Cervantes' finest writing is to be found scattered in his prologues, especially in the introductions to the *Novelas Ejemplares* and the *Ocho Comedias,* along with the appendix to his *Parnaso.* As for the celebrated prologue to the *Persiles,* there is nothing in all his writings, not even the scene beside Don Quixote's death-bed, to equal it in its whimsical courage· before the face of death, its irony without bitterness, and its optimistic faith in the world's eternal youth.

The marvellous year 1492 is also the starting-point for the development of the Spanish *comedia,* as it is the date of Juan del Encina's (? 1469–? 1529) first experiments, which were issued with later efforts in his *Cancionero* (1496). The eight slight Vergilian eclogues in this collection performed the service of secularizing the dramatic *genre,* and were so adapted to simple representation that they rapidly acquired popularity. Encina avoids dramatic situation, and stages only a simple colloquy followed by the announcement of some festival such as the Nativity ; but there is an implied contrast to the naïve jocularity of his shepherds in the actual politeness of the courtiers who acted or witnessed the pieces, and this contrast of the bucolic and the urbane intrudes even into the action. Later editions of his *Cancionero* carry with them sentimental love-stories of Italian origin in loosely juxtaposed scenes with others of comic relief.

But though these works represent an advance in Encina's own technique, they are of less service to dramatic development than his elementary pastoral dialogues.   These it was that influenced the genius of Gil Vicente (c. 1465–c. 1536) to produce similar entertainments for the Court of King Manuel the Fortunate, at first in Castilian, which was the language of that Court.   But from a very early moment Vicente adopts a bolder and more vivid manner of characterization than that of Encina and a more dramatic division of the dialogue.   His was a singularly rapid intellectual development, despite extreme paucity of resources.   He had no stage and no actors, but only an audience of courtiers clamouring for simple entertainment and an opportunity to parade such spontaneous talent as they might possess.   There was nothing to encourage artistic construction, psychological depth, or careful style, and every temptation to improvisation, caricature and display.   Vicente is not incapable of constructing a careful plot ;   in fact, in the *Farsa de Inés Pereira* he tells as regular a story, entirely of his own invention, as his scanty resources allow.   But he does not rely on plot, which with him usually consists of a dexterously contrasted succession of the episodes.   On the other hand, he makes the utmost possible use of character in the form of recognizable types, which he endows with such vitality, like those of Chaucer, that he is the creator of more figures who have a life apart from their context than any other Peninsular dramatist.   His Inés Pereira, Aires Rosado, Beira magistrate, Frey Paço, Mofina Mendes, etc., are recognizable wherever they are met, in a way that the Lisardos and Ciprianos of the later drama are not.   He stages all the varieties of trade and calling, real or unreal, human or superhuman, from the fish-wives of Lisbon to popes and archangels, usually adding felicitous touches of characterizing to each.   In diction Vicente is neither finished nor polished ;   but he is amazingly copious, a master of all shades of dialect, and, above all, a lyrical poet of the most delicate sensitiveness to popular melody.   The merits of the third founder of the *comedia*, Bartolomé de Torres Naharro, are more formal.   His *Propalladia* (1517) anticipates many of the principal traits of the drama that was to be :   it has romantic comedy and comedy of middle-class intrigue, it stages typical figures from hero and heroine, through heavy father, down to the sarcastic lacquey.   His plays are divided into acts, though he chooses five rather than three ;   and he recognizes the need for comic relief in the Calderonian manner of parody by sub-plot.

The middle years of the sixteenth century added to dramatic

resources regular companies of professional players, and the *entremeses* and playlets in prose which Lope de Rueda used for his tours are a considerable advance in professional technique, and determined the list of comic types used for the humorous element of subsequent plays. A little later, in the last quarter of the century, the establishment of the Court at Madrid and that of fixed theatres to amuse the Court led to the rapid advancement of the dramatic art, which now only lacked scenic contrivances, these being advantageously supplied by poetic description. The other service of these decades was to decide the Aristotelian question. Pressure came from the side of Portugal, where Antonio Ferreira's *Castro* was, if not a drama, a dramatic poem of rare dignity written within the supposed laws of Aristotle. This was adapted in the Castilian of Jerónimo Bermúdez (1577), and at once aroused interest. Senecan tragedy proved, however, to be no more than an uninteresting holocaust, and Plautine comedy was not distinguishable from that of Lope de Rueda. It followed that none of the Spanish Aristotelians were able to adopt the whole Aristotelian convention, but that all compromised more or less with popular sentiment, notably in the case of Juan de la Cueva (? 1550–? 1610) whose plays (1579–1583) were among the first to draw on the rich dramatic material in the ballads, and to use that variety of metres which became characteristic of the *comedia*.

In Portugal the drama did not have the support of a public or body of artists dramatically trained. The school of Gil Vicente sank to boorish improvisation and was driven from the Court. Antonio Ferreira's classicism produced not a drama but a narrative poem in dialogue, which formed no school. Camões has three highly interesting pieces, which show him under the influence of both popular and classical schools ; but they are early works, mere parerga in which the poet did not persist. Similarly Jorge Ferreira de Vasconcelos' admirable imitations of the style of the *Celestina*, his *Eufrosina* and *Aulegrafia*, were not technically capable of representation. It followed that, despite Gil Vicente, no school of dramatists flourished in Lisbon ; which leant in this respect, as in certain others, on the Court at Madrid.

It thus happened that all the materials of the future drama had been brought severally into existence before the advent of Lope Félix de Vega Carpio (1562–1635) ; yet the *comedia* is his exclusive creation. Only those proceedings which he adopted passed on to his contemporaries and successors, and nowhere else before him were they to be found in harmonious union. There is little vacillation in his work during all his life, and owing to the difficulties that beset the study of so multifarious a genius it is difficult even to suggest a line of development in his art. He proclaimed public approval to be the canon of his work, to which he was willing to deny the title of art out of deference to Aristotelian criticism. Vacillating in theory, he follows one steady policy in practice, based on his persistent observation of the plaudits of his public, not only in his own plays but also in those of others. He reduces the motivation of action to one cause : love. That is the mainspring that sets his wheels working, whether in tragedy or comedy, and in combination with whatever other motives. Character he does not study, and his personages have no life outside their context : but they have sufficient for that context, and react swiftly to the variations in emotional temperature, thus living an intense existence for the moment. He refuses to distinguish comedy from pure tragedy ; all his plays are mixed, and called, for short, *comedias* ; but there are those which tend towards gravity (*heroicas*) and those which deal with mundane humours (*capa y espada*), so that the inevitable distinction of types is substantially the same. His introductions are among the most skilful in all dramatic literature, as he laid himself out to reconcile the good-will of the public from the start of the piece ; the action is rapid and often complicated, divided by effective curtains, though occasionally the complications are unscrupulous ; the solutions are always unforeseen, and delayed until the last hundred lines of the play, which, however, is too late for them to be submitted to criticism as to their artistic qualities. In diction, the *comedia* employed the whole prosody for the expression of emotional changes, often of very slight nature. It is not based on the octosyllabic quatrain, though that is the usual metre of dialogue ; but on the whole native and Italianate scheme of metres, from the hexasyllables of its laments to the *terza rima* and octaves of heroic description.

In the criticism of Lope de Vega the conception of number is essential. He has no perfect play : but among extant plays alone, without taking into account his extant lyrics, novels, epics, etc., there are *numerically* ten Shakespeares, whose general *average of merit* is above that of Beaumont and Fletcher. So enormous a mass of works, all dramatically suitable and of very high average literary merit, could not but mould the opinions of his contemporaries by sheer weight as well as by artistic pre-eminence ; and we know titles to the number of over seven hundred, while the poet's admirers claimed for him eighteen hundred plays ! These can only be described here by classes, and the classification cannot be altogether precise. There are a few *autos* and minor pieces which do not call for special attention. In Divine and Biblical plays Lope suffered from scrupulous attention to his models, which were frequently more miraculous and fantastical or more disjointed in their narration than was suitable for the stage (*El Cardenal de Belén*). He rises to his full stature in those heroic plays which dealt with national history, either in the bucolic charm of its primitive epochs (*Los Téllez de Meneses*), or in the turbulent insolence of the nobility during the later Middle Ages (*El infanzón de Illescas, Peribáñez*, etc.). Everywhere Lope is epic in his manner, so that these are similar to Shakespearian ' histories ', which degenerate into chronicles as he deals with the affairs of his own time, through excess of data. Foreign and classical history he treats with violence, considering it as the proper province of the marvellous and incredible. In adapting novelistic matter to his own ends his success is various, and is most noted when he can bend his source into conformity with his style in bourgeois comedy (*El Anzuelo de Fenisa*). In middle-class intrigue (*capa y espada*) the stress may be laid on the plot (*El Acero de Madrid*), on the customs (*El Perro del Hortelano*), on character or on one peculiar character (*Los Melindres de Belisa*), etc. As social documents this part of Lope's repertory is not wholly reliable owing to the strong influence upon it of conditions that make for Terentian comedy, and because Lope has erected certain convenient exceptions in ordinary society into the norms of his convention. In these plays Lope is a supreme master of the art of representation, skilful in intrigue within a limited number of types of plot, various in portraiture within general data, with situations that always recur and yet never quite repeat themselves, complex actions leading to unsuspected endings, though these endings are nearly always in the form of marriages all round the stage, and in and through it all brilliant wit and invention expressed through an intentional mediocrity.

Among the contemporaries of Lope de Vega, three can only with difficulty be distinguished from the master : Mira de Mescua (*c.* 1577–1644), Luis Vélez de Guevara (1579–1644) and Juan Pérez de Montalbán (1602–1638). The former is celebrated for the originality of his work at a time when to borrow was no offence ; the second has almost no comic repertory, but excels in heroic plays (*Reinar después de Morir*) and in his attentiveness to popular music (*La Serrana de la Vera*), while he was also, apart from his gifts as a novelist (*El Diablo Cojuelo*), the most celebrated wit of his age ; as for the third, he was the son of Lope's bookseller, and wore himself out at an early age through attempting to rival the spontaneity of his master. Special mention must be made of Pedro de Cárdenas y Angulo, author of the most purely tragic piece on the Spanish stage, *La Estrella de Sevilla*, a work long attributed to Lope de Vega and, in its conception, equal to his best. Very close to Lope de Vega stands his friend Guillén de Castro y Bellvis (1569–1631), author of the *Mocedades del Cid*, from which Corneille drew the plot and language and characters of the first successful tragedy on the French classical stage. Guillén de Castro drew heavily in this as in other *comedias* from the treasures of dramatic situation and characterization offered by the *Romancero*, and his work takes on, like that of Lope's historical plays, a markedly epic tone, which somewhat impairs the dramatic effect by detracting from its concentration. He is somewhat obsessed with matrimonial infelicities and the casuistry of a cavalier's code of honour, but has some excellent comedies *de capa y espada* (*El Narciso en su Opinión*).

The two greatest figures in Lope's entourage are those of ' Tirso de Molina ' (Gabriel Téllez, ? 1584–1648) and Juan Ruiz de Alarcón (? 1580–1639), who, in adopting the technique of the *comedia* in its entirety, carry it out with a high degree of independence. Tirso de Molina is at once one of the most original of Spanish dramatists in his invention of plots, and one of the least varied in manner. His situations are wont to reduce themselves to the activities of a manlike woman or women, contesting with passionate self-abandon for the possession of a lukewarm or averse youth (*Mari-Hernández la Gallega*). He carries his demand for artistic liberty to the point of caprice, making a mock of his readers, his characters, his art, and himself, constructs with supreme disregard of form, and relies on brilliant impressionism. He is rich in vocabulary, and his lines are strong and full of colour, virile in comparison with the effeminacy of Lope's genius, while his witticisms are among the boldest in their malign intention, and flow without stint. As the creator of Don Juan (*El Burlador de Sevilla y Convidado de Piedra*) he is the maker of the third among the national types of Spanish manhood, alongside the Cid and Don Quixote, and of that character which has gained most imitators abroad. There is profound theological purpose in that play as is indicated by the sub-title (addressed by Don Juan to the Deity) ' tan largo me lo fiáis ', and this same theological competence is shown in his play on free-will and illimitable grace, *El Condenado por Desconfiado*.

In *La Prudencia en la Mujer* he found a congenial story of manlike policy in a woman, and in *El Vergonzoso en Palacio* womanlike bashfulress in a man.

In Tirso's manner of construction caprice plays a prominent part ; in Alarcón all is subordinated to moral formula. In his characteristic work Alarcón held the doctrine, later to become official in France, that the aim of comedy was the purgation of social failings through ridicule, and he works out his thesis with greater logic than that of Molière's plots, so that the vice inevitably leads to its punishment. Such vices are habitual deceit (*La Verdad Sospechosa*), slander (*Las Paredes oyen*), interested counsel, vulgarism, etc. Admirable as the logic of these pieces may be, it must be admitted that they unnecessarily limit the scope of imagination, both in plot and in diction. But they wear better than the more gifted works of Lope, Tirso or Calderón, as they contain infinitely fewer exhibitions of bad taste or instances of slovenly workmanship. They have also exercised a notable influence in France, where the first-named supplied the plot of Corneille's inferior *Le Menteur*, and have always been read with satisfaction by French critics who recognize the similarity of Alarcón's comic doctrine to their own.

Between the beginning of Lope's dramatic activity and the death of Calderón a bare century is included, so that the successive generations or ' schools ' of dramatists overlap and are in part contemporaries. Their distinction can, therefore, only be expressed in an approximate manner. In the second period plays show the influence of the growing resources of theatrical decoration, called by Lope ' carpentry ', and mechanical contrivances tend to take the place of a truly dramatic sequence of scenes. Lay figures proportionately increase on the stage and the action falls more rigidly within preconceived limits. There is a notable diminution of originality which is paralleled by the growth of the practice of refunding old plays ; and the types of play used by the dramatists become less numerous, until among the last writers the *comedia* is successful almost solely in comedies of humours (*figurón*). The plaudit-winning devices of soliloquies and set speeches are exaggerated, so that in Calderón both the initial situation and the crisis of action are often covered by lengthy harangues, while others are inserted here and there on the slightest provocation—a royal procession or a recent victory or a change of fashion or a humorous conception. We have to remember, of course, that the drama was the omnibus literature of the age, and was not distant at times from journalism. In respect of diction, the proper use of the *pie de romance* as a narrative metre being lost, set speeches are relegated not infrequently to metres drawn from the Italian prosody, and in Calderón this combines with his gifts as a lyrist to produce an especially altisonant and lyrical type of evolution in the drama.

The transition between the two 'schools' is covered by Francisco de Rojas Zorrilla (1607–1648), whose fame should be based on his comedies of intrigue, such as *Entre Bobos anda el Juego*, were it not for the overwhelming merit of his *Del Rey abajo, ninguno*, which is the most complete representation in Castilian literature of the dignity and honour of the yeoman in face of the exactions of the nobility. It is a type of play which much appealed to Lope de Vega, and with him is normal when treating of Peter the Cruel, 'el Justiciero'. Rojas Zorrilla's contemporary Pedro Calderón de la Barca (1600–1681) is, outside Spain, the most quoted name of the Spanish *comedia*, and, in respect of the plays for which he is so quoted, well deserves the commendation. Lope is the greater, more original, more humane genius ; but his accessibility to every impression leaves him a little devoid of strongly personal traits. Calderón's genius is imitative, mechanical, but also marked by certain definite excellences. Where the two combine their advantages, as in Lope's *Alcalde de Zalamea* refunded by Calderón, we have the broad sympathy and lively characterization of the one perfected by the technique and lyric urge of the other, so as to produce the finest drama of human content, perhaps, in all the range of the *comedia*. But that play is exceptional in Calderón. His European repute depends on a small group of so-called 'philosophical' plays— *La Vida es Sueño, El Príncipe constante, El Mágico prodigioso, La Devoción de la Cruz*—which captured the homage of German Romantic critics and of Shelley. These plays are not deeper in their thought than similar plays by Tirso de Molina which have achieved no great renown beyond the Spanish frontier, and their reputation does in part depend on the ignorance of their foreign readers, who seriously misread their original ; as when Shelley reads his own wild revolt into a Satan whom Calderón conceived, nobly indeed, but in strict conformity with dogma. Calderón is not a philosopher but a casuist. He urges his case, however, with such lyrical force, in such clangorous and metallic verse and with such sweep of fancy as to transcend the limitations of language and to produce profound impressions even on those who know little of the refinements of the Castilian speech. His casuistry appears in his treatment of honour (*El Médico de su Honra, El Pintor de su Deshonra, A secreto Agravio secreta Venganza)*; whereas Lope and other dramatists are concerned to know whether honour extends downward beneath the privileged classes, Calderón is mainly bent on determining the minimum cause for action in defence of one's honour and the most secret manner of carrying it out. Of his comedies of intrigue a generic description has already been given ; his limitations being once admitted, he can be read with pleasure for his extreme technical dexterity and variety of resource (*La Dama Duende, Casa con dos Puertas*). In mythological comedies his skill in ' carpentry ' and his lyrical genius shine forth (*Púrpura de la Rosa*), but he is nowhere quite so much himself as in his sacramental *autos*, variations on the one identical theme of the mystery of the Sacrament, in which an argument in verse and dialogue starts from any premiss—a royal hunt, a parable, a supposed natural law—and seems to advance inevitably to the one edifying conclusion. These plays are not great as theology, for Calderón was addressing only the general public and from it he need fear no contradiction ; but they are superb casuistry, surrounded with the pomp and splendour of lyrical genius and presented with a wealth of allegorical apparatus, calculated to produce, after a day of religious emotion, an effect such as can hardly be recovered.

With Agustín Moreto y Cabaña (1618–1669), who died before Calderón, we are already in the decadence. Moreto invents nothing, and of that which he imitates and refunds only one type is successful, namely, his comedies of customs. But in these he is admirable, and is evidence of the advantages which the greater poets might have gained for themselves had they consented to regard their productions as an art. In character-study, in diction, in wit, in study of manners, Moreto usually improves his originals, and few *comedias* can be read with the same sympathy and pleasure as his *Lindo don Diego, El Desdén con el Desdén, No puede ser*, and others. In the second rank we find redactors, such as Álvaro Cubillo de Aragón, who add to their lack of invention a tendency towards violence in construction and pedantic pomp of style. In them gongorism works its way through Spanish verse, corrupting it to the core. The dramatic manner of Lope's school and Calderón's persisted as far as the mid-point of the eighteenth century, and so almost reached the beginnings of modern drama ; but even before the death of Calderón its inspiration was dead, and its convulsions indicated the progress of its decay, as style lost meaning through excessive strain, and the various Lopean types of comedy successively withered away.

CHAPTER V

SPANISH LITERATURE SINCE 1681

VI. THE EIGHTEENTH CENTURY

THE death in 1681 of Calderón, a writer active almost to the end of his.long life, revealed only too clearly the pitiable weakness which had succeeded the phenomenal fertility of the Golden Age and left Spain without a single writer of first-rate ability. Góngora and the Argensolas, Quevedo and Gracián, Rojas Zorrilla and Moreto, had long since passed away. The once resplendent drama was in the hands of the redactors—not to say plagiarists—mentioned at the end of the last chapter : such were the Portuguese Matos Fragoso, Antonio de Solís, Juan Bautista Diamante. Poetry was practically extinct, and the prose of living writers was for the most part undistinguished. That the robust spirituality of the sixteenth-century mystics should have given place to the enervating quietism of Miguel de Molinos is symptomatic of the decadence which was as manifest in literature as in religion, politics and society.

It is nevertheless too common a misconception that the eighteenth century as a whole in Spain was a barren period in literature. True, neither the eighteenth century nor the nineteenth reached the heights of the age which preceded them, and in the earlier of the two prose took precedence of quality as verse did in the later. But the period of real sterility, which was pronounced enough while it lasted, extends rather from about 1680 to 1750 : the second half of the eighteenth century was steadily, if unconsciously, preparing the way for the revival of Romanticism. Nor was even the reign of Philip V without its significance for Spanish literature. Did it matter that French fiction and French philosophy were as current in Spain as French fashions, if the ground lying fallow after its late glorious harvest was receiving intellectually such constant attention ? The creation of the National Library (1711), the foundation of the Royal Spanish Academy (1714), of the Academy of History (1738), and of the Academy of Fine Arts (1752), the production of the

155

great Academy Dictionary (1726–1739) are all events of a significance which is heightened and expanded by the rise of periodical literature and the publication of important bibliographical volumes like Nicolás Antonio's *Bibliotheca hispana*. It is not lack of culture that makes these seventy years unfruitful, but an exhaustion, perfectly natural in the circumstances, which the most abundant culture could not overcome immediately. Creative literature, in this period, is almost non-existent, while criticism is misdirected by forces which are largely reactive.

Poetry hardly re-emerges. There are graceful lines in the output of the uninspired *capitán coplero*, Gerardo Lobo, and Torres Villarroel, better known for his picaresque autobiography, has as a versifier a certain interest of curiosity. But it seems hard to believe that Lobo was once acclaimed ' Prince of wits ', that he was seriously compared with Vergil, Horace and Ovid, and that, as one contemporary said, ' his praise resided in his very name '. Dramatic activity is concentrated in the imitation of Cornelian tragedy and typified by the *Virginia* (1750) and *Ataulfo* (1753) of Agustín de Montiano. Prose, of its kind, has more merit. The Benedictine, Fray Benito Jerónimo Feyjóo, in spite of his gallicized manner and his unhappily warped sympathies, is held in genuine respect, not only for the encyclopædism of the *Teatro crítico universal* (1726–1739) and the *Cartas eruditas y curiosas* (1742–1760), but for his bold proclamation of his convictions—as behoved a ' free citizen of the republic of letters '— and the scientific spirit in which he often examined matters of which he had little knowledge. Gregorio Mayans is a more purely literary critic, now discredited, who wrote the first biography of Cervantes, edited Vives, Luis de León and Juan de Valdés, publishing Valdés' *Diálogo de la lengua* in his *Orígenes de la lengua castellana* (1737). These two writers, as much for their superb self-sufficiency as for the nature of their contributions to literature, are typical of the prose-writers of their day.

Much of the literary criticism of the early eighteenth century is embodied in the *Poética* (1737) of Ignacio de Luzán (1702–1754), a classical scholar, with a wide knowledge of France and Italy, who had a genuine desire to educate his own country in the canons of good taste. It was in no spirit of servility or flattery to the French that he sought to lead his countrymen into the bondage of preceptists like Boileau, or, as he puts it, ' to restore the use of the rules and so to rejuvenate Spanish poetry and carry it to such a pitch of perfection that we shall no longer need to envy other nations'. That rejuvenation could be produced by rule could only be taught by one with a pedestrian

conception of poetry such as in fact we can read in the frigid
eloquence of his own compositions. The *Poética*, which aspires
to being ' complete, exact and perfect ', is planned on a broad
scale, discussing, first, the origins and history of poetry, then
the pleasure and profit which it may bring, and finally, the nature
in turn of dramatic and of epic poetry. Luzán recognizes freely
the genius of Lope and Calderón—especially the latter,[1]—though
he is rather too generous, by comparison, to Rojas Zorrilla,
Moreto and Solís. Nevertheless, he considers the drama of the
Golden Age barbarous and unenlightened, and the *auto sacramental*, as a *genre*, irreverent to the verge of profanity. The
aim of drama, as of all poetry, is to him purely moral. The
way to write a play is to build it up on some ' moral point ',
fashion it to the rigid pattern of the Unities,—in regard to these
Luzán is stricter than Aristotle—and prune it of all barbarities
of the age now past. Like Boileau, he repudiates tragi-comedy,
but, unlike him, he admits the supernatural machinery of Christianity and the ' son dur et bizarre '. Blank verse he prefers to
rhyme, and against the slavish imitation of the classics which he
recommends must be placed to his credit an insistence on verisimilitude and local colour.

Like Feyjóo in another sphere, Luzán was vehemently
censured for his theories, which were held to be considerably
more indebted to Boileau than they actually were. This mis-
judgment has persisted in later days. The editors of the celebrated quarterly *Diario de los Literatos de España* (1737–1738,
1742), although they were in partial agreement with Luzán's
position, attacked the *Poética* vehemently. Its strictures upon
Lope and Calderón they felt to be over-severe ; even its condemnation of Góngora, though justifiable in the main, they
thought to have passed proper limits. Tragi-comedy and the
use of prose in drama they upheld against him and they demanded
a relaxation of his rigid rules. But Luzán was soon joined by
others. ' Jorge Pitillas ' (Gerardo de Hervás) satirized, in
caustic tercets, and in the *Diario* itself, ' the bad writers of this
age ', while after the short life of the critics' organ was ended,
Luis Josef Velázquez carried on Luzán's work in his *Orígenes
de la poesía castellana* (1754). Whatever the effect of the *Poética*
may have been on the reputations of Lope and Calderón, it
certainly had the effect of condemning their uninspired successors. But the times were completely awry. The ' Academy
of Good Taste ' (1749–1751), which met twice weekly at the

[1] This is considerably less true of the second (revised and posthumous)
edition of the *Poética*, Madrid, 1789.

house of a noble lady in something after the manner of a seven-teenth-century French *salon*, must have had some curious notions concerning the nature of its ideal : Montiano, who with Velázquez, was among its members, had invented a fourth Unity ; Blas Antonio Nasarre had republished Avellaneda's *Don Quijote*, as being better worth reading than the second part of Cervantes'. And though Nasarre to-day is unreadable, Velázquez wrote of his language, in some complimentary verses, that ' should the gods hear it, they will straightway desire to speak Castilian ' ! These men were prominent among Luzán's supporters ; and unhappily, by their own examples and by their exaggeration of his precepts, they brought his name into disrepute. After Luzán's death, the work of the unofficial Academy was continued at the Fonda de San Sebastián, a Madrid restaurant, by a number of writers interested chiefly in the drama. The best of them, Nicolás Fernández de Moratín (1737–1780), was a Romantic born out of due time,—a poet in his inmost soul, but no dramatist, and a misguided enthusiast in his opposition to the Golden Age. His gallicized play *Hormesinda* (1770) failed completely, and two earlier efforts, *La Petimetra*, and *Lucrecia*, were not even produced. Better than these are his ballads, above all the well-known *Fiesta de toros en Madrid*.

We are now in mid-century, and find destructive criticism slowly giving place to a new creative spirit. In the drama, it is true, Moratín's friend José Clavijo enjoyed a prolonged success, both in the review *El Pensador*, of which he himself wrote the whole, and still more in his campaign against the *autos sacramentales*, which in 1765 were prohibited by decree. In the following year all plays by Lope, Tirso and Calderón were forbidden, and translations from French drama were in their stead given official approval. Later than this, the most notable plays of the Golden Age were ' re-written ', with dreadful results. It was preferable to neglect them, as García de la Huerta did in his *Teatro Español* (1785–1786), which consists of sixteen volumes and includes no Lope, Tirso or Ruiz de Alarcón.

Life came into the drama from quite another direction than regular comedy and tragedy. It was Ramón de la Cruz (1731–1794) who, after a false start as a Gallicist, conceived the idea of reproducing the present, while delving deeply in the past, going farther back even than Lope de Vega, and specializing in the one-act play or *sainete*. So the translator of Ducis' version of *Hamlet* became the re-introducer into Spain of the *paso* and *entremés*. In his series of dramatic sketches his originality is seen to go far beyond the adaptation of a single *genre*. Some of them are comedies in little ; others are simply pictures of contemporary customs ; others, again, are skits on those pseudo-classical tragedies which so many were writing at the time but so few could write successfully. Ramón de la Cruz had no great gift of invention, but he was a heaven-sent adapter and reproducer. His *Teatro o colección de los sainetes y demás obras dramáticas* (1786–1791) has been described as ' a huge whispering gallery where you hear all the political and social gossip of the day : all the middle and lower classes of Madrid flit past you, in a vivid and picturesque panorama, light-hearted, careless, full of impertinent grace and wit. It is the drama of the out-at-elbows, the romance of the hard-up, but nobody whines and everybody bubbles over with the sheer joy of life.'[1] It is indeed a joy, after so many years of such monotony, to come again to dramas of which it is possible to use words like these.

Juan Ignacio González del Castillo (1763–1800), an Anda-lusian, carried on the tradition of Cruz, and in too brief a period of activity produced plays which in most respects rivalled those of his master, are read by many with even greater pleasure, and bear sufficient marks of a striking and dissimilar personality to suggest a promise of greater things, unhappily cut short by death. Both authors are highly individual : Cruz is the better *sainctero* ; Castillo is the finer artist and the greater poet.

But when Castillo was starting to write, a no less original and outstanding dramatist was already at work in a more con-ventional field of comedy. Leandro Fernández de Moratín (1760–1828), son of Nicolás, was, though less of a poet than his father, a far better dramatist. Leaving the overworked field of tragedy, he followed in the steps of Molière and Goldoni, and so nearly akin were his gifts to those of Molière that he succeeded in transplanting, not his actual plays (though he did produce versions of some of these), but a surprising portion of the spirit which lay beneath them. *El Viejo y la Niña* (1790), *La Comedia Nueva* (1792), and *El Sí de las Niñas* (1806), his best comedies, are in plot and dialogue the equals of anything of the kind produced in France : if they lack much of Molière's skill in characterization, and have scarcely a touch of his ' high seriousness ', they stand out nevertheless as among the greatest Spanish plays of their century.

Imaginative prose is but little in evidence till it revives with the dawn of Romanticism. The picaresque strain in the novel, which had found a curiously perverted expression in Torres Villarroel, reappears in the *Historia del famoso predicador Fray*

---

[1] James Fitzmaurice-Kelly : *New History of Spanish Literature*, p. 418.

Gerundio de Campazas (1758) of José Francisco de Isla (1703–1781). Isla, a Jesuit banished from Spain in 1767 with his Order, was a satirist of no mean ability who endeavoured to laugh away a pulpit Gongorism by relating the story of a famous (and imaginary) preacher of humble birth and describing a large number of episodes in his career. Isla is also mixed up with the picaresque novel through his translation (1781) of Lesage's *Gil Blas*, which was published posthumously, and claims that, in presenting the famous Santillanan to a Spanish public, it is ' restoring to its native land ' what already belongs to it. This, as might have been seen, was both truth and fiction, but it was the signal for a controversy in Spain over the sources of *Gil Blas* which came to no very certain conclusion.

Turning now to non-dramatic poetry, which is too often associated in readers' minds with the rather lifeless versions of well-known fables made by Félix María Samaniego (1745–1801) and with Tomás de Iriarte's (1750–1791) more diverting and original *Fábulas literarias*, we find that in the second half of the eighteenth century there occurred something not unlike a renaissance. This is associated with two movements, of which the earlier and more important was initiated in Salamanca, and has come to be described, not altogether properly, as the Salamancan School. The home of Fray Luis de León was a fitting birthplace for such a movement, and, still more fittingly, its unconscious begetter was an Augustinian monk, Fray Diego Tadeo González (1733–1794) who, with two friends, formed a circle which grew in size beyond his intention and ultimately embraced most of the poets (in any real sense) of the day. Not the three friends—Delio, Liseno and Andronio, as they called themselves in the conventional nomenclature of the pastoral—were destined to be best remembered among the Salamancans, though Fray Diego drew deeply and with great effect from Fray Luis and but for his excessive reserve might have taken a higher place than that which he occupies in literature. Two University students, who joined the ' Parnassus ' as Batilo and Aminta, outstripped the reputation of its originators : these were Juan Meléndez Valdés (1754–1817) and Juan Pablo Forner (1756–1797). Meléndez is perhaps the earliest poet of the century from whose lyrics one might quote freely with pleasure : from prettiness he suffers often but from prosiness never. His natural facility as a versifier he curbed with due restraint and considerable technical skill; and though, as with many of his contemporaries, his technique outran his inspiration, he fairly earned the title usually given him of chief of the School. Forner, better known as

polemist than as poet, gained the doubtful distinction of being
the subject of a Royal Order—which forbade him to publish
anything at all without special permission.   He was a scholar
deflected into satire : the verses in which he excelled were all
satiric and vehement to a degree ; and he leads us to surroundings far from the imaginary flocks and pastures of the gentle
Delio.   When he and Meléndez were still at the University, a
young soldier named José Cadalso (1741–1782) was stationed
there.   To those acquainted with his poetic output, it is no
surprise that having met Fray Diego he should at once have
joined the School, as Dalmiro.   Cadalso had just produced the
usual rhymed tragedy—a failure, like the rest—in Madrid.   He
now wrote his *Ocios de mi juventud*, and a prose satire, *Eruditos a
la violeta*, but his two finest works are the *Cartas marruecas* (only
published in 1793), a collection after the style of Montesquieu's
Lettres persanes, and the *Noches lúgubres* (1772), a lyrical prose
elegy of great melancholy and passion.   Another celebrated
member of this School, appropriately dubbed Jovino, is Gaspar
Melchor de Jovellanos (1744–1811), whose strong character
reacted on many of its members, though he chafed at their
pastoral artificialities.   Jovellanos was too much of a politician
to be able to devote himself for long periods to literature, but
in his *Defensa de la Junta Central* (1810) we have some of the
century's best prose, and he also essayed drama.   The verse
which he produced, comparatively small as it is in quantity,
reveals something of a poetic temperament too often latent,
the influence of which can be seen in many of the poems of
Meléndez Valdés.

A later group of Salamancans attains much the same degree
of eminence as did the School's initiators.   Almost without
exception, its members foreshadow the lyrists of the coming
century.   José Iglesias de la Casa (1748–1791) is the exception.
His serious poems may still be unearthed in libraries, but only
his elegant and malicious satires live in the memory.   Nicasio
Álvarez de Cienfuegos (1764–1809) is a philosophical senti-
mentalist who was a journalist and politician and died an exile
in France after the events of 1808.   Juan Nicasio Gallego (1777–
1853) has many points of interest : he rises a head above most
of his fellows, both in form and inspiration, and his patriotic
themes are diversified by many signs that he was influenced by
English literature.   Greatest of all these poets, however, is
Manuel José Quintana (1772–1857), whose long life embraces
not only nearly one-third of the eighteenth century, but also
the rise, flower and decline of Spanish Romanticism : born in

the reign of Charles III, he lived to be solemnly ' crowned ' by Isabel II.

Quintana was a pupil of Meléndez Valdés and a friend of Jovellanos ; like the latter he became a victim of political strife, after being editor of the *Semanario patriótico* and Secretary of the Junta Central. Under the *régime* of 1820 he became Director of Public Instruction, but only the death of Ferdinand VII brought him lasting tranquillity. His best known work, a series of *Vidas de españoles célebres* (1807–1833), shows him to be a conscientious historian, the master of a forcible and solid prose style, but never possessing sufficient imagination to save him from frequent dullness. In his verse he is the spokesman of the Liberals : patriotism, liberty and Gallophobia comprise the majority of his themes. At best he is capable of a rousing eloquence and a restrained and noble passion. His faults are those of the eighteenth century, in which, in spirit, he lived till his death ; but his greatest poems : ' Al combate de Trafalgar ' (1805), ' Al armamento de las provincias españolas contra los franceses ' (1808), ' A España después de la revolución de Marzo ' (1808) will hardly, in any age, be forgotten.

Although before the Romantic movement of the nineteenth century had set in, the revival of Spanish poetry by the Salamancan School seemed of greater significance than it really was, it is impossible to deny its importance : it was a Romantic who called Meléndez Valdés ' father or prince of the restored Castilian poetry '. At the turn of the century, influenced strongly by the Salamancans, a second School arose, and this—the Sevilian School—carried the torch of poetry right into the period of Romanticism. Founded in 1793, as another ' Academy of good taste ' and to vindicate the literary fame of Seville, the *Academia de letras humanas* was compelled to justify its existence by printing the poems of its principal members, which unfortunately were soon eclipsed by those of writers of more original genius. The Salamancan School, one feels, might have reacted to Romanticism more sympathetically than did the men of Seville. In spite of their tendency towards the lyricism and the melancholy of the Romantics, the Sevilians were academic to the backbone. It is sufficient to describe three of them. Alberto Lista (1775–1848), a Canon of Seville, was a prudent, conservative critic, a poet of somewhat Lamartinian inspiration, and a personality of more than usual charm. Félix José Reinoso (1772–1841) had often more of facility than of poetry, while José María Blanco (1775–1841), who went to England and took the name of Blanco White, is known principally, even in Spain, by a

sonnet written in English, ' Mysterious Night '.   Other members
of the School were the correct and classical Arjona, Francisco
de P. Roldán, who wrote on Biblical subjects, the pedant Her-
mosilla and the clerical deserter Marchena.   It must be added
that a few poets of merit stand outside both Salamancan and
Sevilian schools.   Of these the chief are the Conde de Noroña,
whose translations from English bring him into one of the
strongest literary currents of the time ; the Gaditano Vargas
Ponce, author of a famous ' proclamation of a confirmed bachelor
to the ladies who aspire to his hand ' ; Francisco de P. Núñez,
an imitator of Herrera, who was closely connected with the
Sevilian School, but turned against it ; and Cristóbal de Beña,
a political writer, who published a volume called *La lira de la
libertad* while exiled in London.

VII.   ROMANTICISM AND AFTER

Romanticism in Spain (if the word be taken in its modern
sense) has had a curious and a chequered history. It can never
fairly be said to have crossed the dividing line which separates a
' movement ' from a ' school ' ; its full possibilities were, except
by an insignificant minority, never realized ; and, although it
has profoundly influenced the whole succeeding course of Spanish
literature, it only lasted, as a militant, constructive and self-
conscious entity, for a period of some ten years at the outside.
    In the literature of France, by which Spain was so strongly
influenced, Romanticism was an intensely individual phenomenon, largely because it contested, not pure classical ideals,
but a vicious pseudo-classicism which had held the field with
tyrannical sway for a century, and had succeeded a period for
the most part classical in its affinities.   In Spain, it must be
remembered, the Golden Age was in essentials a Romantic age,
and, although for long after its passing it was under a cloud, it
never fell entirely into discredit.   Towards the end of the eighteenth century, past epochs in Spanish literature began to be
considered barbaric no longer.   Mediaeval poetry was given a
new interest by Tomás Antonio Sánchez' publication, in 1779,
of the *Cid*, and of other Spanish poems written before the fifteenth

---

[1] As these are my own views and not wholly identical with those
commonly taught, I must refer the reader for my justification of them to
Modern Language Review, XV, pp. 374–391 ; XVI, 281–296 ; XVIII,
37–50 ; XXI, 44–54, and *El Romanticismo en España*, Santander : Biblioteca Menéndez y Pelayo, 1924–5.

century ; Martín Sarmientos' unfinished *Historia de la poesía y poetas españoles* (1775) devotes much space to discussions of the oldest poetry of Spain. Hence, though one aspect of Spanish Romanticism is that of revolt against pseudo-classicism, which came to Spain by way of France, late in time, and greatly tempered in intensity, a more important aspect is the less noticeable one of a slow but sure revival of Spain's Romantic past, a revival which began far back in the eighteenth century, and, gradually gathering force, reached its fullness in the thirties of the nineteenth.

The political happenings between 1808 and 1833 outlined in another chapter affected both these developments, though rather dissimilarly. The revival of Romanticism was perhaps affected the less. Through all the turmoil of these years, and in spite of their wars and revolutions, the periodical Press, now firmly established (though sometimes temporarily suppressed), dealt faithfully, if spasmodically, with literature. The first period of Ferdinand's absolutism (1814–1820) corresponded almost exactly with that of a protracted and significant literary dispute between the German Böhl de Faber and José Joaquín de Mora, which turned largely on the merits of Calderón. The year 1823 saw the foundation at Barcelona of a literary review called *El Europeo*, which rendered its readers the double service of introducing to them foreign Romantics and of discussing Romanticism in its relation to the earlier literature of Spain. The *Romancero* of Agustín Durán (1793–1862) began to appear in 1828, which year saw also his famous *Discurso* on ' the influence of modern criticism on the decadence of the old Spanish drama ' ; in 1832 was published his collection of historical and chivalric romances anterior to the eighteenth century, with its no less famous preface. In creative literature, to take but one example, the Catalan Manuel de Cabanyes (1808–1833) was writing during the latter years of Ferdinand VII's reign and produced his *Preludios de mi lira* in 1833. All these years saw Spain in the throes of unrest, yet they were years of real literary progress.

At the same time we cannot doubt that in an epoch of peace and prosperity the progress would have been greater and more rapid, especially since a number of those who became Spain's greatest Romantics were Liberals suffering exile in France and England. Here, in the intervals of writing and teaching to gain the barest livelihood, they imbibed the principles of English and French Romanticism, and, when the death of Ferdinand permitted their return to Spain, brought these principles with them, and initiated what, for want of a better name, must be called the

Romantic revolt.   At home, too, the ' revolt ' had been maturing. A literary *coterie* which began to meet in Madrid in 1827 included Romantics as pronounced as Larra, Escosura and Ventura de la Vega ; a second and more turbulent one met in 1829-1830, and the dissolution of this led to the formation, at the Café del Príncipe, of the celebrated Parnasillo, which included all the leading Romantics who were not in exile—Larra, Escosura, Espronceda, Ochoa, Salas y Quiroga and many more.

When, after the death of Ferdinand, the Liberals returned to Spain, and inevitably, at one and the same moment, the Romantic revolt broke out and the Romantic revival realized itself, there were certain characteristics generally recognized as being inherent in the double movement which may be considered to constitute Spanish Romanticism. On the positive side, this signified a return to such literature of past ages as evoked the Romantics' sympathy.   In particular, it meant a renewed interest in the mediaeval romances and the drama of the Golden Age ; and secondarily the popularity of ' Ossian ', Southey, Scott, Chateaubriand, Hugo and other foreign writers who stood for some or other of the Romantics' ideals.   On the negative side, there was a general antipathy to classical mythology and also to classical literature and literary theory ; a tendency to throw off all restraint ; and the corresponding proclamation of liberalism in art. So much may fairly be described as the essentials of Spanish Romanticism.   In addition, many of the Spanish Romantics exhibit in greater or less degree traits which some critics consider characteristic, while others do not.   There is a delight in local colour and a turning for it towards the East and especially towards Islamic civilization ; a predilection for what is melancholy, pathetic, funereal, gloomy and even morbid ; an insistence on the disillusion (*desengaño*) to be found in life, which is frequently and loosely called pessimism ; a disinclination to be wholly grave or wholly gay and a consequent return to the principle of tragi-comedy ; an affected sentimentality ; a love of the vague, unformed and unfinished ; and a delight, for its own sake, in the ugly and grotesque.

The biographies of the principal Romantic authors of this time will show how short-lived in Spain was the movement which they represented, and at the same time how lasting in its effects was the evolutionary process upon which their innovations were superimposed.   What the Romantics chiefly lacked was a leader.   Two possible leaders died young : Mariano José de Larra, or ' Figaro ' (1809-1837), whose satirical essays are strongly imbued with *mal du siècle* and whose one historical novel (*El Doncel de Don Enrique el Doliente*) shows much future promise, and José de Espronceda (1808–1842), a Byronic poet of great power who wore out much of his life in exile but will always be remembered for his *Estudiante de Salamanca* and *Diablo Mundo* (1840–1841). The politician Francisco Martínez de la Rosa (1787–1862) began life as a Classicist and later followed other prevailing modes : his prose drama *La Conjuración de Venecia* (1834), for all its immediate success, was nothing more than a single topical incident in his long career. For a time it seemed as though the necessary leader might have been found in Angel de Saavedra, Duque de Rivas (1791–1865), who had certainly all the qualities which fitted him for that position. As a Liberal exile, he lived, before succeeding to his title, in England, Malta and France ; and when he returned to Spain under the amnesty his *Don Álvaro* (1835), the best play of the period, became in a mild way the Spanish *Hernani*. But, alas, between his return and the production of *Don Álvaro*, Angel de Saavedra had become the Duque de Rivas, and he now turned politician, diplomat and *grand seigneur*. Further, it is indisputable that his true genius lay, not in drama, but in the verse romance ; his *Moro Expósito* (1834) had been a notable contribution to the revival of Spanish legendry ; and as he grew older he moved ever farther from France and nearer to mediaeval and sixteenth-century Spain. His *Romances históricos* (1841) and *Leyendas* (1854), which form the principal testimony to this change of direction, are vastly superior to his latest plays. When Rivas died, he was acclaimed as the ' grand old man ' of Spanish letters, but he had only once in his life stood out as a Romantic leader. Even what might have been the important preface to his *Moro Expósito* was the work of his friend Alcalá Galiano.

Three dramas almost contemporary with *Don Álvaro* fall not far short of it in merit. *El Trovador* (1836), by Antonio García Gutiérrez (1813–1884), was the youthful success of an author whose talent spent itself later, for the most part in melodrama. Antonio Gil y Zárate's (1793–1861) *Carlos II el Hechizado* (1837) was the work of one who was no Romantic at heart but an eclectic. *Los Amantes de Teruel* (1837) brought credit to its author, Juan Eugenio Hartzenbusch (1806–1880), but Hartzenbusch, who was primarily a scholar, became director of Spain's National Library and won the gratitude of students the world over, not by his original works so much as by his editions of classical authors.

Only one figure is left which stands out among the Romantics, that of José Zorrilla (1817–1893). Two reasons prevented his taking the leadership : first, he was born ten years too late, so that, when he began to write, the primary enthusiasm for Romanticism had already passed : secondly, he was always more interested in the actual work of art than in the principles underlying it.   Coming into the full inheritance left by the earlier Romantics, he made free and brilliant use of his birthright.   His principal plays, *El Zapatero y el Rey* (1840) and *Don Juan Tenorio* (1844), have a sustained power remarkable in the work of so young a man.   Another side of his genius is shown in the captivating if superficial ' Oriental poem ' of *Granada* (1852), and a vast quantity of less distinguished work in all *genres* exemplifies the fertility of his invention.

While the foremost writers of the day were evincing such lukewarmness for the fortunes of Spanish Romanticism as a movement, the Classicists, few but industrious, were pursuing their way with unconcern, and others followed a middle path between those taken by the opposing parties.   The doctrine of the ' happy mean ' was openly eulogized by men as outstanding as Hartzenbusch, Gil y Zárate and the young author of some sensitively romantic poems and a good historical novel (*El Señor de Bembibre*, 1844), Enrique Gil y Carrasco (1815–1846).   Nothing is more characteristic of the so-called ' Romantic ' epoch than the revival of interest in the Unities (1839, ff.) and the re-emergence on the field of controversy of the ageing Lista.   Another sign of the times is the popularity of the Moratinian playwright, Manuel Bretón de los Herreros (1796–1873), and Ventura de la Vega (1807–1865), both of whom were touched by Romanticism but never converted to it.

The ' Back-to-Lope ' movement and the republication and imitation of the *romanceros* were making steady progress during these years, especially in Catalonia, where a revival of the Catalan language was taking place (see p. 182), and where mediaeval interests were therefore especially strong.   Here very markedly, and more gradually through the whole of Spain, was penetrating the powerful influence of Sir Walter Scott.   To name only a few writers, Ramón López Soler, José de Espronceda, Enrique Gil y Carrasco, José García de Villalta and Patricio de la Escosura all wrote novels which varied from being somewhat close imitations of Scott's manner to romances, professedly original, which plagiarized him unashamedly.   It is significant that while Hugo, Lamartine, Musset, Dumas, Scribe and half a score more of Frenchmen influenced Spanish literature, the influence of Scott surpassed them all, and proved to be more enduring even than that of Byron.

These are the main lines taken by the history of Spanish Romanticism. In addition to the writers already mentioned, there abound others who show individual traits commonly associated with Romanticism in other countries. Juan Arolas (1805–1849) and Gertrudis Gómez de Avellaneda (1814–1873) are religious sentimentalists,—Lamartinians in the main, though they have numerous other sources. Nicomedes Pastor Díaz (1811–1863) affects a resigned form of *desengaño* which becomes more poignant in Gaspar Núñez de Arce (1832–1903), author also of the patriotic *Gritos del Combate*. Local colour is the strong point of ' El Solitario ' (Serafín Estébanez Calderón, 1799–1867), and Ramón de Mesonero Romanos (1803–1882) specializes in essays on *costumbres*, not unlike Larra's, which have given him in later days a new importance to both the social and the literary historian.

None of these writers, however, has more than a secondary importance compared with the four chief figures of the Romantic revival and revolt—Larra, Rivas, Espronceda and Zorrilla. The revival has never entirely ceased, for scholarship has come to the aid of enthusiasm and restored mediaevalism and the Golden Age to places which they are unlikely to lose. The reaction against the revolt began as early as the eighteen-forties : it was a mild and hardly noticeable one, for the would-be revolutionaries, as we have seen, had never gained any real possession of the field. And it was directed against what was the weakest part of the Romantics' armour, their entire indifference to ideas. So completely were they satisfied by brilliance and picturesqueness that even the superficial philosophy of the epigrammatic verses of Ramón de Campoamor (1819–1901) passed for profound thinking : Campoamor, with his *Doloras*, *Pequeños poemas* and *Humoradas*, which are spread over a long literary career, may be said to have led the anti-Romantic reaction. Yet the uselessness of the historian's endeavouring to put order and form into a period of confusion is shown by the dominance at this very time of one of the purest Romantics of the nineteenth century, Gustavo Adolfo Bécquer (1836–1870), whose vividly descriptive tales are as appealing as his verses, are tinged like them with bitter *desengaño* and are full of deep sensibility.

VIII. The Literature of Modern Spain

From 1870 to 1936 the even current of Spanish literature was never interrupted, though the intellectual reaction in Spain to the political disasters of 1898 gave it a fresh impetus at a time when it showed signs of debility, and carried it on to new triumphs. In

spite of the discredit which came to the exotic Romanticism of
the early century, all that was best in it filtered into the literature
of the next era, and the works of every one of the greatest
Romantics made themselves felt on their principal successors.
made themselves felt on their principal successors.

In literary criticism and history this modern period is a
great one, and can show a formidable array of great names.
Few writers, if any, have done more for the Romantic revival
than the Catalan Manuel Milá y Fontanals (1814–1884), a professor of Barcelona University whose more famous pupil, Marce-
lino Menéndez y Pelayo (1856–1912), is Spain's greatest critic.
The latter's *Ciencia española* (1876), *Horacio en España* (1877),
Historia de los heterodoxos españoles (1880–1881) and *Historia
de las ideas estéticas en España* (1883–1891), represent, for all
their importance, but one side of an activity which included
miscellaneous critical essays, a study of Calderón, a monumental
edition of Lope de Vega, anthologies of Castilian and Spanish-
American poetry, and long and detailed if uncompleted histories
of early Spanish poetry and the origins of the Spanish novel.
And all these published works are hardly as extensive as the
projects which Menéndez y Pelayo had in mind when death came
prematurely to him. Beside such a man others can only be
named. Pascual de Gayangos and José Amador de los Ríos are
two great names of the past. More recent critics and historians
of outstanding merit have been Francisco Rodríguez Marín, Emilio
Cotarelo y Mori, Adolfo Bonilla y San Martín and Ramón Menéndez Pidal—all friends or pupils of Menéndez y Pelayo. During the
last few years, a former colleague of Menéndez Pidal, Américo
Castro and Dámaso Alonso, his pupil and successor at Madrid
University, have found their way into the front rank of literary
critics. Of the younger men, José María de Cossío and Guillermo
Díaz-Plaja give promise of distinction.

But it is for its creative force that the modern age of Spanish
literature is most rightly famous. In every *genre* have been
produced works of the very first class ; a certain inequality here
and there is compensated by unusual power ; the note of personal
excellence has made itself uniformly heard, and regionalism has
also had its triumphs. In almost every *genre* Spain's youthful
writers are equal in promise to any of the last three generations.
We must begin by remarking that the historical prose romance,
as modelled on Sir Walter Scott, possessed no real vitality, and
soon became little more than a curiosity. The native current
of Spanish fiction, so strong since the early Renaissance, seemed
to have dried up almost completely in the mid-seventeenth

century. It makes its reappearance, one may say, with *La Gaviota* (1849), the first and greatest *novela de costumbres* of 'Fernán Caballero' (1796–1877). Cecilia Böhl de Faber, to give this writer her maiden name (since she was three times married), was the daughter of the pre-Romantic polemist already mentioned, and partly German by origin. Far from being a Romantic, she leads a reaction against Romanticism by her adoption of a moderate realism in place of the extravagance of the past. (Cf. the preface to *La Gaviota*.) This, the first of her works, is a queer mixture of German sentiment and Andalusian local colour, showing striking gifts of description and characterization. It was acclaimed by Ochoa, and as it proved, correctly, as 'the *Waverley* of Spain . . . the dawn of a glorious day '.

Fernán Caballero continued to publish novels, but none of them, unless it was *La Familia de Albareda* (1856), equalled her first attempt. Nor was the path along which she led the way followed at first by any very notable writer : it was in the eighteen-seventies that the novel suddenly came to life. In 1874, Juan Valera (1824–1905), a mature critic and poet who in his youth had been in the diplomatic service under the Duque de Rivas, produced *Pepita Jiménez*, the first of four psychological novels which made him one of the classics of the nineteenth century. The idyllic story of the love affairs of Luis de Vargas, the young seminarist, and the charming Pepita is told with an excess of sometimes uninteresting digression, but with an insight into character, and an engaging style, which are equally the characteristics of Valera's later books, *Las Ilusiones del doctor Faustino* (1875), *El Comendador Mendoza* (1877), and *Doña Luz* (1879). He wrote for entertainment and not without pretensions to instruct. For all his knowledge of humanity, he is frankly idealistic : ' I will paint things,' he says, ' not as they are, but as more beautiful than they are, illumining them with a light that shall have the power of fascination.'

In the same year as *Pepita Jiménez* appeared the sparkling, humorous and revealing *Sombrero de tres picos* by Pedro Antonio de Alarcón (1833–1891), one of the inimitable masterpieces of Spanish realism, a book to be read by all. While Valera and Alarcón were still writing, a third great novelist, José María de Pereda (1833–1906), came on the scene, and began the long series of mainly regional stories which had been foreshadowed in his *Escenas montañesas* (1864–1871). Of these, the finest are perhaps *Pedro Sánchez* (1883), which deals mainly with life in Madrid, and *Sotileza* (1884), a vividly realistic tale of fisher-life in Pereda's native province of Santander. How great he is in description and characterization can best be realized by comparing him with Fernán Caballero. To his gifts Armando Palacio Valdés (1853–1938) adds a strong Asturian sense of humour, which commends him particularly to the sympathies of English readers. *Marta y María* (1883), *José* (1885) and *La Hermana San Sulpicio* (1889) are all charming tales, easily read and long remembered, distinguished for their vivid, rather than subtle characterization and their observant but kindly outlook upon contemporary life. For a short time, in *La Espuma* (1890) and *La Fe* (1892), Palacio Valdés migrated to a world of Gallic semi-naturalism, from which, however, he fortunately soon returned. True naturalism finds expression in two of the later novels of Emilia (Condesa de) Pardo Bazán (1851–1921), *Los Pazos de Ulloa* (1886) and *La Madre Naturaleza* (1887), where a Galician regionalism, represented more exclusively in some of her other works, combines with a highly developed prose style and some fiercely satirical studies of human character. A path entirely new in this century was carved out by Benito Pérez Galdós (1843–1920) in the series of novels known as *Episodios Nacionales*, which deal with some of the outstanding events in nineteenth-century Spanish history. The production of these spreads over more than thirty years : the closest parallel to them is to be found in the chronicle-plays of Shakespeare. While he was still engaged upon the *Episodios*, Pérez Galdós was also writing novels with a thesis, which have again achieved topicality and governmental disfavour. Somewhat later came the ' novelas contemporáneas ', a series of penetrating and broad studies of Spanish society, of which one, *Fortunata y Jacinta*, is considered by many to be the greatest novel of the century. Some titles are *Doña Perfecta* (1876), *Gloria* (1877), *El amigo Manso* (1882), *Marianela* (1878), *Misericordia* (1897). Other outstanding works are: *Tormento* (1884), *La desheredada* (1881), *Miau* (1888), *Angel Guerra* (1890–1891), and the searching delineation of avarice in the *Torquemada* series (1889–1895). No Spanish author since Cervantes, and few in other countries have described a contemporary society with such a wealth of observed detail, such inexhaustible creative power. The idiosyncrasies, prejudices and virtues of mankind are described with a rich understanding of human frailty which can only be compared with the fullness of Shakespeare, Cervantes and Tolstoi. So that though there can be no doubt in the reader's (or censor's) mind of the Liberal, anti-clerical, anti-authoritarian, progressive intention of the novelist, the fiction absorbs the tract, and this is so even in the later works (novels and plays), in which characters lose some flesh and blood and assume the insubstantiality, not of the earlier thesis caricatures, but of symbols of ideas or types. Galdós' style has been unfavourably criticised. But the ample sentences, the abundant vocabulary, especially of technical and popular words, and the richly varied and frequent dialogues carry the story and the reader along with an almost irresistible power.

High claims are justly made for *La Regenta* (1885), a less equable study of the social and religious milieux of Oviedo, by Leopoldo Alas (1852–1901), who under the pseudonym of Clarín became the most feared and outspoken literary critic of the day, through his articles in ' El Imparcial ', published separately as *Paliques*. The very considerable ' costumbrista ' elements of the story—including magnificent descriptions of the Casino of Vetusta (Oviedo)—serve only as significant background to an epic struggle for the soul (and the person is very desirable too) of la Regenta, an aristocratic married lady, which is waged on many planes between the Magistral of the Cathedral, Don Fermín de Pas, and the provincial Don Juan, Alvaro Mesía. Clarín wrote also some fine short stories. Lesser figures are those of Amós de Escalante, who casts into fiction form his pen pictures of La Montaña in *Ave Maris Stella* ; P. Luis Coloma (1851–1915) who achieved a ' succès de scandale ' with his satire of high Madrid society *Pequeñeces* (1890) ; and the ' erotic ' novelists—including Alberto Insúa, S. González Anaya and Felipe Trigo (1865–1916)—of whom this last goes far to redeem the accusation of pornography by his notable gifts of observation, irony and sincerity in works such as *El médico rural*. J. O. Picón is a stylist with leanings to fiction rather than a novelist ; the best of his work is perhaps *Dulce y sabrosa* (1891).

Regionalism and character-study continued to be the main interest of the next generation of novelists, who exploit their regions for their peculiar characteristics of language, temperament and scenery, among which they do not avoid scenes of physical violence or situations of powerful dramatic intensity. Blasco Ibáñez (1867–1928) has paid heavily for his enormous success as Spain's first cosmopolitan and Hollywood novelist, with works such as *Los cuatro jinetes del Apocalipsis* (1916). But we must not forget the powerful simplicity and vigorous realism of the Valencian novels, *Flor de Mayo* (1895), *La Barraca* (1898)—a masterpiece of dramatic intensity—*Cañas y Barro* (1902), nor the thesis novels, such as *La Horda* (1905).

Pío Baroja (b. 1872) makes play, as Blasco Ibáñez does, with his carelessness of style. It is part of his general attitude of disdain for elegance, art and the formal proprieties—whether literary or social. He will not analyse a situation, or describe an incident fully, but carries his narration along at a fast pace. But in his own abrupt way he is an equally powerful and dramatic chronicler of the ways of Basque scenery and types. He has written a great deal—including in recent years several volumes of *Memorias*— and almost all of it can be read with pleasure, as it was written with gusto and impatience. He is a natural storyteller, whose work overflows very often into trilogies, *El Pasado*, *La vida fantástica*, *El Mar*, *Las ciudades*, *La raza*, of which last, one, *La ciudad de la niebla* (1909) offers a very Basque view of London. A longer series, the *Memorias de un hombre de acción*, unfold the career of a nineteenth-century conspirator Eugenio de Aviraneta (whose real memoirs were discovered and published in 1952). Fine examples of his work are *Camino de perfección*, *El Mayorazgo de Labraz*, *El árbol de la ciencia*, *César o nada*, *Juventud*, *Egolatría*. All these books are vivid, intense and earnest ; they present their author as radical and social reformer, but by no means as such alone. His flashes of description and his gaunt, keen plots are not easily forgotten. He is perhaps less honoured in his own country than in many others.

Galicia has cradled two other novelists, who could not be more different from the Condesa de Pardo Bazán, than they are from each other, though in all three the region finds characteristic expression. Don Ramón María del Valle-Inclán (1869–1935) is above all a poet, a creator, if not of any but his own truth, of haunting beauty ; a weaver of fantasies in which the intricate skeins of brutality, violence, sensuality and pagan adoration of beauty are threaded with the refined artifice of a Renaissance craftsman. The autobiographical emotion, personified in the Marqués de Bradomín, adds drama to the four *Sonatas*, *de Primavera*, *de Estío*, *de Otoño*, *de Invierno* (1902–1905), and to *Flor de Santidad* (1905), and is ever present in all his work, whether novels, *La Corte de los Milagros* (1927), *Tirano Banderas* (1926), the story of a Mexican bandit ; historical narrations, *La guerra carlista* and *El ruedo ibérico* (1928), or powerful plays *Voces de gesta y Romance de lobos* (1908), *La pipa de Kif* (1919), *Cara de Plata* (1923), and poetry. In these works the real and the imagined, the factual and the mysterious, the beautiful and the common, the Galician and the mythical are fused. From a basic realism of scene, character and incident, a powerfully controlled imagination and fancy has, as in a minor key in the ' leyendas ' of Bécquer, created an enchanted world of the senses. W. Fernández Flórez (b. 1885?), the only professional humorist admitted to the Real Academia (in 1934), is known by *Volvoreta* (1917), *Las siete columnas* (1926), *El hombre que compró un automóvil*, *El bosque animado.* Of wider fame but less repute is the work of his fellow Galician humorist Julio Camba (b. 1882).

R. Pérez de Ayala (b. 1881), a thoughtful and distinguished writer, has dropped completely out of the literary world. Yet he is a poet and an artist in words in whom humour wells up refreshingly and character interest asserts itself invitingly as well as forcefully. His early novel, *A.M.D.G.* (1910), is a satire on Jesuit education, *Tigre Juan* (1926), has been widely translated and other notable works are *Luna de miel, Luna de hiel* (1923), *Los trabajos de Urbano y Simona*. But his best known novel, long out of print, is *Belarmino y Apolonio* (1921), which recounts the sayings of two philosophic cobblers, whom the author remembered from his student days in Oviedo. Also from the north are Ricardo León (1877–1943), whose sonorous, archaic style is not to present-day taste, though his ' guía espiritual ' to Santillana del Mar, *Casta de Hidalgos* (1908), is honoured as a classic ; Concha Espina (b. 1877), has not maintained the fame of *La Esfinge Maragata* (1915), while *La casa de la Troya* (1915), of A. Pérez Lugín, a story of student life in Santiago de Compostela, still finds many readers. Other novelists are A. Martínez Olmedilla, Pedro Mata and Alfonso Danvila.

A fastidious artist who never sought popularity is Gabriel Miró (1879–1930), in whose works the temperament, and natural setting of the Spanish Levante—to which the Holy Land is felt to share a family resemblance—is ardently re-created and defined. Though scenes of dramatic, and even brutal realism are not infrequent, together with others of the purest ' costumbrismo ', Miró is most characteristic in his efforts to recapture the timeless gradations of movement, light and shade in the natural settings against which the fictional elements develop. Through the meditations and sayings of Sigüenza—how different an *alter ego* from the Marqués de Bradomín—a more direct expression is found for comment on the contemporary scene. In such works as *Figuras de la Pasión del Señor* (1916), *Libro de Sigüenza* (1917), *Nuestro Padre San Daniel* (1921) and *El Obispo Leproso* (1926), Miró reveals an exquisite sensitivity, a unique love of nature and a wonderful gift of giving form to the evanescent and the impalpable.

A fine novelist of the Republic, Ramón J. Sender (b. 1901), specifically with *Mr. Witt en el Cantón* (1935), has not been well noticed later, a fate shared also by Benjamín Jarnés (1888–1950), and the essayist and critic José Bergamín (b. 1897). One of the most prodigious, ingenious and celebrated writers of prose of this period is Ramón Gómez de la Serna (b. 1891), the inventor of the ' greguería ', of which an example is ' Las gaviotas nacieron de los

pañuelos que dicen adiós en los puertos '. The first appeared in
1910, many collections have since been published. Using the
same technique of the abrupt, intuitive, pregnant phrase, which
endows everything he describes with a vivid animation which just
falls short of true life, he has written biographies of his famous
' tertulia ' in Pombo (1918), of the Madrid *Rastro* (1915), of
Azorín, Valle-Inclán and others, which possess the dramatic
verisimilitude of an eye-witness report. His more specific autobiography is *Automoribundia* (1948). Among his many works of
fiction, which are notable for scenes rather than for characters or
plots, may be mentioned: *El torero Caracho* (1926), *Seis falsas
novelas* (1927),—a very exciting display of virtuosity—and *La
Nardo* (1930).

Since the Civil War, and stimulated by a vigorous publishing
policy which has created a reading public able to absorb in three
or four years, editions totalling twenty to thirty thousand copies,
the novel has flourished. Some of the most successful are: *Nada*
(1944), of Carmen Laforet, now in its eighth edition ; E. Ledesma
Miranda, *La casa de la fama* (1952) ; Elena Quiroga, *Viento del
norte* (1951) ; J. A. Giménez Arnau, *De pantalón largo* ; R.
Sánchez Mazas, *La vida nueva de Pedrito de Andía.* Contemporary
Spain—Republic, Civil War, government of General Franco—is
to be the subject of the trilogy of J. M. Gironella, of which the
first volume, *Los cipreses creen en Dios* (1953), was very widely
praised. The outstanding figures are J. A. de Zunzunegui (b. 1901),
and C. J. Cela (b. 1915). Both take their subjects from the contemporary scene which is described with a powerful, often bitterly
humorous, realism and a wide command of the resources of the
language. Cela experiments with a new technique in each succeeding novel, from the picaresque of *La familia de Pascual Duarte*
1942 (the most read and translated novel of the period) to the
epistolary *Mrs. Caldwell habla con su hijo* (1953). Other works are :
Pabellón de reposo (1943), and *Nuevas andanzas . . . de Lazarillo de
Tormes* (1944). The tangled lives of the denizens of Madrid are
recorded in *La Colmena* (1951) (English translation 1953). His
travelogues about Spain (*Viaje a la Alcarria,* etc.) are highly
regarded. Less varied technically and more relentless in his
depiction of the demoralised post-war society, Zunzunegui is
apparently writing a new series of ' episodios nacionales ' : *El
barco de la muerte* (1945), *La quiebra* (1947), *Esta oscura desbandada*
(1952), *El mundo es así* (1954). It is not a pleasant world he
describes with such power : honour, virtue and constancy are
rarely found in it except in the hearts of some women characters
who are magnificently portrayed. His short stories reveal

unexpected gifts of fantasy, humour and penetration in anecdotes of his native Bilbao : *Cuentos y patrañas de mi Ría* (3 series), *El Binomio de Newton y otros cuentos.*

Spanish drama in the later nineteenth century begins with Manuel Tamayo y Baus (1828–1898), who, in addition to didactic social comedy and Classical tragedy has a fine historical drama, *La Ricahembra* (1854), and perhaps the finest play of the century, in which Shakespeare and Yorick are characters, *Un drama nuevo* (1867). His contemporary, José Echegaray (1832–1916), mathematician, statesman and Nobel prizeman (1905), is now notorious for the exaggerated sensationalism of his Romantic dramas, for his awareness of foreign theatres, particularly of Ibsen, and the violence with which he resolves problems of conscience or conduct, as in *O locura o santidad* (1877), and *El gran Galeoto* (1881). Social injustices, prejudices or conflicts, were dramatised by Joaquín Dicenta who wrote the first ' working-class ' play in Spain with *Juan José* (1895), and by Pérez Galdós, who came to feel that the theatre was a more potent means of revealing society to itself than prose fiction : among the best are *El abuelo* (1904), and *Electra* (1901).

The first contemporary dramatist is Jacinto Benavente (1866–1954), who has written some hundred and eighty plays since the first, *El nido ajeno*, in 1894. His plays require ' a highly educated audience such as (can) appreciate a theatre of ideas, understand philosophical dialogue, rejoice in ingenious and penetrating remarks, answer to suggestion, prefer irony to declamation, seize comical touches presented with the most innocent air and immediately grasp the subtlest allusions '. Taking his characters from the upper and middle classes, which have provided his most regular audiences, he has delighted and disturbed them with skilfully constructed and brilliantly written studies of their foibles both grave and gay. Fine actresses assured the success of many plays in which a woman and love formed the theme : *Rosas de otoño* (1905), *Señora ama* (1905), *La malquerida* (1913), *Cuando los hijos de Eva no son los de Adán* (1931), *La melodía del jazz-band* (1931). Plays about his faithful audience are *Por las nubes* (1909), *La comida de las fieras* (1898), *La Gobernadora* (1901), *Lo cursi* (1901). Since he is more interested in ideas than in people, the characters often acquire symbolic value, as in three of his more disturbing works, *La noche del sábado* (1903), *Alma triunfante* (1902), and the most famous of all, *Los intereses creados* (1909), a skilful pilloring of society's faith in ' appearances '. He has some delightful children's plays. In 1922 he was awarded the Nobel Prize, a fitting acknowledgement of the cosmopolitanism of a

Spanish author who rarely reminds one of his national theatre or predecessors. He continued, almost to the day of his death, to have plays produced. (*Titania, La infanzona, Abdicación.*)

The works of Gregorio Martínez Sierra (1881–1948), possess an unusual delicacy and charm, and such a remarkable command of the art of drawing women characters, that the active collaboration of his wife has been presupposed. Some of his titles are : *El reino de Dios* (1915), *Canción de cuna* (1911)—a favourite with amateur dramatic societies, *Sueño de una noche de agosto* (1918)—translated as *The Romantic Young Lady.*

Serafín (1871–1938) and Joaquín (1873–1944), Álvarez Quintero are pre-eminent in delicacy, grace and wit. Without ever probing into life very deeply, they have given us picture after picture of Andalusia. Their dialogue is marvellous for its tunefulness, shimmer and vitality. They continually blend irony and farce with pure comedy and poetry in prose. Their production is enormous : *El patio* (1900), *La dicha ajena* (1902), *La mala sombra* (1906), *Doña Clarines* (1908), *Malvaloca* (1912), *Puebla de mujeres* (1912), *Don Juan buena persona* (1918), *Las de Abel* (1926), *La cuestión es pasar el tato* (1927), *Olvidadiza* (1943). Many of their works are brief sketches or scenes taken from popular life, a form of play now called the ' género chico ', which is old in Spanish literature and has seen a most brilliant revival in the hands of the Quintero brothers, their Madrid equivalent, Carlos Arniches (1866–1943)—*El puñao de rosas* (1902), *El amigo Melquiades* (1914), brilliant snapshots of ' popular ' life—and in others such as José López Silva, E. García Alvárez. Combined with the music of Tomas Bretón (see p. 244), R. Chapí and others, they gave flavour to the *zarzuela.*

Other dramatists of the early decades of the century, who have fallen completely out of favour, after enjoying a large mead of it, are Manuel Linares Rivas (1867–1938), of whom are *El abolengo* (1904), and *La garra* (1914); the Galician Rey Soto, and the Granadine Francisco de Villaespesa (1877–1936), who in addition to plays, *El Alcázar de las Perlas* (1911), wrote short stories, and some of the earliest examples of ' modernismo ' in poetry.

Poetical drama has achieved new distinction and gained very great popularity in the works of Eduardo Marquina (1879–1946), Federico García Lorca (1899–1936), and José María Pemán (b. 1898). Marquina is a true lyric poet who outgrew his earlier narrative manner. His poems of love, in their passion and sheer beauty, recall Garcilaso de la Vega and St. John of the Cross. He gave dramatic form to his profound belief in the traditional virtues of his race in *Las hijas del Cid* (1908), *En Flandes se ha puesto el sol* (1910), *La Dorotea* (1935), *Teresa de Jesús* (1933), *El estudiante endiablada* (1942). With similar convictions, finely expressed in the poem ' La elegía a la tradición española ', and great dramatic skill, Pemán has defended the Nationalist tenets—not always to the satisfaction of his correligionaries—in tensely constructed plays of great poetic power : *El Divino Impaciente* (1933), *Cuando las cortes de Cádiz . . .* (1934), *La Santa Virreina* (1939), *Noche de Levante en calma* (1941), *En las manos del hijo* (1953). He has translated and transformed plays of Shakespeare and the Greeks, has some very fine essays and is celebrated as an orator.

No writer of contemporary Spain has aroused such passionate interest, at first in his own country and later throughout the world, as Federico García Lorca, whose unforgiven death in the first months of the Civil War has crowned his fame with a martyr's halo. Poet, painter, musician, dramatist, companion, he was almost as oppressed by the richness of his own gifts as he was mortified and overwhelmed by the interpretation given to his works by many of his most ardent admirers : a political interpretation, which he decried, was the ultimate cause of his death. The folk-loric elements of anecdote, type and customs which had served the nineteenth century for so much picturesque description are sublimated by the ardent imagination of Lorca to the status of a racial myth in which the figure of the gypsy in *El Romancero Gitano*, 1928, becomes the symbol of the implacable conflicts within the Hispanic soul of love and hate, loyalty and authority, life and death, survival and destruction. The traditional forms of poetry are similarly subjected to re-creation by the poet of the outstanding surrealist poem in Spanish, *El poeta en Nueva York* (1940). He is at once the most modern and the most traditional of contemporary poets. But whatever the esoteric complexities of language and imagery which the poet of ' vanguardia ' invents, his verses do not for long lose their fundamental qualities of musicality, colour and drama. They are eminently recitable, and it is through recitation, by the author and thousands of others, that many have achieved the distinction of the medieval ' juglar ', of becoming anonymous in an age of print. Lorca in fact resisted publication, and successive volumes garner poems written over several years : *Libro de poemas* (1921), *El poema de cante jondo* (1931). Contrast and conflict coexist with Lorca. When, as he matured, he turned to the writing of plays, he brought to the stage the same combination of traditional anecdote and ultramodern technique, and the same preoccupation with Andalusian and human problems of violent unsatisfaction and primitive impulses. Marriage, as the legendary means of satisfying particularly the call of maternity, is the theme of *Bodas de Sangre* (1933), *Yerma* (1935), *La casa de Bernarda Alba* (1945)—intense tragedies—, of the delicious comedy *La zapatera prodigiosa* (1930), and of the sad history of *Doña Rosita la soltera o el lenguaje de las flores* (1935). In all of them, as in most of Lorca's works, the tension is relieved and accentuated by snatches of pure folklore or lyrical emotion, which spring unbidden, though not uncontrolled, from the rich subsoil of Lorca's marvellous childhood and the Andalusian earth he loved so well.

In lyric poetry both the Classical and Romantic traditions persisted, despite a heightened consciousness of the serious mission of poetry, social and even political, which led in the works of Ramón de Campoamor (1819–1901), and Gaspar Núñez de Arce (1832–1903), to a great development of narrative and philosophic verse. A violent reaction away from such usefulness towards an expression of emotions, impressions and individual ideas of which the ultimate criterion was technical beauty and aesthetic enjoyment, was initiated by Rubén Darío (1867–1916), a Nicaraguan cosmopolitan, whose work revolutionised poetry in Spanish wherever it was written. In his works, which include *Azul* (1888), *Prosas profanas* (1896), *Cantos de vida y esperanza* (1905), *El canto errante* (1907), the poet becomes the master of a strange world of exotic beauty which his own imagination has re-created after the image of paradise, an existence related vaguely to the Orient, the court of Versailles, or some primitive culture. An equal revolution has been effected in the language and form of poetry : vocabulary, rhythms, measures, have been enriched, enlarged, re-created by an adventurous and masterful genius. A poet whose concentration on a region of Spain, Extremadura, removed him from this powerful change was José María Gabriel y Galán (1870–1905). But although not all contemporaries subscribed to the new ' gay trinar ', no other could ignore its very great technical innovations (this is a period of great artistry in verse, represented particularly by an abundance of sonnets), nor escape the obligation to discover the perfect expression of his own individual gifts and vision. The term ' modernism ' is applied to that poetry written and influenced by Rubén Darío, in which aesthetic considerations, the beauty of form, sound and imagery predominate, which, generally speaking, appeared during the ten years following *Prosas profanas* ; and ' postmodernism ' to the more intimate, concentrated and distilled poetry which Juan Ramón Jiménez began to write in his first works : *Rimas* (1902), and *Arias tristes* (1903). A more broadly human note is struck by the many poets who found their inspiration in the earthy timelessness of landscape and custom, or in its relation with the contemporary ' tema español '. Characteristic of the intimacy of these elements, and their separation, is the work of the brothers Machado, Manuel (1874-1947) and Antonio (1875-1939), sons of a distinguished Andalusian folklorist. Manuel is a craftsman to the finger-tips, a Sevillian artist who knows the secret of making sound echo sense in vowel play, rhyme and assonance, and whose choice of metres is so varied and sure that he can convey almost any effect (or so it seems) independently of language. He excels at creating in a few brief lines a portrait of indelible brilliance. Antonio on the other hand, during a long residence in Soria, as schoolmaster, responded to the natural setting and the slow music of humanity which he heard echoing over the barren uplands of Castile, and in *Campos de Castilla* (1912) wrote some of the most powerful lines in Spanish poetry. He had earlier explored the intricacies of his soul—in a moment of modernism—in *Soledades, galerías y otros poemas* (1903). In later prose works and poems, especially in some fine ' elogios ', e.g. to Don Francisco Giner de los Ríos, he revealed a preoccupation with the state of Spain which made him kin with the '98 generation. He was the only poet in verse of this group, and his influence seems as potent on his successors as any of theirs. He is one of the great poets of Spain.

A less profound, but equally true poet of Castile is Enrique de Mesa (1878-1929), in *Cancionero castellano* (1911), and *El silencio de la Cartuja* (1916). Cultured poetry of charming simplicity was written by one of the acutest critics of the period, Enrique Díez Canedo (1879-1944), in *Versos de las horas* (1906), and *La visita del Sol* (1907).

The most distinguished Spanish poet of modernism and the one to whom all later poetry and poets are most deeply indebted for inspiration and example is Juan Ramón Jiménez (b. 1881). With a constancy and dedication rarely permitted by mundane circumstance and human discursiveness, he has devoted his whole life to poetry—to his own poetry, to his Obra: ' Yo tengo escondida en mi casa, por su gusto y el mío, a la Poesía. Y nuestra relación es la de los apasionados ' (J.R.J.). Gifted with an extraordinary sensitivity, an innate taste for simplicity, J.R.J. has striven with undying devotion to give form to his ' Poesía '. At first there was a certain monotony of form and subject—too many evening gardens—in *Arias tristes* (1903), *Jardines lejanos* (1904), and others, though the emotion was sincere and the verse simple. Then at first through added richness and later, and more characteristically, through increasing renunciation of the outward shows of poetry, including rhyme and regularity of line or stanza, the poet isolated

' la poesía de la poesía ' : *Elegías puras* (1908), *Laberinto* (1913), *Sonetos espirituales* (1917), *Eternidades* (1918), *Belleza* (1923), *Diario de un poeta recien casado* (1917), *Antolojía segunda poética* (1922), *Canción* (1936), *La estación total* (1946). In some of the later works, and especially in *Animal de fondo* (1949), a deeper note of triumph has sounded as the poet discovers in the spirit he has been pursuing for almost sixty years a divinity which is harmony and peace. The prose story of *Platero y yo* (1914), recalling incidents of his childhood in Moguer, reminds us of the essentially Andalusian nature of Juan Ramón Jiménez's genius.

Much of the finest poetry written since 1920 is the work of scholars and teachers of literature : Pedro Salinas (1892–1951), Jorge Guillén (b. 1893), Dámaso Alonso (b. 1898), Gerardo Diego (b. 1896). It can be studied in the indispensable anthology of the last named, *Poesía española Antología 1915–1931* (1932), in which the poems are preceded by a photograph, a brief ' Vida ' and a ' Poética ' written by each author in turn. Generations of students have responded to the rich humanity and inspiring teaching of Pedro Salinas and to his stimulating critical studies on *Literatura Siglo XX*, *Gómez Manrique*, etc. Five works published between 1923 and 1936 are gathered in *Poesía junta* (1942), in which the ' aventura hacía lo absoluto ' is pursued with fancy, wit and hopefulness. As dedicated to poetry as J. R. Jiménez, in over thirty years of academic life, J. Guillén has published very little in prose, while his verse has steadily constructed a single volume *Cántico* (1950)—of which three partial editions appeared in 1928, 1936, 1945. Most of a life's work within one volume signifies not poverty of inspiration but the reticence of an exquisite spirit which submits its finest emotions in secret to the unyielding discipline of the mind and taste. Everything which is not poetry is eliminated, and though what remains has been charged with obscurity, to the poet it is ' poesía simple ' (he rejects the term ' poesía pura '). Dámaso Alonso, the outstanding literary scholar of contemporary Spain and interpreter of the whole range of Spanish poetry (*La lengua poética de Góngora* (1935), *Ensayos sobre poesía española* (1944), *Poetas españoles contemporáneos* (1952)) has written also agile, disturbing poems in *Oscura noticia* (1944), *Hijos de la ira*, *Diario íntimo* (1944).

The remarkable contribution of Andalusia to contemporary poetry in Spain has recently been emphasised by the *Antología de poetas andaluces contemporáneos* (1953), edited by J. L. Cano. He is likewise editor of the fine Colección Adonais of new poetry, which in 1954 reached its hundredth volume, an anthology with bio-bibliographical notes. R. Alberti (b. 1902), García Lorca's companion in surrealism, later ventured into political poetry and recently (*Retornos de lo vivo lejano*, 1952) recalls these early days without bitterness. He is an Andalusian of the sea-coast : *Marinero en tierra* (1925), *Sobre los ángeles* (1929), *Pleamar* (1944). Luis Cernuda (b. 1902), is the solitary Sevillian, whose long residence in England and the U.S. seems, from *Como quien espera el alba* (1947), only to have hardened his delicate rejection of the ties of the world. From his first volumes *Perfil del aire* (1927), *La realidad y el deseo* (1936), he handled his verse forms with the ease of a virtuoso who did not readily allow passion to disrupt formal beauty. *Ocnos* (1942) is a fragment of autobiography in prose. Perhaps the most respected living poet in Spain is Vicente Aleixandre (b. 1900), as fastidious and choice a spirit as Cernuda, but of greater power and range, of both emotion and imagery, and much more intimately, and hopefully, disturbed by the inadequacies of our mortal span. Intellect and emotion are violently fused in imagery of great formal beauty which is becoming increasingly personal and universal : *Ambito* (1929), *Espadas como labios* (1932), *La destrucción o el amor* (1935), *Sombra del paraíso* (1944), *Nacimiento último* (1953), *Historia del corazón* (1954). Other distinguished poets of today are Luis Rosales whose volume *Abril* (1935) marks a change of emphasis ; Luis Felipe Vivanco (b. 1907), Miguel Hernández (1910–1942), whose *Obra escogida* was published in 1952 ; Dionisio Ridruejo (b. 1912) ; Rafael Morales (b. 1919) ; José García Nieto (b. 1914). In their slim volumes and ephemeral reviews the post-war poetry of Spain can be admired for its high general level of technical excellence, its serious artistic purpose, reflected in an admiration for Classical poets which has moved, since 1927, from Góngora to Garcilaso and to Fray Luis de León, and for its preoccupation—as widespread as the response to a superior decree—with the mystery of man's existence on earth.

Parallel with the poets of ' modernismo ', a group of writers of prose, which would include Azorín, J. Benavente, M. de Unamuno, J. M. del Valle-Inclán, Ramiro de Maeztu, Pío Baroja, Manuel Bueno (with whom should be included A. Machado), have been called the ' generation of 1898 ', because that historical disaster (see p. 86), stimulated in them a critical reappraisal of the nature, origins, characteristics and future development of their ' patria ', which thus rudely had had destroyed the façade of imperial glory and arranged government which was masking the parlous state of its vital forces. Cadalso, Larra and Galdós had begun to probe beneath the show : Unamuno declared that to be born a Spaniard was to be born a problem. From many regions of Spain these men converged on the Castile described by Antonio Machado :

Castilla miserable, ayer dominadora,
envuelta en sus andrajos desprecia cuanto ignora.

In widely differing ways, as the range of investigation required, they wrote about literature, history, ethnography, ' paisaje ', patriotism, nationality ; they controverted the claims of isolation and ' Europeanization ', of the inspiration and durance vile of tradition, of centralism and regional autonomies, and ultimately, though the group owed little initially to purely religious or political stimuli, of Church and State in education and of Republic or Monarchy in government. Their method was analytical, their aspiration to isolate, describe and revitalise those elements of national life which could be found still valid for the needs of the twentieth century. They read widely, wrote and spoke abundantly and with passion on subjects of which they rarely possessed professional knowledge. The chosen form of expression was the essay, which in their hands acquired a dignity, beauty and variety hitherto unknown in Spanish literature. Prose developed qualities which traditionally belonged to poetry, the gift of representing the truth and beauty of a personality through the use of every known device of rhetoric.

The Granadine Angel Ganivet (1865–1898), correspondent of Unamuno, anticipated and has since constantly stimulated the critical approach with his essay *Idearium español* (1896), (English translation, London 1946). Of less interest are his novels *La conquista del Reino de Maya* and *Los trabajos del infatigable Pío Cid*, 1898. The title of a first novel, *Paz en la guerra* (1897), is as highly symbolical of Miguel de Unamuno's life (1864–1936),—a passionate struggle, ' agonía ', to forge a personality which should withstand the reagents of this world, and the next—, as it has been of all later appreciation of his total production. He was the most controversial figure of his generation by the pungent egocentricity of his patriotism and opinions, and continues to be so, particularly, for his equally passionate and unorthodox views on religious beliefs and practices. A Basque by birth, a Salamancan by adoption, by training a Professor of Greek, a poet by temperament, a Liberal and anti-clerical by conviction, and a philosopher by innermost necessity. *En torno al casticismo* (1902), is one of the many essays (eight volumes were published 1916–1919—many are now being reprinted for the first time by Professor M. García Blanco of Salamanca), which most vigorously characterise an epoch and a personality. The same personality is reflected in endless opinions upon literature in Europe and the two Americas : a very original work is *Vida de Don Quijote y Sancho* (1905). In

Del sentimiento trágico de la vida (1913), and *La agonía del Cristianismo* (1931), Unamuno gave expression to philosophico-religious ideas and emotions which were fundamental to his whole existence. The characteristic urge to uncover the root, cause or form, of a word, idea or belief—endlessly the source of semi-scientific newspaper articles, in fiction (*Niebla*—subtitled ' nivola ' —(1914) ; *Abel Sánchez* (1917), *Tres novelas ejemplares* (1920)), resulted in conflicts of emotions and aspirations which were deprived of the usual fictional covering of description and narration ; in drama (*Sombras de sueño*, (1930), *El otro* (1932)), in similar conflicts which audiences have found it difficult to applaud. His poetry, of which much is only now being published, has made a deep impression : *Antología poética* (1942). Such a great and simple personality is not often seen.

Quite different is José Martínez Ruiz (b. 1876)—for whom the pseudonym ' Azorín ' masquerades even in the Madrid Telephone Directory—whose whole life has been devoted to the reading and writing of literature. In some fifty volumes, mainly of un-emphatic, unhurried essays, he has done more than any con-temporary to reveal the beauties and the traditional values of Spanish literature and custom, which often enough he has dis-covered in the secluded garden, the decaying village, the for-gotten author or work. He is not a ' costumbrista ', but rather the extraordinarily sensitive ' catador ' of the flavour of the past, whose moments of discovery and pleasure are re-created with the emotion and the exquisite language of the poet. Readers in all countries have been enlightened and charmed by him : *El alma castellana* (1900), *Lecturas españolas* (1912), *Clásicos y modernos* (1913), *Al margen de los clásicos* (1915), *Una hora de España* (1924), *Superrealismo* (1929), *Españoles en París* (1939), *El escritor* (1941), *Sintiendo a España* (1942), *Memorias inmemoriales* (1946), *Con permiso de los cervantistas* (1948).

To an extraordinary extent this generation has revealed itself, both as individuals and collectively, in autobiographical writing, and three works of Azorín, *La voluntad* (1902), *Antonio Azorín* (1903), *Las confesiones de un pequeño filósofo* (1904), are not the least valuable of them. (Of great interest are the *Recuerdos de mi vida* (1901, 1917) of S. Ramón y Cajal.) Unlike almost all his com-panions in the group, Azorín has published no poetry in verse. But the unemphatic, fragmentary rhythms of his prose, the detailed precision of his descriptions and nomenclature, the subtle suggestiveness of his impressions and his omissions have gone far to effect a revolution in all Spanish writing.

Of the two professional philosophers who closely followed the generation of 1898, Eugenio D'Ors (1882–1954), has enjoyed the respect of a select audience for his ' glosas '. But the ideas and the literary style of José Ortega y Gasset (1883–1955) have profoundly influenced the entire intellectual growth of Spain, through the fanatical interest, usually favourable, which they aroused in generations of students. In *España invertebrada* (1922) the pessimism of the 1898 generation is justified on historical grounds ; in *El tema de nuestro tiempo* (1931), he develops his theories of ' vitalismo ' and of the need of the intellect to serve life. In works such as *Meditaciones sobre el Quijote* (1914), *La deshumanización del arte* (1925), *La rebelión de las masas* (1930), he develops points of view which became those of many of his contemporaries who held positions of influence. Many of his essays, collected in part in the series of *El Espectador* (1916–1929), have had the effect of tracts for the times ; a service to Spain which he multiplied a thousandfold through the ' Revista de Occidente ' (1923 onwards) and the many editions of notable works—especially of German thought—sponsored by it, under his guidance. Not all his readers have been convinced of the soundness of the historical and psychological premises of his brilliantly composed works ; but no one can deny that he has been one of the major formative influences of contemporary Spain.

Other essayists and scholars whose works are read with the very greatest interest by different readers are Gregorio Marañón (b. 1887), famous doctor and member of many Academies of literary and historical studies ; Salvador de Madariaga (b. 1886), professor, diplomat, historian and multiple critic of literature ; P. Laín Entralgo (b. 1908), Rector of the University of Madrid and historian of *La generación del noventa y ocho* (1945) ; José Manuel Blecua, scholarly editor of texts.

Since the days of Rubén Darío, the literary and cultural relations between Spain and the Hispanic-American countries have grown increasingly close and influential—in both directions. Travel between the countries has been stimulated by political exile, business relations, scholarships and the activities of the Instituto de Cultura Hispánica, Madrid. Important Spanish publishers, established in the Americas, have enormously increased the printing of all Hispanic literatures, both contemporary and Classical. So that a full consideration of Spanish literature would necessarily include ample reference to the Americas, as Professor Federico de Onís has proved in his monumental *Antología de la poesía española e hispano-americana* (1934).

Something similar is happening, within the last twenty years, in the relations between Castilian and Catalan. The publication

by a Barcelona newspaper, *El Vapor*, of Aribau's fervidly nationalist ' Oda a la patria ' (1833) is considered as the decisive event in
the renaissance of the Catalan language. Among the foremost
modern poets writing in Catalan (their number is increasing) who
are at least the equal of their Castilian contemporaries, mention
may be made of Jacinto Verdaguer (1845–1902), Angel Guimerà
(1847–1924), Miguel Costa i Llobera (1854–1922), Joan Maragall
(1860–1911), Joan Alcover (1854–1926), and Gabriel Alomar
(1873–1941). These were matched by scholars of great distinction
without whose contribution to history and literary criticism the
Spanish nineteenth century would be inestimably poorer. Their
distinction has been maintained by later generations, among whom
can be mentioned the scholar poet Carles Riba (b. 1893), Josep
María de Sagarra (b. 1894), Pere Bohigas, Josep Pla (b. 1895), and
a host of new writers of novels and poetry who are achieving
recognition—and often translation—in the rest of the peninsula.

BIBLIOGRAPHY TO CHAPTERS IV AND V

The task of indicating works for the study of Spanish literature is made
easier than it would otherwise be by the publication of the following
excellent little book :

68. Fitzmaurice-Kelly, J. *Spanish Bibliography*. Oxford, 1925.

This includes practically everything that the general reader is likely
to require published earlier than 1925. It may best be supplemented,
for later works, by the quarterly bibliographies of new publications which
appear in the *Revista de Filología española* and the *Nueva Revista de
Filología española*.

The following may be mentioned as the principal current histories of
Spanish literature. For essential and correct information contained in
small compass, the best are probably Nos. 73 and 75. There are good
bibliographies in Nos. 70, 74 and 75.

69. Simón Díaz, J. *Bibliografía de la literatura hispánica*. Madrid,
    1950 ff. This is the first large-scale work on the subject. 3 vols.
    published (1954) on General Studies, I–II, and Edad Media,
    Literatura castellana, III.
70. Brenan, G. *The Literature of the Spanish People*. Second edition.
    Cambridge, 1953.
71. Cejador y Frauca, J. *Historia de la lengua y literatura castellana*.
    14 vols. Madrid, 1915–22. [Should be read with caution.]
72. del Río, A. *Historia de la literatura española*. 2 vols. New York, 1948.
73. Fitzmaurice-Kelly, J. *New History of Spanish Literature*. Oxford,
    1926.
[There are various earlier editions of this work in English, Spanish,
    French and German.]
74. Hurtado, J., y González Palencia, A. *Historia de la literatura
    española*. Sixth edition. Madrid, 1949.
75. Mérimée, E., and Morley, S. Griswold. *A History of Spanish litera-
    ture*. New York, 1930.
76. Northup, G. T. *An Introduction to Spanish literature*. Second
    edition. Chicago, 1935.

77. Ticknor, G. *History of Spanish literature*. 3 vols. Sixth edition. Boston, 1888. [Also in Spanish and German translations.]
78. Valbuena Prat, A. *Historia de la literatura española*. 2 vols. Second edition. Barcelona, 1946.

Among recommendable works on special aspects of Spanish literature, and on the literatures of Portugal, Galicia, Catalonia and Spanish America, are :

79. Azorín [J. Martínez Ruiz]. *Lecturas españolas*. Madrid, 1912. [Almost all the essays of Azorín are valuable to the general reader of Spanish literature.]
80. Barja, César. *Libros y autores clásicos*. Brattleboro, Vermont, 1922.
81. Barja, César. *Libros y autores modernos*. Second edition. Los Angeles, 1933.
82. Barja, César. *Libros y autores contemporáneos*. New York, 1935.
83. Bell, Aubrey F. G. *Portuguese Literature*. Oxford, 1922.
84. Bell, Aubrey F. G. *Portuguese Bibliography*. Oxford, 1922. [This volume is to Portuguese what No. 68 is to Spanish.]
85. Bell, Aubrey F. G. *Castilian Literature*. Oxford, 1938.
86. Bell, Aubrey F. G. *Contemporary Spanish Literature*. London, 1926.
87. Blanco García, F. *La literatura española en el siglo XIX*. 3 vols. Second edition, Madrid, 1909–12. [Should be read with caution.]
88. Bonilla y San Martín, A. *Historia de la Filosofía española*. 2 vols. Madrid, 1908–11.
89. Carré Aldao, E. *Literatura gallega*. Second edition. Barcelona, 1911. [Has a bibliography.]
90. Chandler, F. W. *The Literature of roguery*. 2 vols. New York, 1907.
91. Cotarelo y Mori, E. *Estudios de historia literaria de España*. Madrid, 1901.
92. Cotarelo y Mori, E. *Iriarte y su época*. Madrid, 1897.
93. Cueto, L. A. [Marqués de Valmar]. *Historia crítica de la poesía castellana en el siglo XVIII*. Madrid, 1893.
94. Entwistle, W. J. *The Arthurian Legend in the literatures of the Spanish Peninsula*. London, 1925.
95. Farinelli, A. *Il Romanticismo nel mondo latino*. 3 vols. Torino, 1927. [The third volume has a valuable bibliography bearing on Spanish Romanticism.]
96. Fernández y González, F. *Historia de la crítica literaria en España desde Luzán hasta nuestros días*. Madrid, 1870.
97. Figueiredo, Fidelino de. *Historia da literatura classica (1502–1756)*. 2 vols. Lisbon, 1917, 1922.
98. Figueiredo, Fidelino de. *Historia da literatura romantica portuguesa*. Lisbon, 1913.
99. Fitzmaurice-Kelly, J. *Chapters on Spanish Literature*. London, 1908. [Lectures on ten literary themes.]
100. Ford, J. D. M. *Main Currents of Spanish Literature*. New York, 1919. [A briefer series of lectures than No. 99.]
101. Foulché-Delbosc, R. et Barrau-Dihigo, L. *Manuel de l'Hispanisant*. 2 vols. New York, 1920–24. [Bibliographical.]
102. González Blanco, A. *Historia de la novela en Espana desde el romanticismo hasta nuestros días*. Madrid, 1909.
103. McClelland, I. L. *The Origins of the Romantic Movement in Spain*. Liverpool, 1937.

104. Mendes dos Remedios, J. *Literatura portuguesa desde as origens até a actualidade.* Fifth edition. Lisbon, 1921. [A large volume containing selections as well as history.]
105. Menéndez Pidal, R. *L'Epopée castillane à travers la littérature espagnole.* Paris, 1901. [See also Nos. 7, 38.]
106. Menéndez y Pelayo, M. *Estudios y discursos de crítica literaria.* 7 vols. Madrid, 1941–42. [A new and enlarged edition.]
107. Menéndez y Pelayo, M. *Historia de las ideas estéticas en España.* 6 vols. Madrid, 1939–40. [A new edition with index-volume.]
108. Menéndez y Pelayo, M. *Orígenes de la novela.* 4 vols. Madrid, 1943. [A new edition, enlarged, but omitting the texts of the 1905–10 edition.]
109. Menéndez y Pelayo, M. *Historia de los heterodoxos españoles.* 3 vols. Second edition. Madrid, 1911–18.
110. Menéndez y Pelayo, M. *Historia de la poesía castellana en la edad media,* ed. A. Bonilla y San Martín. 3 vols. Madrid, 1911–16.
111. Milá y Fontanals, M. *De la Poesía heroico-popular castellana.* Barcelona, 1874.
112. Montoliu, M. de. *Manual d'història crítica de la literatura catalana moderna.* 1823–1900. Barcelona, 1922.
113. Morel-Fatio, A. *Etudes sur l'Espagne.* 3 vols. Paris, 1888–1904.
114. Morel-Fatio, A. et Rouanet, L. *Le Théâtre espagnol.* Paris, 1900. [Has a critical bibliography.]
115. Peers, E. Allison. *Studies of the Spanish Mystics.* 2 vols. London, 1927–30. [With bibliography.]
116. Pérez Pastor, C. *Noticias y documentos relativos a la historia y literatura españolas.* Madrid, 1910–14.
117. Peers, E. Allison. *A History of the Romantic Movement in Spain.* 2 vols. Cambridge, 1940.
118. Pfandl, L. *Historia de la literatura nacional española en la Edad de Oro.* Trans. J. Rubió Balaguer. Barcelona, 1933.
119. Piñeyro, E. *El Romanticismo en España.* Paris, 1904. [Short biographical studies.] English translation, enlarged. *The Romantics of Spain.* Liverpool, 1934.
120. Post, C. R. *Mediæval Spanish Allegory.* Cambridge (U.S.A.), 1915.
121. Schack, A. F. von. *Geschichte der dramatischen Literatur und Kunst in Spanien.* 2 vols. Berlin, 1845–46. [Also in Spanish, 5 vols. Madrid, 1885–87.]
122. Underhill, J. G. *Spanish Literature in the England of the Tudors.* New York, 1899.
123. Viel-Castel, L. de. *Essai sur le Théâtre espagnol.* 2 vols. Paris, 1882.
124. Wolf, F. J. *Studien zur Geschichte der spanischen und portugiesischen Nationalliteratur.* Berlin, 1859.
125. Yxart, J. *El Arte escénico en España.* 2 vols. Barcelona, 1894–96.
126. Zurita, R. *Historia del género chico.* Madrid, 1920.
126 (i). Brown, R. F. *La novela española (1700–1850).* Madrid, 1953.
126 (ii). Lain Entralgo, P. *La generación del noventa y ocho.* Madrid, 1945.
126 (iii). Torrente Ballester, R. *Literatura española contemporánea 1893–1936.* Madrid, 1949.
126 (iv). *Diccionario de literatura española.* Second edition. Madrid, 1953.
[See also Nos. 11, 17, 18, 21.]

CHAPTER VI

SPANISH PAINTING

THE history of Spanish painting is not like the history of the painting of any other European nation, in that it is not the history of a popular movement, or a national necessity. In Italy, painting grew as the direct result of a national religious need. In Central Europe, it grew in response to the illustrative instinct. In Flanders, it grew as the result of a two-fold outlook, the religious outlook common to all Christendom, and the entirely sentimental outlook of a people interested in its natural surroundings of personality and of scenery. But in Spain, none of these instincts had anything to do with the growth of painting. The religious need was more readily and more thoroughly satisfied by sculpture, even of the rudest kind. The illustrative need, to a people intensely literal in its power of imagination, or rather largely lacking in imagination, scarcely existed, and in respect of the sentimental outlook upon the environment, it can scarcely be said that this found any artistic expression whatever until the end of the fifteenth century, or, in fact, that it found adequate expression until well down into the seventeenth century. The Spanish temperament is on the one hand tremendously reserved, and on the other tremendously emotional, and between these two extremes there was little or no possibility of adequate expression through the medium of an art which, down to the end of the thirteenth century, at any rate, was in its very essence symbolic. Therefore, we need have no hesitation in seeing in the earlier phases of Spanish painting a struggle between the literal truthfulness of the painter on the one hand and his desire to express the abstract on the other, not realizing the great difficulty with which he was confronted in reconciling the two.

It has long since become a commonplace of artistic history that, in Velázquez, Spain found, in the seventeenth century, the greatest literal exponent of things seen, as opposed to things known, that painting has yet produced, and that the whole of a great technique of painting was built up by this one painter, as a natural heir of his great predecessor, El Greco, for that one clearly realized purpose. What is not so generally understood is that the purpose of Velázquez had been that of Spanish painters from the very beginning.

The beginning of painting as an art of expression—that is to say, as an interpretation of the artist's own view of life and its problems—does not seem, at a cursory glance, to date back very far, but if we come to consider the work of the earliest known Spanish painters, those who decorated the fronts and sides of altars in the twelfth and thirteenth centuries, we shall see at once that there is a marked difference between the Spanish and any other national point of view, with regard to the task in hand. The earliest painters of Spain whose work can be assigned to any definite school are those of Catalonia, and whereas their contemporaries of the thirteenth century in Italy deliberately adhered to the already conventionalized types of Byzantine painting, the Spaniard, from the very beginning, imported into his work the element of personal observation. Mr. Isherwood Kay has remarked upon the ' rustic cumbersome figures, blue eyes and homely genial faces ' of the saints in an altar-piece ascribed to Bernat de Pou, a painter of Barcelona, who worked under the patronage of Alfonso, son of King James II, at Balaguer, in 1314, and this literal and homely character is that which gives the key-note of truly Spanish painting from this time down to the very present day.

Ferrer Bassa (*fl.* 1315–1348) was to a great extent a miniature painter, but work by him survives on the walls of the Convent of Pedralbes at Barcelona in the form of a series of scenes from the Passion, of directly Italian derivation. Those who have seen them assert that it would be difficult to distinguish between them and the work of their Italian source, namely Giotto himself, but, at the same time, it is sufficiently plain that their comparative clumsiness of draftsmanship and coarseness of colour are compensated by an extraordinary vigour and directness of attack. Bassa, in fact, although he had learned the whole of his draftsmanship and composition in Italy, was very definitely Spanish, and very definitely personal in his approach to the treatment of his subject. In a rapid review of this kind, it is impossible to follow step by step the growth of Spanish painting to the point at which it was ultimately able to break loose from Italian influences, but there is no doubt that, during the whole of the fourteenth and the greater part of the fifteenth century, the school of Catalonia was deliberately and consciously eclectic, deriving technical inspiration alike from Florence and Siena, and it was not until the supersession of Gothic by the Renaissance type of archi-

tectural settings that the Italian influence began to lose ground
and to be supplanted, or at least invaded, by Flemish methods.
The great centres of Catalonian culture, Barcelona and Valencia,
are the principal centres of this school, which reached from
Perpignan in the north to Alicante in the south, and was of course
in close and constant contact with Italy ; and the strength of
Italian influence in the early development of Spanish painting is
due to this contact, and to Sienese influence, through the work
of Simone Martini at Avignon.   The brothers Jaume and Pere
Serra (*fl.* 1361–1399), Lorenzo Saragossa (1365–1402) and Luis
Borrassá (1380–1424) all carried on and accentuated this Sienese
influence, and the practice of the Sienese in building up vast altar-
pieces of a large number of small panels set in an elaborate architectural setting was the natural ancestor of the Spanish fashion
of the retablo, which became almost the sole pictorial decoration
of the Church with the coming of the Renaissance in Spain.

Gradually, however, the School of Valencia separated itself
from the true Catalonian School, and began to exhibit characteristics of its own.   Although it is supposed with good reason that
Florentine painting exercised much influence on the School of
Valencia, as exemplified by the remarkable picture of St. Michael
in the Edinburgh National Museum, there is no doubt whatever
of the native Spanish origin of these Valencian pictures.   They
hover strangely between literal and individual observation, and
a large and almost careless tendency towards the generalization
of types, and while on the one hand they retain the national
characteristics of pale faces and fair colour, in contrast with the
stereotyped Italian characteristics of their supposed models, they
make excursions into a literalism which has nothing whatever to
do with Italy, is very natural to Spain, and must be traced in its
origin as an experiment in painting to one source only, namely
Flanders.   It was under the direction of Alfonso V of Aragon that
Netherlandish art gained ground in Valencia.   It is said that, in
1427, Jan van Eyck visited Valencia with an embassy, and at any
rate it is certain that he spent some time in Spain during 1428.
In 1431, Luis Dalmau went from Valencia to Bruges to learn his
craft more perfectly, and in 1445 painted the picture which, in its
place of honour in the Barcelona Museum, is a standing testimony
to the susceptibility of Spanish painters to Flemish influence.
From this time onward, it is scarcely necessary to seek beyond
Flanders for the inspiration of Spanish painting during the whole
of the fifteenth century.   Nothing could be more widely separated
than the Flemish and the Spanish outlook upon man and upon
Nature, except in two points, and these two points are vital.   The

Fleming, like the Spaniard, was enormously interested in every aspect of human emotion, and the Fleming, like the Spaniard, was enormously interested in everything affecting the human being through his environment.   The landscape background is as natural to the materialistic but imaginative Fleming as the gold background is to the philosophic Florentine,—the one cannot see man apart from the world in which he lives, the other cannot see man until he is definitely separated from the world in which he lives.   The Spaniard, grasping with Latin clarity of mind the independence of man from his surroundings, at the same time grasps with Flemish thoroughness the essential unity of man with the world in which he lives.

This may seem to be a fanciful over-statement of the Spanish outlook both upon life and upon painting, but the fact remains that from the beginning of the fifteenth century onwards, the Spanish painter set himself the task of achieving, not the expression of an abstract idea, but the representation of a concrete condition, and from this time onward, the development of impressionistic realism in Spanish painting was a foregone conclusion.

The coincidence, to all intents and purposes, of the entry into Spanish architecture of the Renaissance finality of design, and of the Flemish literalism in representation, determined that the next phase in the development of Spanish painting should be that which arose under the influence of the retablo.   The vast architectural settings which surround the altars of so many Spanish churches have but one representative in British museums, namely, the great retablo in the Victoria and Albert Museum, containing seventeen episodes from the legend of St. George.   This huge design, based traditionally, as has already been pointed out, upon the Sienese model, is here glorified into a picture gallery upon a set subject, in which each panel can represent its episode with a concentration of vigour and design which, while it gives every opportunity of powerful expression, leaves no room for the artist to fall into the manifold traps of composition on a large scale. No style of painting could be more perfectly adapted to the needs of the retablo than that of Flanders, with its minute finish, brilliancy of execution and forcible but generalized representation of types, and to this art the painters of Spain bent themselves for the next three-quarters of a century.   The great masters of the retablo of the fifteenth century are few in number, and their strength lay in their capacity for adapting their ideas from foreign sources.   While it is easy to recognize in any work of Jaime Huguet (*fl.* 1448–1487) and of Bartolomé Bermejo (*fl.*

1474–1495) the influence of Flanders in every line, it is equally possible to trace in Jaime Baço, commonly known as Jacomard (1410–1461), the influence of the Italian Renaissance. To put it shortly, painting was not yet a national Spanish art. No painter, however great his inventive power, however great his religious enthusiasm, was able to build up an art on entirely Spanish lines for the expression of his Spanish outlook, and it is even true that the last named of these painters, Jacomard, was not a Spaniard, but a Frenchman, probably of a descent lying outside the limits of Catalonian influence, and still further rendered cosmopolitan by contact with the Italian painters of Naples and possibly Rome. In the work of Jacomard there is at once an elaboration of detail and a breadth of effect which would excuse the belief that he had come into contact with the contemporary artists of Umbria, and that he was in fact an international rather than a national painter ; but his sobriety of colour and instinctive dignity (even though primitive) of design show his response to the primary desiderata of his Spanish patrons.

Huguet was far more Spanish and far more Flemish both in intention and in method, and in his work we see very strongly developed the grimness of colouring and forcible rendering of things actually seen, which we shall come later to regard as essentials of the Spanish art. The work attributed to him, ' Our Lady enthroned with Child, and Adoring Angels ', in the Birmingham Art Gallery, is an interesting reminder of the fact that the School of Catalonia (as it must still be regarded) practically dominated the more remote possessions of Spain in the Mediterranean, for this work, purchased in Sardinia, is probably not by Huguet, but by a school founded by him either in, or for export to Sardinia. It has every mark of a provincial painting in the somewhat clumsy reproduction of entirely foreign forms, as in the angels above the canopy, who are strongly reminiscent of Campin. Its architectural details are entirely Gothic, its draperies might have been taken straight from any Flemish painter of the fifteenth century, but its two donors, and their young son, kneeling in the foreground, appear as a response to the recorded dissatisfaction of Spanish donors of the fifteenth century, who were constantly demanding recognizable rendering of individuals in place of the generalized portraits which were found among Catalonian painters. In other words, Huguet represents the fusion of the Flemish method with the Spanish spirit far more than either Jacomard or Bermejo (more generally known in this country as Bartolomeo Rubeo), who is almost slavishly Flemish in his handling of his medium.

Bermejo practised the fashion of oil painting then becoming general in Flanders, and, whether in oil or tempera, he sought invariably the brilliance of that medium in his colouring, and the precision of the draughtsmanship appropriate to it. On the other hand, however, he should claim credit as being among the first of Spanish painters to break away from that compromise between painting and sculpture which had characterized all the early phases of Spanish paintings, by representing in paint rather than in built-up gesso or heavy gilding the metallic portions of his design. His St. Michael in the Wernher Collection is a supreme example of the adaptation of the purely Flemish technique to Spanish needs, for in this picture, while every detail of the glittering golden armour set with jewels, and every excursion into grotesqueness which it is possible to impart into his representation of the dragon, is fully indulged, the picture as a whole remains possible rather than fantastic, real rather than purely imaginary.

It was, in fact, in the shaking-off of the trammels of an imagination unnatural to the Spaniard that the task of the Spanish painter in the latter part of the fifteenth and in the early part of the sixteenth century consisted. The Spanish imagination is, according to the way we look at it, either the most vigorous or the most ineffective in the world, for the Spaniard is incapable of visualizing any abstract idea except in terms of the absolutely literal and material world by which he is surrounded, and in which he lives. He had therefore to shake himself free of every vestige of the symbolism which came perfectly naturally to the Italian, and was intelligible to the more speculative painter of Flanders, and to bring down to the level of human experience all those abstract ideas in which he was the most fervid believer, perhaps, of them all.

Religious painting, as it was prescribed by the Church, demanded that the most tremendous abstract ideas should be clothed in a form intelligible to a race brought up in the atmosphere of conflict between two faiths, opposed in their very essence so far as the method of artistic interpretation was concerned. It is impossible to consider the emancipation of Spanish painting from the traditional methods of the rest of Europe without realizing the entirely unique position which Christianity in Spain occupied, so long as one foot of Spanish territory was occupied by an alien race and an alien religion. It is not generally realized, especially in the north of Europe, that it was not until the very end of the fifteenth century that Granada fell to Ferdinand and Isabel, and that the power of the Moor in Spain was finally broken. These mere historical facts may seem to have very little to do with the development of a national art, but if we bear in mind that Christianity was a fighting faith in Spain of necessity until the sixteenth century, and from choice for nearly two centuries more, and that the power against which it had fought for centuries was one which precluded all religious representation, we shall understand better the natural tendency of the Spaniard in the direction, on the one hand, of reticence, and on the other hand of an outspokenness which, to our milder mood, is positively brutal. So long as the task of the Spaniard was that of enlarging the borders of a united Christendom, he had to be content to use the acknowledged and traditional methods of religious expression which had grown up in more fortunate provinces of the faith, but, once the menace was finally removed, it was only the care of the Church, guarding the natural temperament always against extravagance in expression, which prevented Spanish art from becoming barbaric in its expression of Christianity.

The rise of painting, in fact, could but follow upon the heels of the retreating Muslim, and religious art in Italy and Flanders was already far advanced when Spain was taking her first steps. Catalonia, the earliest freed, took her first lessons from Italy, and only later came into contact with Flemish models ; and until well into the fifteenth century, Catalonian painting dominated that of Old Aragon. Castile, long disturbed with war against the infidel, made but slow progress. It was not until the fifteenth century that panel paintings began to appear, and these were almost all the work of foreigners. Some of these, as Nicolás Francés (*fl.* 1430–1468), a Frenchman, worked on the spot, in a manner strongly influenced by the Sienese art of a hundred and fifty years earlier ; for Southern French art was still largely under the spell of the work of Simone Martini at Avignon. At León, where the French Gothic architecture of the cathedral was the setting, the sculptures of the cathedral itself supplied many motives to the painter ; and at Salamanca a Florentine, Dello, decorated the new cathedral with paintings in 1445. Many panel paintings, also, were imported from Flanders, bringing with them the influence of Rogier van der Weyden, Memlinc and Van der Goes. Painters from the Netherlands, settling in Spain, brought with them not only Flemish and Dutch influences, but also characteristics derived from other Northern sources. If his name is any guide, Jorge Inglés may well have been an Englishman; and while the Retablo of the Angels which he painted for the Marqués de Santillana about 1455 shows clearly his Flemish training, it is with something of that literalism which the Englishman shares with the Spaniard that he approaches the rendering of the portraits of his patrons which form part of the retablo. Juan de Flandés was basically Flemish in his technique and in his sensitive treatment of the landscape setting of his subjects, but his work also shows strong French (or perhaps rather Burgundian) affinities, and he stands out among the painters in Spain of his period, the closing years of the fifteenth century and the first twenty of the sixteenth by a certain delicacy and refinement in the features and pose of his figures, and restraint in the expression of emotion, which are rather Gallic than either Flemish or Spanish. His best-known work is the retablo at Palencia, executed about 1506–10 ; but an exquisite example in this country is the ' St. Michael and St. Francis ' in the Cook Collection, in which St. Michael is rather angelic than warrior-like, and—in token of the reciprocal influence of Spain upon the Fleming—the stigmata of St. Francis, and the restrained, almost repressed, ecstasy of his expression, are rendered with uncompromising realism, while the painter's love of landscape has been compressed within the narrow limits of a reflection in the polished steel boss of the Archangel's shield, the background consisting merely of a severely simple arcade, rendered wholly in gold. No Spaniard could have painted the picture, but no one would ever have painted it except for Spaniards.

However, the foreign painters who worked in Spain, for Spaniards, were for the most part already hybridized before their arrival in the country, and were receptive of the influence of Spanish taste, while their own influence upon their native contemporaries was actually less than that of the purely Netherlandish painters who were known in Spain only by imported works ; for the native painters of Spain were able more readily to graft their own personal and national characteristics upon the pure Netherlandish stock than to select from the mixed strains of their foreign competitors those which most nearly approximated to the expression of their own aims. Thus, while the work of Fernando Gallego (c. 1440-1507) honestly avows his debt to Rogier van der Weyden and Dirck Bouts, with a strong leaning to the greater literalism and austerity of the latter, his types are from the first Spanish, and his work is uncompromisingly Spanish both in outlook and form ; and his own influence on his contemporaries is so great that he may fairly be accounted the founder of purely Spanish painting in the whole of north-western Spain.

Moreover, the immense size of some of his undertakings must have necessitated the employment of assistants working to his design and under his close supervision, resulting in the spread and perpetuation of his influence both during and after his lifetime. This employment of assistants, however, does not justify Mr. C. R. Post, in his monumental *History of Spanish Painting*, in relegating the whole of the huge retablo from the Cathedral of Ciudad Rodrigo, always traditionally ascribed to Gallego, to the category of school pieces. It certainly cannot be contended that every part of every one of the fifty or more panels, each five feet high and three feet seven inches wide, with the ten panels of the banco, each half this height, below them, of which the retablo must have consisted when complete, was the unaided work of the master's own hand ; but, as the custodian of the twenty-six panels from this colossal work now in the Cook Collection, I am constrained, as the result of four years of close study and systematic cleaning of them, to record my belief that, with certain recognizable exceptions, the Ciudad Rodrigo panels are rightly to be ascribed to Gallego himself. Moreover, it seems evident to me that the ' Epiphany ' formerly in the Pacully Collection, and now in the Museum of Art at Toledo, Ohio, which is accepted by Mr. Post as an authentic work of Gallego, is a panel from the same retablo, reduced in height by the removal of the blank portion at the top, which was covered by the gilded arcading of the framework when the picture was *in situ*.

Be this as it may (and when Mr. Post saw the panels in the Cook Collection close inspection of them was not easy, and they were much obscured by dirt and bad repainting), the principal contributions of Gallego to Spanish Art, as seen in the San Ildefonso retablo at Zamora, and in his work at Salamanca, were, firstly, the breaking down of the native preference for the gilded background, in favour of landscape and minutely studied architectural settings, and secondly, the realization of purely Iberian types of character in the figures. In achieving this step forward, Gallego opened the way for the expression of the essential realism of the Spanish outlook, the painting of things seen rather than the symbolism of things known, and in so doing, went far towards counteracting the Italian trend which had preceded him at Salamanca ; but on the other hand Pedro Berruguete, working in Toledo and Avila at the turn of the fifteenth and sixteenth centuries, strengthened and continued the Italian influence, so that scarcely any progress towards a truly Spanish School took place. Only in the steady growth of a certain harsh truthfulness can the Spaniard be said to have asserted his national spirit. Spanish painting is still rather a style than a school.

The same sequence of influences operated in Andalusia as elsewhere in Spain, and probably the earliest paintings in Seville, which are markedly Sienese in style, came from Catalonia. Antonio and Diego Sánchez, working at Seville late in the fifteenth century, are almost completely Flemish in their manner, but Spanish in their unsparing realism and dramatic force. There is a fine example of their work, ' Road to Calvary ', in the Fitz-william Museum, Cambridge. The School of Córdoba, to which Bermejo may have belonged originally, was entirely dominated by the character of van Eyck, and it was not until towards the middle of the sixteenth century that Italian influence reasserted itself, and then in the florid and debased form brought back to Spain by Luis de Vargas (1502–1568), from his twenty-eight years' sojourn in Italy, where he studied principally the work of Raphael and Correggio, without learning to reproduce the grace of the one or the charm of the other.

It was again in Valencia, whence so much that was good in Spanish art had already come, that Hernando Yánez de la Almedina, after study in Italy under Leonardo da Vinci, laid the foundations of truly Spanish painting : for, while he grasped the value of freedom of drawing and grace of form, he infused into his use of these Italian characteristics all the vigour of his native outlook, and, in his colour, struck the note of quiet force which was in time to become the glory of painting in Spain. In his beautiful ' Santa Catalina ', in the collection of the Marquis de Casa-Arquedín, he is literally truthful in his rendering of the smallest detail, and yet loses nothing of dignity nor of religious feeling : and, at the other side of Spain, in the remote Extremadura, Luis de Morales (1517–1586), a native of Badajoz, was earning the first national reputation among Spanish painters for his deeply emotional renderings of the Dead Christ, and of Our Lady of Sorrows. In drawing of drapery, and in his very limited range of colour, this painter was a careful follower of Italy, but in the depth of his feeling, and in the harshly literal rendering of emaciated features distorted by grief and pain, he was utterly Spanish, as he was also in his use of black as a ' colour ', by which all modelling becomes almost sculpturesque, and his figures emerge from shadows as though standing out from darkness into light.

A new era now dawned, in which Spanish painters no longer imitated, but used to their own ends, the foreign models brought together in the magnificent collections of the Emperor Charles V. These were largely Venetian, though the Flemish painters of an earlier day still held their ground among them : and gradually there grew up a kind of divergence of these two main streams of influence, the Flemish supplying the technique and style for portraiture, now coming into a position of national importance through direct royal patronage, and the Italian shaping the development of religious painting.

True, the portrait painter of Charles V was Titian, and his

influence is to be traced in much of the Spanish portraiture of the sixteenth century ; but when Philip II followed the precedent set by Charles V, and appointed a Court painter, he chose a Fleming, Antony Mor, from whom the Spaniards Alonso Sánchez Coello (? 1513–1590) and Pantoja de la Cruz learned their art. Of these two painters, Coello adhered the more closely to the tenets of his training, in minuteness of finish, and smoothness of technique ; but even he, as time went on, lost the warmth of colour and softness of shadow of his Flemish master, and approximated to the silvery coldness and austerity of feeling proper to his nationality and to his patron, Philip II. Pantoja de la Cruz broke away sooner and more thoroughly, for while his earliest work is very Flemish, he was soon using a heavier impasto and a harsher and more vital truthfulness, hitherto unattempted by any artist outside Spain. A little coarse in feeling, his portrait of Philip II, now in America, is, with its bold brushwork and sullen reality, a new thing, owing little to any but native inspiration, while Coello's portrait of Don Carlos (Prado) and that of the. Infanta Catalina Micaela, are still, for all their national literalism, thoroughly Flemish in all but spirit.

A contemporary of these painters, Juan Fernández Navarrete (1526–1579), called ' El Mudo ' (the Dumb), exemplifies the continued domination of religious painting by Italy, for he studied in Rome, Naples, Florence, Milan and Venice, and modelled himself avowedly upon Titian. It was quite natural to a Spaniard to follow a Venetian master, for both the Venetian and the Spaniard looked upon religion as part of real life, and visualized it in an everyday setting : and it had this distinct advantage, that it helped the Spaniard to feel and to express his own colour-sense, which tended normally to be rather repressed : and it was also fortunate that, at this precise juncture, the Inquisition stepped in to prevent the Spanish religious painter from lowering the dignity of his art by over-indulgence in a realism which might easily have descended, if unrestrained, to the level of the sordid in form and the picaresque in outlook.

To the discipline of the Church was added the dignity of the Court ; and these two stood as sentinels over the national character, which is that of violent emotionalism labouring under strong restraint, through which it breaks from time to time in moments of great stress : and, as restraint too long maintained is liable to produce sullen apathy, it was fortunate that Spanish art should have found at this moment a leader whose genius was so great and his ties with Spain so slender, as to enable him to defy its traditions and its discipline with impunity.

This leader was a Greek of Crete, Domenico Theotocopouli,

called in Venice, where he learned his art in the studio of Titian,
El Greco, and in Spain, El Griego (*c.* 1548–1614). Coming to
Spain some time before 1577, for no reason that can now be
guessed, he at once found in Toledo his spiritual home. Though
he came as an avowed follower of Titian, whom he echoes vaguely
in his great altar-piece ' The Parting of Our Lord's Raiment ',
in Toledo Cathedral, he broke away immediately from that
allegiance, and, in the ' Martyrdom of St. Maurice and the
Christian Legion ', he gave full rein to his innate passion for the
rendering of solid form and of the plastic rather than the pictorial
aspect of his subject. The picture was commissioned by Philip II
for the Church of the Escorial, but was never hung there, for it
violated every known principle of painting and of design, with its
harsh and livid colour, violent contrasts of light and shade, and
over-modelled and attenuated forms.

In one sense El Greco was a throw-back to the symbolic
formalism of his own Byzantine ancestry in art : in another he
was a daring innovator. In his great masterpiece, ' The Burial
of the Conde de Orgaz ' in S. Tomé at Toledo, the row of mourners
who form the background of the Count lowered to the grave by
SS. Augustine and Lawrence, produces the impression that the
figures in a Byzantine mosaic have suddenly been imbued with
life and have revolted against their age-long immobility. The
wind of life rustles through them as they turn this way and that,
and take each his individual and conscious part in the impressive
moment. Yet, for all the tense vitality of this scene, the upper
part of the picture, which shows the soul of the Count received
into the Divine Presence, is a grotesque and ghastly failure of
imagination. It would be absurd to say that El Greco was not
imaginative, for he was far more ; he was a visionary : but like
the race among whom he made his home, he could not visualize,
nor make visible to others, the visions of his spirit, save in terms
of things known to his material sense of sight. In this lay his
power over Spanish artists and Spanish patrons ; for their
limitations were his own, and he could not ask them to take
flights that lay beyond their powers ; he could only stimulate
them to the effort to go farther and faster along the road to the
achievement of truth in art, as they themselves already understood it subconsciously. He could never be ' popular ', but this
did not matter, for painting was never a popular art in Spain :
nor, perhaps, did he ever achieve complete success, for he wavered
between conservatism and adventure all his life, as though he
mistrusted his own aims : but at least he showed Spain that truth
of vision was above all what it demanded of its artists.

In one respect, however, El Greco went far beyond the national needs and understanding of Spain ; for, though he sought feverishly after the means of realizing the plastic form and atmospheric space in painting, realism was not his aim, but only a means to an end. In all his work there is an inward spirituality, a symbolic intent, that intrigued and baffled his contemporaries, and escaped the notice of his successors altogether. This fiery ecstasy is no mere echo of Italian symbolism and decorative design, but a new thing, that has scarcely found any successor till our own times. No one who has experienced the upward-sweeping force of the stupendous 'Assumption' in S. Vicente at Toledo can escape the conviction that the painter's material vision was controlled, even distorted, by his desire to convey through material forms the presence of a directing inspiration. This was personal to himself, and the fact that no sign of any such impulse occurs in any purely Spanish painter justifies us in considering that it lay beyond the scope of the Spanish mentality.

Nevertheless, the fact that El Greco was in earnest is the important point, for it is this fact which impresses him upon his imitators, and followers, and critics alike. From the time of El Greco onwards, Spanish painting endeavoured, as a whole, to be Spanish, that is to say, to be honest, and a new element is imported into Spanish art, in that it becomes the expression of the individual artist's mentality, rather than merely the echo of his foreign technical ancestry. At first sight, it would seem that the influence of El Greco was short-lived, for the next phase that we have to observe is that of a very strongly Italianizing movement, which is not, as might have been expected, a development of his style, but a reaction from it. The great name of the latter half of the sixteenth century, apart from that of El Greco, in Spain itself, is that of Francisco Ribalta (1551–1628), who, in Valencia, painted in the Italian manner, so far as draughtsmanship and design were concerned, but in the matter of religious and naturalistic outlook is wholly Spanish. His work is characterized by a foretaste of that vaguely human sentiment which becomes later the mark of the School of Seville, although he himself had no affinities with that school. It seems as though the honesty of El Greco had resulted in an acknowledgment by Spanish painters of their natural bent. From this time onward, not only human realism but human sentiment is admitted to the realm of the painter, and Ribalta, in his ' Christ bearing the Cross ', well known in England from its possession by the National Gallery, hovers midway between religious reticence and sentimental outspokenness, presenting both through the medium of a purely Spanish enjoyment of natural but strongly controlled effects of light and shade.

His far more famous pupil, Jusepe de Ribera (1589–1652), carried both aspects of his art far further. Although practising the whole of his life in Naples, in competition and even in savage conflict with the native Neapolitan School, Ribera remained to the end essentially Spanish in his dramatic use of extremes of light and shade, and his relentless representation of the physical aspects of his subject. He is seldom restrained, almost always brutal, and yet never lacks that peculiar quality that the Spaniard seems to inherit as a second nature, of dignity. Though he owed much to that Neapolitan master of chiaroscuro, Caravaggio, he was never an imitator, but always an originator, by his treatment of his theme. Quite early in his career, he produced the terrible St. Bartholomew, now in the Prado, in which the effect is that of a great animated sculpture thrust to within the closest possible focus of the spectator, with at once a sculptural and dramatic effect. Ribera, however, lies outside the true Spanish development, for although he was much imitated, he was never wholly grasped by his contemporaries in Spain itself, and it is rather in the work of Juan de las Roelas (1558–1625) and Francisco de Herrera, the elder (c. 1576–1656), that we must see the true development of Spanish painting.

Although Roelas imitated the Italians on the mechanical side of his art, he has the clumsy honesty of the true Spaniard in his rendering of scenes of emotional and physical stress. His ' Martyrdom of St. Andrew ' in the Seville Museum, although reminiscent of the puerilities of Luis de Vargas, in its unimportant detail, is entirely Spanish in its simplicity of the statement of emotion and of passion. Of Herrera the elder it is difficult to speak with patience. He was a painter who, like all his fellow-citizens of Seville, was the prey of every succeeding emotion, and at the same time, was bound down within the absolute limits of the unimaginative outlook upon the material world. His method of painting is as violent as his method of feeling, his composition is childish, his rendering of character is appalling in its actuality. Herrera's composition was as feeble as his characterization was powerful. He had no spirituality, how-ever, but a compelling humanity, and he achieved perhaps even more than El Greco himself, in his fidelity to the living actuality of things seen as he himself chose to see them. He is the bridge between the two greatest personalities in the history of Spanish painting, El Greco and Velázquez, and in many of the compositions of the latter painter, which have become world-famous, we can see the influence, brief but forcible, of his first impetuous master, Herrera.

There is, however, one painter of the seventeenth century, that Golden Age of Spanish art and letters, who stands out as the indicator of the unattainable goal after which the artists of Spain, apart from Velázquez himself, were striving, during the greater part of the seventeenth century, namely, the reconciliation of a tradition derived from foreign sources, with the essential needs of the Spaniard for visional truth, side by side with spiritual honesty. This was Francisco Zurbarán (1598–1662), who, trained in the first instance as a painter of images, saw life from the first as a scheme of light and shadow falling upon immobile material. It is said that Zurbarán never painted any object without having that object actually before him ; and since he had been trained to colour separate plastic objects with separate coatings of distinct colour, it is perfectly easy, in his pictures, to separate one mass from the other, and to see how he has rendered colour in every case, whether in light or shadow, as a mere graduation of distinguishing tone, belonging inseparably to a distinct object. If it had not been for his instinctive appreciation of the fusing power of light, his work must inevitably have become dull and uninspired, but since Zurbarán aimed, throughout his career, at the presentation not only of actual objects, but also of the atmosphere in which they were enveloped, he may be regarded as the first conscious impressionist in the history of Spanish painting. This seems a strange term to apply to a man whose work is characterized throughout by a singular exactitude in the representation of the individual parts of a subject, but if we consider the degree in which he allowed a predetermined tone, whether of silver or of gold, to dominate every colour and every shade in his picture, we are bound to admit that he is the first of the Spanish painters to convey to us the impression of the visual actuality of the chosen moment.

In this respect, Zurbarán was the successor of El Greco, although their methods are as the poles asunder. His subjects were, for the most part, wholly material and realistic, court ladies in the character of saints (a fashionable freak of the moment), such as his court lady in the character of St. Margaret, in the National Gallery ; vast state portraits, such as the Gonzalo de Illecas, Bishop of Córdoba, at Guadalupe, devoid entirely of formality, and yet full of stateliness,—the natural stateliness of the utterly truthful Spaniard—and clumsy but entirely convincing angels, like the Gabriel at Montpellier, are sufficient to show Zurbarán in the character of a Spaniard of the Spaniards, using

but never succumbing to every foreign example within his knowledge, in turning them into a truly Spanish expression of real life,
real light, real atmosphere and real feeling.

This is especially well shown in Zurbarán's monastic subjects,
such as the Franciscan Friar praying, which is one of the greatest
Spanish pictures in the National Gallery, for in such subjects there
is no superficial charm, whether of colour or of form,—the picture
depends upon the intensity of feeling and upon the utilization of
every scrap of incidental beauty in the play of light and shadow ;
and in the example mentioned, it is solely on account of these
characteristics that the picture compels attention. The figure
emerges from the dark background with dramatic suddenness of
contrast, and the whole of the light is concentrated upon the hands
grasped with a fervour which is almost hysterical in its intensity,
and astonishing in the manner of its presentation.

Thus we come back to the abiding characteristic of the
fully developed Spanish painting, namely the unending search for
absolute truth in presentation of the visible world ; and the name
which is associated with the greatest progress in this direction is
that of Diego Rodríguez da Silva y Velázquez (1599–1660), who,
like Zurbarán, began his career in the School of Seville, and,
studying first under the elder Herrera, learned perhaps no more
than enthusiasm, and later under Pacheco, eventually his father-
in-law, learned perhaps no more than scholarship, but who
contained in himself a frankness and simplicity of outlook upon
the purpose of his art which carried him two centuries beyond his
time. Velázquez was not only a draughtsman, but he was a
draughtsman in three dimensions, that is to say, that from the
very first he sought to portray not only the objects before him,
but the space in which they were set, not merely laterally, but
in the matter of depth also. Atmosphere was included in his
natural vision.

His earliest works are for the most part *bodegones*, that is to
say, interiors crowded with objects mostly of the kitchen, and
containing figures merely to give a *raison d'être* to the whole.
These were no more than drawing exercises, or rather exercises in
the accommodation of draughtsmanship to vision. Laborious
studies of peasant types engaged in culinary operations do not
seem to be inspired subjects for one who was to be a great pioneer
in the art of painting, but they served this purpose, that they
enabled Velázquez to set down upon his canvas, stroke by stroke,
patch of colour by patch of colour, the actual things that he saw
in front of him. These, like his figure studies in the studio of
Pacheco, are hard and brilliant in execution, but entirely lacking

in either spiritual or mental outlook. They served merely to
give him complete command of his materials, and of his accommodation of their use to his use of his eyes. They stand in
relation to the main stream of his art exactly as the practising of
scales stands to the finished art of the pianist.

When, in 1623, Velázquez, on his second visit to Madrid, was
introduced to the patronage of King Philip IV, he was already the
master of his craft, and was so certain in his reproduction of the
things seen that he was able to produce at once a portrait of the
young King which secured for him the position of Court painter,
which he held for the rest of his life.   There could be no more
tranquil or at the same time more exacting setting for his life-work.
The artist who in Seville had painted such pictures as the ' Christ
in the House of Martha and Mary ', which now hangs in the
National Gallery, with its careful rendering of fish, vegetables
and kitchen utensils, and its uninspired but at the same time
wholly colloquial rendering of peasant types, had been unconsciously equipped for his new task and his new surroundings by
the thoroughness with which he had undergone his apprenticeship
in Seville.   Broadly speaking, his work can be divided into three
sections: the first, that which preceded his first visit to Italy in
1629, the second, that of the period between 1629 and 1648, the
date of his second visit to Italy, and the final period from 1649
to his death.   The first period is one in which the painter was
constantly striving after the reproduction upon canvas of the
solidity of form, but without grasping the fact that in order to
represent with absolute fidelity things seen by the human eye,
the presentation of them must reproduce not only the accuracy,
but also the inaccuracy of human vision.   To put it more simply,
Velázquez did not realize, in this first stage of his art, that the
human eye can only see one thing at a time, and consequently,
he endeavoured, by meticulous detail throughout the whole of his
subject, to reproduce everything that was in front of him.   The
result is the development of a remarkable power of characterization (in which perhaps we have the echo of the teaching of his first
master, Herrera) but a complete lack of grasp of the first principles
of tridimensional composition.   Two outstanding examples will
suffice to illustrate this phase, namely, ' The Water Carrier of
Seville ', now in the collection of the Duke of Wellington, which
seeks to represent the recession of vision by laying the strongest
possible emphasis upon a single point of light, where it falls upon
the goblet of water in the centre of the picture, and while sacrific-
ing nothing of detail, subordinating in strength of contrast the
whole of the rest of the picture to this one point ; and second, the

picture upon which he was engaged when the visit of Rubens in 1629 to Madrid fortunately occurred to make a turning-point in his career. This picture was ' Los Borrachos ' ('The Topers' or ' The Village Bacchus '), in which a row of scoundrelly villagers pay mock homage to a semi-nude youth in their midst, who is very self-consciously wearing a crown of vine leaves, and holding a glass of wine in his hand. The picture falls to pieces by the very power of its individual parts. Every single face in it is a brilliant portrait, and an astounding piece of character-revelation, but since the eye must focus separately upon each of these faces, there is no unity about the composition as a whole. The colour is sombre and all the values of the picture are determined in terms of light and shade, and although an earnest attempt has been made to represent distance from front to back of the composition, this object has not been achieved, and the picture is a flat row of faces. On the advice of Rubens, and with the grudging permission of Philip IV, Velázquez now spent two years in Italy, and it is rather surprising to find that his principal preoccupation was not with the works of Michelangelo or of Raphael, then universally esteemed in Spain, but rather with those of Venetian painters, more especially of Titian, though it is certain that the work of Tintoretto must have impressed him profoundly, by reason of its masterly and dramatic handling of light and shadow. Towards the close of this visit to Italy, when Velázquez was suffering from the climate and from overwork, he made the two wonderful sketches (now in the Prado) of the gardens of the Villa Medici, which must have been to him a self-revelation in the painting of atmospheric space. It seems as though in these pictures he had at last grasped the fact that to paint exactly what one sees, one must paint only what one sees, and not what one knows is there. It was so tremendous a discovery, that in his finished pictures it still had relatively little effect, though in the ' Apollo bringing News to Vulcan of the Infidelity of Venus ', and in the ' Joseph's Coat ' in the Escorial, there is a tremendous advance on the single-plane composition of ' Los Borrachos ' and a corresponding gain in actuality of presentation. The former of these pictures at the same time reveals the weakness which neither Velázquez nor any Spanish painter has ever overcome, namely, that of lack of imagination, for the Apollo is nothing more than a rather clumsy peasant model, and there is a certain pedestrian quality in the attempt of Velázquez at the higher flights of imagination, which is more clearly still exemplified in the beautiful picture of the ' Vision of St. Bridget ', now in the National Gallery, in which, while the passionate sympathy of the infant St. Bridget for the suffering of Our Lord seems almost materialized in the single flash of light which stabs the space of centuries of shadow across the picture, the angel who supports the saint is no more than a very stodgy model dressed in serge, and encumbered by a pair of rather furtive wings, tucked away in the shadows of the corner of the picture. Here, then, we have an epitome both of the aims and the limitations of Velázquez, and so of the highest manifestation of Spanish art, and it is a matter for satisfaction that this great craftsman, endowed with the most marvellous eyesight, perhaps, in the world, should have had to spend his life in painting portraits, for this was the thing for which he was most superlatively qualified. In that short period of his seeming retirement, which followed the disgrace of his first patron, the Conde-Duque de Olivares, when he was momentarily freed from the duty of painting royal personages, and was able to exercise his art upon models chosen at his will, he produced that wonderful series of portraits of the court dwarfs, of which the ' Niño de Vallecas ' and the ' Don Juan ' are the most outstanding examples, and was not restrained from free experiment by any undue sense of respect for his sitter ; and it is in these and in such pictures as the ' Aesop ', and the portrait of his friend, the sculptor Martínez Montañés (the latter painted in 1648), that his genius finds full rein. In these, as it were, day by day, the brush strikes more boldly to match the patch of light or shadow, sharp or blurred, which fell upon the mirror of his eye, and so transferred to the canvas, as though it too were a mirror in which the forms were reflected ; and if we look back to the beginning of his career for a moment, and realize that in the background of his picture ' Christ in the House of Martha and Mary ' there hangs a mirror upon whose surface is reflected the group of Christ and the Sisters, dim and blurred, in contrast with the sharp drawing of the figures and objects in the foreground, we shall realize that the development of Velázquez was not accidental, but slowly and painfully deliberate ; that, from the very first, he had set himself the task of treating his canvas as the mirror of the world, which he set it up to portray.

The last phase is that in which he finally achieved his object, the simple object of painting empty space. It must have become obvious to Velázquez, in his lifetime as a Court painter, that one must not count upon finding beauty ready-made in one's subjects, for the physical contours of the King and of the Court gave no encouragement to any such ideas. It was rather in the abstract pleasures of light and shadow, fused and merging colour, that beauty lay. The dwarf pictures were a deliberate testing of a theory evolved from these conditions. The mirror in the early

picture is found again in the ' Venus ' painted about 1649, and
here again we have the contrast between direct and indirect
vision emphasized. The portrait of the Princess Margarita
Teresa, for all its glimmer of grey, and rose and silver, and the soft
gold of the Princess's hair, depends for its greatness, and perhaps
almost for its beauty as well, upon the dusky shadows of the
background, and upon the real emptiness which exists behind the
figure, and in ' Las Hilanderas ' and ' Las Meninas ' we find the
consummation of a life's work, for both of these pictures are
pictures which accidentally possess a subject, the first of the
spinners in a royal tapestry factory, and the second that of a
naughty little princess who needed a deal of coaxing before she
would consent to stand for her portrait, but in fact, are no more
and no less than pictures of the movement of light in space.   In
the former, the light marches like an invading flood, from the
brilliantly lit further room in the background to the dusky room
in the foreground, and in the second, the light is reflected directly
on to the foreground group from the vast mirror that it faces,
and that reflects in its surface (and so upon the canvas) even the
canvas and the painter themselves as well.   It filters in from the
curtained windows at the side, it glares from the open door and
gleams from the mirror in the background, and these invading
streams of light meet upon a central resistance of darkness, a
dusky cloud in the middle distance, which was what the artist had
set himself to paint.

Velázquez, whose conditions of service as Court painter precluded him from painting for money outside that service, was
enabled by this limitation to practise his art as a student all his
life ; and, gifted with the patience and the vision which are necessary to research, he progressed far beyond all his contemporaries
in the discovery and understanding of the basic principles of
impressionistic art. Consequently, though he had several
imitators, to whom we shall turn presently, he left no real successors, and it was not until almost a century had passed, that a
Spanish painter was found to carry forward by a single step the
development of a national art.

It was rather in Seville, and in the hands of a younger contemporary of Velázquez, Esteban Murillo, that the continuity
of Spanish painting with the traditional Italian and Flemish
influences of its early days was preserved and carried forward.
Sometimes it is Ribera, sometimes van Dyck, whose influence
predominates ; sometimes it is the literal brutality of the Spaniard,
as in ' El Tinoso ',. the picture in which Murillo has portrayed St.
Elizabeth in the act of cleansing the hair of a verminous child ;
sometimes it is the gentle dignity of the Andalusian, as in the

' Holy Family ' in the National Gallery, that holds the field ; and
again, after a visit to Madrid at the age of twenty-four, when
Velázquez helped and encouraged him, he shows a delight in the
accidental beauty and lively humour of common life, as exemplified in the ' Melon Eaters ', and many another picture of smiling
ragamuffins of the streets of Seville.   In all his work, Murillo
seeks the lively, the suave, the pleasurable aspect of life, of light
and of colour.   His is the only art of Spain that approaches
laughter, as it is alone, too, in its tenderness.   His many renderings
of the Immaculate Conception are full of sweetness, but wholly
lacking in depth :   they are sincere, but a little flighty.

To find the real Murillo, we must turn to the peasant subjects
in the Dulwich Gallery, for example, ' The Two Peasant Boys ',
or ' The Spanish Flower Girl ', or to the famous ' Boy Drinking '
in the National Gallery, or the marvellous group of similar
subjects, including ' The Melon Eaters ' at Munich.   In these
renderings of the vitality and mentality of the back street,
Murillo is at his best and most characteristic.   In such subjects,
all his natural instinct to capture the adventitious beauty of sunshine and shadow is brought out to the full, and his rendering of
instantaneous mood and fleeting expression places him in a category all by himself in the history of Spanish painting.   He is the
very embodiment in material terms of the picaresque, the modern
novel of manners, and bad manners at that.   In passing, it is
worth note that the Spanish painter, if he is worthy of remembrance at all, is worthy of that remembrance for some aspect of
unrelenting truthfulness.   Murillo was perfectly truthful to the
sentimentally religious outlook of his patrons of the Seville market-
place, and he was equally true to their peculiar sensibility to the
picturesque in the common accidents of their own everyday life.
It is a question worthy of speculation and even of serious investigation as to the extent of the influence of contemporary Dutch
painting upon that of Spain, for it must be remembered that at the
moment that Murillo was producing his most convincing subjects
of low life, Brouwer and Van Ostade were rendering the same
aspect of the life of the newly liberated states of Holland, and that
Dutch artists, in spite of political convulsion, were present and
painting in Spain and even in Seville during the period of his
greatest activity.   It is not at all unlikely that in the work of
Murillo we see the reflection of the contemporary democratic
and nationally constructive movement which was taking place
in Holland, and from this aspect alone we must regard Murillo
as at least as important in the history of Spanish painting as
Velázquez himself.

It has often been a matter for conjecture why, after such a

brilliant outburst of visually inspired production as that of
Velázquez and Murillo, the art of Spain should have subsided into
the deadly mediocrity of the latter part of the seventeenth and
the greater part of the eighteenth century. But it seems evident
that painters of Murillo's naïve and honest sentimentality must
necessarily be rare in a nationality so reserved in temperament
as the Spanish, and that therefore until sentimentality could be
combined not only with virility but actually with something
approaching brutality, it was impossible to hope that it should
produce any further notable development in the representative
art of so reticent a people. It would be idle to fill pages with
the undoubtedly competent productions of del Mazo, the son-in-
law and pupil of Velázquez, for his work was nothing more than
a gradual deterioration from the misunderstood principles of his
master. A journeyman cannot continue the work of a genius,
and while del Mazo might and did quite competently continue
the manner of Velázquez, in the first instance so competently
as actually to cause some confusion to critics of the present day,
between his works and those of the greater man, it is manifestly
not to be expected that he should, with his narrow technical and
mental limitations, carry the art of Velázquez even the smallest
stage further. More importance must be conceded to Valdés
Leal (1630–91), Murillo's younger contemporary at Seville ; for
though, if he be judged by the superficial Italianism of much of
his work, he did little to add credit to Spanish painting, yet, given
the stimulus of an extraordinary subject, he was capable of
revealing tremendous dramatic power. Such a work is his ' St.
Bonaventura', after death, completing his *Life of St. Francis of
Assisi* ', formerly in the Convent of San Francisco at Seville, and
now in the Cook Collection. In this restrained and sombre
picture the macabre idea of the dead Saint, released awhile from
death to complete his task, is conveyed without horror, but with
a startling semblance of truth. From internal evidence it seems
likely that the picture is in fact a portrait of its donor to the
Convent, in the guise of the Saint, in accordance with a peculiar
fashion of the time, of which Zurbarán has left some striking
examples.

As a general rule, however, the repressive atmosphere of
the Holy Office in Seville afforded little scope for strong individualism within the limits of religious painting, and cautious triviality
was the safer road for lesser men ; and so atrophy followed. This,
however, is no real explanation of the decline, for in the domain
of secular painting at the Court in Madrid, things were no better,
and it is not until the eighteenth century is already well ad-

vanced that we find the dismal hiatus in the development of Spain, as a painting nation, closed by the production of a painter who had not only a hand but a mind.

Francisco Goya y Lucientes was born on March 30, 1746, in the little village of Fuente de Todos, not far from Zaragoza. The story of his stormy life has been so often and so well told that it would be a waste of time to recapitulate it here. We need but visualize a painter who, bully, toreador, duellist, bravo, and criminal by turns, was a painter by instinct, a cynic by necessity, and a brute by choice, to understand the extraordinary and inexhaustible vitality of an art which, like that of Velázquez, owed nothing slavishly to history and flung to its contemporaries what they could not understand, and to posterity what it only very slowly learned to use.

Like Velázquez, Goya is a monument of national character, but how different an aspect of that national character! What was in Velázquez slow determination was in Goya impatient insolence; what was in Velázquez direct and coldly analysed vision—vision, that is, of the physical eye, without emotion or imagination to distort it—was in Goya translation into the inexorable facts of form and light and shadow, of a fierce and almost angry personal view of life. After the various vicissitudes which carried him from Zaragoza to Madrid, from Madrid to Rome and from Rome back to Spain, with a trail of violence and lawlessness behind him, he becomes at last acknowledged and settled as the designer of tapestries in the royal factory, and with an aptitude which smells strongly of cynical impudence, models himself for that decorative purpose upon the frivolities of Fragonard. 'The Swing', 'Blind Man's Buff', 'The Greasy Pole' and such productions of this period reveal Goya as a strong man playing at being a Sunday School child, and contrary to all reasonable expectation, not failing therein, but revealing the sinister possibilities of his undeveloped rôle. Goya, as Court painter to a King whom he despised, shows us to what heights ribald disregard of the decencies of his employment could rise, for, in his portrait group of the King in the midst of his family, he painted the most pitiful, because it is the most dignified, caricature in the history of art. Goya as the patriot raging against the obscene brutalities of the 'Dos de Mayo', reveals, with a terrible suddenness and intensity, the awful latent strength of a Spaniard in the days of Spain's torture and humiliation; and as an etcher, in 'Los Caprichos', he tears humanity to tatters with a laugh that hurts.

As his life wore on, and first socially and then politically he was driven slowly from the centre to which his Spanish instinct and his Spanish inspiration clung, he left behind him, one after another, milestones of that undying vitality of his, which enabled him, even in exile in Bordeaux, still to produce an art which, for vigour, for simplicity and for cruelty, is unmatched in the history of painting.

Goya could paint a polite portrait, as for example, that of the Duchess of Alba in the Liria Palace at Madrid. He could paint an insolent portrait, like those of the ' Maja Vestida ', and its astounding echo, the ' Maja Desnuda ',—which are equally portraits of the Duchess of Alba. He could paint a portrait of the Duke of Wellington, which revealed that great Englishman to us in an utterly un-English light, and in which yet we cannot find any direct or deliberate untruth ; and he could almost in the same breath, turn to the production of some astounding plate such as the ' Mala Noche ' in ' Los Caprichos ', one of the most wonderful balances of light and dark in the whole history of monochrome art. Goya was such a giant that we can forgive him the bestialities of giantry, such as ' Saturn devouring his Children ', the picture he painted for his dining-room, for his own beastly delectation ; and we can understand in him the infinite pity, the tremendous sorrow which he expresses in ' The Pesthouse ' or ' The Prison ' in the Bowes Museum.

As at the beginning, so in this, the last really outstanding and national manifestation of the Spanish artistic spirit in painting, truth as the artist sees it is the only consideration, and for this reason it would be idle to carry the story of Spanish painting further. This is not to say that there have not been in the nineteenth century many painters, and some striking painters, in Spain, but it is to say that during the whole of the nineteenth century and so far as the present writer is aware, down to the very present day, there has been no painter in Spain who so relentlessly and so completely expressed the Spanish character as did Velázquez at the one end of the scale, and Goya at the other. It is perfectly true that the work of Mariano Fortuny, with its clear colour and completely dramatic handling of light and shadow, has something of the Spanish spirit, and that the host of more than competent, even dramatically striking Spanish painters of history, such as Carbonero, Lorenzo Valles, Francisco Pradilla, and Checa y Sanz, have contributed very honourably to the history of Spanish painting. But they have not contributed to its development for the simple reason that there has never been and there never will be any development of Spanish painting in the direct sense of the word. From time to time, Spain has produced, and from time to time Spain will produce, great painters, but they never have had and they never will have any antecedents or any successors.

Of modern painters in Spain, probably the two most expressive of their national outlook are Zuloaga and Joaquín Sorolla y Bastida. In the former, vigorous design and careless, almost crude colour combine with a drawing of masses and alternate planes of light, almost comparable, and certainly referable, to the tradition of Velázquez ; and in the latter, a singular felicity in design and an extraordinarily telling and dramatic placing of colour are in each case combined with a kind of simplicity, a kind of obviousness, which ask nothing of the imagination, but demand everything of the observation. To know your Spanish painter of to-day, you must know your Spain, and to know your Spain is not to know it, as so many travelling painters have known it, from the outside, from the point of view of the northern colour sense, which has given David Roberts, Frank Brangwyn and Bertram Nicholls their peculiar outlook upon colour and modelling and design, each in his own kind utterly different from the other and each utterly absorbed in Spain ; but it is to know Spain from the inside, and to realize that the colourlessness of form is not to be translated into terms of a delicate scale of browns or a glorious movement of orange and purple, or a dainty device of line and light, but that it is in itself irredeemably and dreadfully harsh. Zuloaga and Sorolla y Bastida have achieved this ; Fortuny adumbrated it ; but all three lose in force what they have gained by insistence upon action in their subjects, and the ' Bull Ring ' of Fortuny, and the smiling, one might say jesting, peasants of Zuloaga, actually distract the attention by their violence of movement or of expression, from the real beauties of the form in which they are presented to us by artists who are equally, though less forcibly, with Goya and Velázquez, Spaniards of Spain.

There is little to be added to this apparently slighting résumé of the movements of modern Spanish art. We may look any day, every day, for a genius to arise comparable to Velázquez and Goya. He may not come in our time, but, when he comes, if the past history of Spanish painting is any guide, he will owe little more than a common nationality to any of his predecessors, and his successors will not be his followers. He has not come yet, for though, when this chapter was first written, sixteen years ago, Pablo Picasso had already attracted to himself and his work a considerable literature, and was already the subject of a controversy which still keeps his name, if not his work, before a public far beyond the borders of his native country, and indeed more outside than within them, there is no sign that anything that he has ever produced has added, or will add, anything of permanent value to the scope of the painter's art.

This is not a matter of taking sides in a controversy. Picasso is now well over sixty ; if he has not already achieved immortality as a painter, it is fair to assume that he will not do so by any work that he is yet to produce ; and in an outline of the history of Spanish painting, we should by now be able to assess his place in that history.

In order to do this, we are bound, at first, to approach that aspect of it in which it is comparable with the work of his predecessors ; that is to say, we must for the moment set aside all its less readily comprehensible manifestations, and confine our attention to such works as are, like those of all Spanish painters before him, recognizably representational.

This portion of his work reveals an outlook of grave, and for a Spaniard surprisingly gentle, pessimism. The figures in an early work, ' Outcasts ' (1906), remind one of Courbet's ' Enterrement à Ornans ' without either the force or the grandeur of the French work. The composition is simply pathetic in its expression of futility and hopelessness, and reaches its effect with the utmost economy of means. In his exquisite portrait of his wife, painted in 1923, the stillness has become repose, the sadness has given way to quiescence, abruptness of statement to sober refinement of line and tone. Here is a Picasso who is Spanish in all save this strange gentleness.

Yet between these two pictures, and for long periods since the latter was painted, we are obliged to consider the experiments in cubism and in abstract form, and in the distorted and brutalized rendering of the human form, which have been the subject of a whirlwind of words that has done nothing to bring them nearer to the comprehension of the ordinary mind.

The apparent contradiction is in itself an explanation. So long as a painter, working under the restraint imposed by the age-long relation between artist and patron, was obliged to keep his personal reactions to his subject within decent limits, he was not greatly tempted to give way to the impulse to express the grosser or more contentious aspects of those reactions. The often horrific realism of the Spanish primitives, the love of Ribera and Valdés Leal for the macabre, the savage satire of Goya, were an essential element in their personality, kept in check by religious and social restraints. Velázquez found his outlet in the painting of the deformed dwarfs whose very presence at Court was the result of a similar need in their patrons for a purgation of the ugly and grotesque in their natures. But now religious and social restraints, and even those of traditional craftsmanship, have all been swept away, and only self-restraint remains to save the Spaniard from complete domination by that harsh streak in his nature which in other days had been but one of the components of his art. So it seems to me that Picasso, scenting the danger, has adopted the desperate expedient of sublimating the harsher of his reactions in abstract form, leaving the gentler residue to speak for him in plain and intelligible shape. It is to be admitted that this residue is at least worthy of the effort of self-discipline that its expression has involved, but it is hardly the stuff of which immortality is made, and it is a matter for speculation whether Picasso might not still come nearer to greatness if he were willing to make the effort necessary to keep both sides of his personality evenly balanced in a single medium of expression intelligible to all, and challenging all on its undivided merits as the art of a whole Spaniard, rather than as a bowdlerized edition with all the expurgated passages in an appendix. The world would have been spared the spate of would-be interpretative writing on the subject to which I have now unfortunately been obliged to add my quota ; but it might have lost the ' Portrait of the Artist's Wife ', which would have been a pity. Spain still awaits another monumental painter ; but Picasso is at least an outstanding landmark on the way.

BIBLIOGRAPHY TO CHAPTER VI

127. ' Spanish Art ' (*Burlington Magazine Monograph*). London, 1927. [Chapter on Painting by H Tsherwood Kay. This volume also has a useful bibliography.]
128. *The Studio.* Special number entitled *Spanish Painting.* London, 1921.
129. Beruete y Moret, A. de. *The School of Madrid.* Trans. Mrs. Stewart Erskine. London, 1911. Second edition.
130. Beruete y Moret, A. de. *Conferencias de arte.* Madrid, 1924.
131. Caffin, C. H. *The Story of Spanish Painting.* New York, 1910.
132. Cossío, M. B. *El Greco.* Madrid, 1908.
133. Dieulafoy, M. *Art in Spain and Portugal.* London, 1913.
134. Justi, C. *Velázquez und seine Jahrhundert.* Berlin, 1903. Second edition. English translation of first edition : *Velázquez and his Times.* London, 1889.
135. Justi, C. ' Spanish Art ' in Baedeker's *Spain and Portugal.* Leipzig, 1913. [Various other editions.]
136. Mayer, A. L. *Geschichte der Spanischen Malerei.* Leipzig, 1922. Second edition.
137. Mayer, A. L. *Jusepe de Ribera* (Lo Spagnoletto). Leipzig, 1923. Second edition.
138. Mayer, A. L. *Diego Velázquez.* Berlin, 1924.

139. Post, Chandler Rathfon. *History of Spanish Painting.* Harvard University Press, 1933.
140. Sentenach, N. *La Pintura en Madrid desde sus orígenes hasta el siglo XIX.* Madrid, 1907.
141. Sterling-Maxwell, Sir W. *Stories of the Spanish Painters.* London, 1910.
142. Stokes, H. *Francisco Goya.* London, 1914.
143. Temple, A. G. *Modern Spanish Painting.* London, 1908.
144. Tyler, R. *Spain : a Study of her Life and Arts.* London, 1913.
145. Villar, E. H. del. *El Greco en España.* Madrid, 1928.
145.(i). Lafuente Ferrari, E. *Breve historia de la pintura española,* Third edition. Madrid, 1946.

CHAPTER VII

SPANISH ARCHITECTURE AND SCULPTURE

THE story of Spanish architecture and sculpture begins with the Visigothic occupation of the Peninsula in the second half of the fifth century, A.D. But the legacy of Rome was considerable, and Visigothic architecture—crude as it may be—is so evidently a provincial variation of West Roman or East Roman, or both, that such monuments of the Empire as still survive in Spain must be mentioned here.

Toledo, Cádiz, Salamanca, Zaragoza, Seville and Córdoba are all Roman in origin, but the city that has yielded most is Mérida, the ancient *Augusta Emerita*, where the remains include a bridge over half a mile in length containing several of the original piers, and a theatre. The two chief Roman monuments in Spain are, however, the great bridge at Alcántara and the aqueduct at Segovia. The former carried the military road over the rocky gorge of the Tagus, in the modern province of Cáceres, and has been in use continuously ever since it was built by the architect Julius Lacer in A.D. 105. This is one of the earliest buildings in which both the date of erection and the architect's name are inscribed on the structure. It is generally regarded as the finest example extant of a Roman bridge and may well have aroused the admiration of the Arab invaders, who gave it the generic title that one finds in many parts of their former dominions, for *Al-Kántara* means simply 'the bridge'. The Spanish example is over 600 feet long and rises 180 feet above the river. Of its six arches the two central ones have a span of about 100 feet. It is built of large masonry blocks without mortar and still retains its original pavement. Beautifully proportioned, yet massive and severe, it merits the proud boast of its designer : *Pontem perpetui mansurum in saecula mundi fecit divina nobilis arte Lacer.*

The colossal aqueduct at Segovia, rivalled only by the Pont du Gard at Nîmes and commonly called *el puente del Diablo*, was built by Trajan and still provides the city with water from the mountains ten miles away. Built of rough granite blocks without mortar, it is 2,700 feet long and 132 feet high in the centre, where the arches rise 95 feet. Unlike the Pont du Gard, where there is one range of small arches above two ranges of wide ones, at Segovia there are only two ranges of arches and they are of approximately equal width, but the piers between them are rather clumsily diminished in size by means of steps or ' set-offs ' as they rise. In spite of this crude expedient, the whole effect is graceful as well as massive, and the relation of the upper to the lower arcade is most happily proportioned.

Although only these two of the Roman monuments surviving in Spain are of outstanding importance, they must be reckoned among the factors which went to form a native Spanish style of architecture in later centuries. The few remaining examples of Roman sculpture have had little effect on the development of that art in Spain.

Visigothic architecture in Spain has been the subject of violent controversy. Very little of it remains, yet the few tiny churches still standing and the fragments of sculptured detail preserved in museums have considerable importance in the history of Spanish art. The ' barbarian ' Visigoths who had swept over Europe from the Baltic plains to the Black Sea, and then, in forty years, from the Danube to the Ebro, made their Spanish capital in Toledo, where they seem to have attained a high standard in some of the minor crafts. In Spain they built a number of Christian churches until the Muslim invasion of 711 drove them into the mountain fastnesses of Asturias near the northern coast, where they continued to maintain their religious faith and their architecture in spite of the Mohammedan conquerors.

Many small churches, scattered all over the Peninsula, have been described as Visigothic by one writer and another, but of these not more than a dozen merit serious consideration, and some of them are mere fragments. Thus Rivoira, who is the most disinclined of all critics to allow any architectural genius to the Visigoths, only admits the antiquity of the little ruined church at Elche, a part of S. Cristo de la Luz at Toledo, and possibly the crypt of the cathedral at Palencia. But other authorities with a cautious and conservative outlook are disposed to accept a list of genuine Visigothic churches which includes the ruined basilica of Segóbriga at Cabeza del Griego (prov. Cuenca), S. Juan de Baños de Cerrato near Palencia, S. Comba de Bande in southern Galicia, and S. Miguel at Tarrasa, near Barcelona, as well as the three already mentioned, and perhaps S. Pedro de la Nave (prov. Zamora) and S. María de Melque, south of Toledo.

All these nine churches are attributed to a period between the end of the sixth century and the beginning of the eighth. But Segóbriga and Elche are ruined, and neither the Palencia crypt nor the Toledo fragment permit of much architectural speculation. This leaves us with not more than five churches from which to generalize on the nature of Visigothic art. They are all small, rudely built, and difficult of access, for only modest buildings in inaccessible places could have survived the tide of destruction that followed in the wake of religious wars which ravaged Spain for centuries. S. Juan de Baños originally seems to have been a small basilican church with an external colonnade on three sides and a projecting eastern transept. The churches of Bande, Nave, S. Miguel and Melque have a common characteristic : their plan is of the so-called ' Greek cross ' form, though at Nave and S. Miguel the Greek cross is inscribed within a square, so that its shape is not very evident at first glance. Now this ' Greek cross ' plan, which Wren intended to use at S. Paul's and Bramante at S. Peter's (though both were frustrated), generally results in a piling-up of masses buttressing a central tower or dome over the ' crossing ' of the four arms, and in more than one of these tiny churches this remarkable effect is to be seen. Rivoira contends that it is not Greek, that it is a purely Roman invention. The question is whether the Visigothic art of Spain was derived from an Eastern source—Byzantium, Syria, Armenia, or beyond—where such building is found, or from Rome. Here we must leave it unsolved, merely remarking that the evidence for Eastern origin is strong.

Still more obscure is the truth about the so-called ' horseshoe ' arch which appears in these Visigothic churches. Many writers hold that this was a Spanish discovery, but Rivoira again denies it. He argues that the Muslims first used it in the mosque at Damascus early in the eighth century, just about the time of the conquest of Spain. But though he admits the use of horseshoe arches in India centuries before this, he does not credit the Visigoths with the ability to evolve a similar form. There are two kinds of ' horseshoe ' arch, one pointed and one segmental. The Visigoths used the latter form, an arch forming nearly three-quarters of a circle, and, unless one accepts Rivoira,—a voice crying in the wilderness,—one must believe that they invented it themselves or borrowed it from India : either is possible.

For the rest, these little churches are stark plain, and such carved ornament as they possess is of debased Roman type. The capitals of their columns, as well as the rude shafts, are often borrowed from some Roman ruin, but there are Visigothic capitals of barbaric Corinthian type, dating from the fifth or sixth century, in the churches of S. Eulalia and S. Sebastián at Toledo, in S. Miguel at Tarrasa, in S. Pedro de la Nave, and probably in S. Juan de Baños. Beyond these, there is very little sculpture or carved detail surviving, but in the little Nave church, and among the fragments in the museum at Mérida, we can recognize familiar Christian symbols and realize the strength of Byzantine influence.

When the Arab general Tārik invaded Spain in 711, the country was pacific and comparatively civilized. It is sometimes suggested that the Arabs brought to the peoples they conquered nothing more than the scimitar and the Koran. Let us consider whether, at that period, they had developed an architecture of their own worth mention. Of their buildings that can be definitely assigned to a date earlier than 711, the ' Dome of the Rock ' at Jerusalem is so palpably based on Christian types as to be hardly a mosque at all, the Mosque of Al-Aqsà at Jerusalem was built on the site of a church and has been altered again and again, the early mosques of Mecca, Medina, Kairawān and Cairo have been largely rebuilt, that at Kūfah has perished, the mosque of Ukhaidir was barely finished, and that at Damascus had just been begun.

Up to this date, Arab architecture had produced nothing more than the plan of the congregational mosque : a covered colonnade round a rectangular court (the *sahn*), and on the side towards Mecca a deep covered sanctuary, the *līwān*, formed of several colonnades. In the Mecca wall of the *līwān* was a niche, the *mihrāb*, indicating the direction of the holy city. There was generally a pulpit, the *mimbar*, and facilities for ceremonial ablution. But no definitely new architectural forms had yet been evolved by these busy missionary-warriors ; they freely utilized the services of native architects in the countries that they conquered, and as readily they rifled Roman ruins of columns and capitals to support the plain timber roofs of their mosques.

In 786, Abd ar-Rahman I, first of the Western caliphs, laid the foundation of the Great Mosque of Córdoba (now the cathedral). Córdoba had become the Muslim capital of Spain, and this mosque is not only the most important Mohammedan building in that country but one of the most interesting, and certainly one of the most curious, of surviving masterpieces of Arab architecture. Its erection was spread over more than two centuries, for enlargements took place up to the time of Al-Mansur (977–1002) ; and it was considerably altered after the city fell into Christian hands (1236), when it became a cathedral.

The original plan consisted of a *sahn*—still an open court or garden—surrounded by colonnades, and at the Mecca end a deep *līwān* or covered sanctuary, formed of eleven aisles, of which the central one, leading up to the *mihrāb*, was wider than the rest.   These eleven aisles were extended southwards in later years, and then eight more aisles were added west of them; so that the whole block of buildings now consists of nineteen aisles, besides the enlarged courtyard in front of the sanctuary.   The aisles are separated by rows of columns, over 600 in all, rifled from earlier Roman or Visigothic buildings.   Therefore, as in so many early mosques, we find that capitals and columns often do not fit each other, and they have been clumsily adapted to their purpose.   But, from the capitals upwards, we have pure Saracenic—or as it is commonly called in these Spanish buildings, 'Moorish'—architecture.   From the tops of the columns rise horseshoe arches, their striking form accentuated by the red and white stones forming their alternate voussoirs, and above each of these arches rises another arch, this time semicircular but built of the same parti-coloured masonry.   The object of the second tier of arches was to give an internal height proportionate to the great area of the mosque.   On the upper arches originally rested a flat roof formed of carved wooden beams, but to-day we find only a small portion of this roof, and that a modern restoration. All the remaining aisles are spanned by light brick vaults, erected in 1713.   The original minaret of the mosque was only 40 cubits high ; it perished in an earthquake in 860.

The enormous covered area of the mosque as we now see it, some 400 feet each way, divided into nineteen parallel aisles with thirty-three arches in each aisle, has lost some of its original simplicity through later additions, but still retains—up to the roof level—its original form to a great extent.   The horseshoe arches and their striped masonry are characteristic of Saracen taste, though neither feature is so universally used as is commonly supposed. But the mosque at Córdoba has other features that are entirely its own.   The *mihrāb*, normally a niche indicating the direction of Mecca, in this case has the unique form of an octagonal chamber, without any external means of lighting, and richly decorated in marble.   Its roof or ceiling consists of a single block of marble, about 13 feet in diameter, carved out into the form of a shell.

This is, undoubtedly, one of the marvels of Moorish art, but hardly less wonderful are the intricate cupolas formed of interlacing stone ribs over the three bays of the *maqsurah*, or enclosed space in front of the *mihrāb* ; and the' Chapel of S. Fernando ', or

' Chapel of Villaviciosa ', ascribed by Rivoira to the tenth century, by some other writers to a much later date. One bay of the *maqsurah* is enclosed by an intricate pierced marble screen on which is carved the name of its designer, one Bedr. Among special features of this mosque,—besides the interlacing ribs of the cupolas, already mentioned,—there are multifoil or cusped arches (centuries before we find them in English Gothic), and intersecting arches. The great battlemented and fortress-like exterior of the building is characteristic of all early mosques.

Outside Córdoba there are a few considerable works of early Moorish architecture, but nothing to compare with the great monument just described. There is the Aljafería at Zaragoza (eleventh century), the Puerta Visagra (ninth century) and the Puerta del Sol at Toledo, perhaps two small mosques in the same city, and a number of minor examples here and there.

Sculpture as commonly understood, that is, figure sculpture, was forbidden to the Muslims, and such carved ornament as we find in their chief buildings is based on floral or geometrical motives,—hence our term ' arabesque '. The later Mohammedan architecture of Spain, including the Alcázar of Seville, and the Alhambra, will be referred to at a later stage in this chapter.

We must now return to the development of Christian church-architecture in the mountain kingdom of Asturias, where the Visigothic inhabitants had retreated as a refuge from the Arab invaders at the beginning of the eighth century. Their capital was established at Oviedo, and five of the ten surviving churches of this period (*c.* 715–*c.* 915) are to be found within that city or its immediate neighbourhood, while the remaining five are situated within a radius of 30 miles from its walls. There was an active church-building movement in the city under Alfonso the Chaste at the beginning of the ninth century, the king's architect being Tioda the Goth. Several of his works have since perished, but of those remaining may be mentioned the churches of S. Tirso and S. Miguel at Oviedo, and of S. Julián de los Prados at Santullano near by. The first retains little more than its original basilican plan, the second is a mere fragment, but S. Julián is almost intact and is characteristic of the Asturian style. It is an aisled church—that is, a basilica,—but it has a narthex or portico across its western end, a transept, and three square-ended ' apses ' at the east end. Strictly speaking, an apse has a round end, but perhaps Tioda's skill was unequal to this form, which we should expect to find in Italy at that period, and the square-ended sanctuary with flanking chapels is the usual type in Spain. The next group of churches—S. María de Naranco

(848) near Oviedo, S. Cristina de Lena, and S. Miguel de Lino close to Naranco—appear to be the work of one architect, whose name is unknown, but were erected in the reign of Ramiro I (842–850). They form as remarkable a trio as any part of Europe can show from these ' Dark Ages ', and have their parallel only in Asia Minor and Syria. It seems certain that travellers and probably craftsmen came from those countries to Spain along the well-worn Mediterranean trade-route. Naranco was rightly regarded as a miracle of architecture in its own day, for it is completely vaulted in stone, perhaps on account of the Norman raiders who descended on the coast in 843 and were likely to destroy any church with an inflammable timber roof. It consists of a barrel-vaulted crypt, and above it a lofty though narrow church with a ribbed barrel vault. There are external buttresses, beautiful *ajimez* windows (pierced stone slabs), and clusters of spirally-fluted columns carrying the main arches. S. Cristina is smaller, but of the same type, and has a wonderful *iconostasis* or stone screen in the position of a rood-screen, absolutely Syrian in type. S. Miguel de Lino is also small, but has excellent *ajimeces*, and is a fine bit of grouping, rising up to a central cupola in the Byzantine way. S. Salvador at Val de Dios (892) is another example. All these Asturian churches have square-ended ' apses ' and round arches (not horseshoe) are employed. Buttresses are freely used, and stone barrel-vaulting. The *iconostasis* and the *ajimez* are characteristic features.

The next stage in the development of Spanish architecture was due to the exodus of Christian monks and craftsmen from the Moorish cities, especially Córdoba, to the northern districts at the beginning of the ninth century. By this time Northern Spain was throwing off the Muslim yoke, and León had replaced Oviedo as the capital. It is, therefore, in the province of León that we find most examples of this ' Mozarabic ' or Christian-Moorish style that held the field till the coming of Romanesque about the middle of the eleventh century, though there are others in Galicia, Asturias, Castile and Catalonia.

Of the dozen or so of Mozarabic churches that have survived, the best preserved are small, and situated in inaccessible places, thus escaping the wars that devastated Northern Spain during the Middle Ages. Chief among them are S. Miguel de Escalada (913), S. Cebrián de Mazote (? 916), Santiago de Peñalba (*c.* 937), and S. María de Bamba, all in the province of León ; S. Miguel de Celanova (*c.* 937) in Galicia ; S. María de Lebeña (*c.* 924) in the province of Santander ; S. Millán de la Cogolla (929) and S. Baudelio de Berlanga (? eleventh century) in Castile ; S. Pablo del Campo (*c.* 914) and S. Pedro de las Puellas (945) at Barcelona, as well as three small churches in other parts of Catalonia. The two churches at Barcelona have been largely rebuilt, but S. Pablo retains its rounded apses with Lombard arcading. The other Mozarabic churches have the sanctuary of the Asturian type, square-ended outside ; but the inside is often rounded.

The most characteristic feature of Mozarabic architecture is the horseshoe arch, used almost everywhere, and probably borrowed from the Moors, though those people who believe that the Visigoths invented the horseshoe arch independently dispute this. If their view is correct, it is difficult to understand why the round arch was used invariably in the Asturian churches of the ninth century. Other striking features of the style are groined vaulting, projecting eaves carried on bold stone brackets, and some remarkable fluted domes and semi-domes,—notably at S. Miguel de Escalada and Santiago de Peñalba. The most interesting vaulting is at S. Baudelio de Berlanga. Ordinary barrel-vaulting continued in use. also the *iconostasis* and the *ajimez* window. The Visigothic, Asturian, and Mozarabic phases of Spanish architecture thus form a logical and interesting sequence.

Lampérez, a leading authority on Spanish architecture, has well said that ʻSpanish art is alluvial ʼ, by which he means that each flood of invasion brought into the country a fresh deposit to overlay the past. Perhaps that is an over-statement, but certainly architecture was never less distinctively Spanish than in the Romanesque and Gothic periods, when French, Dutch, German, and even, perhaps, English architects were imported as freely as were Italians of the Renaissance in later days.

Ferdinand the Great, who united the kingdoms of León and Castile in 1037, started the movement which gradually pressed the Moors southwards and culminated in the capture of Toledo in 1085. The Christians, exulting in their conquests, launched on a grand campaign of church-building, which synchronized closely with the great era of Norman architecture in England, and similarly they adopted the forms and features which we call Romanesque because they sprang from Roman building traditions in the former provinces of the Roman Empire.

In this brief survey it is impossible to describe more than one of the many Romanesque churches of Spain : the great pilgrimage-church, now the cathedral, of Santiago de Compostela in Galicia. It is the legendary and possibly the actual burial-place of St. James the Apostle. Early in the ninth century his reputed tomb became an object of veneration and the first church then erected on the site attracted pilgrims from all over Western

Europe. In 1078, possibly a year or two earlier, a large new church was commenced, the building of which proceeded with occasional interruptions for some fifty years. On the roads leading to it across France four other important churches of similar type were erected at about the same time : S. Martin at Tours and S. Martial at Limoges (both now destroyed), Sainte Foy at Conques, and S. Sernin at Toulouse. It has often been stated that Santiago Cathedral was copied from S. Sernin by a French architect, and there are many points of resemblance both in form and dimensions. But recent writers hold that the two buildings are contemporary, that the points of difference are too important to be ignored and that there is nothing to prove that the architect was French, though that certainly seems probable. The names of the two men in charge of the building were ' Bernardus ' and ' Robertus ' in Latin. As we now see it, the church is so surrounded and covered with later additions, especially with picturesque and striking Baroque architecture of the seventeenth and eighteenth centuries, that a visitor has some difficulty in disentangling its original aspect from these confusing overgrowths. Yet even the appearance of the exterior at the beginning of the twelfth century may be realized to some extent as one stands outside the front of the south transept, or in the *patio* on the east of the apse, where one can see the round arches of the sanctuary and its chapels. But within the church there is no such difficulty : from floor to ceiling it is a magnificent Romanesque vaulted interior, far more ambitious, far more spacious, and far more complete than any of the earlier Christian churches in Spain. It has an unusually long transept, and the whole effect of the interior is enhanced by the fact that the aisles and the triforium gallery run all round the building, even round the apse and the ends of the transept. There is no clerestory to give space for windows, but the Spanish sun is so strong that this omission is not the defect that it would be in a northern climate. The resulting gloom, however, has the effect of increasing the apparent height of the interior, which is, in fact, only just over seventy feet to the crown of the vault. Originally the church had no less than nine towers and turrets, very different in form from the Baroque steeples that we now see. During the twelfth century it was fortified, till it became a regular citadel, and actually withstood a siege in 1462. The ornate and beautiful Pórtico de la Gloria, of which there is a wonderful cast in the Victoria and Albert Museum, was added to the west front by the architect Master Mateo in 1188.

Other notable Romanesque churches in Spain are S. Isidoro

at León, S. Vicente and the fortified cathedral at Ávila, the Old Cathedral at Salamanca (1120–1178), the Colegiata at Toro, and no less than five churches at Segovia ; while among secular buildings may be mentioned the Exchange at Lérida, the ancient Palace of the Dukes of Granada, and the fortifications of Astorga, Ávila, León, Lugo, Tarragona, and Zamora.

The best examples of Romanesque sculpture are to be found in the churches just mentioned. Among the earliest are those on the south doorway (Puerta de Platerías) at Santiago and at San Isidoro at León, both early twelfth-century works by artists from the School of Toulouse ; the statuary and carving of the west doorway of San Vicente at Ávila in the Burgundian-Cluniac style, and the ' Angelic Salutation ', a more realistic work, over the south porch of the same church, again suggesting a master from Toulouse ; and the curious sculptures in Zamora Cathedral, apparently based on Roman prototypes. The Templars' Church in the same city also contains two remarkable tombs. But the most magnificent example in Spain is the Pórtico de la Gloria at Santiago, described by one recent writer as ' the darling of antiquarians ' and again as ' a typical piece of Cluniac expensiveness ', but by M. Dieulafoy as the greatest work in sculpture of the whole period.

It will be realized that Moorish architecture continued to develop abreast of Christian building all through the Middle Ages, right up to the fall of Granada in 1492. Of many examples still surviving the most important are the Alcázar at Seville and the Alhambra at Granada, but both these cities contain several other Moorish buildings of interest, and at Seville Cathedral the beautiful Giralda tower or minaret (1184–1196), the Puerta del Perdón, and the Patio de los Naranjos are relics of the earlier mosque.

The name Alcázar is the Arabic word *Al-Kasr* (= the castle or citadel). Formerly the palace of the Moorish rulers, it was originally built in 1181 by a Toledan architect named Jalubi. When Seville was captured from the Moors in 1248, it became the palace of the Christian kings, and was largely rebuilt by them in the late fourteenth and early fifteenth centuries in the ' Mudejar ' (Christian-Moorish) style. It consists of a series of rooms and one small court, grouped round a larger central court, the arcaded Patio de las Doncellas (= Court of the Maidens). This fine *patio*, erected in 1369–1379, but much altered as regards its upper story by Charles V, has pointed and richly cusped arches, above which the wall-surfaces are carved into a rich open-work pattern. The Saracen artists were masters in this mode of geometrical surface-decoration, well suited to the strong sunlight of the South. Other notable features of the Alcázar are the Hall of the Ambassadors, a domed and gorgeously decorated apartment, 33 feet square ; the small Patio de las Muñecas (= Court of the Dolls) with horseshoe arches ; and the external façade (1364), a perfect example of graceful *mudéjar* work, with cusped arches and a great overhanging pent-roof on brackets.

The name ' Alhambra ' (Arabic *al-hamrá* = ' the red ') was given by the Moors to the buildings erected by them on the plateau of the hill commanding the city of Granada. It is a strong natural position, encircled by massive and lofty walls which form a striking contrast to the dainty architecture of the Moorish palace that occupies a part of the enclosed area. A wing of this building was destroyed by Charles V to make room for the grandiose palace which he commenced in the Renaissance style (1526–1635). The remaining Moorish buildings were mostly erected in the fourteenth century, long before Granada fell to the Christians, and form the only considerable example of a Saracen royal palace remaining to us of many which were built in the great days of Islam. Magnificently situated, with far-reaching views, it consists of a series of apartments, varying greatly in shape and design, disposed round two large garden-courts lying at right angles to one another : the Patio de la Alberca (= Court of the Pool) and the Patio de los Leones (= Court of the Lions). Beautiful as these two courts are, the construction of the surrounding arcading above the marble shafts is only of lath and plaster, and though it has survived for five centuries in the brilliant sunshine of Andalusia, during recent years steps have had to be taken to arrest the alarming ravages of decay. This flimsiness of construction is not, as has sometimes been stated, characteristic of Saracenic architecture as a whole, but the Alhambra is one of the lightest and gayest examples of the style. Here, as at the Alcázar of Seville, we find a plentiful decorative use of ' stalactites ', originally structural features employed in building a dome over a square space, but later used quite illegitimately, as in this case, as an ornament to be repeated in rows and tiers for mere effect. Other characteristic details are the gorgeous geometrical wall-patternings in stucco and *azulejos* (glazed tiles), the inlaid doors, the pierced windows, and the Arabic characters worked into decorative friezes. The principal apartments of the Alhambra all have domes on stalactite ' pendentives ', and there is a small mosque or oratory with a *mihrāb*. On a neighbouring hill stands another famous Moorish building, the Generalife, which has lost some of its charm owing to neglect, but should be visited for its fine old gardens.

The subject of Gothic architecture in Spain is difficult to compress into the limits of a few pages, for in many respects its history differs fundamentally from that of English or French Gothic, and several of the most famous Gothic cathedrals in Spain are among the least Spanish of that country's buildings. The transitional period, from the Romanesque examples already described to the full-fledged Gothic of Toledo and Burgos, and the few examples remaining from that debatable time, have inspired some writers to state that it was a sterile and negligible period, whereas others find in it a manifestation of native Spanish genius.

Without venturing far into this controversial field, one may cite as examples the cathedrals of Sigüenza, Lérida, and Tarragona ; but in some of the Romanesque buildings already mentioned there are pointed arches, bold buttresses, and other features heralding the approach of Gothic ideas. The introduction of Gothic architecture into Spain may be attributed with certainty to the Cistercians, and its three chief masterpieces of the first period are as undoubtedly the cathedrals of Toledo (1227), Burgos (1221), and León (c. 1240).

During the previous period the Cluniac Order had been mainly instrumental in building churches, of which Santiago is the principal example, and at first the Burgundian type was followed, barrel-vaulted naves and groined aisles being common. In the next phase the buildings of Western and South-western France served as models, though Spanish individuality still remained evident. But the Cistercians who entered Spain in the first half of the thirteenth century brought with them the fully-developed Gothic of the Ile-de-France, and the three cathedrals mentioned above are of the same family as Notre Dame de Paris (1163), Bourges (1190), Chartres (1194), and Amiens (1220). At first the Cistercians suppressed the profuse ornament and the picturesque steeples favoured by the Cluniacs, relying for effect rather on bold vaulted construction, good proportion, and sound craftsmanship ; but as time elapsed their practice became less severe. Their work is to be seen not only in their own houses such as Poblet, Santas Creus, and Las Huelgas near Burgos, but also in many secular cathedrals where their influence was strong. Their buildings in Spain for a hundred years show remarkably little variation, and conform, more or less, to a standard French type. In their present form it is not always easy to visualize the original effect intended and produced by the builders, for additions and alterations have almost buried their exteriors, while the *coro* (choir) has been erected in the nave (as at Westminster Abbey) with high walls or screens, in such a way that one cannot obtain a good vista from the west door, and usually the view across the transept from the north or south door is the more attractive. Moreover, nearly all Spanish cathedrals are crowded with screens, altars, tombs, and other ' bric-à-brac ' of late and florid design, obscuring the stark Cistercian arcades. The English architect Street, who devoted so much research to the history of Spanish Gothic buildings, discovered the names of a great number of their architects, but was unable to determine the nationality of Master ' Petrus Petri ' who designed Toledo, or of Master ' Henricus ' whom he suspects of having designed León, but he considers that both must have been Frenchmen, and that the architect of Burgos must have been an Angevin.

Of these three great Cathedrals, that of Toledo is generally agreed to be the finest. Its enormous area is surpassed by few Gothic churches, and its internal width (178 feet) only by Milan and Seville cathedrals. Street regards the building as equal in some respects to ' any of the great French churches ' and aptly describes it as ' a grand protest against Mohammedan architecture '. It has five aisles, and a *chevet* (an ambulatory with radiating apsidal chapels) at the east end, in which the ingenious vaulting system is noteworthy. The bold flying-buttresses, the ' dog-tooth ' mouldings, and the position of the cloister on the north of the church are also features to be observed. Best seen looking across the transept from the north doorway, the interior fails to convey an impression of its great size for, as in the Cathedral of Florence, the scale is so enormous that one does not realize the height of the vaulting, in this case 100 feet above the floor. Later additions to this cathedral are numerous, including most of the principal doorways and the north tower at the west end.

León Cathedral closely resembles Amiens and Rheims in type. It has only three aisles to the nave, but there is a *chevet*, as at Toledo, with polygonal apsidal chapels. It has a considerably smaller area than Toledo, but the vaulting is of approximately equal height. But León is a more delicate and a more daring design ; too daring, in fact, for it has not lasted well. The area of the supports is small, and the width of arches and windows between them is great. It has good geometrical traceried windows which still contain much stained glass, but the fabric generally has been thoroughly restored, if not over-restored. Like Toledo, it has a cloister on the north. León Cathedral as it stands must present an aspect very closely resembling its original form, the fifteenth-century southern tower on the west front being one of the few additions.

Burgos, on the other hand, has been so much transformed, both inside and out, that hardly any photographs show us its original aspect. From the west, the usual view of the exterior, one sees only the rich western towers built in 1442–1458 by Hans of Cologne and the rich octagonal lantern erected by a Burgundian architect in 1567, while illustrations of the interior are confused by elaborate Renaissance fittings, and the most striking of the many subsidiary chapels is that of the *Condestable*, built in the Plateresque style in 1482. But inside and behind all these florid trappings there remains the bulk of the fine three-aisled French church with its transept, *chevet*, and double flying-buttresses   Though perhaps finicking in some of its detail (thus being in direct contrast to the over-large scale of Toledo), and inferior in boldness of design to León, it is still one of the finest and one of the most interesting Gothic cathedrals in Spain.

The work of the fourteenth century,—which we may call the ' Middle Pointed ' period for convenience,—may be found in most parts of the country, but its most remarkable achievements are in Catalonia, a province always somewhat apart from the rest of Spain. From the time when it was part of Charlemagne's ' Spanish Marches ', through its transition and growth from the independent County of Barcelona to the Kingdom of Aragon, it retained its artistic individuality as well as its political independence. It owed little to Mozarabic influence, received the Cluniac and Cistercian incursions, but, curiously enough, in view of its proximity to France, was never completely possessed by the Burgundian ideas which counted for so much in the architecture of the remainder of Spain. Nor did it accept from the Cistercians, ready-made, the building styles of the Ile-de-France that we have seen in the three great cathedrals just described. On the other hand, Lombard or Italian influence was always strong in this kingdom, which at one period ruled the Italian islands. During the thirteenth century architecture made no remarkable progress in Catalonia, but during the fourteenth it produced the most important buildings erected in all Spain, for Catalonia was rich and prosperous. Hence its building activity embraced, not only cathedrals and churches, but municipal buildings and other evidences of a flourishing corporate life. This movement also extended to the neighbouring kingdom of Navarre.

Some of the chief architects appear to have been foreigners, and one of them paid six visits a year to Gerona Cathedral during its erection, carrying on his practice at Narbonne in the meantime. But the greatest of them all, Jayme Fabre, was a native of the Balearic Islands, and thus a Spaniard by birth. Street has preserved a great deal of interesting information about the personal aspect of this period of Spanish building, and his account of the procedure adopted by the Gerona Cathedral chapter, to ensure that their architect's project of building the widest vaulted nave in Christendom was practicable, forms excellent reading. Briefly, it may be said that the great Catalan churches of the fourteenth century are primarily places for congregational worship on the grand scale, thus resembling the large churches of the friars in Italy, but surpassing them by having vaulted instead of wooden roofs. They lean to the contemporary German rather than the French type. Their tracery is geometrical and somewhat stiff. They have very wide naves and a *chevet*. Their carved ornament is restrained. They are well designed to suit a sunny climate, the windows being comparatively small and placed high up.

The three chief examples are the cathedrals of Barcelona (1298) and Gerona (1312) in Catalonia, and Pamplona (13 7) in Navarre. At Barcelona the scale is well contrived, so that one realizes the size of the building on entering. The cloisters and west front are later additions. The exterior of Gerona has been greatly altered, and its importance lies within, where the immense span of the nave (73 feet), which is roughly double that of Westminster Abbey, is the most striking feature. The length of the nave is, however, somewhat too short for perfect proportion. Pamplona is a skilfully designed cathedral which has suffered little alteration since it was first built.

The last phase of Gothic architecture in Spain includes the fifteenth century, but it extended well into the sixteenth, long after the first appearance of the Renaissance. Its chief characteristics may be ascribed once more to foreign influence, this time from a new quarter. The architects, sculptors, and craftsmen who invaded Spain during the fifteenth century were mainly Flemings or Germans, such as Hans of Cologne who designed the western towers of Burgos Cathedral in 1442, or the Egas family of Brussels who worked at Toledo. In the Spaniards they found receptive pupils. The work of this period is somewhat florid, but it has the merits of good scale and grouping, it contains much picturesque detail, and it is admirably suited to the Spanish climate. Moorish influence is often apparent in the ornament.

The most important examples of the period are the cathedrals of Salamanca, Segovia, and Seville. Salamanca ' New ' Cathedral adjoins the older Romanesque church (fortunately preserved for the most part), which it dwarfs by its size and swamps by its exuberant decoration. It was begun in 1512 by the architect Juan Gil de Hontañón, following an elaborate commission of inquiry quite in the modern style, when nine practising architects were asked to report on the best method of dealing with the new cathedral and the old one. It is a three-aisled cruciform church with a *square* east end, thus differing from all the other Gothic churches described hitherto. Over the crossing is a lantern, a favourite feature in Spanish buildings. The interior is of great width and very impressive, but the exterior displays an abundance of mixed and mediocre Gothic-Renaissance detail. Segovia, commenced by the same architect in 1522 and finished by his son only about fifty years later, so closely resembles Salamanca in many respects that even the cautious Street suggests that the same plans may have been used. Like Salamanca, it has side-chapels to both aisles of the nave. There is a cloister with flamboyant tracery, crocketted pinnacles, and cresting of somewhat Moorish design. Externally, horizontal parapets are prominent, and they conceal all the roofs. The huge cathedral at Seville was begun in 1402 and completed about a century later. It occupies the site of the mosque that the Christians used as a church after they captured the city in 1248, and the Giralda Tower, the Puerta del Perdón, and the Patio de los Naranjos are relics of the old Saracen building. The architect's name is unknown : he may well have been a German. The cathedral forms a complete rectangle, and has five aisles. Of these the *side aisles* of the nave are approximately equal in width and height to the main nave of Westminster Abbey ! This gives some idea of the enormous scale of the cathedral, the largest mediaeval church in the world, and as to its interior very similar in design to Milan Cathedral, its rival in point of size.

Gothic sculpture in Spain is mainly architectural in its nature, that is, it formed part of the buildings already described, and therefore its development followed on somewhat similar lines. There is a fairly continuous sequence of examples showing the gradual transition from the conventional and rather archaic Romanesque statues of the Pórtico de la Gloria at Santiago to the Ile-de-France sculptures of the late thirteenth century. The Cistercians, with their puritanical severity in matters of taste, at first discouraged figure-sculpture, so that when it appears in their buildings it is of an advanced and mature type. Work of this period is to be seen in the central west portal at León and on various portals at Burgos, resembling French sculptures at Chartres and Bourges, the Burgos statues forming a museum in which one can follow the gradual advance towards the realism of the fourteenth century. Yet even in these examples there is something distinctively Spanish.

The use of colour in connection with sculpture developed throughout the Gothic period, and polychrome statues are common. In the Old Cathedral at Salamanca there are four fine examples. Other notable early Gothic works include the tomb of Bishop Manrique at León, the statues of Ferdinand the Saint and Beatrice of Swabia in the cloisters at Burgos, and an interesting series in Tarragona Cathedral. Besides the numerous effigies of saints and apostles, and the rather conventionalized portrait-statues on tombs, there are many admirable statues and statuettes of the Madonna, to be seen over altars and *retablos*, a subject in which the Spanish artists of the day seem to have excelled. At Zaragoza Cathedral the recumbent effigy of Archbishop Lope Fernández is one of the outstanding works of the late fourteenth century.

In the fifteenth century portrait-effigies show a rapid movement in style towards accurate realism, as in the fine statue of Archbishop Juan de Cervantes (d. 1453) in the cathedral at Seville, by Lorenzo Mercadante of Brittany. Among the pupils of this celebrated French sculptor were Dancart, who began the great *retablo* at Seville, and the Spaniard Pedro Millán, who executed the beautiful Virgen del Pilar there. Other notable *retablos* of the fifteenth century are to be seen in the cathedrals of Tarragona and Zaragoza, both by Pere Johan of Tarragona. The work of Gil de Siloe may best be studied at Burgos, in the cathedral and the Cartuja de Miraflores.

In sculpture as in architecture, there is a marked difference in style between the various provinces of Spain. Up to about 1400 French and Burgundian influence had predominated, French especially in Navarre, while the Mediterranean towns of Catalonia leaned towards Italy, and as early as 1440 we hear of a great *retablo* being imported from Genoa. In Castile and Andalusia the fifteenth century saw the arrival and settlement of a large number of Flemish and German sculptors, notably the Egas family of Brussels, who developed the tendency towards realism, so that Christ came to be represented as an emaciated figure and the Virgin as a middle-aged woman. Finally, in the work of Gil de Siloe and Diego de la Cruz we see the first signs of the Renaissance, before the fifteenth century had closed.

The Renaissance in architecture may conveniently be defined as the revival of interest in Roman building, followed by the application of its main features, and afterwards its principles,

to modern practice. It reached France some time after it had
become accepted in Italy, England later still, but its course of
development in Spain is perhaps the most puzzling part of all
the complicated history of Spanish architecture. The period—
if it can be called a period—may be divided into phases, the
Plateresque, the Middle Renaissance, the Baroque, and the
Academic Revival. But each of these subdivisions overlaps its
neighbours, so that we find Gothic buildings still being erected
after Charles V had commenced his great palace at Granada in
the Italian style of the ' Middle ' period. Nor is it easy for any
but a practised student to distinguish between some florid Plateresque works of the early sixteenth century and certain Baroque
buildings of the late seventeenth : extravagance of ornament
is no criterion in Spain.

Towards the end of the fifteenth century signs of the new
movement begin to appear, in architecture as in sculpture. The
most obvious feature of Renaissance architecture in all countries
is the Roman ' Order ', a column or pilaster with its entablature
designed according to rules. But at first Spain did not take the
Orders seriously, and they were used for the most part as applied
decoration, mingled carelessly with flamboyant Gothic or even
with Moorish detail. Thus the cloister of S. Esteban (1524) at
Salamanca has Gothic vaulting on Renaissance pilasters, and the
Lonja (1541) at Zaragoza has Gothic vaulting on Ionic columns.
Plateresque architecture was, in fact, a fashion in decoration rather
than a serious revolution in structural methods. Its singular
name is derived from the word *platero* (= goldsmith) and M.
Dieulafoy goes so far as to ascribe the source of the whole movement to a Catalan goldsmith who returned from Italy about
1458, settled at Toledo, and had a great influence on Enrique
Egas, son of the Flemish architect of the cathedral there. Egas
subsequently became one of the chief exponents of Plateresque,
and indeed he had so large a practice that he was dismissed from
his post as cathedral architect at Granada because his visits
there were so infrequent. The crowded façades of the churches
of S. Pablo and S. Gregorio at Valladolid are characteristic of
Plateresque, but there are many other Spanish towns abounding
in examples, especially Salamanca, Zaragoza, and Alcalá de
Henares. The Ayuntamiento or Town Hall of Seville (1534–
1572), by Diego de Riaño, is more Italian in type, but the various
Renaissance details are massed together with a profusion that
is not Italian.

It may have been Moorish tradition that made Spanish
architects revel in surface decoration, which perhaps reaches its

apogee in the extraordinary Casa de las Conchas at Salamanca, an abuse of craftsmanship : but the somewhat similar Casa de los Picos at Segovia, with its faceted stones, has an Italian prototype or rival in the Palazzo de' Diamanti at Ferrara. The noble cornices of Florentine palaces of the fifteenth century are seldom found in Spain, though the Lonja (1541) at Zaragoza has one, but the Plateresque architects preferred an open loggia on the upper story of houses, providing a secluded promenade and lounging-place for the women. This feature, with a deep eaves and boldly projecting brackets, again suggesting Moorish influence, relieves the usually plain exteriors to the street, elaborate decoration being reserved for the often beautiful *patio* and apartments within. The monastery of S. Marcos at León (1514–1549) actually has a Moorish arch in its façade. But in spite of all these cross-currents and complications, the Plateresque style was an Italian product ; it was the outcome of Italian ideas imported mainly through aristocratic and ecclesiastical channels at a time when Spanish soldiers and Spanish clerics were closely in touch in Italy ; and it owes its unique character to the exuberant and splendour-loving tastes of the Spanish people, then at the zenith of their prosperity.

The second phase of the Renaissance in Spain is much more obviously Italian in its nature and inspiration, as definitely Italian, indeed, as the designs of Inigo Jones in England which it preceded by almost a century. The Roman ' Orders ' are employed everywhere, structurally as well as decoratively, and other classic features assume an increased importance, while planning becomes regular and symmetrical. Once more Spain subordinates her individuality for a short time to the genius of an alien race, just as she did during the period when her three chief early Gothic cathedrals were built in the French style. As examples of the mid-Renaissance three more cathedrals may be mentioned : Granada (1520), Málaga (1538), and Jaén (1532). The two former are churches of the first class, so far as dimensions are concerned, while Jaén is also a considerable building. Each has a width approximating to two-thirds of its length. The architect who commenced Granada Cathedral was Enrique de Egas (of the Flemish family already mentioned), but he was superseded, two years after construction had begun, by the Spaniard Diego de Siloe for the reason previously explained. A five-aisled church, flanked on each side by chapels, and with an east end designed in the form of a *chevet*, its plan is surprisingly mediaeval, and in fact nave and aisles are completely roofed with Gothic vaulting, resting on curious piers with engaged fluted

Roman columns, and with an entablature above their capitals. Málaga has a three-aisled plan with chapels and a *chevet*, but it is roofed with domes on arches, so that it is a step further towards Renaissance purism, but even at Málaga the Orders have not begun to be used effectively.

Charles V's Palace in the Alhambra at Granada (1526), by Pedro Machuca, is far more recognizable as a child of the Renaissance. Its central court is something of an absurdity, and the whole building is utterly out of tune with the Moorish masterpiece which it partly replaced, but it is characterized by the unity and restraint of the Italian School. The courtyards of the Alcázar at Toledo, of the Colegio del Patriarca at Valencia (1586–1604), and of the Hospital of S. Juan Bautista at Toledo (1584–1587) are all akin to the work carried out in Genoa and Milan at that time by such architects as Alessi and Tibaldi. The victory of Italian ideas was partial and short-lived, but it appears at its best in the enormous block of buildings commenced by Philip II in 1559, and known briefly as 'the Escorial' from the mountain village of that name which it adjoins. Comprising a monastery, a church, and a royal palace, it forms a noble group, magnificently situated. But its prevailing characteristic is stark severity, relieved only by the masterly grouping of its dome and towers. It is said that Philip himself devoted much attention to the design and progress of the building, but we must assign chief credit for its success to his architects, Juan de Toledo and Juan de Herrera. The former, who had studied in Italy, died in 1563, just after the foundation-stone had been laid. Herrera, who succeeded him, had studied in Brussels, had served in Italy as a soldier under Charles V, and designed, among other buildings, the Lonja (Bourse) at Seville, and the Colegio del Patriarca at Valencia (already mentioned), as well as the Cathedral at Valladolid, completed with considerable alterations after his death.

After a short transition period, of which the Jesuit church at Alcalá de Henares (1602), by Ordóñez, is a typical product, we arrive at the Baroque phase of the Renaissance, which was taken up greedily and enthusiastically in Spain, where it naturally found a spiritual home. For Spain, of that day at any rate, was essentially a place of 'pomp and circumstance', whose people must have chafed under the severities of Palladian architecture, and, after a very brief spell of restraint, her architects, who had barely forgotten the Plateresque fantasies of their fathers, gladly welcomed the message of liberty, splendour, and revolt that had arrived from Italy as an antidote to Vitruvius. And in Spain, where we can see Baroque at its worst, we can also find, if we look, illustrations of its more worthy aspects : ingenuity and dignity in monumental planning, nobility of grouping, picturesqueness of effect. In my book *Baroque Architecture* (1913) I have dealt with the characteristics of the style, and have devoted a chapter to Spain. Here only a few of the innumerable Baroque buildings in that country can be mentioned, but it is desirable to remark that the unfortunate architect Churriguera (1650-1725), whose name has been coupled with the worst excesses in design of that period, was comparatively reticent in his taste. The façades of Santo Tomás and San Cajetano at Madrid, the Town Hall and Jesuit College at Salamanca are examples of his style.

Of the following examples, typical of the century or so from 1650 to 1750, some are wild and flamboyant, others quite sober : the great Jesuit College at Loyola (1683–1738) near San Sebastián, by the Italian Carlo Fontana ; the royal palaces at Madrid (1738–1764) and La Granja (1721–1723) by the Italians Juvara and Sacchetti ; the palace at Aranjuez (1712) by Idogro and Bonavia ; the façade, ' El Obradoiro ' (1738), of Santiago Cathedral, by Casas y Novoa ; the cathedral façades of Jaén, Granada, Valladolid, and Murcia ; a number of striking towers ; churches and palaces everywhere ; the Tobacco Factory at Seville ; and some fine fountains and gardens. Salamanca, Madrid, and Valencia are rich in examples. Towards the end of the eighteenth century, the Baroque phase ended, and with the introduction of cosmopolitan *Academismo* Spain concluded one of the liveliest chapters in her architectural history, and from that point her architectural history becomes merely European, though there have been occasional exceptions, notably the recent productions of the Catalan School.

Sculpture during the Renaissance followed a somewhat similar course. Italian humanistic influence appears in the work of Damián Forment, who studied in Italy, followed the style of Donatello, and died in 1533. Among his masterpieces are the *retablos* of Nuestra Señora del Pilar and S. Pablo at Zaragoza, the *retablo* at Huesca Cathedral, and perhaps the fine tomb of Martín Vásquez de Arce at Sigüenza Cathedral. His work is marked by refinement and by a sensuous appreciation of human beauty. Another sculptor captured by Renaissance ideas was Philip of Burgundy (Felipe de Vigarni), who began work on the reredos at Toledo Cathedral in 1501 in the flamboyant Gothic manner, but was carving alabaster reliefs at Burgos like an Italian a few years later, and reached a high standard of realism in his remarkable polychrome effigy of Isabel the Catholic in the

Chapel Royal at Granada. Contemporary with him was Barto-lomé Ordóñez, a Catalan sculptor imbued with the spirit of the Renaissance, who also worked on the royal tombs at Granada, as well as at Ávila and elsewhere. Besides these and other Spaniards of note, there were native-born Italians who came to Spain mainly to design and carve tombs in churches. Among them may be mentioned Miguel the Florentine, Francesco Pisani, and Pietro Torrigiano—fresh from his work at Westminster—who settled in Seville but left no authenticated work in Spain except the statue of S. Jerome in the Seville Museum.

Sculptors of the middle period include Alonso Berruguete (c. 1480–1561), Gaspar Becerra (1520–1571), and Juan Juni (1507–1577). The first two, at least, spent a long time in Italy, and all three were considerably influenced by the work of Michel-angelo. They seized with avidity on his notions of dramatic posing and anatomical accuracy, with the result that their statuary, while undeniably clever and striking, has a restless effect somewhat disturbing to the repose of a church interior. The Spanish taste for polychromy still continued.

Into the excitement of the Baroque phase the sculptors of Spain plunged with joy, revelling in the spirit of revolt that actuated it. Whirling masses of pagan saints and cherubs scrambled among marble clouds and golden sun-rays above every glittering altar. Taken separately, the statues and carved orna-ments of the seventeenth and eighteenth centuries are often admirable, but the very profusion with which they are scattered in almost all Spanish cathedrals prevents us seeing the wood for the trees. The iron *rejas* (= screens or grilles), the wood choir-stalls, the alabaster *retablos* and the tombs : all these individual details are usually well designed and executed, but they tend to destroy the effect of architecture—that ' Mistress Art ' whose handmaidens they should be—by the exuberance which is, after all, the prevailing note in Spanish art.

BIBLIOGRAPHY TO CHAPTER VII

[The following list is of books in English, French, German and Spanish, each group being arranged in alphabetical order.]
146. Amador de los Ríos, J. (etc.). *Monumentos arquitectónicos de España*. Many vols. Madrid, etc., 1859–95.
147. Bevan, B. *History of Spanish Architecture*. London, 1938.
148. Braun, I. *Spaniens alte Jesuitenkirchen*. Freiburg, 1913.

149. Briggs, M. S. *Baroque Architecture* (Chap. XIV, ' Spain '). London, 1913.
150. Byne, A. and Stapley, M. *Spanish Architecture of the sixteenth century.* New York, 1917.
151. Byne, A. and Stapley, M. *Spanish Gardens and Patios.* New York, 1924.
152. Byne, A. and Stapley, M. *Provincial Houses in Spain.* New York, 1925.
153. Calvert, A. F. *Moorish Remains in Spain.* London, 1906.
154. Calvert, A. F. *Sculpture in Spain.* London, 1912.
155. Caveda, I. *Geschichte der Baukunst in Spanien.* Stuttgart, 1858.
156. Conant, K. J. *Early History of the Cathedral of Santiago.* Cambridge, U.S.A., 1926.
157. Dieulafoy, M. ' Les Églises asturiennes préromanes ' (in *Mélanges Vogüé*). Paris, 1909.
158. Durán, F. *La Escultura medieval catalana.* Barcelona, 1919.
159. Gómez Moreno, M. *El Arte románico español.* Madrid, 1934.
160. Gómez Moreno, M. *Iglesias mozárabes.* 2 vols. Madrid, 1919.
161. Gromort, G. *Jardins d'Espagne.* 2 vols. Paris, 1926.
162. Güell, Conde de. *Escultura policroma religiosa española.* 1925.
163. Haupt, A. *Geschichte der Renaissance in Spanien.* Stuttgart, 1927.
164. Jones, Owen, etc. *The Alhambra.* 2 vols. London, 1842–5.
165. King, G. G. *Pre-Romanesque Churches of Spain.* Bryn Mawr, U.S.A., 1924.
166. Lafond, P. *La sculpture espagnole.* Paris, 1908.
167. Lampérez y Romea, V. *Arquitectura civil española.* 2 vols. Madrid, 1922.
168. Lampérez y Romea, V. *Historia de la arquitectura cristiana española en la edad media.* Madrid, 1908.
169. Mayer, A. L. *Architektur und Künstgewerbe in Alt-Spanien.* Munich, 1921.
170. Mayer, A. L. *Mittelalterliche Plastik in Spanien.* Munich, 1922.
171. Mayer, A. L. *Spanische Barock-Plastik.* Munich, 1923.
172. Nizet, C. *La Mosquée de Cordoue.* Paris, 1905.
173. Porter, A. K. *Romanesque Sculpture of the Pilgrimage Roads.* Boston, U.S.A., 1923.
174. Prentice, A. N. *Renaissance Architecture and Ornament in Spain.* London, 1893.
175. Puig y Cadafalch, J., etc. *L'Arquitectura romànica a Catalunya.* 3 vols. Barcelona, 1909.
176. Schubert, O. *Geschichte des Barock in Spanien.* Esslingen, 1908.
177. Sitwell, S. *Spanish Baroque Art.* London, 1931.
178. Street, G. E. *Some Account of Gothic Architecture in Spain.* 2 vols. London, 1865.
179. Tyler, R. ' Architecture '. *In Spanish Art* (Burlington Magazine Monograph). London, 1927.
180. Villa-Amil, G. P. de. *Arquitectura civil española.* 3 vols. Paris, 1842–50.
181. Waring and Macquoid. *Examples of Architectural Art in . . . Spain.* London, 1850.
182. Weise, G. *Spanische Plastik aus sieben Jahrhunderten.* Reutlingen, 1905. .
183. Whitehill, W. M. *Spanish Romanesque Architecture of the eleventh century.* Oxford, 1941.

184. Whittlesey, A. *Renaissance Architecture of Central and N. Spain.* New York, 1920

185. Wurz, H. *Von Spaniens alter Baukunst.* Munich, 1913.

186. Wyatt, Sir M. D. *An Architect's Notebook in Spain.* London, 1872.

CHAPTER VIII

MODERN SPANISH MUSIC

THE art of music in Spain of the present day is the newest of all Europe. It is more recent even than that of Finland and Great Britain. The first of the ' new Spaniards ', Isaac Albéniz, was born three years later than Edward Elgar, the first undoubted genius of the English renaissance. He was certainly born five years before Sibelius, the head of the Finnish group ; but whereas Sibelius belongs to the grand line of European masters, Albéniz is but one of the relatively minor composers, and until he came under the influence of the French musicians, his music was little more than conventional. When in 1909 he died at the age of 49, his work in its new phase was perhaps unfinished ; yet he had done enough to show that his gifts were not those of the supreme creators of music.

The modern art of France, formed and led by Debussy, asserted itself during the last ten years of the nineteenth century, so that it gave a lead even to Albéniz. The second great French composer, Maurice Ravel, was born in 1875. The first Spaniard of universal power, Manuel de Falla, was born in 1876. But while Ravel came to maturity without delay, so that he wrote some of his best music while yet in his twenties, Falla's development was postponed until he had in his turn drawn sustenance from the Frenchman, and he was well advanced into the thirties before he could exercise his powers to the full. (The renaissance in Hungary and the Near East generally is still *sub judice* ; for the art of Béla Bartók, born in 1881, has not yet proved itself.)

Thus the new music of Spain is so exceedingly recent that few in Spain or elsewhere can know much about it. And both at home and abroad its rise and promulgation have been hindered by two conditions. One of these is the lack of interest displayed by Spaniards themselves in their own native music, whether folk or art. The other is the excessive popularity, no less in Spain itself than in Western Europe, of a conventional type of music which, though Spanish, is not true and complete Spanish.

Throughout the nineteenth century this commercialized Spanish music flourished. Every composer who served a market of piano students wrote his serenades, seguidillas, Andalusian songs, gipsy dances, habaneras, and the like, when in doubt naming them *danses espagnoles* or affixing such titles as *guitarre*. The makers of this music lived in England, France, Germany, Austria, Scandinavia, the United States of America, and the Iberian Peninsula.

About the middle of the nineteenth century certain of the Russian composers began to penetrate more deeply into the true music of Spain, so that from them came the first impetus to the recovery of a vital art. Some thirty years later, the French composers did the same, but far more thoroughly ; and when the nineteenth century passed over into the twentieth, the way was open for native Spaniards to take part in the work. The Spanish musicologists and collectors of folk-music had already been active for more than a generation, discovering that in no quarter of Spain during the eighteenth and nineteenth centuries had the ' folk ' abandoned their natural music, that each locality retained its dances, and that the gipsies of the south lived in and by music as fully as the gipsies of any other country. Thus the preserving labours of the students of folk-music were not hindered by serious decay in any direction ; and from the time when Felipe Pedrell (1841–1922) began to preach his religion of a national school of musical art, material for that art was available.

The conventional pieces of the nineteenth century did no harm. They did not delay the production of the true music, because the time was not ripe for that to appear. Indeed, they did good in that they kept alive some measure of interest in certain lively rhythms, bright turns of melody, and highly individual emotional moods. The music was romantic. It portrayed a race and a country which every one liked to be in touch with, quickening the general imagination of Europe. Bizet's *Carmen*, a work of pure genius, is the climax of achievement in this direction, and much of its fame is due to the fact that everything in it is of a familiar cast. The Toreador's song, the habanera (a piece written, as it happens, by Yradier, a Spaniard whose *La Paloma* is known all over the world), and the music of the opening scene of the last act, were recognized as ' Spanish ' the moment their introductory phrases were heard ; and whenever the new, essentially Spanish art-music makes its way into foreign countries, it is aided by *Carmen* and the host of smaller works of the same type.

The educated classes in Spain were not interested in native music during the nineteenth century. Like all such classes throughout Europe (Germany and Austria excepted only in part) they yielded to the Italian opera. But the educated Spaniards made use none the less of conventionalized Spanish music. The pieces interested them much as if they themselves were foreigners, so that for every ten of such pieces written by musicians of another race, probably fifty were written by native-born musicians. The average professional composer, compelled to live by serving his home market, and by nature disinclined for change, did not welcome the revival in its first stages : he probably laughed at the enthusiasms of the folklorist, and he certainly caused Pedrell to withdraw into his native Catalonia in 1894, disappointed, and in bad health. All of Spain that he wanted to express could be put into the song, the violin or piano solo, and the *zarzuela*. And the public at large knew nothing of the work of Pedrell and his fellows.

Before Pedrell was in his 'teens, one Russian composer had been inspired to the creation of serious art-music upon Spanish themes. This was Glinka (1803–1857), first of the Russian nationalists, and termed by Liszt the Prophet-Patriarch of musical Russia. Glinka visited Spain in the late 1840's, studied the native music there, making friends with guitarrists and all kinds of people, and then wrote his two overtures, *The Jota Aragonesa* and *A Night in Madrid*, thereby initiating a revival that was destined to await the passing of another generation before it could manifest itself further.

It was natural that a Russian should write *à la espagnole*. Spanish music is primarily Oriental, and Russian music contains many Oriental elements. We should not confuse a Russian *orientale* and a Spanish : no Albéniz or Granados could have composed the *Islamey* of Balakirew ; yet the fundamental non-European spirit of native Russian and native Spanish music draws them more closely together than any other two sections of European musical art.

The next creative influence exerted by Spain upon a foreign composer (next, that is, in respect of works that are in frequent use to-day) is that which brought into being the *España* of Alexis Emmanuel Chabrier (1841–1894), a Frenchman born in the same year as Felipe Pedrell. Chabrier observed with great thoroughness the idomatic qualities of Spanish music ; and his rhapsody, originally written for piano (1883), and then arranged for orchestra, is to-day a very frequently played piece of music. It incorporates the jota and the malagueña, and is in every way

Spanish in spirit and style ; yet it is not of the kind that inspires other musicians, and although different in every way from the commercialized Spanish music of the nineteenth century, it is not likely that it has done anything to foster the present development of Spanish art-music. To such other works as the *Symphonie espagnole* of Édouard Lalo (1823–1892) the same remark must be applied.

The fertilizing power that came out of France, to which the leading Spanish composers of to-day constantly pay tribute, was developed by a musician who wrote, not *à la espagnole*, but *en espagnol* (the phrasing is Manuel de Falla's). The musician was Claude Debussy (1862–1918). But Albéniz, the first highly gifted Spanish musician of the period, had already run half his course before Debussy had done any work in this direction to influence him and his countrymen. Sarasate, the violinist (1844–1908), Tomás Bretón (1850–1923), and others, came too early to be influenced by the new French school, even if their musical natures had been susceptible : Sarasate's pieces are but pleasant trifles ; Bretón's operas and zarzuelas, although performed in Europe, have not gone permanently into the repertory of a foreign opera house. (Bretón's music is pure, clear, sweet and strong ; the *Jota la más famosa* from the opera *La Dolores* is fascinating.) Except when he was writing for money—and his pockets were often empty—Albéniz during the first period of his life wrote none but the best conventional Spanish music. But this word conventional must be applied to many of his compositions only because of the later development in his own art ; for the hundred or so short piano pieces in the Spanish manner written before his removal to Paris are finer music, and more representatively Spanish, than any of the same class written by any other musician, native or foreign. We can, indeed, learn all we need to know of nineteenth-century Spanish music from these alone. They have everything but poetry in its finest distillation, and they range into every province.

That finest poetry, without which music, however varied and energetic, is not pure music, was first drawn from the heart of things Spanish by Debussy, who knew nothing of Spain but what was conveyed to him by pictures, literature, and collected folk-songs, and who was in the country but once, and that only for a few hours. Perhaps none of his works on Spanish subjects (which will be particularized at the end of this chapter) has the magic of his *L'Après-midi d'un Faune* ; but no other modifying remark is permissible : the orchestral work entitled *Iberia* (which was recorded for the gramophone by the Columbia Company in January, 1928) is ideally Spanish. Drawn partly by Debussy, but mainly by the general modern conditions of music prevailing in Paris, Albéniz went to France, and by his subsequent compositions (as Pedro García Morales has said) he ' revealed to the world the artistic significance of Spanish music, and awoke musical Spain to the reality of a modern sensibility '.

The Spanish renaissance dates from this moment. Ravel extended in his own highly individual manner the work begun by Debussy. Granados, writing in a less specifically Spanish manner than Albéniz, and with none of Albéniz' modernism, contrived by means of his *Goyescas* to remind the outside world of the importance of the new energy that was active in his country. Spanish music was in the air, and Manuel de Falla was ready to inspire it and render it forth in the finest works yet created by a Spaniard.

It would seem that, for reasons obvious to all acquainted with Spain, the true art-music must come of the South. Pedrell, Albéniz, and Granados were Catalonians. Falla is an Andalusian, and he is an infinitely more complete musician than any of his predecessors. He stands, in the opinion of most critics, in the foremost rank of present-day creators. Others have produced more. Others, by reason of circumstance, position, character of work, or organized publicity, have become more widely known to the general public. Others again, because of their situation in the cosmos of European music and the adaptability of their subjects to the grand constructions (Spanish music cannot identify itself with the classic Teutonic forms), have written works better suited for everyday performance here, there, and everywhere. But Spain has in Falla one of the indubitable masters of this generation, and her renaissance has evolved this great musician early in its second generation.

Falla's poetic genius is naturally the counterpart of his musical genius. Its range is wide, comprising pathos, and therefore humour, as much wit as good music wants, sentiment that ranges from the gardens of the Alhambra on summer nights to the merrymakings of country-folk and the high spirits of holidays, —indeed, everything that forms the true character of that entity known as the South of Spain. His musical genius is altogether modern, but his technique and style are such that he is neither atonalist, polytonalist, futurist, neo-classicist, nor anything else which the strange development of music in Central Europe has forced into naming. The manner of music-making which he has evolved is an instrument for the utterance of his own thoughts and feelings ; it is this that brings him ultimately into line with tradition, and proves the stability of the renaissance of Spanish art-music. The intellectual revival in Europe has been accompanied by two theories of art : in Italy, for example, the young literary men are split into two factions, the *Strapaese*, or nationalists, who would have Italian art confine itself to provincial subjects, and the *Stracitta*, or universalists, who would have it opened at once to subjects that are entirely general. Falla begins with purely Spanish subjects, and he never departs from them ; but before he has perfected an expression of them in his art, their common human value has become clear, and his art is made universal.

The Spanish musical renaissance, or the research that prepares the ground for it, extends into every province. The interest in regional music is as individual as are the districts themselves, —and nowhere else in Europe are the various departments of a country so curiously individual. We can therefore obtain collections of native songs from every part of Spain, though as a rule these mean little to foreigners until—as is the case with the Hungarian folk-songs and Béla Bartók—they have been re-cast by a great musician. Hitherto such imaginative treatment has been effected in the remoter provinces only by composers of very moderate ability, so that the pieces produced are frankly dull : e.g. R. Villar's *Canciones Leonesas para piano* and *Danzas Montañesas* from León, and the *Veinte Melodías Asturianas para piano* of Anselmo G. del Valle,—yet the six Asturian rhapsodies of Valle are attractive. It may perhaps be that only the native music which is ' full of the warm south ' can ever pass into the great art of the concert world, or into the greatest art ; the Basques incline more to a lofty religious music, the Catalans (as is shown by the work of Eduard Toldrá and Juli Garreta) to big-sized, very dry essays in the classic manner or to compositions that are beautiful only in the established universal way of romantic music. But at any moment a genius may arise in any province to prove this thought wrong.

A case in point may be cited. In 1887 was born in Guipúzcoa a musician who, had fate been kind, might have done for the north what Falla has done for the south. This was José María Usandizaga, a native of San Sebastián. Usandizaga had the power to carry into effect the long, widespread desire to create Basque opera. His second work for the stage, *Las Golondrinas* (Madrid, February 5, 1914), brought him fame literally overnight, for within twenty-four hours of the first performance he became a national hero of music. But he died twenty months later, and his music does not appear to have travelled abroad.

Allowing for the new style of present-day composers, which obscures contemporary works for men and women not musical by nature, one leading difficulty in respect of modern Spanish music is admitted and explained. Another, more serious, is that Spanish music is quite different from the Italian or Teutonic upon which most of us in England have been trained. Spanish and German music express two different worlds. Between Schumann and Albéniz, for example, between the *Fantasiestücke* of the one, and the *Azulejos* of the other, lies a gulf as deep as that between the Catholic religion of Andalusia and the Protestant of Saxony, or between the organ and the guitar. This gulf is traversible. There are many ways from the one side to the other. But until we perceive the ways, and until we have lived long enough on the Iberian side to be at home there, the Spanish does not content us as does the German.

Nor do professional performers always help us in the right way. Until the dawn of the twentieth century, music for the Central and Western European meant (as already implied) German music or Italian. The Italian, being vocal or operatic, may be left out of the present count. Thus, speaking broadly, the main world of music, for us of Western Europe, meant for a hundred years that which is signified by the names Bach, Handel, Haydn, Mozart, Beethoven, Schubert, Weber, Wagner, Brahms. Now all this vast range of music expresses a sensibility or sentiment which we call Teutonic. And the entire course of training for pianists, violinists, and orchestral musicians during the nineteenth century was determined by that sensibility. Imagine speakers trained to Shakespeare (in all his moods), Milton, Wordsworth and Browning, and taught by implication that there was only this one type of poetic art—diverse, it may be, yet essentially the same—and taught further that the way to speak it was the only right and proper way to speak verse. Imagine now these speakers confronted with a form of poetic art that is the counterpart of the swift *opera buffa* of Italy or the sparkling intellectual comedy of France,—say the comedies of Sheridan cast into a light verse. Obviously the speakers would deliver this fancied Sheridan verse in quite the wrong manner. Their technique, vocal and mental, would be the wrong technique, and we should not receive from them the verse as it should be received. Consequently we should not understand it, because we should not be seeing the thing as the thing really is. Much the same mistake will occur when musicians of Western Europe play Iberian music to us. They invest it with a quality of sentiment which it does not contain. They adopt a type of touch for music deriving from the guitar which belongs only to music deriving from the organ. They purvey a passion which Spaniards do not know in their art, because it is not in their lives. They strive after a richness of tone, a clinging refinement of meditation, and a spiritual *misterioso*, that are the very essence of Northern music, but of that alone.

Not too much is to be made of this critical objection, but enough should be made of it to justify our questioning any performance of Spanish music in which conflicting interests seem to enter, and particularly to justify our questioning the remarks made by professional critics about the music. For as the performers approach the music from the Northern, not the Southern, point of view, so critics may do the same. To those of us who have not brought thought and patient experience to mediaeval music, that music sounds all alike, the love songs as heavy as the dirges ; whereas actually it is as different when necessary as the poetry which it accompanies. The same is the case with music of remote foreign countries,—Spain, Finland, Czecho-Slovakia, and particularly the Orient. Two strongly antithetical lines from one of the lyrics in *The Princess* might always be in the minds of musicians when in contact with Spanish music :

> That bright and fierce and fickle is the South,
> And dark and true and tender is the North.

Taking the Northern music as a standard or criterion, we can make the following objections against the Southern. Its melodies are brief to the degree of fragmentariness. Its rhythms are confined to a few characteristic figures. In the matter of form it is rhapsodic, not finely wrought fugally or cast into grand symphonic architecture. Spiritually it seems by contrast almost shallow. Intellectually it is erratic, in that where with Northern music we have well packed logical development, with the Southern we may have long flights of apparently irresponsible melismata or florid cadenza. Then whatever the piece, its mood, purpose, or form, it seems bound to bring in the same conventional melodic turns and the same continuous subsidence upon the dominant of the key.

These objections are fatal, in view of the assumed standard. But since that standard is false, the objections are to be struck out. In other words, Spanish music must from the outset be regarded from a totally different position. It reflects the high lands of the Central Provinces or the orange groves of the Southern, not the broad rich plains of Germany. Its moonlight is not that of the Thuringian forests, but that of richly perfumed

Granada. And it has come, not from the great congregations of the Lutheran Church or the great worldly operatic public of Austria and Italy, but primarily from the burning Orient and the gipsies. In the ultimate issues, music must become universal, as must poetry : the greatest poetic expressions will pass with but little change into every language capable of conveying the same thought and mood, and the greatest musical expressions will win a response from people of every race, Oriental and Occidental alike. An Arabian or Bengali singer, though his art may seem ludicrous at first, can in the end find the way into our hearts and move us almost as profoundly as a European singer of the Schubert songs. But this is only in the ultimate issue, and neither Spanish music nor we ourselves have as yet risen to that point. We have thus to be educated into the Spanish form of musical art. The process is not complex or confusing. Given first a radical sympathy and some personal musicianship, it requires no more than an understanding of the national poetry, art, philosophy, and average mental and emotional conditions.

It is not necessary to cross the seas and gather knowledge of primitive Oriental music. If we learn a little of Hebrew, Arabian, Persian, and Hindu music, and of the gipsy of Europe in general, we are certainly made open-minded to the *variety* of music, and forced to recognize that what we are familiar with from the cradle is not the only kind ; but this is not actually necessary here, for the reason that everything in Spain has long been assimilated into that which has its own *raison d'être*.

A bibliography of English and American essays on Spanish music cannot be brought into this chapter, or compiled as an appendix to it, for the reason that very little of importance has so far been produced. Three of the English musical periodicals not infrequently have reliable articles ; these are the *Chesterian* (11 Great Marlborough Street, London W.1), *Music and Letters* (22 Essex Street, London, W.C.2) and the *British Musician* (53 Barclay Road, Birmingham). J. B. Trend has written two books,—*A Picture of Modern Spain* (Constable), and *The Music of Spanish History to* 1600 (Oxford University Press). The only other book in English is Carl van Vechten's *The Music of Spain* (Kegan Paul), a lively, jumbled, often inaccurate piece of journalism which still manages to convey to the reader some idea of the renaissance and the average interest taken in Spanish music abroad.

General articles by English and American critics, and special articles called forth by particular occasions (such as the production of a Falla opera or the death of a composer like Granados), are not authoritative, because not written by musicians who are thoroughly grounded in the subject. Almost the first article of value to which the reader can be directed is one by Ernest Newman on the *Goyescas* of Granados, which appeared in the *Musical Times* for August, 1917.[1]   J. B. Trend's contributions to *Music and Letters* include essays on the Dance of the Seises in Seville Cathedral (December, 1920), Music in Spanish Galicia (January, 1924), and ' Falla in Arabia ' (April, 1922).; another paper of his, entitled ' A Background of Spanish Music ', appeared in the British Music Society's *Bulletin* for December, 1923.   In the *Chesterian* for November, 1924, there is an article by the present writer on the piano works of Albéniz.   Manuel de Falla wrote in the October, 1926, number of *Musical Quarterly* (New York) on Arabic influences in modern music, and his famous essay on the Cante Jondo was translated for the first time into English and published in the *British Musician* for June and July,[2] 1926.   To the latter was appended a considerable mass of editorial notes and explanations, with some musical quotations to illustrate details referred to only verbally by Falla, and this presentation of the leading Spanish composer's ideas as to the primitive origins of Spanish music affords the most complete introduction to the subject available in English up to the moment of writing.

The same numbers of the *British Musician* contain other articles on Spanish music, one of them a poetical rhapsody, ' Spain and her Music ', by Katharine F. Boult, which displays a sensitive Englishwoman's response to the natural musical conditions of the country.   In the *Dictionary of Modern Music and Musicians*, published by Dent (1924), the student will find the names of practically every Spanish musician of note or promise born since 1850 ; and the third edition of *Grove's Dictionary of Music and Musicians* (1928) for the first time in the history of

[1] The character of most earlier articles can be gathered from J. S. Shedlock's ' Spanish Music ', a short paper published in the *Monthly Musical Record* for June, 1906 (' . . . her national music is remarkable for its rhythmic life, its charm, and its quaintness : the Basque songs, the boleros and seguidillas of Old Castile, the beautiful melodies of Andalusia, and the North Spanish national dance, the *jota*. . . .').

[2] Add Edgar Istel's essay on Albéniz published in the *Musical Quarterly* for January, 1929. Istel, a German musician resident in Madrid, has incorporated much first-hand information in his article ; and he has quoted thirty-six themes from the works of Albéniz, referring these to their native (folk-song) originals, so that the reader may make use of this article as a guide to the chief melodic and rhythmical figures of Spanish music.

that work deals with Spanish music fairly completely. A guide
to the extensive literature in French and Spanish (with a few
references to that in German) is given in Trend's *A Picture of
Modern Spain*, pages 202–212.

Far more useful than books and essays is the music itself.
The scores are to be procured from the Unión Musical Española
(Carrera de San Jerónimo, Madrid ; Cruz, Bilbao ; Puerta del
Ángel, Barcelona ; Wad-Ras, Santander ; Peris y Valero,
Valencia ; and Santiago, Valladolid) or from the Paris publishers
who issue works by Spanish composers. A London clearing-
house for Spanish music is J. and W. Chester, Ltd., 11 Great
Marlborough Street.

The pianoforte appeals strongly to Spanish composers, owing
to the ease with which it can be made to reflect the guitar.[1]
They have extended its technique ; and, except in the case of
Falla, we can study their music thoroughly by means of this
instrument. Even Falla's music is in process of transcription
for the piano, so that already we can obtain whole ballets and
operas in the pianoforte score.

The piano music is naturally difficult, far beyond the power
of any but exceptionally gifted amateurs. Therefore we have
to turn to the player-piano, and it is a fortunate circumstance
that the catalogue of the Aeolian Company, New Bond Street,
London, contains many titles of works by modern Spaniards.
Except when otherwise stated, all the compositions in the following list are available in Aeolian Company music rolls ; duplicate
issues in a number of cases may be found in the Ampico (Regent
Street, London) and the Animatic (Blüthner and Co., Wigmore
Street, London) catalogues. About twenty-five of the pieces are
further available for the electric reproduction pianos of the Aeolian
Company, the Hupfeld (Blüthner and Co.) Company, and the
Ampico.

Opportunity is sought in this list of player-piano music rolls
to give some information about individual pieces and to indicate
further the character of Spanish composition.

I. ALBÉNIZ. The *Suite Espagnole* is the early set of pieces
that first gave Isaac Albéniz a general reputation in Europe and
America. No. 4, entitled in the Suite ' Cádiz ', and subtitled
' Saeta ', became the famous Spanish Serenade of the 1890's ;
it was played in every hotel and restaurant and was as regular
an item in the repertory of amateur pianists as the first movement

[1] Andrés Segovia, a famous guitarist, records for the H.M.V. Gramophone Company.

of the *Moonlight Sonata*. No. 6, ' Aragón ' (' Fantasia '), and No. 7, ' Castilla ' (' Seguidillas '), are better known to-day as ' Jota Aragonesa ' and ' Seguidillas ' ; the latter is one of the best examples of this dance available, and it is among the more popular works in the player-piano repertory. No. 5, ' Asturias ' (' Leyenda '), a very interesting piece of music, became afterwards the Prelude of the *Chants d'Espagne*, of which No. 7, the seguidilla just mentioned, became the finale. It was a business-like habit with Albéniz to issue the same work under different titles.

The remaining numbers of the *Suite Espagnole* are : No. 1, ' Granada ' (' Serenata ') ; No. 2, ' Cataluña ' (' Curranda ') ; No. 3, ' Sevilla ' (' Sevillana ') ; and No. 8, ' Cuba ' (' Capricho '), said by the composer to be in triple-time by his time-signature, but actually in a duple-time, and derived from the tango or habanera.

There has always been difficulty in expressing Spanish rhythms in musical notation, and the carelessness—amounting to ignorance—of the Spanish composers has not eased it. As with certain Oriental systems of music, notably the Hindu, attempts to write Spanish music on paper date back over only a few generations. The rough-and-ready methods of some composers, and the ambiguity attending upon the methods of even the careful ones, set a further problem for foreign musicians who are trained in the exact notational systems of Teutonic and Italian composers.

One detail may be instanced here : the 6–8 rhythm, which is a duple-time,—

$$(a) \quad \left| \begin{smallmatrix} 6 \\ 8 \end{smallmatrix} \quad \flat\flat\flat \quad \flat\flat\flat \right|$$

when syncopated, should be expressed thus,—

$$(b) \quad \left| \begin{smallmatrix} 6 \\ 8 \end{smallmatrix} \right|$$

This figure (*b*) in ' straight ' or direct rhythm becomes a triple-time,—

$$(c) \quad \left| \begin{smallmatrix} 3 \\ 4 \end{smallmatrix} \right|$$

and as such the syncopated 6–8 of (b) is often written by Spaniards. Yet the Spaniards themselves play in a syncopated rhythm right through a phrase, as in,—

(d)

in despite of their notation of,—

(e)

Returning to the Albéniz compositions: the remaining numbers of the *Chants d'Espagne* are No. 2, an ' Orientale '; No. 3, an habanera, ' Sous le Palmier '; and No. 4, ' Córdoba ', a lovely serenade-meditation based upon this poetic motto: ' In the silence of the night, something interrupts the whisper of the aromatic zephyrs through the jessamines,—the guzlas [1] sound, accompanying the serenades and diffusing in the air ardent melodies and notes as sweet as the vibrations of the palms in the high heavens.'

A third set of early, and therefore conventional, pieces by Albéniz are the *Recuerdos de Viaje*: No. 1, ' En el mar ', a barcarolle; No. 2, another barcarolle, of the ballade or *leyenda* type; No. 3, ' Alborada ' (not the northern song, but a ' morning mood '); No. 4, ' En la Alhambra '; No. 5, ' Puerta de Tierra ', a bolero; No. 6, ' Rumores de la Caleta ', after the malagueña; No. 7, ' En la Playa ', a third barcarolle. Two pieces derived directly from Moorish forms are the ' Zambra ' (*Douze pièces caractéristiques*, No. 7) and the ' Serenata árabe ', an isolated composition. No. 12 of the *Pièces caractéristiques* is a serenata, ' Torre Bermeja ', which illustrates the elementary transcription of the guitar style to the piano. Not provided for the player-piano, but well within the technique of a good amateur pianist, is a *Rapsodia Española*, written probably about 1890, which incorporates: (1) the ' Petenera de Mariani ', (2) an original jota, (3) the ' Malagueña Juan Breva ', and (4) that very happy Salamanca dance, ' Estudiantina '.

The works for piano written by Albéniz in the last period of his life, when he lived in Paris and yielded to the inspiration of the new school of French composers, are among the finest creations for that instrument, and entirely representative of the first stages in the modern development of the art of music. They

[1] The guzla is a type of one-string violin.

are mostly difficult ; Albéniz himself, becoming stout in his last years, could not play all of them. They are difficult even for the player-pianist, and some, as the ' Jerez ' of *Iberia*, are not effective upon the player-piano, owing to the involved writing.

Two pieces, a Prelude and an Asturias, are brought together under the title *Espagne*. The Prelude is a long, beautiful, comparatively simple *andantino* in D flat major. The Asturias is a song, *allegretto non troppo*, in F sharp minor. Experienced music lovers, desiring to enter at once into the absolute music of this composer, might make use of these two pieces. Amateur pianists whose experience is limited might select for the same purpose the set of six ' album leaves ' entitled *España* : Prelude (in the Zaragoza manner), Tango, Malagueña, Serenata, Capricho Catalan, and Zortzico. These are not provided for the player-piano.

The zortzico, a northern dance in five-time, is worked by Albéniz into an exquisite composition which appears to have been written when he was on the threshold of his final period. This piece is named *Zortzico*, and is published by the Bureau d'Edition de la Schola Cantorum, Paris. Two great posthumous works for piano, left unfinished by thè composer, are the *Azulejos*, a prelude inspired by the Alhambra, and *Navarra*, an elaborate art-expansion of the jota : the former was completed by Granados, the latter by Deodat de Sévérac ; and both are published by the Bureau of the Schola Cantorum.

The set of twelve pieces wherein Albéniz fully asserted the high qualities and wide range of Spanish art-music is the *Iberia*. No. 1, ' Evocation ', expresses the very heart of Spanish music, in poetic terms that are rare with Albéniz, who for all his interest in Spain was always a Catalan. Navarre and Andalusia are the regions he brings into this prelude to *Iberia*. The eleven numbers that follow are brilliant pictures of the localities implied in the titles : El Puerto, Fête-Dieu a Séville, Triana,[1] Almería, Rondeña, El Albaicín, El Polo, Lavapiés, Málaga, Jerez, and Eritaña. It is necessary to remain with *Iberia* for a long while in order to penetrate to the spirit behind the notes and rhythms and to discover the individuality of the various pieces. And it is probably essential that the student and music lover shall have acquired elsewhere a knowledge of Spanish music.

[1] Leff Pouishnoff, the Russian pianist, tells an amusing story of *Triana* and its treatment by a Manchester music critic. He plays the music in a version made by Godowsky. The critic remarked that Godowsky's amplification of the notes seemed to have converted the originally charming girl of Albéniz' fancy into an over-blown courtesan.

II. GRANADOS. The nineteenth-century music of Liszt, Chopin, Grieg, and in less degree Schumann, so much influenced Granados that his music is less Spanish than general. He is a Spaniard in the way Rachmaninoff, for example, is a Russian : he writes to national, even regional, subjects, and native rhythms, melodies, and colours enter into his work at every turn ; yet his work is not that of a national revivalist, nor again is it that of a modernist composer. The *Danzas Españolas*, twelve in number, are issued without determinate titles ; and though we can refer some of them to their native origins, they are chiefly of interest as pieces of late nineteenth-century music. The Spanish flavour is more strongly marked in the *Seis Piezas sobre cantos populares españoles,*—Añoranza, ' Ecos de Parranda ', Vascongada, Oriental March, Zambra, and Zapateado. The *Capricho Español*, Op. 39, is moderately attractive. The *Rapsodia Aragonesa* (1901) is refined, elegant, and (to the student who observes the art-treatment of the jota of Aragon) distinctively poetic. But only the *Goyescas* lift Granados into the foremost line of twentieth-century musicians, and of these it is chiefly by two numbers, *El Pelele* and *La Maja y el Ruiseñor* (' Quejas '), that he is proved a writer of genius. The first of these is rhythmically brilliant ; the last is one of the most delicately poetical pieces of music in existence. Three further numbers from the *Goyescas,*—' Los Requiebros ', ' Coloquio en la Reja ', and ' El Fandango de Candil ',—display the composer's very exceptional musicianship, though without the thoroughness of the other two.[1]

III. MANUEL DE FALLA. Opera and the ballet have been the medium for the expression of Falla's mature art ; and by the year 1928 only the first dance from *La vida breve* and the ' Danse Rituelle du Feu ' had become familiar as piano pieces and found place in the player-piano (Ampico). The music written by him for piano consists only of four Spanish pieces from 1908 (*Aragonesa, Cubana, Montañesa,* and *Andaluza*), and a *Fantasía Baética* (1925). The four pieces, of early composition, yet marked by Falla's later refinement, strength, and exact poetic intelligence, are available for the player-piano ; the very advanced *Fantasía* was recorded for the gramophone in 1926, but the record was withdrawn.

A work for piano and orchestra, *Noches en los jardines de España,* represents the purest poetry of the new Spanish music. It is occasionally to be heard at English concerts. The *Siete Canciones populares españolas,* Falla's most entirely familiar compositions, form an exquisite assembling of some of the more

[1] Eleven of Granados' compositions were played by the composer for the Hupfeld Electric Reproducing Piano.

distinctive elements of Spanish native music ; these vocal pieces
are : (1) ' El Paño moruno ', (2) a seguidilla of Murcia, (3) an
Asturiana, (4) a Jota (a particularly charming song), (5) a Ber-
ceuse, ' Nana ', (6) a piece described simply as ' Canción ', and
(7) a specimen of the vivacious polo. Falla's *Homenaje*, a piece
for guitar written in memory of Debussy, is probably the most
highly organized composition for the Spanish guitar. An
orchestral suite of dances from the ballet of *El sombrero de tres
picos*, which is heard at English concerts, is among the opera
and ballet selections that are published for piano solo.

IV. JOAQUÍN TURINA. In Turina's music the sharp, bright,
hard qualities of Spanish art are even more pronounced than in
that of Albéniz. Turina was born at Seville in 1882, and he
has become known abroad chiefly by means of his *Procesión del
Rocío*, an orchestral composition. Although his music is not so
grateful to foreigners as is Falla's, he is one with Falla (and
Conrado del Campo) in both the desire and the power to elevate
Spanish art-music.

It happens that an exceptional quantity of Turina's works
have been made available for study at the player-piano : *Coins
de Séville* (No. 4, ' A los toros ') ; *Sevilla* (' Sous les Orangers ',—
' Le Jeudi Saint à Minuit ', a procession,—and ' La Feria ') ;
Recuerdos de mi rincón (a ' tragedia cómica ', unintelligible with-
out the printed copy of the music) ; *Album de viaje* (' Retrato ',
—' El Casino de Algeciras ',—' Gibraltar ', with the British
National Anthem,—' Paseo Nocturno ',—and ' Fiesta mora en
Tánger ') ; and *Femme d'Espagne* (' La Madrilène Classique ',—
' L'Andalouse sentimentale ',—and ' La Brune Coquette ').

V. THE FRENCH COMPOSERS. The following list includes
the principal works on Spanish themes that are provided for the
player-pianist.

DEBUSSY : *Estampes*, No. 2 (' Soirée dans Grenade ') ; *Pré-
ludes*, No. 9, Book 1 (' La sérénade interrompue ') and No. 3,
Book 2 (' La Puerta del Vino ').

With all music *en español*, it is helpful to know not only the
region, or the town, or building, or event, expressed in the
music, but even the particular portion of the locality or the
individual detail of the event ; and Spanish composers frequently
give clues in their titles that we should follow up : Debussy
adopted the native custom when he calls the second of these
preludes ' La Puerta del Vino '.

RAVEL : *Miroirs*, No. 4 (' Alborada del gracioso ' : very
graphic music) ; *Rapsodia Espagnole :* (1) ' Prélude à la Nuit ',
(2) a Malagueña, (3) a Habanera, and (4) ' Feria '

CHABRIER : *España* (Animatic music roll). SAINT-SAËNS :
La jota Aragonesa (Animatic). MASSENET : ballet movements
from *Le Cid* and *Don Quixote* (of little musical value.)

VI. LISZT wrote a *Rhapsodie Espagnole* on the old melody,
' Folies d'Espagne ', and the jota of Aragon. MOSZKOWSKI
wrote some dozens of conventional Spanish pieces : the *Album
Espagnole*, the *Boabdil* Ballet, the *Spanish Dances*, Op. 12, a
number of detached pieces (*Guitarre*, *Habanera*, etc.), and—best
of all—the *Caprice Espagnol*, Op. 37, in A minor.

VII. There are innumerable compositions by Spanish
writers of the second rank which are pleasant in themselves and
instructive in the matter of Spanish rhythms, melodies, and
moods. Many of these are to be had for the player-piano, as
de la Cinna's *Jota Aragonesa*, Larregla's *Viva Navarra !* (or
' Siempre Pa Alante '), Nogués' *Jota Aragonesa*, and the *Rhapsodia Española* of Anselmo G. del Valle. And modernist composers often bring into their works Spanish rhythms and turns
of melody, as Stravinsky in his *Étude pour Pianola* (Aeolian
Company, London, Roll No. T 967).

Gramophone records are made in Spain and in Spanish
America for local markets. These are rarely of a high musical
value. The catalogues of the great companies in England and
the United States contain many Spanish compositions, and as
other works become known to the concert public the list will
be expanded.

BIBLIOGRAPHY TO CHAPTER VIII

The bibliographical indications belonging to this chapter will be found
in the text, pp. 249–251.

CHAPTER IX

SPAIN SINCE 1898

(i) THE EPOCH OF ALFONSO XIII (1898–1931).

TO Spain, as to England, the end of the nineteenth century brought war and change. The loss of her last American colonies, as has been said (p. 86), was followed by a revision of national values. Cánovas had been assassinated in the preceding year and the Republican Castelar died in 1899. Although eloquence did not die with him, there was a growing feeling that one must get down by penetrating analysis to the bedrock of fact underlying hollow speeches and pompous display. The learned Aragonese, Joaquín Costa, demanded that seven turns of the key should be given to the Cid's tomb. The dead were to bury the dead. Spain never shows up better than when confronted with misfortune and the way in which at the beginning of the twentieth century Villaverde took in hand and restored the national finances without failing to honour any of Spain's foreign liabilities was worthy of her past history and permanently enhanced her credit abroad, even though his efforts to impose stringent economy proved unavailing.

The compact, begun in 1885, by which Liberals and Conservatives alternated in power continued to work with fairly satisfactory results until the War of 1914 brought new conditions to bear on an outworn system. The steady, discreet and courageous rule of Queen María Cristina during her seventeen years' regency (p. 85) was of material assistance in preserving the throne for her infant son, who, like his father, began to reign at the age of sixteen (May 17, 1902). His marriage, four years later, to an English princess was another sign of a new period in Spain's history. It showed recognition of the fact that England, although in history she has often been Spain's enemy, is her natural friend and ally. The saying, generally applied to Portugal, is true of Spain : ' Con todo el mundo guerra y paz con Inglaterra.' [1] Spain hitherto in her external relations had maintained an attitude of courteous isolation, and at the outbreak of the Cuban conflict,

---

[1] ' War with everybody and peace with England.'

followed by war with the United States, she had found herself alone.

The first years of the new century saw political changes as great as those of the last years of the nineteenth. The leader of the Federalists, Pi y Margall, died in 1901, and the Liberal leader, Sagasta, in 1903. In the latter year Nicolás Salmerón, one of the Presidents of Spain's First Republic (p. 84), was chosen as leader of the Republicans. It proved less easy to find an undisputed successor to Sagasta. The votes for Montero Ríos and those for Moret were so nearly equal in number that neither of them felt able to accept the leadership, while the hour of the more Radical Canalejas had not yet come. The Conservative Party was more fortunate, for, although it also suffered from too many blue ribands, it possessed several men, and especially one man, of character and outstanding ability to carry on the traditions of Cánovas. In 1906, Maura, who had been Premier in 1904, succeeded to the leadership of the Conservative Party. He was the chief personality of Spanish politics during the first quarter of the century, and possessing, in addition to a sensitive temperament, a keen practical sense and skill in parliamentary debate, set himself to reform a hidebound and corrupt political system, and became a very splendid failure.

When the Liberals returned to power they were at sixes and sevens, and more stable government came in only with the return of Maura, who was Premier during two and a half eventful years, from January, 1907 to October, 1909. The elections of 1907 emphasized the dissension in the Liberal ranks, which gave some opportunity to Republicans, Catalanists and Carlists ; but the final results, an overwhelming Conservative majority, placed Maura in a strong position. His attention was engrossed by his Bill of Local Administration, which with unwearied patience and skill he piloted through the Chamber in the face of continual obstruction. His conciliatory attitude was rewarded by the voting of the Bill by the Chamber of Deputies in February, 1909. He also introduced a Bill for the reconstruction of the Navy.

Maura's action was hampered by terrorist outrages and serious bomb-throwing at Barcelona. Despite this and the murder of the King of Portugal on February 1, 1908, King Alfonso courageously visited the Catalan capital a few weeks later and met with an enthusiastic reception. The Government, politically so strong, had to face a serious situation in Morocco in the summer of 1909, when the Moorish tribes made a fierce attack on Melilla. Acting as any government worthy of the name must have done, it immediately sent out the regiments which could most quickly

relieve Melilla, those of the Barcelona garrison. The elements of
disorder at Barcelona seized the occasion, and, after promoting a
defeatist demonstration at the departure of the troops, organized
a general strike on July 26. There followed the notorious ' Tragic
Week '. Barricades were erected in the streets, fierce attacks
were made on the convents, and even while the fighting was going
on round Melilla a hundred persons were killed in the Catalan
capital. The Government once more acted with decision, many
arrests were made, the ' lay schools ' were closed, and one of their
promoters, Francisco Ferrer, arrested earlier in the year, was tried,
like the rest, by court martial and shot. A week later, the Government fell, and Moret was in office. The new Government appointed
General Weyler Captain-General of Catalonia, and his action was
moderate and conciliatory.

This tragic episode, at the end of July, 1909, proved how closely
related were Spain's three chief internal problems, maintenance
of order, the clerical question and Catalanism. The unpopularity of the war in North Africa was taken full advantage of
by Anarchist and other agitators, who, by misrepresenting the
objects and reasons of the campaign, promoted their own revolutionary aims.

The Conference of Algeciras in 1906 gave international recognition to Spain's rights in Morocco, and, at the same period, in
1904 and in 1907, a closer bond was drawn between Spain and
France and England. This served Spain's real interests : with
Germany, as the Conde de la Mortera remarked at the time, she
had no interests in common. More than one incident made it
plain that in Morocco at least the action of Germany could not be
beneficial to Spain. Differences arising with France led to the
Treaty of 1912. Spain's international action in the Morocco
question was hampered throughout by the absence of a strong
united public opinion in Spain itself. As her share in Morocco
Spain had received a barren mountainous region, inhabited by
warlike tribes, which was of a nature to tax any country's energies
and resources. Some prominent politicians were of opinion that
there could be no peace until the whole region was conquered ;
others wished to limit Spanish enterprise to the utmost, consistently with the security of a narrow strip along the coast. The
Morocco question was further complicated by the status of
Tangier. ' The internationalization of Tangier ', said the Conde de
la Mortera, ' reduces the problem of Morocco to that of a city,
but keeps it alive in its entirety.'

In the first half of the year 1909, the Conservative Government's request for a special vote of credit for Morocco in order

to restore order in the Spanish zone was denounced by the Liberals as a policy of conquest. On July 27 the Spanish met with a severe reverse and the Barranco del Lobo was added to the tragic names of Spain's history. This collapse of the Spanish arms in Morocco was repeated on a more disastrous scale when, in the summer of 1921, the Moors, under command of the Riff leader Abd-el-Krim, attacked and isolated the Spanish advanced positions. During the retreat from Annual the Spanish losses were most severe and the Moors surged up to the very walls of Melilla. General Silvestre, who himself lost his life during the retreat, either at his own or at the enemy's hands, was blamed by public opinion for his precipitancy, while General Berenguer, sent out subsequently, incurred censure for delay. The Army retaliated by fixing the blame on the hesitations, contradictions and delays of the politicians at home.

At the beginning of 1910 Moret was succeeded as Premier by Canalejas, whose attention was mainly taken up with the so-called religious question. This came into Spain with the new century : partly it was the effect of French Radical doctrines on Spanish Liberals and Radicals ; partly it was due to the expulsion of the monks from France, when many of them took refuge in Spain, thus raising the question of the status of foreign members of religious communities in Spain. In 1901 Pérez Galdós' play *Electra*, which dealt with the undue influence of members of religious Orders in the family, was the occasion of excited scenes in the streets of Madrid. Maura's Convenio of 1904 had confirmed the Concordat of 1851 and authorized the existence of the religious communities in Spain while rendering them liable to equal taxation with other Spanish subjects and abolishing communities of under twelve members ; but Maura fell before his Bill had been voted by the Chamber. In the autumn of 1906 a new Law of Associations, revising that of 1887, was presented to Parliament. It subjected all religious Orders in Spain, with the exception of those mentioned in the Concordat of 1851, to the civil authorities, to the Spanish State. The Concordat had mentioned by name two Orders (St. Vincent de Paul and St. Philip Neri), and a third anonymously, and the ingenious interpretation was put forward that two and one did not necessarily make three ; the third Order might be a third Order in each district or diocese.[1] Maura's Convenio of 1904 was denounced to the Vatican. In Parliament the Conservatives opposed the new Bill ; a formal protest was received by the Government from the Archbishop of

[1] On this interpretation, however, see E. Allison Peers : *Spain, the Church and the Orders*, London, 1939, pp. 81–5.

Toledo in the name of the Spanish prelates ; there were demonstrations and counter-demonstrations.

In 1910, the clerical question again became acute. The
Government of Canalejas embarked on negotiations with the
Vatican for the revision of the Cóncordat of 1851, but meanwhile, in May, 1910, it enacted that all Orders in Spain except
the three of the Concordat must be registered civilly, thus putting
in force a decree of Sagasta dating from 1902, the year before
his death. In June the Government further allowed non-Roman-
Catholic religions in Spain the use of the external signs of their
religion, as, for instance, crosses on their churches. A provisional
measure, known as the padlock, ' Ley del Candado ', now forbade
the establishment of more religious houses in Spain pending the
result of the negotiations with Rome. This, said some critics,
was to lock the religious Orders not out of but into Spain after
they had been allowed free entry on their expulsion from France.
There were anti-clerical demonstrations at Madrid, followed by
huge clerical demonstrations at San Sebastián and elsewhere.
Before the end of the year the Spanish Ambassador to the Vatican
had left Rome. The artificial character of the clerical question
in Spain was shown when soon after this it collapsed and ceased
to be a prominent factor in practical politics, although Moret
and other Liberal leaders had called it the most important question
of the time. The religious Orders have rendered great services in
agriculture, education, culture and research ; and there seems
no reason, provided they have no unfair privileges, why they
should not be allowed to render similar services in industry and
commerce.

In April, 1911, Canalejas reconstructed his ministry. He
was kept in power as a kind of buffer state between the Conservatives and the extreme Left. The Republicans and Socialists
attacked him, but without a real wish to overthrow him, fear-
ing that his fall would lead to the return of the Conservatives ;
the Conservatives regarded him as a protection from the Radical
revolutionaries. Between them they maintained him in office
but paralysed his action. Yet, when faced by revolutionary
strikes, he showed a firmness and a decision which sealed his
doom. After his murder (1912) he was succeeded as Premier by
Count Romanones, one of the ablest statesmen of his time.

In October, 1913, Romanones' Government gave place to a
Conservative ministry under Dato, who was in office at the outbreak of the War of 1914–18. He was characterized by unfailing
discretion and moderation ; it was said of him that if he were
to meet the Devil he would offer him a cigarette ; but he held

definite views and could speak out on occasion, as when he com-
mented on the revolutionary strike of August, 1917, or after the
murder of Canalejas demanded that the penal laws should be more
rigidly applied, pronouncements which paved the way for his
own assassination in 1921.

In 1914 Spain at once declared her neutrality ; it was the only
possible course, as statesmen of all parties agreed, and it was
more of a triumph for the Allies than the Allies generally realized.
The Allies had comparatively little to offer Spain, while Germany
held out the glittering baits of a free hand in Portugal and the
possession of Gibraltar and Tangier. The Allies had little to fear
from their enemies in Spain, for the latter were well aware that
Spain must remain neutral and that her destinies were bound up
with those of France and England. On the other hand, the Allies
had a good deal to fear from their friends. In the first place there
were the Catalans ; Catalan pro-Ally intrigues were in the rest
of Spain felt to be primarily anti-Spanish or anti-Castilian. It was
indeed easy for the Catalans to declare that had Catalonia been
independent she would not have been neutral : had Catalonia
been independent of Spain she *could* not have been neutral.
Count Romanones was consistently pro-Ally, as were also the
eloquent Don Melquíades Alvarez, the enigmatic politician Señor
Lerroux, the Republican novelist Blasco Ibáñez and the provocative Unamuno. None of these champions could do much to
further the cause of the Allies in Spain. The Spanish army admired
German discipline ; the Church did not admire recent French
legislation. Maura could declare, in September, 1916, that
France and England, through three centuries of history, had been
hostile to Spain's progress, and that they had systematically
weakened and belittled her since the days of Richelieu. Spaniards
of character and learning were grateful to Germany for the part
she had taken in the study of Spanish literature and art, and
perhaps failed to realize as clearly as Menéndez y Pelayo had
done that the Germany of the twentieth century was a very
different Germany from that of Goethe.

Spain's neutrality throughout the War, as loyal as it had been
inevitable, was greatly appreciated in France, whose southern
frontier was thus secure from attack. Spain was early able to
distinguish between English and German methods in warfare : by
September, 1916, she had already lost thirty thousand tons of
merchant shipping by the action of German submarines ; and the
Germans persisted blindly in this course in the face of every
Spanish protest. This gradually estranged Spain from Germany ;
while the prolonged and devoted labour of King Alfonso in tracing

French and other prisoners won for him the permanent gratitude of the Allies.

King Alfonso's personal popularity had sensibly weakened the Republican Party, and the Carlist cause had faded out of practical politics. On the other hand, the Socialist Party flourished, more perhaps than its intrinsic strength in the country warranted, owing to the prestige of its leader, Don Pablo Iglesias. The Unión General de Trabajadores, founded in 1888, had 127,000 members in August, 1912. In its moderate socialism it contrasted with the later and more revolutionary Confederación Nacional del Trabajo. The division between Socialists and Syndicalists was clearly marked, and in 1920 the moderates, being in a majority, were able to turn the scales against decision to adhere to the Third International. The danger of revolution arose chiefly from subversive ideas, of non-Spanish origin, disseminated among the workmen of the large towns and in the army. At Barcelona, where politically Catalanism made so much play, the artisans were always tending to turn from it towards anarchism and syndicalism.

In the summer and autumn of 1917 ministries began to topple over like ninepins. The Marqués de Alhucemas succeeded Count Romanones in April, but resigned in June; Dato fell in October; and, after half a dozen political leaders had in turn found it impossible to accept the task of forming a ministry, the Marqués de Alhucemas was again sent for and became Premier in November. Thus there were four Governments in the year and many intervals of crisis. It was not expected that the path of the new Government would be easy, and in February, 1918, a lengthy crisis only ended when Maura was sent for and formed a National Government of ex-Prime Ministers, including Romanones, González Besada, Alhucemas and Alba. This ministry was too eminent to last; in the beginning of November it broke up and one of its members, Alhucemas, formed a Government, with Romanones as his Foreign Minister. This arrangement proved fleeting, and in December Romanones became Premier; but stable government was as far off as ever.

A rapid succession of ministries marked the year 1919. In April, Maura came into power, but the elections held in the summer proved unfavourable to the Government and in July he was succeeded by the veteran Conservative Sánchez de Toca, who in turn made way for the Maurist Allendesalazar in December. In May 1920, Dato returned to power, ten months before his murder by anarchists. He was succeeded by Allendesalazar, with La Cierva as Minister of Public Works. Much was expected from

the latter's energy, and he did in fact devise an elaborate plan
of national reconstruction ; but it was not to be carried out in a
few weeks and the Government fell in January, 1922. Maura then
came into power, but fell in March, and his successor, Sánchez
Guerra, resigned in December. The ministry then formed by the
Marqués de Alhucemas lasted for nine months—the last Spanish
constitutional government before Primo de Rivera's dictatorship.

The cinematographic succession of ministries during the five
years after the War were necessarily weak, and in their weakness
the problems menacing Spain grew and prospered. Government
completely lost control of the finances ; it failed to maintain
order ; it hesitated and waited upon events in Morocco and in
Catalonia. In the year 1921 Anarchist, Syndicalist or Communist
outrages were of almost daily occurrence. Governments rose and
fell, and Parliament continued to debate eloquently. Well might
the King complain in his speech at Córdoba that Parliament
talked and nothing was done. All Spain's internal problems were
closely connected with the disaffection at Barcelona. This city
was the hotbed of terrorism, and the curious paradox resulted that
Catalonia, in some ways the most progressive region' of Spain,
constantly acted as a drag on Spain's progress. It is equally true,
however, that there were failures in understanding and administration on the part of the Madrid Government.[1]

Catalanism was organized by small political groups, often
mutually antagonistic, at Barcelona, and its final aims were
always ill defined, transparently clear as might be its immediate
programme. It began as a regionalist movement ; regionalism
developed into nationalism ; and many nationalists, despairing
of Madrid declared for separatism. To win certain positions, not
as a final settlement, but as a basis and fresh starting-point for
a further advance was constantly the Catalanist policy. Its real
demands were tersely if cruelly described by an opponent as
' autonomía con subvención '. We must be independent but not
separate, said the Catalans. The delicate distinction might be
paraphrased as follows : ' You are to recognize us as a free state,
with separate parliament, government, laws and language ; but
you are to continue to protect our industries by a high tariff, you
are to prevent us from being absorbed by France or any other
foreign power, you are to provide us with railway and postal
services, you are to guarantee our prosperity and independence
until we are in a position to absorb you '. It was a caricature,

_____

[1] The following paragraphs, on the Catalan question, represent a
compromise between the views of the two authors : for those of Mr. Bell,
the reader should consult the first edition of this book, pp. 261-4 ; for
those of Professor Allison Peers, his *Catalonia Infelix*, London, 1937, *passim.*

but a plausible caricature, of the position of the Catalan federalists : it is understandable that the action of the Central Government should have been inhibited by the feeling that they were
treading on a quicksand.

Modern political Catalanism dates from the last years of
the nineteenth century, and it developed rapidly on such occasions
as the war with the United States, the war in Morocco and the
War of 1914–18. It was in 1882 that Valentí Almirall founded the
Centre Català, and five years later dissidents from this formed the
Lliga de Catalunya. Fresh divisions led to the foundation of
the Unió Catalanista in 1892, which in its meeting at Manresa
adopted as its political creed a programme known as the Bases
de Manresa. The same year marked the beginning of terrorism
and bomb-throwing at Barcelona. In 1899, after the war with
the United States and when General Polavieja in office had
proved powerless to carry out his Catalan programme, the
presence of a French fleet at Barcelona was made the occasion
of anti-Spanish demonstrations, rendered the more significant
by the fact that Admiral Fournier, perhaps in ignorance, stood
up to the singing of the revolutionary ' Els Segadors ' Scenes
not dissimilar were witnessed after the War of 1914–18, when
Marshal Joffre visited Barcelona. When Dato, then Minister of
the Interior, was at Barcelona in the spring of the following year
(1900), he was systematically hooted in the streets of the generally
so courteous and hospitable Catalan city.

The Catalan Polaviejustas had founded the Unió Regionalista,
while dissidents from the Unió Catalanista joined to form the
Centre Nacionalista Català ; after their success in the elections
of 1901, these two new groups coalesced to form the Lliga Regionalista. It was at this time that the Radical and Republican
Lerroux obtained a strong political hold on the masses at Barcelona ; he was held by his opponents to be an emissary of the
Liberal Government at Madrid, a kind of lightning conductor to
render the Lliga innocuous. When in 1904 King Alfonso visited
Barcelona, he was welcomed by part of the Lliga with Cambó as
its spokesman ; those members of the Lliga who did not approve
of this action severed themselves from it and founded the Centre
Nacionalista Republicà. On November 25, 1905, in retaliation for
a caricature in a Catalan comic paper insulting the Spanish Army,
a group of officers wrecked the offices of the Catalan newspaper
La Veu de Catalunya, an act which excited great indignation at
Barcelona and ultimately led to the notorious ' Law of Juris-
dictions.' This subjected persons accused of offences against the
Army or the Navy to military tribunals, and made it an offence to

issue publications, prints, engravings or caricatures, or to make ' gestures or allusions ' directed against ' regions, provinces, cities or peoples of Spain.'

The advent of a Conservative Government at Madrid had strengthened the Lliga at Barcelona, and it triumphed in the elections of 1905 ; and, after Regionalists, Unionists, Integralists, Federalists and Nationalists had united at Gerona (February 11, 1906) to form the Solidaridad Catalana triumphed again over Lerroux in the elections of April, 1907. In the following year, however, Solidaritat was defeated by the Radicals, and in 1909 Federalists, Republicans, Nationalists and Unionists left it and founded the Unió Federalista Nacionalista Republicana, which broke up five years later, when in 1914 the Nationalists united with Lerroux and the Radicals to contest the elections. In 1909 Cambó, an able and active politician with a strong sense of reality and a reasonably opportunist policy, had supported Maura's Local Government Bill in the Chamber. Two years later, the Catalan proposal that the four Catalan provincial Governments of Barcelona, Tarragona, Lérida and Gerona should be fused into a single Catalan administration was accepted by Canalejas, who passed a bill to that effect through the Chamber of Deputies in July, 1912. After his murder the matter was taken up by Count Romanones, and finally Dato as Premier passed the measure by royal decree. Thus, in April, 1914, the Catalan Mancomunidad was constituted under its first president, Prat de la Riba.

During the War large fortunes were made by Catalans through trading with the Allies, and if Catalan manufacturers scarce had time to put themselves on a permanent basis of prosperity, part of Catalonia nevertheless was prosperous when the War ended as never before. Naturally impressed by President Wilson's pronouncement in favour of nationalism and self-determination, Catalonia was not slow to put forward her demands. It was in fact but a few days after the Armistice that (November 29, 1918) a demand for full autonomy, with a regional parliament, and the right to exercise functions corresponding to those detailed in the Bases de Manresa, was presented by the Catalanists to the Premier, the Marqués de Alhucemas, who refused to commit himself. The answer to the Catalanist message was given by his successor, Romanones, on December, 1918. It did not evade but postponed the issue and took the form of appointing a committee to inquire into the possibility of granting Home Rule to the various regions of Spain. For the Catalan movement for autonomy had found an echo in Valencia, in the Basque Provinces and even in distant Galicia.

The committee, in due course, produced some proposals which the Mancomunidad considered inadequate and countered by submitting proposals of its own, previously approved by 1,046 out of its 1,072 municipalities. These, being unacceptable to the Cortes, were allowed to lapse and no further solution of the ' Catalan question ' was attempted. Between 1919 and 1923 the gulf which separated Madrid and Barcelona widened; Francesc Macià, later to be Catalonia's first President, formed a party, called Estat Català, which advocated separation from Spain as a prelude to federal union ; and a progressive group seceded from the Lliga and formed Acció Catalana, the organ of which, *La Publicitat*, became the mouthpiece of left-wing nationalism during Primo de Rivera's dictatorship, when the founder and most of the adherents of Estat Català were in exile.

Before coming to the *pronunciamiento* of September, 1923, it may be well to remind ourselves that the quarter of a century had been for Spain a period of steady progress. Two vital reforms, afforestation and irrigation, still awaited the continuous attention of a stable Government ; yet even here there was no stagnation : a little more land was afforested every year and a little more *secano* was converted into *regadío*—a chance which would often increase its value tenfold. Large estates tended to break up, and in May, 1921, a Bill was introduced with the object of promoting small holdings and thus dealing with the agrarian question. This has always been a difficult problem in Spain, where conditions vary widely in the various regions. The chief result of the sale of the land of the religious Orders in 1835 had been their acquisition by rich usurers and the number of small properties had not increased ; in the south, especially, there has always been a tendency for land to accumulate in the hands of a large proprietor ; in the provinces of Andalusia, Extremadura and Toledo figures show that two hundred proprietors own between them over a million acres ; in Galicia, on the other hand, property is minutely and intricately subdivided, and in the province of Segovia small holdings are common ; in the greater part of Castile, indeed, the broad undivided wheat-fields are no sure indication as to the division of property.

A few figures will give some idea of the amount and variety of wealth possessed by Spain. In 1918 her total mineral wealth stood at about fifty-five millions sterling (at par) as compared with about ten millions sterling twenty years earlier ; its further increase depended partly on the extension of railways, of which in 1919, the country possessed 9,130 miles, and the cheapening of the cost of transport. With a population of about twenty-five millions, Spain has about ten million acres under wheat and about eight more million acres under barley, maize, oats and rye. In 1917 there were over five million fig-trees, fourteen million almond-trees, fifteen million orange trees (chiefly in Valencia and Andalusia), six million chestnut trees (especially in Galicia and the north-west). Spain, moreover, produced in 1914 over £100,000 worth of lemons and nearly half a million sterling of apples (in Asturias and the Basque Provinces). When one remembers the vast treeless wheat-growing plains in the central region, one can imagine that much of the rest of the country is a continuous orchard. Owing to the ravages of phylloxera the extent of the vineyards (about three million acres in 1918) has not increased ; olive-yards, on the other hand, showed an increase of over two and a half million acres during the years 1914–18. Livestock showed a similar increase : in the first twenty years of the century the number of pigs more than doubled, attaining the huge figure of four millions, while the number of goats advanced from two to four millions, that of cows from two to three millions, that of sheep from thirteen to seventeen millions. These are certainly remarkable figures. It is not surprising that the deposits in the savings banks rose from under six million sterling in 1900, divided among 202,315 investors, to over thirty-four millions sterling, divided among 1,334,693 holders in 1919. [These are the figures at par of 25 pesetas to the pound sterling, which, however, stood at 33 pesetas in 1900, 26 in 1913, 16½ (the highest to which it has ever risen in Spain) in 1918, and 32 in 1921.] Progress was not confined to Spain, for in Morocco similar advance was made in agriculture, and excellent roads were built from Melilla and Tetuan and a railway between Tetuan and Ceuta. The most marked progress, however, was that of the cities of Spain. Vigo grew up like a mushroom ; Bilbao, whose population had doubled and trade trebled during the last quarter of the nineteenth century, made even more rapid progress during the first quarter of the twentieth ; Barcelona and Valencia spread and prospered ; Madrid became a magnificent city. An attempt was made to revive the Spanish silk-growing industry and to grow rice and tobacco on a larger scale ; and, with even greater prospects of success, to foster cotton-growing. The number of acres under beet-sugar cultivation increased, between the years 1911 and 1918, by 75,000. A good example of the elasticity of Spain's prosperity, an elasticity common to agricultural countries (and in Spain a quarter of the population is engaged in agriculture).

is the fact that her mercantile marine, which in the year before the War had a tonnage of 877,000, with 864 boats, two years after the War (during which it had suffered heavy losses by German submarines, amounting to about a hundred thousand tons) had a tonnage of a million, with 1,192 boats.

Spain, the country of the bullfighter and dancer, is also the country which, with the painter Picasso, initiated Cubism and has given to the world the La Cierva gyroscope. Both in motoring and in flying, two activities congenial to individualism, she has won triumphs. But in no field of intellectual life, during the twentieth century, can it be said that she has lagged behind. To mention but one or two names, where a dozen could be given, painters such as Sorolla and Zuloaga, musicians such as Arbos and Falla, men of science such as Ramón y Cajal, scholars such as Menéndez y Palayo and Menéndez Pidal, sculptors such as Mariano Benlliure, Inurria or Julio Antonio ; orators such as Maura and Melquíades Álvarez, singers such as Fleta, an actress such as María Guerrero : these are names of which any country might be proud. In literature there has been at once a revival and a revolution. The Generation of 1898, enemies of rhetoric, have been succeeded by a generation even more subtle, and sometimes unintelligible to the profane ; some of them are literary cubists and some are regarded as being the full expression of that earlier generation ; indeed, we find Azorín thirty years later, in 1928, exhorting young writers to become even more radical in their methods. This brilliant group of young writers it is still too early to judge ; but a country which has recently produced such writers as those dealt with in Chapter V (see pp. 169–86), can be denied by none a place of honour in the modern literary world.

In certain respects, such as failure to keep pace with a mechanical civilization which has but little attraction for a nation of individualists and artists, or to adopt the ideals of size and speed for their own sake, Spain has been a backward country, but she has never been a decadent country. Spain, whose social legislation is in some ways in advance of that of the other countries of Europe, has been backward in matters of schools, railways, roads and sanitation ; but in these respects, in all of which much progress has been made of recent years, she is not to be judged by foreign, northern standards or without intimate acquaintance with her climate, geography and character. A dry, sunny climate may support conditions which in a wet, gloomy climate would be fatal. The average of mortality stands high in Spain, and the

sanitary conditions prevailing in the poorer quarters of some of
the large towns have seemed calculated to encourage it ; but there
has been much improvement here. As to the roads and railways,
only those who have travelled in this abrupt and mountainous
country can realize the difficulties to be overcome ; but here
again Spain's principal communications were a revelation to
those who revisited the Peninsula, after an interval of a quarter
of a century, around 1930.

On the matter of education foreign travellers in Spain usually
have a sad tale to relate. They are completely horrified to
discover that in some districts over half the entire population
is illiterate, although by law attendance at school has been compulsory for generations ; they declare that there is a shortage of
several thousand schools ;   and they relate with unfeigned
amazement that they have seen or heard of a village mayor who
was unable to sign his name. There is a great deal of ignorance in
all this criticism. Spain has not yet entirely confused intelligence with book-learning. The peasant mayor who cannot read
or write has sound sense and a knowledge of men and of the
management of affairs. Those who know Spain best know that
the uneducated Spanish peasants who have preserved their
ancient traditions are in intelligence, originality and essential
practical knowledge as superior to the mechanical product of
modern schools as they are in sobriety, dignity, good manners
and the very purity of their speech. Most travellers in Spain,
even when bewailing the backwardness of book-learning, have
paid glowing tributes to the splendid qualities of the illiterate
Spanish peasantry. Spain has been, and will again be, a happy
country, and those who visit it are made to realize that civilization is as much a matter of the heart as of the head.

Spain's finances have been thoroughly artificial since the
advent of a metallic unremunerative wealth brought in gold
bars from the New World in the sixteenth century. The Treasury
has fed on, instead of fostering, the resources of the country.
it cannot be said, however, that a budget of some forty millions
sterling, as it was before 1914, was too large for a country of
great agricultural wealth and other resources. In 1905, Villaverde,
and after him Echegaray, Finance Minister in the Montero
Ríos Cabinet, was balancing the budget at a thousand million
pesetas. Before 1914 this had increased by about one-fifth.
The first post-war budget, that of 1919, for the first time exceeded
two thousand millions, and this rapidly rose to three (roughly
equal to a hundred millions sterling) From 1898 to 1908, budgets
had shown a small surplus ; from 1909 to 1913 there were deficits,

less large on paper than in reality, owing to the method of provid-
for supplementary supplies by means of loans. This easy rather
than sound system was continued after the War, when a series
of weak Governments proved unable to cope with the financial
groups on which they depended for loans, and they failed likewise
to derive advantage from the growing wealth of the country.
Alba, as Finance Minister, attempted in vain to tax war profits
in 1915. The estimates for the budget of 1921–1922 gave an
initial deficit of twenty millions sterling ; that of the preceding
year had resulted in a deficit of over thirty millions, nearly the
whole pre-war revenue. Even so, the acknowledged deficits gave
no true idea of the State finances ; successive Governments
became more and more inclined to drift and to cover expenditure
by means of loans which were usually raised with facility and
pointed to with pride as an indication of the country's prosperity,
but which really drained away money from being remuneratively
employed in the soil, industries and mines. Thus the paradox
continued of a naturally rich country being only artificially prosperous and of a country of great resources remaining partly
stagnant. In July, 1920, a three hundred million pesetas four and
a half per cent. loan was covered in four weeks. In February and
March, 1927, under the Military Directory, Calvo Sotelo's funding
operation appeared to be introducing a sounder financial era.
It provided for the conversion of 5,225 million pesetas from
Treasury notes into fifty-year five per cent. bonds, which would
mean an ultimate saving to the nation in 1977 of close upon a
thousand million pesetas.

The floating debt, consolidated in 1905 and again in 1909,
stood on October 1, 1919, at 12,456 million pesetas. In the
three thousand million budget of 1919–20, half the expenditure
went in service of the Debt (1,383 millions) and pensions (88
millions) ; the War Office (375 millions) and Spain's action in
Morocco (141 millions) accounted for over one-sixth. Clearly
there could be little left for expenditure on education (107
millions) or public works (211 millions). Of the revenue 176
millions came from the State lottery, 159 from the tobacco
monopoly, 184 from the Customs. Thus a very small part of
the yearly expenditure was of a remunerative nature. A special
reconstructive budget, introduced by the Directory in 1926,
provided for the expenditure of sixteen hundred million pesetas
on public works (railways, roads and harbours), 1,508 millions
on national defence (the Army, Navy and Aviation) and two
hundred millions for education. Sixteen hundred millions is
about half the total expenditure of an ordinary budget. That of

the year 1927 showed a small surplus of 26,800,000 pesetas (or about one million sterling), with a total revenue of 3,215,500,000 pesetas. For the first time in twenty years no loan was raised, so that the surplus was not a merely nominal one, while expenditure in Morocco sank to under three millions sterling.

A greater gain than any immediate wealth was brought to Spain during the War of 1914–18 by the closer relations with Spanish America, which had hitherto often only approached Spain through Paris. Many excellent Spanish products had been sold under foreign trade-marks, partly owing to the fact that if admitted to be Spanish they would have been less appreciated, partly also with the connivance of the Spanish seller in order to escape payment of a higher tariff. Spanish olive-oil was sold as of Genoa, Spanish wines and preserves were French, boots of Bilbao or Madrid masqueraded as Viennese, fans and mantillas as articles fabricated in Paris ; Catalan cotton-goods received a Hamburg mark, Toledo knives were marked Solingen, even the swords of Eibar and Toledo were not admitted to be Spanish, and sardines caught in Spanish waters became French as soon as they were tinned (in Spain). A change now occurred in this, but even more important were the new intellectual and spiritual ties that bound the Spanish-speaking world to Spain.

Spanish manufacturers after the War were still prosperous, but their wealth was more precarious : they were faced by foreign competition ; their plants required renewal ; the War demand for their goods was at an end ; salaries and the cost of transport rose ; strikes and labour trouble grew more frequent. On the other hand, wealth became more equally distributed throughout the country, the rise in prices benefiting the agricultural towns of the interior, and emigration, amounting to at least 200,000 yearly before the War, received a permanent check. While Spanish imports diminished there was an increased demand (due to the many new rich in Spain and the difficulty of importation during the War years) for motor-cars and other luxuries. The balance of trade in Spain's favour in 1917, showing an excess of exports over imports to the value of about five hundred million pesetas, veered round to an unfavourable balance of roughly the same amount in 1920. Some idea of Spain's position before, in and after the War may be derived from figures of some of the exports in the years 1913, 1917 and 1918 : manufactured articles, under a million pesetas in 1913, rose to twenty-one millions in 1917 and stood at fourteen millions in 1918 ; the figures for cotton for those three years were three, twenty-five and six millions ; olive-oil, thirty, eighty-one and twenty-three ; ordinary wines, ninety, one hundred and forty and forty-eight ;   rice, eight, thirty-three (in 1915) and five.

General Primo de Rivera, who on September 13, 1923 raised the standard of revolt at Barcelona, had been born in Jerez in 1870, the nephew of a general of the same name who had played a prominent part in and after the Second Carlist War. His *pronunciamiento*, which led to a dictatorship lasting for six years and four months, was inspired by a desire to carry out much-needed reforms and by a conviction that this would never be done under the parliamentary system. Elections were corrupt ; the political *caciques*, or local bosses, could constantly interfere with taxation and the administration of justice ; and a flock of officials came in and went out with each change of ministry. The Army, too, was top-heavy with an excessive number of officers of high rank : five hundred of these, in 1923, were employed at the War Ministry alone. Primo de Rivera's sense of the hopelessness of continuing party government was widely shared. If Maura, with all his energy, talent, sincerity, probity and good-will, with his strong character and wide prestige, had failed to reform the bureaucratic administration and to make politics a vital interest instead of a machine worked from the Ministry of the Interior, the system would not and could not be altered by constitutional methods.

So Primo de Rivera " pronounced " for his dictatorship, and the King signified his acquiescence. The Dictator first said that he had come for only three months, in order to prepare the country for a purified form of democratic rule. But very soon this period became indefinitely lengthened. In 1925 a Civil Directory was substituted for the Military one, and in 1927 an attempt was made to give the system a democratic colour by the creation of a so-called National Assembly. What actually brought it to an end was general discontent. The peseta was lower than at any time since the beginning of the century ; disturbances were multiplying ; the project for drawing up a new Constitution had failed. Then Calvo Sotelo, the Dictator's Finance Minister, resigned, and no one could be found to succeed him. So Primo de Rivera put himself into the hands of the senior officers of the Army and Navy, and they in turn referred him to the King, who accepted his resignation. This was on January 28, 1930 : just over six weeks later Primo de Rivera, self-exiled to Paris, died.

Many of his material accomplishments had been of great value. Roads and railways benefited ; the two trans-Pyrenean railway tunnels were completed ; large irrigation schemes began ;

hotels were improved, a State tourist service was created and two enormous exhibitions brought visitors to Spain from all over the world.

But Primo de Rivera's greatest success was his termination of the war which since 1909 had been dragging on in Morocco. During the late summer of 1925, he launched an attack, in collaboration with the French, which led ultimately to a much desired settlement in the following May. Against this, and against his material reforms, must be set such abuses as the constant repression of free speech, the censoring of the Press, the abolition of associations, the imposing of religious tests on State officials, and the high-handed treatment of Catalonia. Because he had abolished the Mancomunidad and forbidden the public use of the Catalan language, his supporters claimed that he had ended the movement for Catalan Home Rule. Because he made strikes, trade unions and political parties illegal, they said that he had quelled the disturbances caused by organized labour. But all he had done in reality was to drive these activities underground. Even while his benevolent rule appeared to be proceeding with the greatest smoothness, reactions were in preparation, which reached their full force nearly a decade later.

(ii) THE SECOND REPUBLIC (1931–1936)

The initial reaction from the Dictatorship came more slowly than might have been expected and in its early stages was peaceful. A temporary Government, under General Dámaso Berenguer, appointed to prepare the way for a return to democratic rule, held office till February 1931, and the Government which followed it fixed municipal elections for April 12, parliamentary elections to be held shortly afterwards. Meanwhile, the Republican party grew by leaps and bounds, and on August 17, 1930, a Revolutionary Committee, pledged to bring in a Republic, concluded the Pact of San Sebastián with the Catalanist leaders, promising them, in return for their support, to bring in a Catalan Autonomy Bill as soon as it should be in power.

After an abortive attempt, made in December 1930, to overthrow the Monarchy by force, six members of the Revolutionary Committee were arrested and tried for treason. The trial, however, was little more than a Republican demonstration and both the imposition of nominal sentences and their remission within twenty-four hours indicated the direction of the prevailing wind. The municipal elections passed off quietly but produced a spectacular result. Though the full returns were never published, and the only figures issued showed that the Monarchists had secured

22,150 seats to the Republican's 5,875, practically all the large towns recorded Republican majorities, which reached their height in Madrid and Barcelona. So Sr. Alcalá Zamora, President of the Revolutionary Committee, took the bold course of demanding the abdication of King Alfonso. After some rapid negotiations, the King undertook to "suspend the exercise of royal power and leave Spain '—in order, as he put it in a message to the people, ' to abstain from any course which might plunge my compatriots into a fratricidal civil war.' He never abdicated ; and the wording and tone of the message make it clear that he expected before long to be recalled. Actually, he died, still in exile almost exactly ten years later (February 28, 1941).

In July 1931, when the newly elected Cortes of the Second Republic met to draw up a Constitution, the prospects for peace and reform in Spain looked extremely bright. The Government was a genuine coalition, including talented men of widely differing views—Conservatives, Liberals, Radicals, Socialists and Autonomists, united in their determination to work those long-needed reforms which the Monarchy had failed to produce either by constitutional rule or by dictatorship. But unfortunately the coalition was unable to cohere. In October, the Prime Minister, Niceto Alcalá Zamora, and the Home Secretary, Miguel Maura, resigned from the Government, while in December the Radicals, too, went into opposition, leaving the administration predominantly Socialist. This started the successive reactions within the Republic which were one cause of its failure. Another cause was its lack of a leader strong enough to keep it from falling into the hands of extremists on the one side or the other. The régime was accepted alike by Communists, Anarchists and Syndicalists, but only as a stage towards the particular type of proletarian revolution that each desired, and they used the large measure of freedom which it allowed them to keep up a succession of revolutionary strikes, varied with occasional burnings of churches (e.g., in May 1931) or open revolts (e.g., in January 1932, January and December 1933) which they considered as rehearsals for the eventual Day. On the other side, General Sanjurjo led an unsuccessful rising in August, 1932, and in the following year the formation of the Falangist, or Spanish Fascist, party set in motion the machinery which in 1936 was to bring about civil war.

On the surface, however, the newly-born Republic seemed to be making great progress. The new Constitution, completed, in December 1931, by a unicameral parliament in which the Left had a two to one majority, defined Spain as a ' democratic republic of workers ', with ' no official religion ', respecting the

' rules of international law ' and ' renouncing war as an instrument of national policy.' It prohibited federalism but authcrized
the granting of autonomy to regions which could justify their
demand for it. Both men and women were to be given the vote
at twenty-three. Titles of nobility were abolished. Property and
wealth would be ' subordinated to the interests of the national
economy ', and might be expropriated on payment of an indem-
nity. The President of the Republic, to hold office for six years,
would be chosen by an Electoral College to consist of all the
deputies to the Cortes and an equal number of members elected
ad hoc. The Constitution could be amended, but not until at
least four years after its promulgation.

The clauses in this document which had excited most opposition were those relating to religion. The Church was to be dis-
established and the State payment of clergy (a form of compensa-
sion for past expropriations, agreed upon in the 1851 Concordat)
was to cease. Those Religious Orders which demanded a vow ' of
obedience to an authority other than the legitimate authority of
the State '—this in practice meant the Society of Jesus—were
to be dissolved and their property was to be impounded. Other
Orders were to be regulated by a special law controlling their
activities and none of them was to engage in industry, commerce
or education.

It was these clauses affecting religion which led to the resignation of the Prime Minister and the Minister of the Interior.
Alcalá Zamora, subsequently elected first President of the Republic
was succeeded as Premier by the War Minister, Manuel Azaña,
who for two years led a determined campaign for fundamental
reforms in an atmosphere of revolts, strikes and general unrest.
The Agrarian Law of 1932 expropriated certain large estates,
indemnifying their owners, and created a State-subsidized
Institute of Agrarian Reform, representative of both owners and
workers. The Catalan Statute of Autonomy, approved on the
same day as the Agrarian Law, provided that Catalan and Castilian should be ' co-official ' languages in Catalonia and gave
the regional Catalan Government (which in April 1931 had
assumed the historic title of Generalitat) the power to maintain
educational institutions of its own, to control museums and
archives, to organize its own police service and to execute various
kinds of legislation. The Law of Religious Confessions and Congregations was hotly debated for seven months, chiefly because
it forbade all teaching after the end of 1933, by members of
religious Orders. Since the country was already short of both
schools and teachers, this measure would deprive at least 350,000

children of education, and even some anti-clericals thought that the Orders should have been left alone till enough State schools had been built, and teachers trained, to provide for all children who had none.

Before the end of 1933, however, the left-wing régime had ended. Despite its bold attempts at reform, many of its original supporters had been alienated from it by the drastic powers of suppression and suspension which it gave the Minister of the Interior, its inability to deal with revolutionary strikes and its tactless handling of more serious insubordination. Under the new régime, however, which, like its predecessor, lasted for two years, activity and unrest gave place to lethargy and depression. Seats in the new Cortes were much more evenly allotted than in 1931 : the Right had now 207 ; the Centre, 167 ; and the Left, 99. The Centre thus held the balance of power, and it was the Centre, rather than the Right, which governed, its general policy being to hold up the legislation of 1931–33, presumably until the end of 1935, when the Constitution could legally be amended. So the Government postponed the closing of the schools of the Orders, restored to the clergy a part of their stipends, delayed the transference to Catalonia of powers granted her by the Statute of Autonomy ; and passed a new Agrarian Law more favourable than the last to the landed proprietors. Soon this régime, like its predecessor, found opinion running against it, and that violently. In October, 1934, revolutions broke out simultaneously in Asturias and in Catalonia : the former, after a week of nothing less than a localized civil war, was suppressed with extreme severity ; the latter, whose ostensible aim was the establishment of a federal Republic, collapsed more quickly, the Catalan ministers were imprisoned and Catalonia had once again to be ruled from Madrid. But these revolts, quelled though they were, served the purpose of their promoters by vastly increasing the general discontent. Azaña, imprisoned after the Catalan rising, tried, set free and then re-arrested, became almost a national hero. When the Cortes were dissolved and elections fixed for February 16, 1936, he was acclaimed as leader of the progressive groups not only by the left-wing parties, but by the Syndicalists, Anarchists and Communists, who temporarily sank their differences to form a ' Popular Front '.

In the Cortes which emerged from these 1936 elections the Left had a majority of 39 votes over the Right and Centre, but precisely what they would have done with it will never be known, since the country experienced a new high level of disorder and the five months which followed the elections were months of chaos.

Prisons were stormed ; land was seized by peasants, who defied
the law to take it from them ; churches, religious houses, seminaries, clubs, newspaper offices and the residences of persons with
right-wing sympathies were set on fire, while revolutionary
strikes and similar acts of insubordination occurred daily.

Politically, too, there was a characteristic upheaval when
Alcalá Zamora, who as President of the Republic had attempted
for so long to steer a middle course between Right and Left, was
deposed from his office by an all but unanimous vote in the Cortes
of Right and Left combined. With a corresponding degree of
unanimity, Azaña, still believed to be the ' strong man ' of Spain,
was elected his successor.

But no political upheaval, however fundamental, could have
had consequences as serious as another movement already afoot
in the country. Extremism on the Right, as well as on the Left,
was rising to a climax. Strikes and arson began to be accompanied by murder. The inevitable crisis was precipitated by the
assassination of Calvo Sotelo (once Primo de Rivera's Finance
Minister and now a prominent Falangist), in revenge, it was said,
for the murder of a lieutenant in the military police. Two months
previously, the newly appointed Prime Minister, Casares Quiroga,
had defined the Government's attitude to Falangism. The
purpose of this movement, he had said, was ' to attack the
fundamental principles of the democratic Republic. Here the
Government cannot maintain an attitude of neutrality. In its
relations with Fascism, the Government is a belligerent.'

Now the Falangists, as they prepared to take up the challenge,
might reasonably have asked why the Government was not
equally a belligerent in its relations with Anarchism and Communism, whose purpose was also to attack its fundamental
principles. Far from adopting belligerency with regard to these
groups, the Government had accepted their support and was thus
their ally. However, the time for logic had passed ; it was the
hour for action. And, less than a week after the murder of Calvo
Sotelo, the action came.

On July 17, 1936, under General Francisco Franco, an army
revolt against the Republic took place in Spanish Morocco. On
the next day General Franco landed in Andalusia and revolts
broke out in garrison after garrison all over Spain. In Madrid,
on the Basque coast and in the east, the Republic held firm ; in
the whole of Galicia, in most of León, in part of Asturias, in Navarre
and in some Castilian cities—such as Burgos, the rebels' ' capital ',
Salamanca, Valladolid and Segovia—the revolt was successful.

On the mainland, Casares Quiroga had declared, when the

news of the Moroccan revolt came through, ' nobody, absolutely
nobody ' had taken part in this ' absurd scheme '. When the
nature and extent of its absurdity became known, Casares
Quiroga had of course to go ; and Azaña, hoping perhaps that a
Government of a more moderate type than the last might make
terms with the rebels, nominated as Premier the President (i.e.,
Speaker) of the Cortes, Martínez Barrio. This he was entirely
within his rights in doing, since Article 75 of the Constitution of
the Second Republic empowers the President ' freely to nominate
. . . the Prime Minister '. Unhappily the leaders of the extremist
groups insisted that the new Government should not be of the type
that Azaña desired and he was forced to nominate another Prime
Minister than the man of his choice. On that day, two things
came to an end. First, the legend that Azaña was Spain's
' strong man ' : from now until his resignation in 1939 he was
no more than a figure-head. Second, the legality of the Government—and for that matter of the Constitution itself, which was
termed by one responsible minister a ' paper Constitution ' and
was taken seriously by none.

(iii) The Civil War (1936–1939)

From July 19, 1936 to March 31, 1939, Spain was at war, the
two contending parties being the Republicans, nominally defend-
ing a democratic régime but in reality ruled by anti-democratic
extremists anxious to declare a proletarian revolution at the first
possible moment, and the rebels (or Nationalists, as they dubbed
themselves), who were quite frankly fighting in order to establish
a right-wing dictatorship.

The Nationalists began badly by losing several of their
leaders, but, having the bulk of the Army and the armed police
to do battle with the Popular Front's untrained or half-trained
militia, they quickly made progress. By taking Badajoz, in
mid-August, they united their southern army with their northern.
In September, the capture of Irún and San Sebastián secured the
western French frontier ; and when, at the end of the month, a
force moved rapidly upon Madrid, it looked as if the War might
soon be over. Had not this force made a détour to relieve a group
of Nationalists besieged in the Alcázar of Toledo, Madrid might
easily have fallen. But the few days' grace allowed a body of
foreign volunteers known as the International Brigade to be
moved up to the Madrid front, and, instead of storming the
capital, the Nationalists had to besiege it for two years and four
months before it fell.

Though the huge majority of the combatants in this war

on both sides were Spaniards, there was, almost from the beginning, a considerable degree of foreign intervention. The Republicans received war material from Soviet Russia, and, to a lesser
degree, from Mexico, while the efforts of the International
Brigades were reinforced by the help of the Red Army's technicians. To the Nationalists came combatants, technicians,
aeroplanes and large supplies of war material from Germany and
Italy. France, fearful of an extension of the conflict to other
parts of Europe, approached the leading Powers on the matter ;
and a Non-Intervention Committee, representing twenty-seven
nations, was set up in London. Though active, however, the
Committee cannot be said to have been very successful, and intervention, to a varying degree, continued till the War ended.

The early stages of the War were marked, on both sides, by
great ruthlessness, and atrocities committed by supporters of
the Republicans included the murder of ten Bishops and many
thousands of priests and religious. It must be remembered,
however, that a huge proportion of the forces of order had gone
over to the rebels, and, in such circumstances, discipline, especially
in the midst of a war, cannot easily be improvised. Nor in the
Popular Front itself was either discipline or unity much easier of
attainment. After the fall of Irún, when the Socialist leader,
Largo Caballero, became Prime Minister, its Government was
enlarged to embrace Communism ; and, when Madrid was
threatened, Syndicalism. None the less, a serious Anarcho-
Syndicalist rising took place in Barcelona from May 3 to 10, 1937,
as a result of which Syndicalists were excluded from the Cabinet
for nearly a year. It was now that Largo Caballero gave place
as Prime Minister to Dr. Juan Negrín, who was still holding that
office at the end of the War.

After a winter and early spring in which they had achieved
little beyond the capture of Málaga, the Nationalists cleared the
North by taking Bilbao in June 1937, Santander in August
and Gijón at the end of October. Early in December, however,
before they could turn eastwards, the Republicans began an
offensive in Aragon and won their only spectacular success of the
War by capturing Teruel. But in less than two months this city
was re-taken in a new offensive, which the Nationalists continued
by raising the siege of Huesca, capturing Barbastro, penetrating
into Catalonia, taking Lérida and thence pursuing the enemy up
the Segre valley as far as Tremp. At the same time, farther south,
they cut Republican Spain in two by forging themselves a broad
corridor to the Mediterranean. The Republican Government,
which, when Madrid was threatened, had migrated to Valencia,

had moved again, in face of the fresh danger, to Barcelona. Madrid, therefore, became completely isolated.

As early as October 1, 1936, General Franco had declared himself head of Nationalist Spain and outlined the main features of a régime which he described as ' broadly totalitarian ' : abolition of popular suffrage and regional autonomy ; equitable taxation ; complete religious tolerance ; a new Concordat with Rome ; and, in foreign affairs, avoidance of ' Sovietic contacts ' and preferential treatment of ' nations of related race, language or ideology '—i.e., Portugal and Latin America. On April 19, 1937, the two main Nationalist groups—Falangists and Traditionalists, corresponding respectively to the Left and the Right within this right-wing régime—were fused into a single party with a National Council and a powerful executive committee, and all other political parties were dissolved. A Labour Charter (*Fuero del Trabajo*) on the Fascist model, issued on March 9, 1938, gave the worker an undertaking (here and there rather nebulously worded) that the New State, as Franco's régime came to be called, had not come merely to restore the past. Work, the right and the social duty of all, would be demanded of all who were not disabled. The State would limit working hours, prohibit night employment of women and children, give married women humanitarian guarantees and provide all workers with cultural and recreational facilities and an annual vacation with pay. A minimum living wage would be fixed, together with family allowances. An agrarian policy would aim at giving every peasant family a small holding and improve sanitary and housing conditions in rural districts. There would be increased social insurance to cover old age, disablement, unemployment, maternity and accidents or illnesses arising from the worker's occupation. All factors of the country's economic life, together with the liberal and technical professions, would be incorporated, under State direction, in Vertical Syndicates, in which all the elements devoted to fulfilling the economic process within a particular service or branch of production would be combined into a single organism. These Syndicates would study problems of production, intervene in the regulation of conditions of work, establish employment bureaux and have the right to initiate organizations of any kind concerned with production. The Syndicates, whose verticalism was peculiar to Spain, were so essential a part of Franco's system that it took the title, unpleasantly suggestive of Hitler's régime, of ' National-Syndicalism '.

Meanwhile, the War dragged on, though signs that the Republicans, who had fought so well against such odds, were at last envisaging defeat came in April, 1938, when Dr. Negrín formulated an irreducible minimum of thirteen ' points ' which must be conceded to him before he would sign an armistice. Some of the Powers would gladly have supported proposals for peace talks, but General Franco insisted throughout upon unconditional surrender, which eventually he obtained. None the less, when from July to November, 1938 he was held up on the Ebro, some observers believed that the Republicans might hold out till Hitler should land Europe in a war now seen to be imminent. But their determined stand was to prove the Republicans' final effort. Two days before Christmas General Franco began a determined advance on Barcelona, which fell in just over a month. The Republican Government fled northwards—and Dr. Negrín, as a last gesture, reduced his thirteen points to three. But Franco took no notice. By February 5, he had conquered the whole of Catalonia. Azaña crossed into France and at the end of the month resigned his office, but Negrín and his Government returned by air to Madrid, prepared to hold out there until the end.

This was not long in coming. The capital, on which the Nationalists were now about to concentrate their attack, had long been all but devoid of heating and food ; every day scores were dying of starvation. Within a week of his arrival Negrín was back in France again—driven out by the revolt of a so-called ' Council of Defence '. But the Council's real aim was not defence but the negotiation of a surrender and on April 1 General Franco was able to issue the last communiqué of the campaign, ending with the words : ' The War is over.'

(iv) THE DICTATORSHIP OF GENERAL FRANCO (1939–1946)

After civil war must always come a slow and painful period of reconstruction—both material and moral. Of Franco's attempts at moral reconstruction the less said the better. Had he, like General Grant after the Civil War in the United States, declared, not only ' The War is over ' but ' The rebels are our countrymen again,' the subsequent history of Spain might have been different. Unfortunately such an attitude represented the very antithesis of his policy. Instead of issuing an amnesty to his late opponents he clapped hundreds of thousands of them into prison, and later committed acts of unreasoning vengeance like the shooting of the Catalan President, Lluis Companys. Instead of making concessions to regionalism, he suppressed it with an iron hand. Year by year the anniversary of each of his major victories was celebrated with pomp and display. One after another, the cities of Spain received him in state, applauded his eloquent perorations and presented him with the customary gold medal. All over the country, mass demonstrations were held on such patriotic festivals as May 2 and October 12, and the bodies of dead Nationalist heroes were disinterred and brought in solemn processions across Spain for ceremonial reburial. And it is worth noting that the grandiose memorials erected to the victims of the War commemorated only those who had fallen ' for God and for Spain '— that is to say, for General Franco.

This policy of imposing himself as a conqueror only hardened the subterranean opposition of masses who would have rallied behind a more tolerant and generous leader bent on burying the past as soon as might be and pursuing a steady course of much-needed reform. International events, however, were to make it impossible, for some years, for the opposition to declare itself. And meanwhile material reconstruction made as much progress as in the conditions could have been expected. The rebuilding of shattered towns and villages began in earnest. Food was distributed by an energetic women's organization known as ' Auxilio Social ', which at one time was providing over a million free meals daily. Schools and universities were re-opened and new education laws set in motion. Programmes of public works were drawn up which, if ever they were carried out, would be of the greatest benefit. But these activities had barely been proceeding for five months when prospects of reconstruction were darkened by the outbreak of the European War.

General Franco, who, on September 27, 1938, at the height of the Munich crisis, with German troops still in his country, had made a declaration of Spain's neutrality in the event of such a conflict, lost no time, when it began, in reaffirming this position, as in the interval he had done several times already. It is true that, at the end of March, 1939, Spain had joined the anti-Comintern *bloc*, but at about the same time she had made a treaty of non-aggression and friendship with Britain's oldest ally, Portugal. General Franco's often-expressed hostility to Soviet Russia made it advisable for him to ignore the Russo-German pact of August, 1939, while he could hardly have approved the Russo-German dismemberment of Catholic Poland. In any case, had he wished to join in the War between September, 1939 and June, 1940, he could not have done so, for France stood between Spain and Germany, the French fleet kept guard in the Mediterranean and the British blockade would have prevented a hostile but half-starving Spain from importing the food which she needed to sustain bare life.

Even when Germany invaded the Low Countries Franco was

still a good neutral. 'I command all Spaniards,' he proclaimed, ' by the present decree, to observe the strictest neutrality.' It was a month later, when France fell, and the victorious Germans occupied the Basque coast as far as Irún, that the possibility of Spain's following the lately ' non-belligerent ' Italy into the War seemed such a real one. Not only was France now controlled by Germany, but the French fleet had gone : the sole obstacles to intervention were the British blockade and the risk, once the Spanish Army was occupied with a foreign war, of a Republican revolution. For the moment, Franco contented himself with declaring that Spain, previously a strict neutral, would hence-forward be a ' non-belligerent '. Few expected that she would remain on that fence for long, especially when in October 1940 Hitler, in his capital, received an imposing Spanish mission, led by Franco's brother-in-law, Serrano Súñer, and when, after various consultations between Hitler, Serrano Súñer and Mussolini, Franco himself had a meeting with Hitler at the Irún-Hendaye frontier. Previously, he had profited by the weakness of France and Britain to seize Tangier, and both his Press and his Falangist organizations indulged in a good deal of loose talk about a ' Second Empire ', which, it was understood, would be inaugurated by the incorporation into Spain of Gibraltar—when Germany had won the War. ' For two hundred years,'· declared Serrano Súñer, ' we have been meek and abject. Now our only cry is ' ¡ *Arriba España* ! ' (' Up, Spain ! ').

But bold words filled no stomachs which the ravages of a Civil War, an officially patronised Black Market, and bad harvests of 1939 and 1940 kept empty. General Franco, resisting the blan-dishments of the Axis and the exploits of the volunteer Spanish Blue Division on the Eastern Front, did well to maintain a policy of non-belligerence, which in general greatly benefited the Allies. His first task was to restore normality to a country so drained of resources as to be incapable even of profiting from neutrality, and so ostracised by the Allies as a Dictatorship which flouted many passionately held creeds that in an epoch of mutual lease-lend and Marshall Aid it was excluded from all such communal encourage-ment and assistance, and regarded (Portugal and Russia were allies) as a monstrous anachronism in the New Europe! Im-poverished and isolated, Spain was to be encouraged only to change her form of government. In December 1947, after much sincere but not altogether altruistic debate, the U.N.O. broke off diplomatic relations with her, at least formally, by the withdrawal of the person of the Ambassadors. But neither this pseudo-action —which profoundly stirred the patriotic allegiance of the Spanish people, nor the equally pseudo-closing of the Franco-Spanish frontier which enriched local barrow boys and taximen—could long resist the plain facts of trade, Spain's hostility to Communism, her strategic geographical position and the sympathy of the Hispanic nations on the American continent. Wool was traded by New Zealand and wheat by the Argentine while the U.N.O. debated the form of its disapproval. France unilaterally reopened the frontier on September 1, 1948 ; by September 14 diplomatic relations had been re-established by six Hispanic countries. In May 1949 the U.N.O. voted to grant freedom of action to all the member nations, and within a few weeks of its decision of October–November 1950 to restore general diplomatic relations, Ambassadors had been exchanged with the U.S. (December), Great Britain (January 1951) and France (March). The régime was enormously strengthened in prestige. Spanish meanwhile (December 1948), had been accepted as the third official language of the U.N.O., and the constant advocacy of her sister nations gradually won Spain an invitation to participate in many of the specialist, scientific and humane activities of the organization. This international contact also strengthened the ties of blood, religion and tradition between the members of the Hispanic family of nations which it became a cardinal point of policy of General Franco to reaffirm and exalt. Through institutions such as the Consejo de Hispanidad (founded 1940), and the Instituto de Cultura Hispánica (1946) (of which the first Director, Sr. J. Ruiz Giménez, became Minister of Education not long afterwards), the concept of ' Hispanidad ' was renewed, diversified and blazoned abroad by congresses, lecture tours, numerous and diverse publications, the foundation of Colegios Mayores, interavailability of many academic and professional qualifications and very particularly by the warm welcome given in Spain to students (now some 3,000 a year) from the Hispanic-American countries. Never in the palmiest days of Empire had the metropolis so vigorously served as the centre of the Hispanic world. Less successful was an attempt made in April 1952 to re-establish cordial relationships with the Arab world.

Meanwhile the U.S.A., distracted from her mission of constructing a solvent counterpoise to the Soviet bloc by the discordant voices of Europe, decided independently to adopt a ' realistic ' attitude to Spain, that is to ignore her form of government as a means of integrating her military potential, if not into the North Atlantic Treaty at least into the Atlantic defence system. A first great international loan to her by the Chase National Bank of New York (February 1949) to complete her purchase of the U.S. Telephone holdings in Spain, was followed by a governmental loan of $62,500,000 (August 1950)—the reduction from 100 million by Congress later made good by other credits— by the visits of influential senators and businessmen, and finally, after two years of world suspense, by the signing in September, 1953 of three pacts : The ' Convenio relativo a la ayuda mutua para mutua defensa ', the ' Convenio sobre ayuda económica ' and a ' Convenio defensivo '—the first two valid until notice to end them was given, the last for ten years with automatic extension for two successive periods of five years each. By the first document the two governments agree ' to foster international peace and security, to promoting understanding and goodwill and to main- taining world peace ', towards which end—as far as might be consistent with the Charter of the United Nations—they promise to exchange military equipment and technical information and to control trade with nations which threaten world peace. In the second document the assistance to be supplied to Spain by the U.S. is surrounded with every sort of guarantee, security and explicit direction to ensure its fit and proper application : adequate supervision, quarterly statements, frequent public and private supply of information, firm control over Spanish industry, labour, capital and governmental budget to ensure a stable currency and price level ; full freedom to observe and report on the working of the Agreement is granted to the American Press. But Spain is not only a debtor requiring supervision. Both the U.S. government and her nationals expect facilities to do business with her, the government for stockpiling—she is prepared to encourage the production of goods she needs, and the nationals for normal trading. Both require assurances on the supply of ' pesetas ' and the second on their freedom to transfer balances back to the U.S. By the Defense Agreement, to which a reference is inconspicuously made in the second ' Convenio ' (Article V subsection b), the U.S. agrees, with the co-operation of Spanish industry to ' satisfy the minimum requirements for equipment necessary for the defense of Spanish territory ' by the Naval and Air Forces, and to ensure that ' the armament and equipment of the Army Units be as far advanced as possible ' (Art. I section 3). To this end she will be allowed to develop, maintain, and to exercise internal security over certain areas and facilities, which will however remain the property of the Spanish government, will be available for joint utilisation, and remain under the Spanish flag and command and within a Spanish external security service. It is clear that General Franco has by no means sold his country for a mass of dollars, and that any Spanish property ceded to the Americans bears so little relation to that ceded by Great Britain under Lend-Lease, that to call the sites Bases is highly misleading. One understands from Press reports (February, 1955) that the Americans are learning to appreciate this distinction the hard way. But as the simple—though not very specific—clauses of the Agreements are transmuted into men and materials, no amount of cautious deflation on the one side and prudent restraint on the other can lessen the sense of wonder which this reputed invasion of the Old by the New World has stirred in the Spanish people and their economy. It may be that more than at any time in her past Spain is interested in the prospect of being conquered : certainly the juxtaposition of old and new on her soil is rich with possibilities—not all of which will agree with the present régime, or the traditional way of life of the country.

The relations of Great Britain with Spain have been a little obscured by the ' realistic ' honeymoon she is enjoying with the U.S. Britain's formal observance of the rulings of the U.N.O. and the free expression of antagonism to Spain's form of government have been held against her particularly : and several influential members of the Falange have used opportunities to publicise their anglophobe opinions. But the principal cause of friction has been a nationally organised campaign to exacerbate the regret and pique which for some 200-odd years the British presence on the Rock of Gibraltar has caused many Spaniards. The Head of the State has created opportunities—which the disciplined ranks of the Falange have fervently echoed—to incense the nation, and violent propaganda has sought to make the question of Gibraltar an article of pride—if not of faith—with the many who had never thought of it before. The visit of Queen Elizabeth and the Royal family to the Rock (May 10–11, 1954), on their return from the Commonwealth Tour was described as the final insult. In the face of British equanimity General Franco—more wittingly perhaps than the irate Henry II—certainly with an unwonted rashness—gave notice that such an insult would so wound the susceptibilities of some patriot that he could not answer for the consequences. The visit passed off tumultuously, but the irritant which has been injected into official British-Spanish relations will not soon be assuaged. The irritation fortunately for both countries does not hinder either trade, or the tourist industry, which by 1951 was handling over 1,000,000 visitors a year. By both means Great Britain continues to be a leading contributor to the supply of foreign exchange which is always one of Spain's major problems.

Her relations with other countries—with two exceptions—have followed her interests and her needs. In a world of planned scarcity, it is a sign of the diversity of her needs that she should have signed trade agreements with the Argentine (October 1947), England (March 1948 and December 1949), the Benelux Countries (April 1949), France (June 1949), Greece (February 1950), Norway (January 1951), Turkey (June 1951), etc. With Russia diplomatic relations continued broken : with Portugal they are ineffectively fraternal and frequently brought before the public eye.

After almost twenty years of power (he was elected Head of the Spanish State by the National Defence Council on December 29, 1936), no group or creed has been or seems able to challenge the inevitability—even the desirability—of the supreme dominion in Spain of Generalisímo Francisco Hermenegildo Franco, ' Caudillo de España por la gracia de Dios ' as the inscription on the coinage reads since December 1947. No other potential central power promises with half his success to maintain an equilibrium which during the last 150 years has been disturbed by the selfish struggles for autocratic power of the Army, the Church, the Monarchy, the Liberal parliamentarians, the federalists and regionalists. With greater or less conviction and aspiration towards national statesmanship his governments have imposed on a centrifugal, anarchical nation a system which is essentially centralist and syndicalist—with some considerable allowance left for predilections among the governors. Madrid has become the metropolis, and under its officials very few activities in the country —economic, social, cultural, religious—have escaped ' integration ' into a national ' sindicato ', ' consejo ' or ' instituto '. From Madrid flows a constant stream of advice, subsidy and support when the project meets with approval : without which, as frequently in Catalonia, projects are often stillborn. Regions, towns and local entities are encouraged—under central stimulus—to honour their peculiar virtues and traditions. A characteristic foundation is the Consejo Superior de Investigaciones Científicas established in 1939 (November 24) ' to foster, guide and coordinate research in Spain '. Research in any field, publication in book form or in one of a hundred or so periodicals, scholarships, stipends, recommendations, Summer Schools, Associations of the most diverse sort, attendance at international or national congresses, organization, distribution and support of these and manifold other activities throughout the kingdom fall within the authority of the C.S.I.C. It could be added that never has publication in Spain been so voluminous, subsidized and profitable. Industry—under the Instituto Nacional de Industria (I.N.I.)— is organized into vertical syndicates, by industry, in which labour, management and technicians elect representatives from the local to the national level.

There is one unexpected break in this chain of organizations : for the first time since 1812 Spain does not possess a written Constitution. It has instead a series of Basic Laws, which must be observed by any Head of the State and can be changed only by a national Referendum. The most important of these are :

1938 : January 30. The transformation of the Technical Council into the Government of Spain, of which the victorious General was elected President, and the Vice-President was dispensed with in 1939 (August 8).

1938 : March 9. The ' Fuero del Trabajo ' (Labour Charter) given more legal form in 1945, July 17, as the ' Fuero de las Españoles ' (The Spaniards' Charter).

1942 : July 17. The creation of the Cortes, its code of Rules followed in 1943, January 5, and modifications were introduced later in 1946, March 9 and July 15.

1945 : July 17. Bases of Local Government—both Provincial and Municipal.

1945 : September 29 and October 22. The reform of electoral procedures and the creation of the Referendum.

1947 : June 8. The Law of Succession to the Headship of the State—approved by the Cortes and in 1948 by National Referendum.

1953 : August 27. The Concordat between Spain and the Holy See.

No more than the briefest of summaries of these Laws can be given here, with the additional caution that under an autocratic government the disparity which traditionally obtains in Spain between the letter and the operation of the Law is naturally exaggerated. Though the prisons may long ago have seen the last of the ' Reds ', a roseate-hued past, however pale or however acquired, is a very real hindrance to millions of Spaniards who are still virtually ' on parole '. Perhaps the most depressing, and inexplicable, characteristic of a régime which apparently strives by its social and industrial policy to raise the standard of living of all Spaniards and to fuse them into one united nation, is in fact just this stubborn, provocative denial of the human rights of the conquered. The heroes and the fallen who are so regularly and with such primitive intensity honoured and recalled in Hitlerian demonstrations still belong exclusively to one sort of Spaniard. It must rub salt into the wounds of hundreds of thousands of the other Spaniards.

By the Spaniards' Charter, all Spaniards are guaranteed equal rights to educational opportunities, to service to the State both in war and peace, in government and in daily life : they enjoy freedom of speech, of residence, of meeting, of habeas corpus and of petition—which freedoms may however be suspended by a *Decreto-ley*. The family is honoured as the fundamental unit of society. Work is the right and the duty of all Spaniards and the State will ensure not only that the worker receives a fair share of the results of his labour, but that in time of need (unemployment, sickness, maternity, old age, incapacity, etc.), he shall receive assistance. Private property is recognized under the overriding claims of the State. No person will be molested because of his religious beliefs, but no ceremonies or external manifestation of any other than the Catholic Religion will be permitted. A vast system of social insurance is now being developed to honour these promises, and though the allowances are often small—the economy is not a rich one—much distress is receiving some alleviation and much ignorance being dispelled.

The Cortes is a single chamber to which Procuradores are elected and nominated in three groups : (*a*) high administrative officers of the government, Presidents of the Council of State and Supreme Law Courts, Rectors of Universities and representatives of cultural bodies ; (*b*) professional and syndical organizations (representing industry and the professions, and within industry the three groups : workmen, technicians, and management) ; (*c*) provincial and municipal authorities including the mayors of fifty provincial capitals. The Head of the State may nominate up to fifty members. All Spaniards of the age of twenty-one and over may be elected provided they enjoy full use of ' los derechos civiles y no sufren inhabilitación política '. The Cortes is in session for three years : it meets in plenary session for several weeks each year to hear the informative addresses by Ministers on the activities of their Departments and to vote on the laws which its Commissions have elaborated, but not initiated. It has no executive power and can easily degenerate into a consultative body which is informed of action rather than asked for counsel or direction. It has almost no echo in the life of the country. Government is presidential, not parliamentary ; ministers are responsible to the Head of the State only, the General Secretary of the Falange Movement has the status of a Minister.

Provincial and municipal government repeats the same tripartite membership—administrators, intellectuals and syndicalist representatives. All the key posts are filled by Central nomination.

We learn from the Law of Succession that the Head of the State shall normally be assisted in all matters ' which are within his exclusive competence ' by a Council of the Realm, composed in addition to the Council of Regency (President of the Cortes, highest ranking Prelate and Captain-General) of the General-in-Chief of the General Staff, Presidents of various bodies (Supreme Court, etc.), four Procuradores and three nominees of the Head of the State. The Head of the State may at any time submit or withdraw the name of anyone to succeed him—either as King or Regent. If the Headship falls vacant, the Council of the Realm shall propose to the Cortes the person of Royal descent possessing the necessary qualifications, which are : male sex, a Spaniard of thirty years of age at least, Roman Catholic and to take an oath to observe the Basic Laws of the Nation and the principles of the National Movement.

It will be remarked that the present Head of the State has preserved for himself complete liberty of action to suggest, withdraw or blackball a successor to himself, who may or may not be of Royal descent, to serve either as King or as Regent. Galician wit ' hila muy delgado '.

Of all the groups which in recent years have exercised power in the land, only the Church and the Falange seem to have consolidated themselves—almost to an unspoken degree as rivals—in the present régime. The rump Republican Government—in exile—is less than the shadow of a shade. It is difficult to estimate how much more substantial within the country is the memory of that Republic which persistent propaganda and great material changes in daily life have forced into an unreal past. That it has evolved would seem to be the lesson of the violently un-Spanish strikes of workers—against industrial conditions in Bilbao, in Barcelona against the fares of municipal transport—which were apparently spontaneous, peaceful and totally self-disciplined—but much more effective and uncrushable than any ever seen before in Spain. Dignified passive resistance would be a new force in Spanish history and not an entirely surprising development under the present régime. On the other flank the Monarchists and traditionalists make a braver public show but may strike a less profound echo in the country. Some of the traditionalist individuality was absorbed in the compulsory merger with the official party of the Falange, whose voice seems to be powerfully expressed in government by its Secretary, Fernández Cuesta, who has the status of Minister, and in public life, among others, by Rectors of several Universities, and other intellectuals. That it still has the power, and funds, to move the multitudes is demonstrated by

rallies such as the monster one of October 24–28, 1953 (the first
National Congress of the Falange), which filled the biggest
football stadium and all Madrid with travel-stained enthusiasts
from every corner of the country, while the world on compulsory
holiday looked on. Many distinguished scholars and writers
belong to the Falange, which also attracts the younger generation
who, such is the special atmosphere of this Dictatorship, support
it, by contrast, as a liberalising and independent power in the
land. The Falange is the protagonist of the ' Movimiento ' : the
' Cruzada ' is the continuing preoccupation of the Church. Not
since the sixteenth century has Spain experienced such a profound
and widespread revival of religious faith as now is evident in
public and private life alike, in the publication of religious literature, including—as a best seller—a new translation of the Bible
for the common man, in the respect for the cloth and devotion to
exhortations of the priesthood. Not since that distant epoch has
any country probably witnessed such a successful struggle of a
Church to make its influence felt in all spheres of national life and
activity. The foreign historian, who recalls the fierce and often
bloody rejection by the modern world of the theocratic State, must
marvel at the ceaseless labours of the Spanish Church to burden
itself with a voice and a vote in all temporal matters—which
might range for example from the State recognition of degrees
awarded by Apostolic Universities or religious technical colleges
to proposals for an alliance with Arab countries. A characteristic
though minor expression of this struggle has been the creation of
a new Spanish Religious Order, blessed by the Pope on June 16,
1950 (though founded as early as 1928 by its actual President,
Monsignor Escrivá), the Sociedad Sacerdotal de la Santa Cruz y
del Opus Dei. The lay members of the Order (the Opus Dei) who
take in private the vows of poverty, chastity and obedience, are
directed by the priestly members of the Sociedad, in their mission
of inculcating a more austere and orthodox manner of life and
thought among the leaders of national opinion. Though the Order
now has some 100 houses in twenty countries, and is credited with
influential members, especially in University circles, it is not dis-
respectful to record that in the popular imagination its activities
are rumoured with something of the fearful awe once reserved for
the Inquisition, then for the Jesuit Order, and still later for the
Masons.

The crusading zeal, the economic dependence and the universal
aspirations of the Spanish Church were justified and blessed in
solemn Concordat between Spain and the Holy See, signed in the
Vatican City on August 27, 1953. In thirty-six articles with eleven

of Addenda, specific (could one say dogmatic?), definition is given
to the rights, privileges, prerogatives, titles, immunities and
warranties of the Church in its relations with the Holy See, and
with the laws and responsibilities—economic, social, military,
legal, educational—which otherwise govern the relation of the
Spanish State with its citizens. It is implicit only that these
privileges are essential to the Church's ministry in the country, in
which (Article I) ' The Catholic Apostolic and Roman religion
continues to be the only religion '. By Articles II–XIII the Church
is assured of independence to publish Papal ordinances, to own
and manage property, to make appointments to dioceses and
benefices, which can be created and altered freely ; Articles XIV
and XV exempt clergy from public offices and military service ;
by Article XVI the jurisdiction of Ecclesiastical Courts in their
relation with the Civil Courts is firmly defined ; Articles XVIII–
XXI specify the manifold ways in which the State shall contribute
financially to the maintenance of the property, personnel and
activities of the Church and of the Religious Orders (including
Seminaries, educational establishments, missionary work, pensions
funds), all of which—not excluding the gardens and orchards
attached to any such properties—shall be exempted from State
and local rates and taxes ; with similar precision the Church's
right to ensure that the teaching in all educational institutions
conforms to the Dogma and morals of the Catholic Church, to
provide instruction in the Catholic religion which is a compulsory
subject in them and to found at will its own universities, schools
and colleges is confirmed in Articles XXVI–XXXII, and in
Articles XXXII–XXXIII is enlarged to include religous ministry
in the Armed Forces and among patients, and staffs, of all
hospitals. Among the Addenda which in general dot the i's and
cross the t's of separate articles, but include also comments on the
Concordat of General Franco, *L'Osservatore Romano* and the
Foreign Minister, A. Martín Artajo, two might be mentioned.
Addendum III records that the Spanish State pursuant to ' the
constant and munificent reverence ' historically professed to the
Holy See undertakes to pay to it annually 8,000 gold pesetas in
renewal of a pledge given to it in 1647 by Philip IV as ruler of
Naples and Sicily, which later governments, since the Treaty of
Utrecht of 1713, have been more than reluctant to assume.
Addendum VII in relation to Article I quotes the relevant
Article VI of the Spaniards' Charter that ' No one shall be
molested for his religious beliefs or in the private practice of his
worship. No other external ceremonies or manifestations than
those of the Catholic Religion shall be permitted. '

Three other important elements in contemporary Spain remain to be discussed in this regrettably brief survey : the Armed Forces, Business and the Monarchists. Though the Armed Forces, with the other forces of internal order, are exceedingly prominent and absorb over one-third of the National Expenditure (Budget of 1950) the most remarkable feature about them during the past fifteen years or so has been their unexceptional loyalty to the régime : not the whisper of a ' pronunciamiento '. Even more conspicuous, and perhaps of less steady faith in the régime is the business world, from which the régime has drawn not only much financial blood but also a good many teeth, by taxation, fines and industrial legislation. But no business world is mortally hurt by the enforced share-out of steady returns on capital invested, and such one would judge Spanish business to be enjoying, not only by the range of goods newly manufactured at home but by the opulent display of marble, brass and wrought iron in the fashionable 'Banking Imperial' style of architecture.

There was a period just after the Civil War when many fervid Republicans believed that the only solution to the problem of government lay in the return of the Bourbons. The Law of Succession, very guardedly, assumes that a royal dynasty will follow General Franco. Yet it is difficult to assess the actual warmth and strength of monarchical aspirations in the country. The uncertainty arises not from the existence of a lively Republicanism—memory and propaganda have made this an enigma which few sensible men would solve dogmatically. It arises in part because a monarchy is not essential to the programme of the Falange, and could hardly increase the authority and primacy now enjoyed by the Church, in part also because with the passing of the years monarchy has lost both its significance as a shibboleth to divide, and its attraction as a practical aspiration and creed for which the majority of Spaniards would hazard the present relative tranquillity and prosperity.

Of the four sons of Alfonso XIII, the two eldest, Alfonso and Jaime (b. 1907 and b. 1908) early renounced their rights to the succession. The third and only surviving son, Juan (b. June 20, 1913), one time a midshipman in the British Navy, and for some years a resident of Lisbon, is now the accepted head of the Spanish House of Bourbon, with whom the Head of the Spanish State has had several interviews. But it is rumoured that General Franco feels a preference—as his own successor—for Don Juan's eldest son, Juan Carlos, who in fact with his brother has studied for and passed the Bachillerato examination in Madrid and is now (January–February 1955), at the age of seventeen, to take up residence in Spain ' where he will complete his education . . . in order to serve his country better in the future according to the rank he occupies in the dynasty ' (Official Note, December 1954, issued after an interview of Don Juan and General Franco). From these non-committal terms it would seem that General Franco is, as so often in the past, directing his policy by the wisdom of the traditional axiom ' Dar tiempo al tiempo ', which Philip II interpreted, unhappily, as ' El tiempo y yo para otros dos '. Certainly if his mind is that way inclined, he can afford, from the security of his position and the exemplary health of his sixty-two years, to delay decisive action at least for the four years that Juan Carlos lacks his majority. He may even experience a strategist's (or Galician's?) delight in containing each and every claimant for the post when he, and they, recall that the sole right of nomination lies in his hands, that by the Law of Succession—susceptible to change only by a National Referendum which it is also his privilege to initiate—all claimants must be not twenty-one, but thirty years of age. We may well see further negotiations before a successful Dictator goes into a voluntary eclipse.

BIBLIOGRAPHY TO CHAPTER IX

187. Alba, S. *Problemas de España*. Madrid, 1916.
188. Alcalá Galiano, A. *La Caída de un trono*. Madrid, 1933.
189. Alcalá Galiano, A. *España ante el conflicto europeo*. Madrid, 1916.
190. Altamira, R. *Problemas urgentes de la primera enseñanza en España*. Madrid, 1916.
191. L'Alvarez del Vayo, J. *Freedom's Battle*. London, 1940.
192. Borkenau, F. *The Spanish Cockpit*. London, 1937.
193. Brandt, J. A. *Toward the New Spain*. Chicago, 1933.
194. Brenan, G. *The Spanish Labyrinth*. Cambridge, 1943.
195. Calvo Sotelo, J. *Mis servicios al Estado*. Madrid, 1931.
196. Castillejo, J. *Wars of ideas in Spain*. London, 1937. [On Spanish Education.]

197. Chapman-Huston, D., and Princess Pilar of Bavaria. *Don Alfonso XIII*. London, 1931.
198. Cossío, M. B. *L'Enseignement en Espagne*. Madrid, 1908.
199. Estelrich, J. *Catalunya endins*. Barcelona, 1930.
200. Eza, Vizconde de. *El Problema agrario en España*. Madrid, 1915.
201. Fernández Almagro, M. *Historia del reinado de Alfonso XIII*. Barcelona, 1933.
202. Foss, W. and Gerahty, C. *The Spanish Arena*. London, 1939.
203. García Morente, M. *Idea de la Hispanidad*. Buenos Aires, 1939.
204. Giner de los Ríos, F. *La Universidad española*. Madrid, 1916.
205. Gómez de la Serna, J. *España y sus problemas*. Madrid, 1916.
206. Lema Marqués de. *Spain since 1815*. Cambridge, 1921. [A brief recapitulatory lecture.]
207. Madariaga, S. de. *Anarquía o jerarquía*. Madrid, 1935.
208. Madariaga, S. de. *Spain*. London, 1942. [Second edition, enlarged.]
209. Maeztu, R. de. *Defensa de la Hispanidad*. Madrid, 1934.
210. Maeztu, R. de. *Hacia otra España*. Madrid, 1899.
211. Marvaud, A. *L'Espagne au XXe. siècle*. Paris, 1913.
212. Marvaud, A. *La Question sociale en Espagne*. Paris, 1910. [Bibliography, pp. 461–468.]
213. Maura Gamazo, G. *Bosquejo histórico de la Dictadura*. 2 vols. Madrid, 1930.
214. Maura Gamazo, G. *La Cuestión de Marruecos*. Madrid, 1905.
215. Maura Gamazo, G. *Historia crítica del reinado de Alfonso XIII durante su menoridad*. Barcelona, n.d.
216. McCullagh, F. *In Franco's Spain*. London, 1937.
217. Mousset, A. *La Política exterior de España*, 1873–1918. Madrid, 1918.
218. Ortega y Gasset, J. *España invertebrada*. Madrid, 1922.
219. Ortega y Gasset, J. *Rectificación de la República*. Madrid, 1931.
220. Orwell, G. *Homage to Catalonia*. London, 1938.
221. Peers, E. Allison. *Catalonia Infelix*. London, 1937. [With Bibliography.]
222. Peers, E. Allison. *Spain in eclipse*. London, 1943. [With Bibliography.]
223. Peers, E. Allison. *Spain, the Church and the Orders*. London, 1939.
224. Peers, E. Allison. *The Spanish Tragedy*. Sixth edition. London, 1937. [With Bibliography.]
225. Romanones, Conde de. *El Ejército y la política*. Madrid, 1920.
226. Romanones, Conde de. *Las Responsabilidades políticas del antiguo régimen. De 1875 a 1923*. Madrid, 1924.
227. Romanones, Conde de. *Las Ultimas Horas de una monarquía*. Madrid, 1931.
228. Rovira i Virgili, A. *El Nacionalismo catalán*. Barcelona, 1917.
229. Sencourt, R. *Spain's Ordeal*. Second edition. London, 1939.
230. Sencourt, R. *Spain's Uncertain Crown*. London, 1932.
231. Toynbee, A. J. (and others). *Survey of International Affairs*: 1937, Vol. II; 1938, Vol. I. Oxford, 1938, 1941.
232. Trend, J. B. *The Origins of Modern Spain*. Cambridge, 1934.
233. Uña y Sarthou, J. *Las Asociaciones obreras en España*. Madrid, 1900.
234. Young, Sir G. *The New Spain*. London, 1933.
[See also Nos. 3, 8, 10, 13, 16, 17, 49, 54, 60, 67, 143, 144.]

INDEX

No references are given to the Bibliographies or to the bibliographical pages of Chapter VIII. The letters 'ch', 'll' are treated as in English spelling and not as in Spanish: the Spanish 'ñ' follows 'n'. Pages denoted by a heavier type contain the most important references to the subject to which they refer.

Carpio, *v.* Bernardo
Carrión, 95
Cartas eruditas y curiosas, 156
Cartas marruecas, 161
Carthage, 21
Carthaginians in Spain, 30, 31
Casa-Arquedín, Marquis de, 198
Casa con dos puertas, 154
Casa de la Troya, 174
Casas, Bartolomé de las, 134
Casas y Novoa, 237
Casta de Hidalgos, 174
Castelar, Emilio, 84, 258
Castellanos, Juan de, 138
Castiglione, 128
Castile, 1, 2, 3, 6, 7, 8, 10, 11, 14, 15,
    16, 19, 22, 41, 42, 44, 45, 48, 49, 50,
    51, 52, 53, 55, 56, 60, 67, 89, 90, 94,
    96, 97, 99, 105, 107, 112, 115, 117,
    118, 119, 121, 122, 138, 144, 180, 182,
    195, 223, 233, 268
Castilian, *v.* Spanish
Castillejo, Cristóbal de, 126
Castillo, Enríquez del, 116
Castillo, Hernando del, 113
Castillo Solórzano, 144
Castro, Américo, 16, 17, 144
Castro, Guillén de, 151
Catalan architecture, modern, 237
Catalan language, 8, 9, 16, 96, 103, 109,
    121, 167
Catalan literature, 9, 96, 99, **107–10**,
    124
Catalan music, 246, 254
Catalan painting, 190, 191, 193, 195
Catalan renaissance, 167, 186
Catalanist movement since 1898, 259,
    260, 263–8
    Catalina Micaela, Infanta ' (of Coello),
    199
Catalonia, 6, 7, 8, 9, 11, 40, 41, 42, 47,
    48, 52, 53, 55, 67, 68, 69, 70, 71, 79,
    80, 84, 108, 117, 118, 119, 137, 167,
    169, 223, 230, 231, 233, 234, 238,
    243, 265, 273–8, 281, 283
Cateau Cambrésis, Peace of, 63
Catholic Monarchs, 59 n. (*v.* also Ferdi-
    nand V, Isabel I)
Cea Bermúdez, *v.* Zea
Cela, C. J., 175–6
Celanova, S. Miguel de, 223
Celestina, 18, 142, 148
Celtiberian race, 30
Celtic words in Spanish, 13
Celts, 5, 30
Centre Català, 266
Centre Nacionalista Català, 266
Centre Nacionalista Republicà, 266
Cepeda, *v.* Teresa
Cerdagne, 68

Cernuda, Luis, 182
Cervantes, Archbishop Juan de, 233
Cervantes Saavedra, Miguel de, 6, 12,
    19, 24, 27, 205 n., 124, 133, 140, 141,
    143, **144–6**, 156
Ceuta, 73, 116, 269
Chanson de la Croisade, 104
Chanson de Roland, 24, 38, 42, 90
character, Spanish, *v.* Spanish
Chabrier, 243
Charlemagne, 8, 37, 91, 93, 230
Charles I of Spain (Emperor Charles V :
    v. 60 n.), 19, 25, **60–3**, 66, 123, 137,
    198, 199, 226–7, 234, 236
Charles II of Spain, **68–9**
Charles III of Spain, **72–4**
Charles IV of Spain, **74–6**, 78, 80, 162
Charles of Anjou, 51, 52 ; — son of
    Philip II of Spain, 65 ; — Viana,
    Prince of Navarre, 52 ; — Archduke
    of Austria, 69, 73 ; — son of Isabel
    Farnese, 71 ; — brother of Ferdi-
    nand VII, 79, 81
Charles Martel, 36
Chartres, 228, 232
Chateaubriand, 23, 165
Chaucer, 114, 147
Checa y Sanz, 212
Cherinton, Odo of, 117
Chile, 62
Chindaswinth, 35
chivalric romance, 141, 145, 146
Chopin, 255
' Christ bearing the Cross ' (of Ribalta),
    201
' Christ in the House of Martha and
    Mary ' (of Velázquez), 205, 207
Chronicle of James I of Aragon, 108
Chronicon Mundi, 101
Church and State in Spain, 73, 74, 82,
    123, 261–3, 293–4
Churriguera, José, 237
Cicero, 13, 31, 118, 132
Cid Campeador, 42, **45–6**, 89, 91, 94,
    104, 120, 151, 258
Cid Poema de Mio (or *Poema del Cid*),
    14, 17, 18, 24, 42, 93, **95**, 163
Ciencia Española, La, 169
Cienfuegos, *v.* Álvarez
Cieza de León, 135
Cifar, El Caballero, 105
Cintio, 143
Cisneros, Jiménez (*or* Ximénez) de, 57,
    59
Cistercians, 47, 228, 230, 232
Ciudad Rodrigo, 77, 197
' Clarín ', 172
Clásicos y Modernos, 184
Clavijo, González de, 51, 116
Clavijo, José, 158

INDEX

318 SPAIN